Music at World's End

Music at World's End

Three Exiled Musicians from Nazi Germany and Austria
and Their Contribution to Music in Iceland

ÁRNI HEIMIR INGÓLFSSON

Cover credit: Photos © Sibyl Urbancic (top left) and © Elín Þ. Ólafsdóttir. Used with permission.

Published by State University of New York Press, Albany

© 2025 State University of New York

All rights reserved

Printed in the United States of America

No part of this book may be used or reproduced in any manner without written permission. No part of this book may be stored in a retrieval system or transmitted in any form or by any means including electronic, electrostatic, magnetic tape, mechanical, photocopying, recording, or otherwise without the prior permission in writing of the publisher.

Links to third-party websites are provided as a convenience and for informational purposes only. They do not constitute an endorsement or an approval of any of the products, services, or opinions of the organization, companies, or individuals. SUNY Press bears no responsibility for the accuracy, legality, or content of a URL, the external website, or for that of subsequent websites.

This project, grant no. 217,386, was supported by the Icelandic Research Fund.

For information, contact State University of New York Press, Albany, NY
www.sunypress.edu

Library of Congress Cataloging-in-Publication Data

Name: Árni Heimir Ingólfsson, author.
Title: Music at world's end : three exiled musicians from Nazi Germany and Austria and their contribution to music in Iceland / Árni Heimir Ingólfsson.
Description: Albany : State University of New York Press, [2025]. | Includes bibliographical references and index.
Identifiers: LCCN 2024018727 | ISBN 9798855800685 (hardcover : alk. paper) | ISBN 9798855800708 (ebook) | ISBN 9798855800692 (pbk. : alk. paper)
Subjects: LCSH: Music—Iceland—20th century—History and criticism. | Exiled musicians—Iceland—History—20th century. | Jewish musicians—Iceland—History—20th century. | Róbert Abraham Ottósson, 1912–1974. | Edelstein, Heinz, 1902–1959. | Urbancic, Victor.
Classification: LCC ML314.5 .A696 2025 | DDC 780.92/294912 [B]—dc23/eng/20240516
LC record available at https://lccn.loc.gov/2024018727

Contents

List of Illustrations		vii
Note on Spelling and Naming		xi
Introduction: Lives Saved through Music		1
Chapter 1	Beginnings	3
Chapter 2	Without a Home	27
Chapter 3	World's End	57
Chapter 4	"A Country Free of Jews . . ."	89
Chapter 5	New Realities	109
Chapter 6	Work to Be Done	129
Chapter 7	Conflict and Controversy	167
Chapter 8	Endings	199
Postlude		229
Acknowledgments		233
Notes		235
Bibliography		283
Index		305

Illustrations

1.1	Dr. Ernst Urbantschitsch with his two sons, Victor and Erich, ca. 1910.	5
1.2	Hildegard Urbantschitsch with her two sons, Erich and Victor, in the garden of the family home at Gymnasiumstraße 59, Vienna.	7
1.3	Victor Urbancic at age twenty-three in Vienna, spring 1927.	9
1.4	Melitta Grünbaum, ca. 1927.	10
1.5	The title page of *Caprices mignons* op. 1, Urbancic's first published work.	13
1.6	Heinz Edelstein in his early twenties.	15
1.7	Charlotte Schottländer, ca. 1928.	17
1.8	Otto Abraham at the piano as his wife Lise looks on, ca. 1911.	20
1.9	Otto and Robert Abraham in Berlin, ca. 1917.	22
1.10	Robert Abraham aged fifteen, in 1927.	25
2.1	Heinz Edelstein in Freiburg, ca. 1932.	33
2.2	Charlotte Edelstein with her newborn son Stefan, 1932.	34
2.3	Members of the Frankfurt Jewish Culture League symphony orchestra performing Tchaikovsky's Serenade for Strings under the direction of violist Richard Karp, Frankfurt, April 1937.	36

2.4	Robert Abraham in Berlin, ca. 1929.	39
2.5	Emmy Schulz, Robert Abraham's fiancée in Berlin.	40
2.6	Robert and Peter Abraham with Lis Jacobsen in Denmark, ca. 1935.	42
2.7	Victor Urbancic rehearsing singers for a performance at Mainzer Stadttheater, ca. 1930.	46
2.8	Victor and Melitta Urbancic with Melitta's parents, Ilma and Alfred Grünbaum, ca. 1936.	54
3.1	The Hljómskálinn Pavilion in central Reykjavík, ca. 1935.	60
3.2	Ragnar Jónsson, chairman of the Reykjavík Music Society.	61
3.3	Robert Abraham's choir at a concert in the New Cinema (*Nýja bíó*), Akureyri, in March 1939.	67
3.4	Robert Abraham conducting his choir at a Spring Festival in Svarfaðardalur, a valley in Northern Iceland, June 1939.	72
3.5	Charlotte Edelstein with her son Wolfgang, ca. 1933.	75
3.6	Wolfgang and Stefan Edelstein in Freiburg, probably in 1934.	79
3.7	Robert Abraham and Guðríður Magnúsdóttir on their wedding day, May 17, 1942.	87
4.1	Hermann Jónasson, Iceland's Prime Minister and Minister of Justice from 1934–1942.	90
4.2	Albert Klahn at his home in Reykjavík, ca. 1950.	94
4.3	The Reykjavík Music School Trio in November 1938: Heinz Edelstein, Árni Kristjánsson, and Hans Stepanek.	96
4.4	Ludwig Misch in Bonn, ca. 1965.	98
4.5	Ilma Grünbaum in Vienna, ca. 1937.	105
4.6	Robert and Peter Abraham with Margrethe and Niels Bohr, Rigmor Adler (Bohr's cousin), and Hans Bohr, in Copenhagen, ca. 1937.	107
5.1	Melitta Urbancic with her three children in downtown Reykjavík shortly after arriving in Iceland.	114

5.2	Proud siblings: Ruth, Sibyl, and Pétur Urbancic with their newborn sister, Eiríka.	118
5.3	Heinz Edelstein in the Icelandic highlands, ca. 1948.	122
5.4	Charlotte Edelstein in Reykjavík, 1947.	126
6.1	Victor Urbancic, the Music Society Choir, and the Reykjavík Orchestra at their performance of Bach's *St John Passion* at Reykjavík's Free Church in 1943.	133
6.2	The Reykjavík Music School Trio, ca. 1942: Heinz Edelstein, Árni Kristjánsson, and Björn Ólafsson.	137
6.3	Heinz Edelstein, ca. 1950.	140
6.4	Robert Abraham at a concert with the Craftsmen's Choir in 1947, with pianist Anna Pjeturss.	142
6.5	Robert Abraham with the National Radio Choir and string orchestra in the Reykjavík Cathedral, 1949.	145
6.6	Victor Urbancic with two of his children, Ruth and Pétur, in Reykjavík, ca. 1944.	152
6.7	The cover of *Ten Songs by Johann Sebastian Bach*, edited by Victor Urbancic in 1952.	154
6.8	Victor Urbancic conducting the recording of Jórunn Viðar's score for the film *The Last Farm in the Valley* (*Síðasti bærinn í dalnum*) in January 1950.	158
6.9	Victor and Melitta Urbancic with their children and son-in-law, 1952.	164
7.1	Robert Abraham with the Icelandic Musician's Union Orchestra and the Harpa Choral Society in Tjarnarbíó, May 1944.	169
7.2	Victor Urbancic conducts the Music Society Choir in rain and wind on Iceland's Independence Day, June 17, 1949.	176
7.3	Victor Urbancic in Reykjavík, ca. 1950.	180
7.4	Olav Kielland, Chief Conductor of the Iceland Symphony Orchestra, 1952–1955.	182

7.5	Aram Khachaturian with Heinz Edelstein and his students at the Reykjavík Music School in 1951.	190
7.6	Students from the Children's Music School rehearse under the direction of Robert Abraham, spring 1961.	194
7.7	Heinz Edelstein conducts students from the Children's Music School at a public concert in May 1955.	195
7.8	Robert Abraham with his wife Guðríður Magnúsdóttir and their son Grétar Ottó Róbertsson, May 1959.	197
8.1	Victor Urbancic with his mother Hildegard in Vienna in summer 1954, four years before his death.	201
8.2	Charlotte, Stefán, Heinz, and Wolfgang Edelstein reunited for the last time in Freiburg, Christmas 1958.	207
8.3	From Robert Abraham's doctoral defense at the main hall of the University of Iceland, November 1959.	210
8.4	Robert Abraham rehearsing the Philharmonia Choral Society and the Iceland Symphony Orchestra in Brahms's *German Requiem*, November 1961.	212
8.5	Robert Abraham after an orchestra rehearsal in March 1960.	217
8.6	Robert Abraham and his wife, Guðríður Magnúsdóttir, listening to the Philharmonia Choral Society singing on their doorstep on Abraham's sixtieth birthday, May 17, 1972.	221
8.7	Eiríka Urbancic unveils her mother's bust of Victor Urbancic in the National Theater of Iceland on what would have been his seventieth birthday in 1973.	225

Note on Spelling and Naming

Note: This book uses Icelandic spellings of all Icelandic names and texts. The special characters used to write Icelandic are preserved here, not transliterated to an approximate English spelling. The special characters used include the following: the consonants þ (upper case Þ) and ð (lower case only), pronounced as the first sound in English "thin" and "this" respectively and often spelled with *th* or *d* in English transliteration. Also, æ [ai̯] and ö [œ] are considered letters in their own right, as are the dipthongs represented by an acute accent mark over the letter: á [au̯], é [jɛ], í [i], ó [ou̯], ú [u].

Icelanders employ, in general, a patronymic system in which the suffix *–son* or *–dóttir* is added to the genitive form of the father's first name. (In recent years, some Icelanders instead use a matronymic derived from the mother's first name, though this does not apply to any of the individuals discussed in the present book.) Although Icelanders always refer to each other by first name, this book refers to them by patronymic and treats these in the same manner as family names.

Robert Abraham adopted an Icelandic form of his name (Róbert Abraham Ottósson) in 1949, but to avoid confusion he is referred to by his German name throughout. Also in 1949, Victor Urbantschitsch changed the spelling of his family name to Urbancic. Apart from early references to his family in Vienna in chapter 1, the latter spelling is used throughout.

Introduction

Lives Saved through Music

Iceland has one of the shortest Western classical music traditions of any European country. This remote island in the North Atlantic, settled by Norwegians in the ninth century CE, has long prided itself on its literary heritage, which includes magnificent medieval stories and poems. For most of its history, however, its musical culture was far more humble. The first performance in Iceland by a full symphony orchestra took place as late as 1926, when the visiting Hamburg Philharmonic gave a momentous series of concerts in the nation's capital, Reykjavík. It was only in the aftermath of this event that local performing ensembles and a music school were established, but even then, progress was slow due to limited resources and lack of adequately skilled players.

An unforeseen convergence of factors led to Iceland's musical revolution, when it did finally occur, happening at an astonishing pace in the 1940s and 1950s. Iceland had been a colony of Denmark for centuries, and though it became a sovereign nation in 1918, it was still ruled by the Danish king until 1944. With the establishment of a republic came a desire to become "a nation among nations," which in turn demanded the cultivation and public financing of music, theater, and other hitherto neglected art forms.

At the same time, millions of people of Jewish origin were desperately attempting to save their lives by fleeing Nazi terror in Germany and Austria and seeking refuge elsewhere. Iceland had an unyielding immigration policy, shaped and controlled by a xenophobic prime minister, yet two musicians of Jewish origin, and a third whose wife was Jewish, were allowed entry between 1935 and 1938. These three men—Robert Abraham, Heinz Edelstein, and Victor Urbancic—would lay the groundwork for the classical music scene in

Iceland, bringing their invaluable skills as choral and orchestral conductors, performers, educators, arrangers, and scholars. Under normal circumstances, Iceland would never have been a sensible, let alone attractive, career move for musicians of their caliber. They arrived in a country that had yet to hear even the fundamental works of the classical canon: the passions and oratorios of J. S. Bach, the Requiems of Mozart or Verdi, the symphonies of Brahms or Mahler—to name but a few. With extraordinary skill and effort, and in collaboration with enthusiastic local musicians, they were able to shape an entire musical culture in only a few decades. A particularly poignant irony in their situation vis-à-vis the Nazi government is that they were allowed to make their new home in a country whose existing culture, not least its medieval literary heritage, was worshipped by the Nazis as embodying the "pure" and "strong" aesthetic of the "Nordic" race, and thus became a model for artistic creation in the Third Reich.[1]

This volume largely constitutes a triple biography, with subchapters dedicated to each of the three musicians woven into an overarching narrative. Chapter 1 depicts their formative years in Germany and Austria, while chapters 2 and 3 trace the rise of Nazism and the three musicians' flight to Iceland. In chapter 4, I digress from their personal stories to examine Iceland's hostile immigration policy in the 1930s, the recently discovered stories of other Jewish-born musicians who were refused entry there, as well as the fates of some of the three main protagonists' family members. Chapter 5 returns to the main narrative, with a focus on the acculturation of the three musicians, as well as their wives and children, in a new and unfamiliar land. Their professional accomplishments in the 1940s and the cultural transfer that ensued are the subject of chapter 6, while the frustrating setbacks that led them to explore other career options in the 1950s are detailed in chapter 7. The eighth chapter traces their final years and evaluates their overall influence on the Icelandic music scene. A brief postlude tells how their stories have been remembered in the twenty-first century, often in the form of a history lesson within a larger debate on current immigration policies.

Robert Abraham, Heinz Edelstein, and Victor Urbancic were outstanding musicians who survived the horrors of Nazi Germany only by a twist of fate. By seeking refuge on a remote island where classical music was virtually unknown, they were able to save their own lives as well as those of their families, while also having a significant and lasting impact on the music culture of an entire nation. Their remarkable stories, told here in detail for the first time, deserve to be much better known.

1

Beginnings

Among the thousands of young men studying music in Germany and Austria in the first decades of the twentieth century, three would become colleagues later in life in a faraway land. They were all sons of esteemed doctors, born into upper-middle-class families between 1902 and 1912: Victor Urbancic was born in Vienna, Heinz Edelstein in Bonn, and Robert Abraham in Berlin. As became increasingly obvious in their teenage years, they all excelled in classical music, whether as performers, composers, or scholars, and they all seemed destined for fulfilling careers in Germany and Austria. Their impressive talents were already being recognized, when their entire world was suddenly—and violently—turned upside down.

Urbancic: A Doctor's Son in Vienna

For centuries, Vienna has been one of Europe's leading musical centers. The city that Haydn and Mozart, Beethoven and Brahms, Schubert and Mahler called home, it was where many of classical music's greatest works were heard for the first time: Mozart's *The Marriage of Figaro* and *The Magic Flute*, and the symphonies of Beethoven and Schubert, to name only a few. By the late nineteenth century, the nexus of Vienna's music scene was to be found in two imposing buildings situated within a few hundred feet of each other: the Court Opera (now the Vienna State Opera) and the Musikverein concert hall, a veritable temple of music in neoclassical style. Vienna's citizens were reputed to be a rather conservative crowd, flocking in the early years of the twentieth century to see and hear popular operettas such as Franz Lehár's *The Merry Widow*. At the same time, a younger and more progressive group of composers led by Arnold Schoenberg and his pupils had begun exploring the limits of tonality, ushering in a new era of modernism in music.

Vienna's lavish architecture and way of life were fitting for the capital of the enormous Austro-Hungarian empire, which spanned not only Austria and Hungary but a substantial part of Middle and Eastern Europe, from Croatia in the south to Ukraine in the east. Vienna was also a cultural crucible, a bastion of the arts and sciences. In the early years of the new century, Sigmund Freud published his landmark theory of the meaning of dreams, while Gustav Klimt and Otto Wagner perfected the ornamental style of visual art and architecture known as *art nouveau*. Describing these years decades later, author Stephan Zweig referred to this period as "the golden age of security"—the glorious final years of the Austro-Hungarian empire, before Europe was plunged into a catastrophic war.[1]

In the affluent Währing area, the so-called eighteenth district near the edge of the Vienna Woods in the city's northwestern section, the renowned otologist Dr. Ernst Urbantschitsch and his wife Hildegard made their home in a splendid three-story house at Gymnasiumstraße 59, now the residence of Lebanon's ambassador to Austria.[2] Dr. and Mrs. Urbantschitsch were both Roman Catholics, and they had been married for just over a year when their first child, Victor Ernest Johann, was born on August 9, 1903. Two years later, Hildegard gave birth to another son, Erich, who died in infancy of appendicitis. A third son, also named Erich in memory of his deceased brother, was born in 1907 (see fig. 1.1). The Urbantschitsch family had its roots in the Slovenian town of Preddvor and rose to prominence there in the nineteenth century. One distant relative, Josipina, was even a promising composer and poet, though she died tragically of a combination of childbirth and measles at only twenty years of age.[3] In Slovenia, the family name was spelled according to local custom, *Urbančič*—which later in life inspired the older son to take up the simplified spelling of *Urbancic*.

The young Victor was born into a family of distinguished medical doctors. His grandfather and namesake, Viktor Urbantschitsch, today still considered among the founders of modern otology, was an associate professor at Vienna University and led the otology department at the city's main hospital. His son Ernst followed in his footsteps, becoming chief physician at the Emperor Franz Joseph Hospital in 1913 and eventually presiding over the Austrian Otological Society.[4] Yet another physician in the family was Ernst's younger brother, the renowned psychologist Rudolf Urbantschitsch.

Figure 1.1. Dr. Ernst Urbantschitsch with his two sons, Victor (right) and Erich (left), ca. 1910. *Source:* © Sibyl Urbancic, private collection. Used with permission.

He studied human sexuality, was on friendly terms with Sigmund Freud, and later had a distinguished career in California. Rudolf's grandson is without a doubt the most internationally renowned member of the Urbantschitsch family: the Academy Award–winning actor Christoph Waltz.

The spacious and elegant Urbantschitsch home in Währing was a typical residence of the Viennese intellectual bourgeoisie, made all the more lively by the presence of several schnauzers. In the large back garden, amidst countless fragrant rose bushes, were a small gazebo and a giant swing that could accommodate up to five people at a time.[5] In charge of running the household, Hildegard Urbantschitsch was rather strict and rigorous, while her husband Ernst had a warm, humorous disposition that verged on the amusingly eccentric. He was one of the first automobile owners in Vienna but never learned to drive—he had to protect his hands, he said, so that he could rely on them to do impeccable work at the operating table. His devoted chauffeur, Leopold, made certain that he arrived promptly for his appointments, which were anything but conventionally timed. Each morning, the doctor left the house at exactly thirty-three minutes past six, and the morning's first operation began at precisely four minutes to seven. Years later, when his daughter-in-law asked him to explain his quirky scheduling habits, he replied that only in such a way could he guarantee the absolute punctuality of his staff. When told to appear on the hour or half-hour, he observed, people were far less meticulous.[6]

The Urbantschitsch household was a profoundly musical one; Ernst played cello in his free time and Hildegard was a skilled pianist. They delighted in making music both as a duo and in larger ensembles with their friends, whom they regularly invited to their home for chamber music soirées. These ambitious, sophisticated programs habitually included sonatas, trios, and quartets by all the major composers, as well as four-hand piano arrangements of Mozart and Beethoven symphonies. At these soirées, young Victor was permitted to stay up later than usual, and he always asked to sit by the piano, next to his mother. Once, he later recalled, she performed a work that ended with a loud, decisive note in the bass register. The boy promptly memorized this, and, at the conclusion of the next piece, he himself reached forward and pressed the same note on the keyboard, his face beaming with pleasure and conviction. Unfortunately, that piece was in a different key and thus his contribution was far from the success he had anticipated. Even decades later, his family would jokingly refer to this as his first "wrong note" as a performer.[7]

Victor began piano studies at the tender age of four, guided by the watchful eye of his mother, who took care that he practiced daily and would correct his playing when needed.[8] His progress was impressive; by the age of ten he had mastered several of Grieg's shorter piano pieces, and soon after that he began to tackle far more substantial works. According to a notebook from 1917–1918, when he was fifteen years old, he already had ten of Beethoven's piano sonatas under his belt, as well as a sizeable selection of music by Bach, Mozart, and Chopin.

For a young and talented music student in the early 1900s, Vienna offered an endless variety of live performances of the highest caliber. In a series of notebooks, the young Victor carefully listed each of the concerts and operas he attended during his teenage years, a fascinating chronicle of how his musical horizons expanded. In 1918, for example, he heard the Vienna Philharmonic perform all of Beethoven's symphonies, as well as his Violin Concerto and *Missa Solemnis*, all conducted by Felix Weingartner, the orchestra's renowned chief conductor. He attended up to seven operas

Figure 1.2. Hildegard Urbantschitsch with her two sons, Erich and Victor (standing), in the garden of the family home at Gymnasiumstraße 59, Vienna. *Source:* © Sibyl Urbancic, private collection. Used with permission.

a month, either at the Court Opera or the Volksoper, the city's newest opera house and only a short stroll from his family home. Thus, the young Urbancic—from now on, we shall use the spelling he adopted later in life—experienced many of opera's great masterworks in performances that could hardly be outdone: Mozart's *Don Giovanni* and *The Magic Flute*, Richard Strauss's *Salome* and *Elektra*, all of Wagner's major operas. Most of them he saw repeatedly, season after season. He also began purchasing full scores of the symphonic and operatic repertoire, listing his acquisitions carefully in a separate notebook. It seems that even as a teenager he dreamt of one day becoming so intimately familiar with these great works of music that he would be able to conduct them himself.[9]

As far as can be determined, Victor Urbancic first began to write down his own music at the age of thirteen. Several sketchbooks from 1916–1917 show how his notation becomes gradually more secure, the shape and development of his musical ideas more convincing. A modest leap forward was a *Forest Suite* for piano that he wrote in summer 1917, at the age of fifteen. Half a year later, his name day gift for his father was a new work, *Three Pieces for Cello and Piano*, presumably premiered by the composer and dedicatee in the Gymnasiumstraße living room. In his teenage years, Urbancic wrote a substantial number of Lieder for voice and piano, combining his interest in music and literature (see chapter 6). When he enrolled at the gymnasium or secondary school that was only a stone's throw away from the family home—hence the street name, Gymnasiumstraße—he became still more immersed in composition, and a few of his works were even performed in public in Vienna and Budapest. Another important milestone was his debut conducting the student orchestra at his own gymnasium.[10]

While music was a steady force in the young Urbancic's life, the outside world was becoming increasingly unstable. In June 1914, with tensions already simmering among the major European powers, the heir to the Austro-Hungarian throne was murdered in Sarajevo, triggering a brutal war that proved more deadly than anyone could have imagined. Victor Urbancic was nearly eleven when World War I broke out, and fifteen when peace was finally restored. His family was certainly better off than many others, but the hardships of war left no one unscathed. In Vienna, food shortages soon became acute: by 1915, bread was being rationed, and soon the same was true of other staples, whether meat, coffee, milk, or sugar.[11] The devastating famine was further exacerbated by an outbreak of tuberculosis that the city's hospitals, already overfull with thousands of injured soldiers, were ill-equipped to deal with.[12] When peace was finally restored, the brilliant optimism of the century's first decade had yielded to anxiety and doubt. The immense Austro-Hungarian empire had collapsed and its ruling family had been driven into exile, while Vienna was but a shadow of its former self, the capital of a small, destitute state. For Urbancic, like all of Austria's citizens, the lessons of the Great War were not easily forgotten: that fortune's wheel can turn in an instant, forcing one to try to simply survive in the most challenging circumstances.

As he completed his secondary education in 1921, it had become clear that music was the young Urbancic's passion. He chose not to follow in the footsteps of his physician father and grandfather, enrolling instead at Vienna's leading conservatory, *Akademie für Musik und darstellende Kunst*, where he studied composition and theory with the school's dean, the renowned composer Joseph Marx. He also took piano lessons with Paul Weingarten and studied conducting with Clemens Krauss, who would only a few years later be appointed director of the Vienna State Opera and Vienna Philharmonic.

But Urbancic also had a scholarly inclination. His keen interest in the history and analysis of music led him to enroll, concurrently with his conservatory studies, as a student of musicology at the University of Vienna. There, he became a pupil of the legendary Guido Adler, one of the founders of musicology as a discipline, as well as his younger colleague Egon Wellesz, a composer-scholar of Jewish heritage who would later flee Austria for England. Urbancic thus received a stellar education, studying with many of Vienna's most prominent musicians and scholars. In 1925, he completed his doctorate at the remarkably young age of twenty-two—the youngest musicologist to complete that degree from the University of Vienna. His dissertation, a study of Brahms's use of the sonata form, was an impressive work of scholarship, and its main findings were published two years later in Adler's renowned journal, *Studien zur Musikwissenschaft*.[13]

While Urbancic's dissertation research must have consumed most of his time and energy, his life took an unexpected turn in summer 1924

Figure 1.3. Victor Urbancic at age twenty-three in Vienna, spring 1927. Photo: Georg Fayer. *Source:* © Austrian National Library. Used with permission.

when he made the acquaintance of a young woman who also studied at the university and, like him, loved both music and literature. Melitta Grünbaum was a year older than Urbancic, born in Vienna in 1902 (see fig. 1.4). She was raised in the Jewish faith, the daughter of Alfred, a lawyer from Teschen (today divided into Cieszyn in southern Poland and Český Těšín in the Czech Republic), and Ilma, who was of Czech heritage but born and raised in Vienna. The Grünbaum household was also a musical one: Melitta studied piano as a child and formed a trio along with her two sisters, Jenny, who played cello, and Alberta, who played violin. Their mother was also a fine pianist, and their father had a splendid tenor voice; after returning home from his office, he would often entertain his family with songs by Schubert and even excerpts from Wagner's operas.[14] In what must be regarded as a remarkable coincidence, Alfred Grünbaum's legal office in central Vienna was located in the same building as Ernst Urbantschitsch's doctor's office—yet neither knew of the other's existence until their children became romantically involved.[15]

Victor Urbancic was immediately smitten by Melitta, or Litty, as she was affectionately called by her friends and family, yet he apparently lacked

Figure 1.4. Melitta Grünbaum, ca. 1927. *Source:* Photo: Trude Fleischmann. © Sibyl Urbancic, private collection. Used with permission.

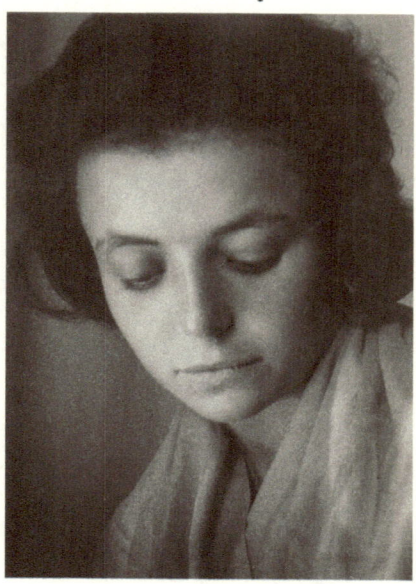

confidence in winning her heart, at least at the outset. On the evening of their first, serendipitous meeting at the university, he wrote in his diary that he now knew he would never marry—since he had already found the only woman he could ever love, and surely she was far out of his league.[16] In the end, it all turned out much better than he had hoped. Victor and Melitta went on their first date in the small park in front of Vienna's Town Hall, just a stone's throw from the university, and soon discovered they were soulmates, developing a relationship built on love and genuine respect. "They had incredibly many interests in common," relates their daughter Sibyl, "whether it was literature, music, history, or politics."[17] Yet, as personalities, they could hardly have been more different: Victor was a remarkably modest and unassuming man, while Melitta had a fiery, passionate temper. Politically, both were committed social democrats, a stance that somewhat baffled the senior members of the bourgeois Urbantschitsch family.[18]

Melitta Grünbaum was a woman of many talents, but literature was her main passion. This was also true of her best friend since childhood, Erika Mitterer. So great was their admiration for the renowned Austrian poet Rainer Maria Rilke that Erika not only wrote an epistolary poem dedicated to their literary idol but also had the audacity to send it to him by mail, along with several of her other verses, including one titled "An Melitta" (To Melitta). The two were completely taken by surprise when the master replied with a series of poems of his own, one of which was dedicated to both of them, titled "Die Liebenden (Erika und Melitta)," or "The Lovers (Erika and Melitta)."[19] Such unexpected near-contact with a literary icon only fueled Melitta's admiration for Rilke, who would remain a primary source of inspiration for her own poetry later in life. For a while, she studied literature, philosophy, and English at Heidelberg University under the tutelage of philosopher Karl Jaspers and renowned literary scholar Friedrich Gundolf, the author of an important study on "Shakespeare and the German Spirit." She was deeply impressed by their erudition and later in life wrote a memoir of her studies with Gundolf, in whom she perceived a kindred spirit; it was published for the first time in 2012.[20]

Through her love for literature, Melitta found her way to the stage. For a while, she took a leave of absence from university to work under the tutelage of renowned director Max Reinhardt in Vienna, but when he departed for Hollywood she again returned to her study of literature. She completed her doctorate in 1927 with a study of poetics, specifically on the use of iambic pentameter in the works of nineteenth-century playwright Christian Dietrich Grabbe. Such a detailed analysis of poetry intended for the stage was an ideal topic for Melitta, allowing her to combine her two main passions in life.[21]

Having completed his own doctorate, Victor Urbancic remained in Vienna for a while. He had a temporary contract as rehearsal pianist and conductor at Theater in der Josefstadt, a small but beautiful theater with a rich history, also in terms of music. Ludwig van Beethoven had composed his overture, *The Consecration of the House*, for its opening festivities in 1822, and Richard Wagner's *Tannhäuser* was given its Vienna premiere there in 1857.[22] During Urbancic's tenure, the Josefstadt theater was under the direction of Max Reinhardt, who thus exerted a formidable influence on both Urbancic and his fiancée in the mid-1920s.

Urbancic also began to draw attention as a composer. In 1926, his first work was published by the renowned Viennese publishing house Doblinger: *Caprices mignons über ein Kinderlied* op. 1 for piano, written in 1922 (see fig. 1.5). In this set of variations, Urbancic creates a delightful contrast between the theme itself—a simple children's song from Humperdinck's opera *Hansel and Gretel*—and the chromatic, late-Romantic ethos of the variations themselves. Technically, Urbancic places heavy demands on the performer, suggesting that he was a formidable pianist himself. Also written in 1922 was his Sonatina for Piano op. 2, and two years later he composed two substantial chamber works: a Sonata for Violin and Piano and a *Fantasy-Sonata* for clarinet and piano, the latter dedicated to Melitta. By the end of the 1920s, with his undeniable talent as a pianist, conductor, composer, and scholar, it appeared as though Victor Urbancic could pursue virtually any path he desired as a musician.

Edelstein: A Cellist in the Rhinelands

Compared to the bustling cultural activity of Vienna or Berlin, the town of Bonn in western Germany was a somewhat provincial place, with only 50,000 inhabitants in 1900. In the annals of music history, the town has two major claims to significance: Ludwig van Beethoven was born there in 1770, and Robert Schumann died in a mental institute in nearby Endenich, then an independent municipality, in 1856. Yet, apart from Beethoven in his teenage years, neither was active as a musician in the town—which comes as no surprise since its musical resources were limited. A symphony orchestra, the so-called Städtisches Orchester, was founded in Bonn as late as 1907, and opera was not offered there until later.[23] To enjoy cultural

Figure 1.5. The title page of *Caprices mignons* op. 1, Urbancic's first published work. *Source:* Private collection of the author.

activities on a larger scale, one had to make the brief journey to Cologne, twenty miles to the north.

Heinz Theodor Edelstein was the oldest of the three musicians discussed here, born in Bonn on June 5, 1902. His father, Emanuel Edelstein, was a merchant's son from Bingen, a small Rhineland town best known as the site of an abbey founded by Hildegard, the twelfth-century abbess and composer of music. Emanuel moved to Bonn to study medicine at the local university, completing his dissertation in 1897. Four years later, he married Ida Oberländer, a local merchant's daughter. Heinz was born six months into their marriage, and a daughter, Ruth, followed four years later. Dr. Edelstein's medical practice was located in the old town center, and the family home was also nearby, only a few hundred feet from the house where Beethoven was born.[24]

Emanuel Edelstein was an observant Jew who took an active part in Bonn's Jewish congregation and was among the leaders of the German Zionist movement in the Rhinelands. He contributed articles on Judaism for a leading Zionist publication and also corresponded with Max Bodenheimer, the movement's leader in Germany, who later settled in Palestine.[25] Heinz Edelstein was a committed atheist later in life, but his father appears to have been devout in his religious practice. It therefore seems likely that both Heinz and Ruth Edelstein also received a religious upbringing, although the few surviving sources from their childhood do not confirm this.

With the outbreak of World War I, Dr. Edelstein was summoned for duty at a military hospital on the Eastern front. He served in Jarosław, southeastern Poland, under horrible conditions, as an epidemic of cholera and typhoid fever ravaged the area. Edelstein returned from the battlegrounds severely ill, and passed away on January 21, 1917, at forty-five years old.[26] "He could save everyone but himself," the rabbi of Bonn's Jewish congregation lamented at his funeral.[27] Local papers noted that Edelstein's funeral procession drew an uncommonly large and diverse crowd; not only did all the males of the Jewish congregation in Bonn attend, but so did many local doctors, Edelstein's former patients, as well as survivors from his battalion in the war.[28] It must have been a terrible blow for his son Heinz, then in his fifteenth year, to lose his father so tragically. One can even speculate as to whether this loss, in such a formative period, had a long-lasting psychological impact. Later in life, Heinz Edelstein was reputed to be a rather stern personality, and he was described by several colleagues and acquaintances as dry, acerbic, and not particularly sociable (see chapter 6). His later antipathy toward religion may also have been rooted in the fact that not even prayers were able to save his devoutly religious father's life.

Otherwise, little is known about Heinz Edelstein's childhood and adolescence. He rarely discussed this period later in life, and few surviving documents shed light on the family's life in Bonn. Both siblings studied music, with Heinz learning to play cello and his sister Ruth playing the violin.

Theirs was a warm and playful relationship; decades later, Ruth reminisced that they would sometimes play-act dramatic duels using their instrument bows as make-believe swords, much to their parents' consternation.[29]

Although Edelstein's talent as a cellist must already have been evident by his late teens, he initially intended to study pedagogy at university, according to his gymnasium certificate. In autumn 1920 he moved from Bonn to Freiburg am Breisgau, the city that would become his home for the next decade and a half, and enrolled at its prestigious university. It is clear from Edelstein's course schedule that he had varied intellectual interests: he studied philosophy with the renowned Martin Heidegger, as well as pedagogy and musicology. As his studies progressed, it became clear that music was destined to become his main subject. Among the courses reported in his school records are seminars on medieval notation, music analysis, instrumental music of the Baroque era, and the works of Robert Schumann.[30] Later in life, he would find ways to combine music and pedagogy, not only as a respected cello teacher both in Germany and Iceland, but particularly in teaching innovatory preschool music classes for young children in Reykjavík.

Figure 1.6. Heinz Edelstein in his early twenties. *Source:* © Benjamin Edelstein, private collection. Used with permission.

While nothing suggests that Edelstein was dissatisfied in Freiburg, his early years at university were a rather restless period. Having completed three semesters in Freiburg, he returned home to Bonn in autumn 1921, enrolling at the local university with musicology as his main subject. He remained there for a year and a half, but by summer 1923 he had moved to Berlin, studying at the Friedrich-Wilhelms-University—now Humboldt University—for just one semester.[31] He then returned to Bonn, and resumed his studies in Freiburg only in summer 1924.[32] These were distressing times in Germany, and the political and economic situation may explain his nomadic lifestyle. Rampant hyperinflation made life difficult for everyone, not least university students, and perhaps Edelstein had no choice but to move back in with his mother and sister for a while. Even so, Bonn was hardly a tranquil city; like all of the Rhineland in the aftermath of World War I, it was occupied by French troops until 1930.[33]

Perhaps Edelstein also wished to take a break from his academic work and focus on playing cello. His principal teacher was Gustav Thalau, leader of the cello section at the Cologne Opera, but he also took lessons with the legendary Emanuel Feuermann, then considered one of Germany's finest cellists. Although Feuermann was only a few months Edelstein's junior, his talent was so prodigious that he was offered a professorship at the Cologne Conservatory at only sixteen years of age. It is unclear exactly when or for how long Edelstein was Feuermann's pupil, but it was likely in 1921–1923, during Edelstein's sojourn in Bonn. Perhaps it was Feuermann's move to Berlin in 1923 that sparked Edelstein's decision to study there for a while. In any case, it must have been profoundly inspiring for him to learn from such a brilliant performer and teacher as Feuermann.[34]

Having once more settled in Freiburg, Edelstein completed his doctorate in musicology under the supervision of Wilibald Gurlitt, a respected scholar who himself would later be blacklisted by the Nazis due to his partially Jewish heritage.[35] Edelstein's dissertation is a study of Saint Augustine's views on music as expressed in his *De Musica* (On Music), believed to have been written in 387–388 and thus predating the *Confessions*, his far better-known work. Edelstein's doctoral defense took place in February 1928, and the dissertation was published the following year.[36] Although little is known of Edelstein's university years beyond what can be gleaned from official records, the memoirs of his schoolmate Leopoldine Schwalbach, published in book form in 1997, provide a fleeting glimpse. There, she depicts Edelstein as belonging to a circle of talented philosophy students and admirers of Heidegger, noting that he was highly regarded by teachers and fellow students alike.[37]

By the time Edelstein defended his dissertation, he had already met his future wife. Charlotte Therese Schottländer was two years younger than he, born in Lauban, Silesia (now Lubań in Western Poland, roughly eighty miles east of Dresden), in 1904 (see fig. 1.7). Her parents were Adolf, a factory owner, and his wife Jenny (*née* Danziger), whose brother, Ludwig Danziger, was a distinguished painter. The family name Schottländer came from a suburb of what was then the Prussian town of Danzig, now Gdańsk, Poland. When Jews were forbidden to live in the town's center, they moved to a suburb that had been settled by Scots and was thus known as Alt-Schottland (*Stare Szkoty*) or Old Scotland. Charlotte—or Lotte, as she was known—was a talented and ambitious young woman who had studied economics at the universities of Frankfurt am Main, Basel, Munich, and finally Freiburg, where she met her future husband. She defended her dissertation, on the idea of "solidarism" as an economic concept, on December 10, 1928, and ten days later she and Heinz Edelstein were married.[38] By that time, Lotte was already expecting their first child, Wolfgang Michael, born in June 1929 and named after her older brother, a casualty in the Great War. Another son, Stefan Emanuel, was born in December 1931.

Figure 1.7. Charlotte Schottländer, ca. 1928. *Source:* © Benjamin Edelstein, private collection. Used with permission.

Although Edelstein devoted significant effort to his dissertation and was a promising scholar, the cello was his passion and life's work. He had already played with the orchestra at the Düsseldorf Opera House during his student years, and he continued working there after earning his doctorate. He also performed chamber music with orchestra members, tackling demanding new works such as Béla Bartók's String Quartet no. 2 in spring 1925. He taught cello privately, reviewed concerts for local newspapers, and was a regular substitute with the city's symphony orchestra.[39] Around 1930, he began teaching at Birklehof, a progressive boarding school near Freiburg, where great emphasis was given to introducing students to the fine arts. Nearly all of them played an instrument and sang in a chorus, and Edelstein had twelve cello students there in addition to his private pupils in the city.[40] For extra income, he also performed three times a week with an ambitious salon ensemble at Ganterbräu, a popular tavern in Freiburg's old city center. This was located in a medieval house—destroyed in World War II—that once was the home of renowned scholar Erasmus of Rotterdam, at the old "Potato Market" Square (*Kartoffelmarkt*). All in all, Heinz Edelstein appears to have led a busy yet fulfilling existence as a freelance musician during the final years of the Weimar Republic. He was happily married, had two young sons, and was building a career that allowed him to explore and expand his two main interests, as performer and teacher. At the Birklehof school, he also had the opportunity to develop his skills teaching young children—an experience that would come in good use later, under radically different circumstances.

Abraham: A Young Musician in Berlin

By the early twentieth century, Berlin—a late bloomer among Europe's capitals—had become established as a leading cultural center. It boasted of some of the world's most outstanding orchestras and opera houses, had a first-rate conservatory, the *Hochschule für Musik*, as well as the Prussian Academy of the Arts, the city's most renowned arts institution. Berlin was also a place where new and progressive art was met with an unusual degree of enthusiasm. The city teemed with first-rate musical talent, including composers Arnold Schoenberg, Paul Hindemith, and Ferruccio Busoni, pianist Artur Schnabel, and cellist Emanuel Feuermann.[41]

Music was also highly regarded at the home of Otto Abraham in Genthiner Straße, a quiet street in the Tiergarten area near the city center.[42] Abraham, a born and bred Berliner, had completed his doctorate in gynecology in 1894, and ran a medical office on the ground floor of the building where he lived. But Dr. Abraham led something of a double life, since he was also an ambitious and innovative scholar of music.[43] Even long after his death, his family recalled that after his passing, many of his patients had been surprised to hear that their doctor had also been a prolific scholar, while those who knew his articles on music were no less taken aback upon discovering that the erudite academic had a "secret life" as a gynecologist.[44]

As a scholar, Otto Abraham's key contribution was in the fields of music cognition and transcription. From 1896, he was assistant to the psychologist and musicologist Carl Stumpf at the newly founded Berlin Institute of Psychology, where Abraham researched what is commonly known as "perfect pitch," but which he preferred to call "absolute tone consciousness." He developed an extensive questionnaire, informed by novel methods of large-scale surveys being applied in the emerging social sciences and humanities at the time, and distributed it among a hundred test subjects to investigate their musicality. Among his results was that musical ability was less a natural talent than something learnable, arising from a tailored musical background and education.[45]

In 1900, Abraham and Stumpf founded the Berliner Phonogramm-Archiv, which soon developed into a leading collection of music from all corners of the globe. The entire project was made possible by the recording technology developed by Thomas Edison in the 1880s, using soft wax cylinders attached to an external horn. In 1900, Abraham and Stumpf made the first-ever recording of what was then referred to as music of "exotic" peoples, with a Siamese court orchestra in Berlin. Soon Abraham and Stumpf were joined at the Archive by yet another influential scholar, Erich Moritz von Hornbostel. The three were among the pioneers of a new discipline that examined the music of the West and other civilizations by means of comparative study, what was known in the German language as *vergleichende Musikwissenschaft* or comparative musicology. By documenting and comparing music from every corner of the world, they hoped to understand its origins and nature in a completely new manner. Abraham documented music from Japan, India, and Syria, among other places, and developed a method of notating it using the traditional Western system.[46] He authored several articles in collaboration with Hornbostel, including a seminal text in which they codified the methods and symbols employed in the transcription of non-Western music.[47]

In his leisure time, Otto Abraham enjoyed traveling north of the border to Denmark. He had close friends in Copenhagen but also enjoyed the more rural setting of the small Danish island of Bornholm in the Baltic Sea. It was there that he made the acquaintance of another Berliner, Lise Golm, who would become his wife (see fig. 1.8).[48] By the time they met, Abraham was already a confirmed bachelor, but they soon developed a loving relationship. The fifteen-year age difference was of no concern: when they married in February 1911, he was thirty-nine years old and she was twenty-four. Like her husband, Lise Golm was of Jewish heritage, but her family, which included esteemed members of Berlin's intellectual circles, had long ago converted to Protestantism. Her father, Eugen, ran a book store and publishing house; her maternal grandfather, Ferdinand Benary, had been a professor of Old Testament exegesis at Berlin University. A maternal

Figure 1.8. Otto Abraham at the piano as his wife Lise looks on, ca. 1911. *Source:* © Elín Þ. Ólafsdóttir, private collection. Used with permission.

great-grandfather, Moritz Daniel Volkmar, was an influential banker and a friend and benefactor of the composer Giacomo Meyerbeer.[49]

Around the time of his marriage, Otto Abraham appears to have withdrawn from his work at the Berlin Phonograph Archive to focus on his medical practice. This is suggested by his diminishing output as a scholar, as what had been a steady stream of published articles for roughly a decade largely runs dry after 1910.[50] Perhaps, with his prolonged bachelorhood at an end, he wished to enjoy domestic life and found that a private practice gave him more control over his own time. On May 17, 1912, a year after Otto and Lise Abraham were married, she gave birth to a son named Robert Louis Eugen. He was a true delight to his parents; Otto Abraham wrote to a friend in Copenhagen that he himself felt "like an infant" when face to face with such a bright and wonderful boy.[51] The couple's younger son, Peter, was born three years later.

The entire Abraham family was absorbed by the father's musical interests, including the household pet. As he conducted his research on pitch memory, Otto Abraham acquired a parrot to see if he could train the bird to develop perfect pitch. For months, Abraham would repeatedly sing to the parrot the opening notes of Beethoven's Fifth Symphony, and, eventually, the bird astonished its owner by learning to whistle the theme at absolutely correct pitch.[52] Abraham took this as proof that animals were able to develop exceptional musical skills through intensive practice. Even more surprisingly, the parrot turned out to be highly sensitive to musical transposition: if, in its presence, Beethoven's theme was whistled at a different pitch, the bird went completely mad and only gradually regained its composure.[53]

Robert Abraham began to play piano at an early age and was at first instructed by his father, who was eager to put his theories on musical ability into practice. Robert later recalled that he had mastered the rudiments of music before learning how to read: when asked to recite the alphabet at school, he insisted that it began *a, h, c, d*—the notes of the scale in German spelling.[54] At seven years of age, he composed his first short piano pieces, which his father wrote down for him. He also developed perfect pitch at an early age, hardly a surprise given his father's extensive research on the subject.

The earliest compositions to survive in Robert's own hand date from 1923, when he was eleven, namely, a song written for his mother on her birthday, and another for his father at Christmas.[55] This soon became a household tradition; the precocious Robert would gift new compositions to his closest family members on their birthdays and major holidays. As the pieces grew in scope and ambition he began to call them "symphonies"—a substantial overstatement since these are fairly short piano pieces. Yet the music does have dramatic flair, and he may well have imagined it being played by a full orchestra. Abraham later recalled that as a child he had considered only three jobs for his future profession: a conductor, a train operator, or a chef. He made up his mind at thirteen, he said, having been given the opportunity to direct his school orchestra. During his teens, Robert—or Rob, as the family called him—attended the Klindworth-Scharwenka music school, considered one of Berlin's finest pre-college institutions.[56] It was a particularly convenient arrangement, as the school was also located in Genthiner Straße, only a few yards from the Abraham family home.

It appears that Robert Abraham enjoyed a pleasant and carefree adolescence—until losing his father at the age of fourteen. Otto Abraham,

Figure 1.9. Otto and Robert Abraham in Berlin, ca. 1917. *Source:* © Elín Þ. Ólafsdóttir, private collection. Used with permission.

fifty-three, died from kidney failure on January 24, 1926, his wife's thirty-ninth birthday.[57] His untimely death was a profound loss to all who knew him. According to Erich von Hornbostel, he was the perfect colleague: highly intelligent, kind hearted, and humorous.[58] A few months later, Lise Abraham confided to a friend in Copenhagen that her husband's death had "shattered" her "sweetest, most beautiful" family life: "I live on, and still have my friends, but deep inside there is always my dreadful sorrow."[59]

Perhaps the sudden death of his musically gifted father made Robert even more determined to make music his profession. Having completed his gymnasium studies at age eighteen, he enrolled in the musicology department at Humboldt University, but after a year he changed course and decided on a career as a practicing musician instead. He began studying composition and conducting at the Berlin Academy of Music (*Staatliche Akademische Hochschule für Musik*), where his primary teacher was Walter Gmeindl, a former student of renowned composer Franz Schreker. At around this time, Robert's compositions became larger and more ambitious. He had already written a work for four-hands piano that he felt was worthy of being his "opus 1," and in 1933 he composed a *Scherzo rusticale* for winds as well as a fugue for piano solo—his audition piece at the Academy.[60] Besides his lessons with Gmeindl, he studied piano with Valesca Burgstaller and harpsichord with Eta Harich-Schneider, as well as attending the renowned lectures in music history given by Curt Sachs, one of his father's former colleagues and director of the Academy's extensive collection of historical instruments.[61]

During the heady years of the Weimar Republic, Berlin was a thrilling place for a young music student. Several of Germany's most famous conductors had permanent positions there: Wilhelm Furtwängler led the Philharmonic orchestra, Erich Kleiber directed the State Opera, while Otto Klemperer introduced new and progressive works at the Kroll Opera, near the Reichstag parliament building. These included the first staged performance of Stravinsky's *Oedipus Rex* in 1928, with the composer—and a fifteen-year-old Robert Abraham—in the audience.[62] While Otto Abraham was alive, he would often bring his son to concerts and operas, and for the rest of his life Robert recalled his excitement at being allowed, in his early teens, to visit backstage after a concert in the old Philharmonic Hall, and shake the legendary Furtwängler's hand.[63]

Yet the young Robert's musical idol was yet another conductor: Bruno Walter, who held the post of music director at the Städtische Oper in the Charlottenburg district, where the Deutsche Oper now stands. At age twelve, Abraham had been completely enthralled by Walter's performances with the Philharmonic, and even created a special notebook in which he entered information on each of Walter's concerts that he attended. He found an all-Mozart concert in March 1929 "wonderful" and described Verdi's Requiem a month later as "sublime." That spring, he also heard Walter conduct Rachmaninoff's Piano Concerto no. 2 with the composer himself as soloist.[64] He devotedly attended Walter's opera performances, which included Wagner's *Tannhäuser* and *Tristan und Isolde*. "It was magnificent," the sixteen-year-old Robert wrote in his copy of the program book after hearing the latter.[65] Judging by the surviving programs in his collection, Robert Abraham frequented all the city's major concert halls from 1926 to 1933, attending piano recitals by Vladimir Horowitz, Artur Schnabel, and Igor Stravinsky, Bach's Passions under the direction of Otto Klemperer and Wilhelm Furtwängler, as well as countless other performances, large and small. He witnessed the English composer Dame Ethel Smyth conduct the Berlin Philharmonic in 1928, a landmark event in its own right, and in the more intimate hall of the Singakademie he became acquainted with the chamber music of the Baroque era.

Abraham later recalled how he and his schoolmates would exert themselves to get the first-come, first-served balcony seats to the Berlin Philharmonic's concerts that were made available to music students. As soon as the hall opened, they would "run past the fatherly policemen, past the smiling cloakroom attendants—onwards, onwards, through the Philharmonie's endless hallways. We leapt over steps and handrails, climbed over rows of seats, and, when the goal was near, you had to focus on a specific seat and throw yourself on it with the force and precision that only experience could teach."[66] In his later teens, Robert Abraham joined the Bruno Kittel Choir, a large symphonic chorus that collaborated regularly with the Berlin Philharmonic. This gave Abraham invaluable experience, since he was able to perform the great works of the choral/orchestral literature under the batons of both Walter and Furtwängler, including Beethoven's Ninth Symphony and Verdi's Requiem—both works he would later conduct himself.

While Robert Abraham idolized Walter more than any other musician, he only made his personal acquaintance in 1935, when he traveled from Copenhagen to Brussels just to see him conduct once again. By then, both were in exile; as one of Germany's most successful Jewish musicians, Walter had been a prime target for Hitler's contempt.[67] Walter soon began a new life in the United States, but again crossed paths with Abraham in Edinburgh in autumn 1947, when he conducted the Vienna Philharmonic at the newly established arts festival. The two corresponded briefly in the

Figure 1.10. Robert Abraham aged fifteen, in 1927. *Source:* © Elín Þ. Ólafsdóttir, private collection. Used with permission.

1950s, when Abraham asked his mentor for advice on selecting repertoire for the newly established Iceland Symphony Orchestra.[68] After Walter's death, Abraham received one of his batons as a gift from the conductor's daughter, and cherished it as a relic for the rest of his life.[69]

As a new decade dawned in 1930, it seemed that fortune was smiling upon these three prodigiously gifted musicians. Two of them, Heinz Edelstein and Victor Urbancic, had already completed their doctorates in music, and while permanent employment was hard to obtain in the midst of a global recession, their talents were already drawing attention. The youngest of the three, Robert Abraham, was just about to begin university and appeared destined for a brilliant career. But danger was looming, and the progressive "Golden Era" of the Weimar Republic would soon come to an abrupt end. With the rise of the Nazi Party and the enactment of its virulent anti-Semitic policies, there was now a distinct possibility that these three musicians—along with millions of other men, women, and children—would no longer be able to live and work in the countries they called home.

2

Without a Home

Monday, January 30, 1933, was an ominous day in history, particularly for the more than 500,000 Jews then living in Germany. On that day, Adolf Hitler, the forty-three-year-old leader of the National Socialist German Worker's Party, was appointed the country's chancellor. He had led his party for more than a decade, and as local conditions deteriorated in the wake of the international financial crisis, the party had seen a dramatic rise in support. But Hitler's aim was never to lead a democratic society. When the Reichstag, home of the German parliament, burned down due to arson only four weeks after Hitler took power, he suspended most civil liberties and had thousands of communist supporters arrested. The Nazi Party's electoral success had not least been due to its opposition of Jews and communists, whom Hitler decried as enemies of the German state. It was thus only to be expected that once in power, the Nazis would enact their cruel policies. As stated in a memorandum by the Nazi security service a year later: "Germany must be a country where Jews have no future."[1]

An important goal for the Nazis was to make life unbearable for people of Jewish heritage. On April 1, 1933, the Nazi Party staged an economic boycott targeting Jewish-owned businesses. Nazi paramilitaries (SA, or *Sturmabteilung*) also stood menacingly in front of the offices of professionals such as doctors and lawyers, and, throughout the country, acts of violence were perpetrated against individual Jews and Jewish property.[2] A week later, the so-called Law for the Reconstitution of Civil Service was passed, excluding Jews and political opponents from all civil service positions.[3] In September, the Reich Music Chamber (*Reichsmusikkammer*) was established, membership of which was required for any professional musician in the German state. A primary goal of the association, especially in the early years, was the "cleansing" of the German music scene, and it barred entrance to anyone who lacked the required "reliability and suitability"—including Jews, foreigners, and political opponents.[4] Thus, within months of seizing power, the Nazis had created a framework for eliminating all Jews from Germany's public musical life.

The Nazis shaped their own definition of the term "Jewish." Religious practice in itself was not their main concern, as Jewishness was for them largely a matter of race. Thus it became of crucial importance whether any ancestors of a given individual could be shown to have had "Jewish blood." If a person had three or four such grandparents, they were a "full Jew" (*Volljude*), but if only one or two grandparents had been of Jewish heritage, they were classified as "part Jews" (*Mischling*). Even people of Christian faith who had never entered a synagogue could be Jewish or of mixed heritage according to the Nazi's racially motivated definition. In the coming years, people of Jewish heritage saw their civil rights gradually stripped away. The so-called Nuremberg Laws of 1935 defined a citizen only as a person who was "of German or related blood." Jews, defined as a separate race, were thus stripped of German citizenship. Also, intermarriages and sexual relations between Jews and people "of German or related blood" were prohibited, on the grounds that "mixed-race children" would undermine the purity of the German race.[5]

The gradual eradication of civil rights for Jews was an enormous blow for their community, not least since the decades following the founding of the German Empire in 1871, a period of relative liberalism overall, also saw economic and cultural prosperity for Jews.[6] After Germany's humiliating defeat in World War I, and the ensuing political and economic instability, the situation deteriorated again. For some, Anti-Jewish attitudes were driven by socioeconomic concerns, including hyperinflation and unemployment, while others saw Jews mainly as a threat to German culture and national solidarity.[7] Even more common and widespread was what has been called "moderate antisemitism," a vague sense of unease that stopped short of wanting to harm people of Jewish heritage but may have "helped to neutralize whatever aversion Germans might otherwise have felt for the Nazis."[8]

Yet it should be emphasized that Jews—or Jewish Germans, to use a more appropriate term—were by no means a homogeneous group. They covered the entire spectrum of society, whether in their political, religious, or philosophical attitudes.[9] Many of Jewish heritage had converted, some generations earlier, and had a long road of acculturation and assimilation behind them. An area in which they enjoyed particular visibility and success was that of the arts: music, film, theater, poetry, painting, and architecture. According to a 1925 census, Jews, defined by religion, constituted 0.9 percent of the German population, but they made up 3 percent of those engaged in the combined theater and music trades.[10] Countless Jews considered themselves German as much as anything else, proclaiming their patriotism while also preserving a sense of ethnic solidarity.[11] Even if their dreams of complete acceptance had never been fully realized, they were patriots who had entered and embraced German culture.[12] For hundreds of thousands of German Jews, "their" composers were Bach, Beethoven, and Brahms—even Wagner.

Not everyone agreed. As anti-Semitism grew in Germany, the view became increasingly prominent that Jews could have no role as performers of German music since their interpretation was inherently "un-German," to quote a term used by Nazi sympathizers to describe Bruno Walter's musicianship.[13] Such rhetoric had solid roots in Germany's past, particularly in the writings of Richard Wagner. In his notorious 1850 article, "Judaism in Music" (*Das Judentum in der Musik*), Wagner had accused Jews of being unable to create true art because they were unable to grasp its true essence; instead, they could offer only an imitation of art, which they conceived of as a form of commerce.[14] The Nazis agreed. In their opinion, German music, inherently "pure" and "untarnished," could only be "corrupted" by Jewish influence, which thus had to be eradicated. In a speech at the Reich Music Festival (*Reichsmusikfestwoche*) in 1938, Minister of Propaganda Joseph Goebbels reminded his audience that only a few years earlier, the country's "own great masters" had been "deformed and derided through distorted performances" by Jews—and this in Germany itself, "the classic land of music."[15]

In order to eliminate the "corruption" they believed to be inherent in Jewish music, Nazis soon proscribed music by Jewish composers from German musical life. Most famously, works by Felix Mendelssohn and Gustav Mahler were banned, although both had converted from Judaism in their lifetimes as a necessary career move in an already highly anti-Semitic society. In November 1936, the statue of Mendelssohn situated in front of the Gewandhaus concert hall in Leipzig was pulled down and destroyed by Nazi sympathizers. Mendelssohn's scores proved more durable, however, not least his ever-popular incidental music to Shakespeare's *A Midsummer Night's Dream*. In order to come up with a viable alternative, Nazi culture chiefs aggressively solicited new scores for the play, including one from the Munich-based composer Carl Orff. Dozens of scores by "acceptable" composers were tried out between 1933 and 1944 as replacements for Mendelssohn's much-loved work, but in each case the results proved lackluster. Eventually, the despairing Nazi authorities were forced to allow Mendelssohn's music while mention of the composer's name was omitted.[16]

Another direct consequence of the Nazis' virulent anti-Semitism was the publication of dictionaries listing the names of boycotted Jewish musicians. The most notorious of these was the *Lexicon of Jews in Music* (*Lexikon der Juden in der Musik*), a volume of nearly four hundred pages, first published in 1940 and sponsored by the Nazi Party itself. The *Lexicon* was the brainchild of Herbert Gerigk, a musicologist and critic who soon rose to prominence within the Nazi cultural hierarchy. He wielded considerable power as cultural adviser to Alfred Rosenberg's organization, responsible for supervising the entire ideological and intellectual program of the Nazi party. Among the names listed in the *Lexikon der Juden in der Musik* was the Freiburg cellist Heinz Edelstein, although he had emigrated by the time of the book's publication.[17] Yet the volume's contents turned out to be rather selective. For example, it was discovered shortly after Austria's annexation in 1938 that Johann Strauss's ancestors were of "mixed" racial origin. Not even the most virulent Nazis were willing to deprive the Third Reich of such a widely admired composer as the "Waltz King" himself, and thus this information was kept secret and his works were performed as frequently as before.[18]

In the second half of 1933, Jews were dismissed from all their previous positions in German musical life, whether as instrumentalists, singers, teachers, or scholars. Many saw the writing on the wall and emigrated as soon as they could; in the first year of the Nazi regime, over 37,000 Jews fled Germany. Still, the majority viewed the situation as a temporary phenomenon, believing common sense would soon prevail. Some were married to "Aryans" or had a distinguished military record and hoped this would guarantee a more humane treatment by the authorities. Also, not everyone had the opportunity to go abroad, be it for personal or financial reasons.[19] Nazis made emigration even more difficult by a stringent property tax on émigrés, the "Reich Flight Tax" (*Reichsfluchtsteuer*) that discouraged citizens from leaving and became a form of legalized theft to confiscate Jewish assets.[20]

Despite a constant stream of emigration in the ensuing years, the preponderance of the Jewish population remained in Germany until after the notorious *Kristallnacht* or "Night of Broken Glass" in November 1938, when Nazi paramilitary forces along with crowds of civilians ransacked Jewish homes, hospitals, and schools, burned synagogues, and assaulted and incarcerated tens of thousands of Jews. From 1933, Nazis had established prison camps and other incarceration sites for a number of purposes. In the early years of their reign, these were largely populated with political prisoners and people accused of "socially deviant" behavior, but later they grew in number and became more focused on the "Final Solution"—the genocide or mass destruction of Jews.

Over a million people of Jewish heritage were made to suffer persecution in Germany, Austria, and Czechoslovakia from 1933 onward. Of that number, it is believed that roughly half a million were able to flee, including over four thousand musicians.[21] Getting to safety was not always easy, and success depended in large part on the country involved. After World War I, the United States had returned to isolationist politics and introduced stringent limitations on the number of immigrants to be accepted from each country. All in all, it is believed that 132,000 refugees made it from Germany and Austria to the United States, including 1,500 musicians.[22] Seventy thousand Jews were given asylum in Great Britain, and over 55,000 settled in Palestine. A comparatively large number also made it to China and Argentina, while Australia, Canada, and South Africa were far more reluctant to accept refugees.[23] In Latin America, agrarian countries such as Cuba, Mexico, and Columbia showed little interest in receiving exiled artists and intellectuals; these countries either closed their borders or insisted that the refugees take up farming.[24]

For most of the musicians who left Germany after the Nazi takeover, freedom came at a price. Even those fortunate enough to find work appropriate to their vocation had to adjust to circumstances often drastically different from their previous ones. Composer Arnold Schoenberg, who had taught master classes to advanced students in Berlin, settled in California and expressed his frustration at having to instruct beginners in the fledgling music department at UCLA.[25] Kurt Weill, known for his satirical music theater work, adapted to life in Manhattan and began writing musicals for Broadway.[26] Many lesser-known musicians experienced poverty and sorrow in their new circumstances and were never again able to make full use of their talents.[27]

Needless to say, the exodus of Jewish musicians in the 1930s was a substantial loss for all fields of German culture and science. At the same time, other countries benefitted from the significant transfer of knowledge and talent that exiled Germans could provide.[28] Some have gone so far as to call this fortuitous result of Nazi racial policy "Hitler's Gift" to the rest of the world—the title of a book, published in the year 2000, exploring the careers of scientists expelled by the regime.[29] The irony of the situation was hardly lost on contemporaries. "Hitler is my best friend," renowned art historian Walter Cook, chairman of New York University's Institute of Fine Arts, famously quipped—"he shakes the tree and I collect the apples."[30]

Although every exile faced substantial challenges, musicians were in some ways more fortunate than other artists forced to leave Germany. They could communicate through their instruments, compositions, or physical gestures, in a nonverbal medium often considered international, unfettered by geographical or linguistic boundaries. Thus, many musicians found it easier to obtain work in their field than did actors or writers, who first had to master a foreign language.[31] In addition, the tradition of classical music was commonly regarded as "cultural capital"—a resource that could be converted into social or economic advantage.[32] Their country of origin even worked to their benefit, since, despite the tense political situation, music lovers across the globe still understood "classical" music to be primarily an Austro-German art form. Thus, it was widely, if often only implicitly, assumed that musicians from Germany and Austria were endowed with an innate understanding of the art form in all its nuanced meanings.[33]

Edelstein: A Jewish Orchestra in Frankfurt

In Freiburg im Breisgau, the charming university town at the edge of Germany's Black Forest, Heinz Edelstein's performing career came to a grinding halt in the spring of 1933. In April, he was forced to give up his salon orchestra job at the Ganterbräu tavern when storm troopers from the Nazi's paramilitary group threatened to boycott the establishment if a Jew was seen playing there again.[34] He was no longer eligible for freelance work at the Freiburg Symphony Orchestra, and most other projects also evaporated. Before long, his only remaining part-time job was as music teacher at the Birklehof boarding school. There, school authorities were sympathetic to the plight of their Jewish students and teachers and tried to protect them for as long as possible.[35]

Yet even this was a precarious situation, as it was only a matter of time before Nazi authorities would gather the information required to dismiss Edelstein on racial grounds. During the first year of its existence, the *Reichsmusikkammer* dispatched questionnaires to all professional musicians in Germany, demanding a detailed report on their racial ancestry. This was the letter that every Jewish person dreaded receiving, and in June 1934 it landed in Heinz Edelstein's mailbox. While he had no choice but to admit his status as a *Volljude*, he attempted to refute the impending ban on the grounds that his father had sacrificed his life for Germany in the Great War.[36] Nazis could sometimes be swayed by such arguments, although they never offered more than a brief respite.[37] At the Birklehof school, Edelstein's colleagues did what they could to secure his continued employment. In November 1935, the schoolmaster wrote to the Nazi authorities on Edelstein's behalf, noting that he had "in a short time achieved wonderful results, both technically and artistically, and he has been remarkably successful in stimulating the children and awakening their interest in their music studies. We would very much regret if he were no longer allowed to instruct at our school."[38] But such efforts were all in vain. In July 1936, Edelstein was officially denied membership in the *Reichsmusikkammer*, and thus it was clear he could no longer teach music anywhere within the Third Reich.[39]

Facing total unemployment, Edelstein was desperate to somehow provide for his family.[40] He took the only job he could find, as a traveling salesman. In summer and autumn 1936, Edelstein traveled among neighboring towns near Freiburg on his bicycle, selling soaps and other cleaning products door to door—a truly humiliating situation for such a talented musician, but he had no other choice. Even more than seventy years later, the cleaning product's brand name remained fixed in his son Wolfgang's mind: *Ofix*.[41]

Figure 2.1. Heinz Edelstein in Freiburg, ca. 1932. *Source:* © Benjamin Edelstein, private collection. Used with permission.

Charlotte Edelstein's situation was no less desperate. She had occasionally contributed columns on economics to the daily *Freiburger Zeitung*, and hoped to be able to build an academic career once her sons grew older.[42] But she had become just as unemployable as her husband: according to the rules of the *Reichsschrifttumskammer*, the Nazi association of writers, only "Aryan" authors were allowed to publish in newspapers and periodicals. In this time of frustration and hardship, Charlotte sought refuge in religion. She was baptized into the Catholic faith in 1935 and had her two sons baptized soon thereafter.[43] Heinz Edelstein, on the other hand, was an atheist and largely disapproved of organized religion. Charlotte's fervent devotion to her faith became a major obstacle in their marriage, which began to deteriorate around this time.[44] Fortunately, her religious contacts were able to secure a modest source of income. Beginning in 1936, when money had become alarmingly scarce, Charlotte was covertly employed by Caritas, the Catholic relief organization. She administered their archives and was even allowed to write short, anonymous articles in their monthly newsletter, although this was strictly forbidden by law.[45] For her work, she earned only one hundred marks each month, nowhere near enough to feed a family of four. Her son Wolfgang later recalled that in these years she became increasingly despondent and that the entire situation weighed heavily on her.[46]

Figure 2.2. Charlotte Edelstein with her newborn son Stefan, 1932. *Source:* © Benjamin Edelstein, private collection. Used with permission.

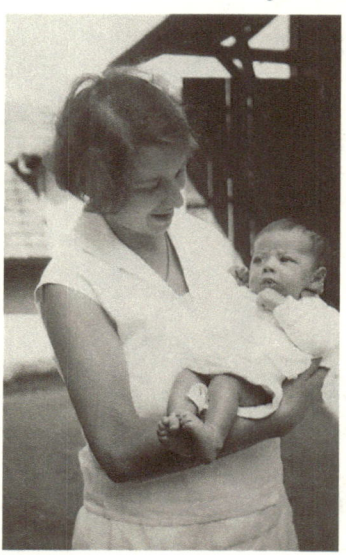

After 1933, the only employment open to Jewish artists in Germany was through the Jewish Culture League, or *Jüdischer Kulturbund*, an organization that presented various forms of entertainment within a strictly regulated framework. Only Jews were allowed to perform at the League's events, which only other Jews were allowed to attend. Events could be advertised or reviewed only in specifically Jewish publications. The center of the League's activities was Berlin, where a third of all German Jews lived, and in 1933 a symphony orchestra was established there consisting only of Jews, and operating with the approval and support of the Nazi party.[47] This enterprise proved so successful that the following year a second orchestra was founded in Frankfurt am Main, consisting of thirty-five players who had lost their posts in other orchestras or were being refused further training at conservatories.[48] In autumn 1936, Heinz Edelstein joined this orchestra as a cellist, and thus his career as a traveling salesman came to a welcome end.[49]

The Jewish Culture League was a kind of artistic ghetto for Jews. Its activities were to some extent useful to the Nazi regime, which exploited the entire project as propaganda. The League's very existence supposedly proved that Jews were not being mistreated, but rather were encouraged to find their own forum for cultural expression.[50] By creating a strict framework, authorities could keep a tight grip both on the concerts and the individuals who took part in them. The programs of the Jewish Culture League's orchestras were unusual in that they consisted in part of works by Jewish composers who were otherwise banned within the Nazi realm, including Mendelssohn and Mahler, as well as more recent works by Arnold Schoenberg and Ernst Toch. The orchestras were also allowed to perform music by foreign composers, particularly those of Slavic heritage (such as Dvořák and Tchaikovsky), since the Nazis considered the Slavic race to be "subhuman," and thus, presumably, saw performing their music as a suitable task for Jewish musicians. However, works by German "Aryan" composers—such as Beethoven and Wagner—were soon forbidden, and with the annexation of Austria in 1938, the same applied to the music of Mozart, Schubert, and others.[51]

Edelstein joined the Jewish Culture League orchestra at a critical moment in its history. Although the Frankfurt synagogue and individual donors had done their best to keep the orchestra financially viable, it had been facing serious financial difficulties. Eventually, its activities were restructured so that instead of giving concerts only for a local audience in Frankfurt, the orchestra toured all of Germany, providing musical entertainment for Jewish communities near and far.[52] The orchestra also faced another substantial challenge: as more and more Jews left the country, recruiting talented musicians for the ensemble became increasingly difficult. In 1936, several members joined the Frankfurt orchestra's founding director, Wilhelm Steinberg, in emigrating to the Holy Land, where they formed the Palestine Symphony Orchestra (later the Israel Philharmonic Orchestra); others began new lives in the United States. Steinberg's successor in Frankfurt was Julius Prüwer, an experienced conductor in his sixties who had led the first performance in Russia of Wagner's *Tristan and Isolde* in 1898. He had formerly been professor of orchestral conducting at the Berlin Conservatory but was among those dismissed in 1933 due to his Jewish heritage.[53] Under Prüwer's baton, Edelstein performed a variety of repertoire, including symphonies by Haydn and Schubert, Dvořák's *Slavonic Dances*, and various works by Mendelssohn (see fig. 2.3). He also took part in even larger projects organized in collaboration with soloists and choirs in the Frankfurt area, such as a concert performance of Verdi's *Rigoletto* in January 1937.[54]

Figure 2.3. Members of the Frankfurt Jewish Culture League symphony orchestra performing Tchaikovsky's *Serenade for Strings* under the direction of violist Richard Karp, Frankfurt, April 1937. Heinz Edelstein is furthest to the right of the orchestra's four cellists. *Source:* © Jüdisches Museum Frankfurt. Used with permission.

Edelstein was also invited to join the League's resident string quartet, known as the *Streichquartett des Jüdischen Kulturbundes Rhein-Main*. This ensemble was led by the orchestra's concertmaster, Ernst Drucker, an outstanding violinist who traveled to Iceland in 1938 and gave several concerts on behalf of the local Music Society. Later that year, he immigrated to the United States and eventually joined the Metropolitan Opera Orchestra; his son Eugene is also a noted violinist, and a founding member of the Emerson String Quartet. The Jewish Culture League's quartet had to comply with the same repertoire restrictions as the symphony orchestra, and its programs largely consisted of works by Jewish and Slavic composers. They traveled widely in Germany, giving concerts to enthusiastic response in cities such as Aachen, Dortmund, Essen, and Cologne.

Many of those who worked for the Jewish Culture League or attended their concerts later testified to the positive psychological impact of its activities. In its stubborn refusal to "give up its bond to Europe and to deny its intellectual tradition," it offered a fleeting escape from the daily challenges that confronted the Jewish community.[55] In such situations, many were grateful for the chance to enjoy a deep and fulfilling artistic experience. Oboist Kurt Michaelis characterized the League's performances as "normal," a means of living life without focusing exclusively on the surrounding horrors.[56] Martha Hirsch, a pianist who frequently attended their concerts, recalled that those in attendance were "deliriously happy" at the concerts "because it was another evening where they didn't work on their emigration and where am I going to go and how can I get out of here and all these sad things. We forgot for a couple of hours or otherwise we would all have been in the insane asylum."[57] The same perspective can be seen in reviews of Edelstein's performances with the League's string quartet, for example, of a concert in Hannover in spring 1937 where they performed works by Mendelssohn, Dvořák, and Ernst Toch. A critic for the local Jewish paper lavished praise on the quartet's inspired performance, noting in particular the "joy and uplifting, all the deliverance from the burdens of daily life" that their art brought to the audience.[58]

The orchestras of the Jewish Culture League did not survive for long after Edelstein's departure for Iceland. The Frankfurt ensemble gave its farewell concert in April 1938, but the Berlin orchestra played on until September 11, 1941, when all activities by the League were banned throughout the Nazi realm. Most of its members were arrested and sent to concentration camps, which only a few survived.[59]

Abraham: Exile in Paris and Copenhagen

In Berlin, the young Robert Abraham had just begun his studies at the Berlin Academy of Music when the Nazis took power. He was a *Volljude* according to Nazi typology, but both his parents had long ago converted to Christianity; he was raised as a Protestant and confirmed at the Church of the Twelve Apostles (Zwölf-Apostel-Kirche), down the street from his childhood home. Later in life, he noted that his upbringing had been "typically German," adding—with a specifically Icelandic twist—that he "didn't think about being Jewish more often, or any differently, than a boy from Reykjavík would think about having parents who came from the north of Iceland."[60]

Under the Nazi regime, the situation at the Berlin Academy of Music soon became unbearable. The Academy had been a rather conservative institution until Franz Schreker, a Viennese composer of international standing, took over as director in 1920. He created a liberal atmosphere signaled by an openness to contemporary trends, and was able to lure artists of international stature to join the school's faculty. This all changed when the Nazis took power. Among the leading cultural associations of the early Nazi years was The Militant League for German Culture (*Kampfbund für deutsche Kultur*), a nationalist, anti-Semitic society formed by party ideologue Alfred Rosenberg and committed to defending German culture against what was seen as the threat of liberalism. On February 9, 1933, seven members of the League disrupted a recital of Walter Gmeindl's composition class at the Academy, loudly protesting against the students, many of whom were Jewish, and complaining that such "miserable stammering" was being presented as "German art at a German music academy."[61] Since composition with Gmeindl was Robert Abraham's main subject, he was probably present at this concert although no direct evidence for this has survived.[62] The League for German Culture also fought for the removal of Schreker, the school's director, who was dismissed in April that year. By summer 1933, the "re-organization" of the Academy of Music was well underway. Twenty-seven teachers lost their positions or left of their own volition, including legendary pianist Artur Schnabel and cellist Emanuel Feuermann, who had been Heinz Edelstein's teacher a decade earlier.

The situation at the Academy deteriorated further in spring 1934. Students were required to take part in the Nazi May Day parade, and, beginning with the summer semester, courses in political indoctrination were added to the curriculum in order to introduce students to the "ideas of the National Socialist movement and to the doctrines of the National

Figure 2.4. Robert Abraham in Berlin, ca. 1929. *Source:* © Elín Þ. Ólafsdóttir, private collection. Used with permission.

Socialist State."[63] Earlier that year, Robert Abraham had been informed that, as a *Nichtarier*, he would not be allowed to conduct the school orchestra. At that moment, he understood that Germany no longer held a future for him, and he began to plan his departure.[64] His brother Peter had left for Copenhagen in spring 1933, soon after completing his secondary education. The Nazis were also quick to degrade their father's scholarly accomplishments. Otto Abraham was among those listed in the infamous *Lexicon of Jews in Music*, and his former colleagues at the Berlin Phonograph Archive were summarily dismissed from their posts; Erich Hornbostel immigrated to England, and Curt Sachs to New York.[65]

As he bid farewell to Berlin, Robert Abraham had to leave behind not only his family and friends but also his fiancée, Emmy Schulz, a talented pianist and schoolmate at the Academy of Music (see fig. 2.5). They had been a couple for a few years, and in 1932 he had dedicated to her one of his

Figure 2.5. Emmy Schulz was Robert Abraham's fiancée in Berlin. This photograph accompanied a letter from her to Robert in 1935. *Source:* © Elín Þ. Ólafsdóttir, private collection. Used with permission.

more substantial compositions, for four-hands piano—presumably intended for them to perform as a duo.[66] In the memoirs of Emmy's daughter, Heide Sommer, published in 2019, she relates that while her mother was keen to follow Robert abroad, she was reluctant to sacrifice her piano studies in Berlin for a completely uncertain future.[67] A few years later, Emmy married Artur Grenz, another schoolmate at the Academy and a good friend of Robert's. Grenz was both a violist and composer, having studied with Paul Hindemith until the latter left Germany.

Heide Sommer recalls that, later in life, her parents would often reminisce about Abraham's prodigious talents, claiming he had been among the Academy's most exceptional students.[68] After the war, Emmy and Robert resumed their correspondence, and whenever he found himself back on the continent he would try to visit his old friends, who later founded a music school near Hamburg. He also ensured that Emmy, Artur, and their three children—who affectionately called him "Onkel Robert"—received food packages from the Red Cross and warm clothing, as they suffered great hardship after the war.⁶⁹ In 1966, when Abraham and Heide discovered they would be in London at the same time, they arranged to meet. She recalls that he was so overwhelmed at her likeness to the woman he had loved more than thirty years earlier that he could barely utter a word.⁷⁰

Paris was Abraham's first destination in exile. Since he spoke French, he may have hoped to either resume his studies or secure a job there, yet he stayed for only a few weeks in the summer of 1934. The short-term attraction was the opportunity to study with Hermann Scherchen, a legendary figure who had conducted the premiere of Schoenberg's *Pierrot lunaire* in 1912. Scherchen's disgust for the Nazi regime had prompted him to leave Germany, and he settled for a while in Paris, where he organized a two-week summer course in conducting and general musicianship called *Deuxiéme Session d'Études de Hermann Scherchen*. The course was attended by eleven students who received intensive lessons from the master himself, as well as attending lectures and performances by other renowned musicians. The musically inclined Princess Edmond de Polignac, whose real name was Winnaretta Singer and who was heir to the Singer sewing machine fortune, invited all the participants to her palace, where Bach's *Musical Offering* was given its first known Paris performance. A few days later, Scherchen organized a concert of important works by leading modernist composers, including *Pierrot lunaire* and Stravinsky's *Les noces*.⁷¹

The final concert of Scherchen's course occurred on July 4 in the hall of the Sorbonne's Institute for Art and Archeology, then a new and imposing edifice. Scherchen divided the movements of Beethoven's Fourth Symphony among four students, and his demands were stringent: everything had to be conducted from memory and with no prior rehearsal, as Scherchen maintained that a good conductor could suggest his interpretation with physical gestures only. Robert Abraham conducted the first movement, and although he had conducted student orchestras in Berlin, this was his public debut.⁷²

No sources have survived to tell whether the concert was a success, but in any case it led to no further opportunities for Abraham in Paris. For more than a year, musicians had been streaming across the border to escape the Nazi regime, and the job market had never been more competitive. Henry Prunières, editor of the monthly periodical *La Revue musicale*, had lamented as early as May 1933 that France was "actually gorged with conductors, pianists, violinists and teachers of harmony with no work. How [to] find employment for the hundreds of Jewish musicians who continue to arrive? With the best will in the world, the situation is too vast to be coped with, and people are asking themselves anxiously what will become of these refugees in a few months, when the emergency funds raised on their behalf have been exhausted."[73]

Having completed Scherchen's seminar and with no prospects of work or further study in France, Abraham left Paris for Copenhagen. There, he benefitted from the long-standing friendship between his family and Lis Jacobsen, a renowned philologist and archeologist (see fig. 2.6). Her father, Marcus Rubin, a statistician and head of the Danish National Bank, had been a close friend of Otto Abraham, but both had passed away. Jacobsen was in her early sixties, herself of Jewish heritage and a woman of considerable means. She lived rather opulently in Copenhagen, drove a black Buick, and moved in the highest intellectual circles; among the guests at her luxurious dinner parties were composer Carl Nielsen and influential scholar Georg Brandes. She was also a devoted humanitarian who assisted many Jews in their plight during the 1930s. When the Nazis occupied Denmark, she was herself persecuted by the Gestapo, fleeing in 1943 to Sweden where she resided until the end of the war.[74]

Figure 2.6. Robert and Peter Abraham with Lis Jacobsen in Denmark, ca. 1935. *Source:* © Elín Þ. Ólafsdóttir, private collection. Used with permission.

For Abraham, Lis Jacobsen proved to be a remarkably magnanimous and supportive patron. She found him a place to live, gave him money for living expenses, introduced him to leading cultural figures, and used her influence to provide him with performance opportunities.[75] She even had a grand piano delivered to her summer house near the Øresund strait so he could make music there, and decades later she recalled how Abraham had "so lavishly" brought the joy of music into her life.[76] Peter Abraham was already studying at Copenhagen University, and the brothers were thus reunited after a year apart. Peter had also profited from Jacobsen's generosity, not least when she introduced him to a remarkable couple who took him under their wing: the renowned physicist Niels Bohr and his wife Margrethe. Peter studied with Bohr and for a while lived as a guest in their home, which he described as "pure heaven."[77]

Initially, Robert Abraham hoped to land a job in Copenhagen as the conductor of the Danish Radio Choir, but this came to nothing. Danish authorities had recently passed a law that made it nearly impossible for foreigners to obtain work permits, and thus his chances for any job in Copenhagen—let alone a highly coveted one—were slim.[78] Lis Jacobsen took matters into her own hands, using her considerable clout to arrange a series of three orchestral concerts in the main hall of the Ny Carlsberg Glyptotek, an imposing art museum of antique sculptures, with Abraham conducting the orchestra of The Young Musicians' Society (*Det Unge Tonekunstnerselskabs Orkester*).[79] The concerts, which took place in January and February 1935, presented an overview of instrumental music in the seventeenth and eighteenth centuries, as suggested by the overall title: "From Baroque to Classical: Three Historical Music Evenings" (*Fra Barok til Klassik: Tre historiske Musikaftener*). This musical journey began with concertos and sinfonias by Italian Baroque composers Corelli and Vivaldi, while the final evening culminated with Beethoven's Symphony no. 2. Abraham was already well versed in historical performance practice, and the programs were the result of careful research at the Copenhagen Royal Library; he even prepared some of the performing materials himself. The orchestra was fairly small, which was both a stylistic and economic advantage, and Abraham led from the harpsichord when appropriate.[80]

The concerts were prominently featured in Danish newspapers. Possibly Lis Jacobsen, who partly funded the enterprise, used her influence to ensure good publicity.[81] Since no concerts had been allowed in the Glyptotek museum for a long while, a certain element of novelty may also have drawn attention to the series.[82] Yet, despite a sold-out hall and a positive audience reaction, critical reception was decidedly mixed. This was Robert Abraham's first appearance as a professional conductor and, though he was a prodigious talent, he had much to learn. One critic praised him as a "refined musician with a good understanding of style," while another found his interpretation too romantic, his dynamic shaping unclear, and his fast tempi too exaggerated.[83] The harshest review was by Sven Lunn, a staff member at the Danish National Library and later director of its music division. He found the series to have been "a huge disappointment" and claimed not to have sensed in Abraham's conducting "the least personal connection with this old music."[84] Given how difficult it had become for foreigners to obtain a Danish work permit, it must also have been a severe blow when two local critics—including renowned musicologist Erik Abrahamsen—asserted that Denmark had plenty of young conductors who were at least as talented as Mr. Abraham.[85]

Abraham's fiancée, Emmy Schulz, had visited him in Copenhagen in autumn 1934 and became acquainted with his new friends there, but soon returned to Berlin where she resumed her piano studies. Her surviving letters express her affection and heartache. As she wrote him shortly before Christmas 1934: "Robert, you are so good and kind. I long for you day and night. You're always there. I think of you always. I love you always."[86] She found it heartbreaking to miss his conducting debut at the Glyptotek, and by spring 1935 she scolded him for not writing more often: "You're too far away and you give me too little. And yet you're the only person to whom I am always attracted and whom I trust completely. With you, I have never felt anything but kindness. But sometimes I find it so absolutely necessary to talk to you and to sense the harmony between us once more. (Well! Now the waltz from *Der Rosenkavalier* is playing on the radio! How am I supposed to bear listening to it all by myself?) Robert, in short: I need you, just you. How long has it been since I last saw you? I don't want to figure it out—it hurts far too much."[87]

It soon became clear that all paths would remain closed for Abraham in Denmark. The Danish Musicians' Society (*Dansk Tonekunstnerforening*) had approved his participation in the Glyptotek concerts only because he was not being paid for his work, a one-time gesture of good will.[88] In February 1935, Abraham had been rehearsing a full Lieder program—songs by Schumann, Brahms, and others—with a young soprano who was a student of Danish opera singer Henry Christoffersen, a friend of his late father's. Her application for Abraham to accompany her in a public concert in March was rejected by the Musicians' Society, and the Ministry of Justice declared, only a week before the scheduled date, that the concert would not be allowed to occur as planned.[89]

Thus, in spring 1935, Abraham's future seemed completely uncertain. He was made to report regularly to the Danish police, and surviving files suggest that by this time he was exploring options in several other countries. At a police interview in April, he claimed he was considering further study in Vienna, but only a day later, Lis Jacobsen told police that her protégé was seeking employment in Russia. In August, Abraham once again had to disclose his plans to the authorities, and by that time, he said, he had hopes of getting to South America.[90]

Yet none of these places were destined to be Abraham's final destination. Jacobsen had introduced him to many of her friends and colleagues, including a few Icelanders who had told him about their country and its shortage of top-level musicians. Among them was philologist Jakob Benediktsson, who later recalled feeling certain that Abraham's "passionate spirit" would come to good use in Iceland.[91] Eventually, Abraham agreed that going to this faraway place, even if only for a short while, might be a way out of his dilemma.[92] His acquaintances arranged a meeting with Sveinn Björnsson, then Iceland's ambassador to Denmark, who in 1944 became the first president of the Republic of Iceland. The ambassador listened politely to Abraham's ideas, reminding him that his country had little to offer such a gifted musician: there was no symphony orchestra, no mixed choir of any reputation, and the entire music scene was only beginning to take shape. In the end, he remarked: "If you want to go to Iceland to get wealthy, then don't give it any further thought—but if you really want to help, you'll find a warm welcome there."[93] After more than a year in Copenhagen, the time had come for Robert Abraham to relocate once again.

Urbancic: Vexation in Mainz

Victor Urbancic was employed in his native Vienna for several months after completing his doctorate in musicology there, but in 1926 he received his first permanent position, as rehearsal pianist and assistant conductor at the municipal theater (Stadttheater) in Mainz, Germany (see fig. 2.7). This city of approximately 130,000 inhabitants, on the banks of the river Rhine, near Frankfurt, would be his home for the next seven years. Urbancic and his fiancée Melitta initially had a long-distance relationship, as she enjoyed a brief but successful acting career in Baden-Baden, around ninety miles south

Figure 2.7. Victor Urbancic rehearsing singers for a performance at Mainzer Stadttheater, ca. 1930. *Source:* © Sibyl Urbancic, private collection. Used with permission.

of Mainz. After completing her own doctorate in 1927, she instead took another theater job in Koblenz, only sixty miles to the north.[94]

Eventually, Melitta moved to Mainz and gave up acting to start a family. She and Victor Urbancic were married in autumn 1930; a year later, their son Peter was born, followed by their daughter Ruth in 1932. Urbancic had a busy career at the Stadttheater rehearsing and conducting operas, including Offenbach's *The Tales of Hoffmann*, which was a particular success in spring 1931.[95] He also took on freelance work for the Schott music publishing house, which had its headquarters in Mainz, preparing piano reductions of scores such as Paul Hindemith's *Lehrstück*, Erich Wolfgang Korngold's one-act opera *Violanta*, and a two-piano arrangement of Manuel de Falla's *Nights in the Gardens of Spain*.[96]

As time passed, Urbancic grew increasingly frustrated with his job at the Mainz theater. He had an exhausting workload of rehearsals and performances, yet he was poorly paid, and, according to Melitta, his employers took advantage of his dedication and selflessness. "It pains my heart," she wrote to her mother in spring 1931, "to see a person of his worth so completely exploited and ripped off."[97] It was thus something of a godsend when the following year Urbancic was offered a position at the Mainz Conservatory of Music, an institution led by an old friend and colleague from Vienna, composer Hans Gál. The Mainz Conservatory was a renowned institution, with roughly a thousand students and sixty teachers, most of them in part-time positions.[98]

During the 1932–1933 season, Urbancic divided his energies between the municipal theater and the Conservatory, but shortly before the Nazis took power he signed a full-time contract at the latter institution. Under the new regime, however, it soon became evident that these plans would come to nothing. In local newspapers, Gál was publicly attacked for having employed a teacher who was not only a foreigner but also married to a Jew, when Germany had plenty of talented musicians to replace him.[99] Within a few weeks, Urbancic was informed he had no support for further work in Mainz, whether at the Conservatory or theater. Urbancic was of course not alone in this situation; all Jewish teachers at the Conservatory were summarily dismissed, including director Hans Gál.

Urbancic strongly protested his dismissal and, in April 1933, demanded a formal explanation in a letter to the mayor of Mainz. Two weeks later he received the reply that his discharge was inevitable as he could not be trusted to "always act wholeheartedly on behalf of the national state," as was required by the new Nazi legislation on civil servants.[100] An additional disadvantage was that Melitta Urbancic had been an active member of a pacifist organization in Mainz and had even consented to give a speech for the local association of women's clubs in March 1933 on "The Opponents of World Peace." With the Nazis in power, to publicly suggest that Germany might present a threat to world peace was a risky endeavor, and the event was canceled at short notice. According to a staff member at Mainz's city hall, Mrs. Urbancic withdrew her participation voluntarily, fearing it might harm her husband's already precarious situation.[101]

It is curious that the Mainz authorities should blame only Melitta's political unreliability for her husband's dismissal, while not mentioning her Jewish heritage at all. Yet they were fully aware of it, as shown in a memo from a Town Hall staff member to Wilhelm Jung, a lawyer and enthusiastic Nazi who became mayor of Mainz in spring 1933.[102] Possibly, the Mainz authorities wished to tread gently when it came to the new legislation on civil servants, and preferred to use the laws' fourth paragraph (on political unreliability) instead of the third (on Jews and "Aryans") when they had the choice.

Urbancic was deeply distressed by the situation and only reluctantly bid farewell to Mainz. After seven years as a devoted and hard-working employee, he found it preposterous that a new turn in politics should result in his forced dismissal. He resisted the outcome as long as he could, hiring a lawyer to plead his case with city officials, and requesting that the Austrian consul in Mainz send a formal complaint to the mayor, as this was a violation of the rights of an Austrian citizen.[103] Like so many Nazi victims, Urbancic initially believed the situation was only a temporary setback, and that he could still enjoy a promising career in Germany if he persevered for a while longer.

As it turned out, the Urbancic family departed Mainz in a hurry. For years, Melitta had frequented the store of a local merchant who appears to have been well informed in political matters. According to her daughter Sibyl, the merchant whispered to Melitta one day that she had been blacklisted by the local Nazi party, and asked her to be careful. It appears that rumors of her Jewish origin and political "unreliability" had begun to spread, and this ominous warning was the final straw. They decided to leave as soon as possible, leaving behind their furniture and most of their other belongings and heading back to Vienna, where both the Urbantschitsch and Grünbaum families lived.[104] It seemed like a safe haven—for the time being.

Urbancic: A Fortuitous Exchange

Finding employment in Austria in 1933 was no easy task. Following the Nazi takeover, thousands of Austrian Jews who had previously resided in Germany had returned to their homeland and were looking for work—a situation in which the Urbancic family now also found itself. But Victor Urbancic was a calm, practical man who used his time wisely, taking the so-called state examination in piano in the hope that it could lead to other opportunities later on. He also authored several articles in local music periodicals, and appeared as a guest conductor in Serbia, directing performances at the Belgrade Opera House in spring 1934.

Fortunately, this period of uncertainty soon came to an end. In 1934, Urbancic was offered a position at the Graz Conservatory of Music, considered one of Austria's finest music schools, founded in 1816 at the initiative of the Steiermark Music Association (*Musikverein für Steiermark*). In his new position, Urbancic could draw on his uncommonly broad expertise, teaching music theory, piano, music history, and composition, as well as supervising the school's opera studio. In addition, during the winter months, a concert series took place in the main hall of the conservatory, and Urbancic frequently appeared there as pianist, organist, or conductor.

In the 1930s, Graz was (and remains) Austria's second-largest city, with a total of 200,000 inhabitants including the suburbs. The tree-clad Schlossberg hill, with its ancient clock tower, looms over the city center, and the river Mur weaves gently through the town nearby. In Graz, Victor and Melitta Urbancic found an apartment in a three-story building in Brunnengasse, a quiet street in the St. Peter suburb, south of the city center. Their landlord, Mr. Wiesler, lived on the main floor, and his children would often play with young Peter and Ruth Urbancic. By a remarkable coincidence, Wiesler's granddaughter, flautist Manuela Wiesler, would much later also make Iceland her home. She made an important contribution to music there in the 1970s and 1980s, not least by commissioning and premiering a substantial number of new works for flute by Icelandic composers.[105]

Urbancic's first large concert in Graz was as continuo organist in Bach's *Christmas Oratorio* in December 1934, but his performances there were remarkably varied: he appeared as organist and pianist, played chamber music with his faculty colleagues, and conducted the university orchestra and a madrigal choir.[106] Only six months after his arrival, the dean of the conservatory was called to Ankara as a special music consultant to the Turkish government, and during his absence Urbancic assumed the post of acting dean. He also taught theory and counterpoint at Graz University from spring 1935 onward, with such favorable results that the philosophy faculty expressed its special satisfaction with the arrangement.[107] Despite this daunting schedule, Urbancic still found the time to compose music, including a Partita for cello and piano, and vocal settings of poetry by Hermann Hesse. His daughter, Sibyl, is still amazed by his productivity, and by his ability to carry out his varied tasks with such tranquility. "My father was just so calm and composed, one never had the feeling that anything could distress him. I've never known anyone else who has exuded such calm and patience towards everyone, and still achieved all the things that he did."[108]

Urbancic soon became a fixture of the Graz music scene, and reviews suggest his talents were well appreciated there. For example, a December 1935 concert of excerpts from operas by Mozart, Smetana, and Weber, with students at the conservatory, was said to have shown musical depth and passion. In particular, the reviewer of the *Grazer Tagespost* noted the "especially outstanding work" of Urbancic, an "eminent instructor and conductor" well worthy of the enthusiastic applause he received.[109]

But his situation soon became precarious. Graz was an early breeding ground for Nazism in Austria, and the situation there soon became arduous for people of Jewish heritage or in "mixed" marriages. Melitta was particularly worried about the children, who were growing up in an environment so different from what she had known as a child. Although the Nazi Party was forbidden in Austria from 1933–1938, many supported their goals in secret, and she sensed that the cruelty on which Nazism was built was gradually taking hold of even ordinary civilians. In January 1937, she wrote to her father in Vienna, expressing concern for her children's future in a world that seemed ever-more deranged: "Our children find themselves in an environment that is based on humiliation and disadvantage from the very beginning. They are intimidated by their fellow humans, oppressed and disgraced. Back in our day, we were able to defend ourselves, but now such cruelty has become an officially sanctioned way of life."[110] Melitta's greatest fear was that her son, Peter, who was just about to begin school and was a kind and gentle spirit, would, as a "half-Jew," be unable to stand up for himself in such a barbaric environment, and his "spiritual development" might be damaged for good.

Such hostile attitude could also be sensed within the walls of the Graz Conservatory, where several of Urbancic's colleagues made no attempt to hide their Nazi fervor. Their leader was Ludwig Kelbetz, two years Urbancic's junior, himself born and raised in Graz. He was appointed Associate Professor of Music Education in 1936, but his passion for shaping future generations through music found another outlet as well: he was music advisor to the Hitler Youth.[111] It was not least through Kelbetz's patronage that the Graz Conservatory became a haven for various local Nazi organizations. Since the Nazi Party was still officially banned, its supporters would gather informally under a different pretext, the "open singing" (*Offene Singstunden*) held once every few weeks in the conservatory's main hall. There, about two hundred Hitler supporters assembled to sing German and Austrian patriotic songs, and since police authorities were also sympathetic to the Nazi cause, such meetings were left undisturbed. Occasionally, Victor Urbancic was even required to take part as accompanist, although of course he had no affinity for such events or their political message.[112]

When Nazi troops marched into Austria on March 12, 1938, it was clear the Urbancic family would have to emigrate. Although Nazi officials hinted that Urbancic could remain in Graz if he would only divorce his wife, his love for Melitta and their children was much too strong for him to consider such an option. He first turned his attention to the United States, enquiring about available teaching positions via the American Musicological Society and enlisting the aid of a friend from Vienna, the exiled psychologist Fritz Redl, who attempted to help via the Emergency Committee in Aid of Displaced Foreign Scholars in New York, but with no success.[113] He also applied for a conducting post with the Swiss Radio Orchestra, also to no avail.[114]

Surviving correspondence by Austrian officials suggests that Urbancic's work had left such a formidable impression that even resolute Nazis would have preferred that he stay in his post. In April 1938, the aforementioned Kelbetz, recently promoted to dean of the conservatory, wrote to a high-ranking Nazi official in Vienna, praising Urbancic as an "outstanding and unusually talented musician" who was virtually indispensable to the school.[115] Reading between the lines, Kelbetz seems to be requesting an exemption to Nazi law on the grounds of Urbancic's rare talent. While there are a few examples of Nazis turning a blind eye in similar situations, in this particular case they would not be swayed.[116] A month later, the Graz Musikverein's board noted they had petitioned the authorities on Urbancic's behalf, since he was "truly indispensable," but without success.[117]

Urbancic found an unexpected way out of this seemingly hopeless situation. He had heard that Viennese musician Franz Mixa, a former schoolmate of his at university, was currently employed in Iceland but wished to return to Austria. Mixa had traveled to Iceland in 1929, soon after completing a dissertation on Mozart's use of the clarinet, to rehearse the recently founded Reykjavík Orchestra for its most ambitious performances thus far, at the millennial celebrations of the Icelandic parliament in 1930. His work there was deemed so successful that he was given a permanent contract, conducting the orchestra and teaching piano and music theory at the newly established Reykjavík Music School. Mixa had taken a leave of absence during the 1931–1932 school year, traveling back to Vienna, and it was there that he enrolled in the Nazi Party on January 16, 1932—his membership number was 782,617.[118] He then returned to Reykjavík, resumed his position at the music school, and married a talented local pianist, Katrín Ólafsdóttir.

Mixa's friends in Austria sensed the changing political situation and encouraged him to return home for good. One of them was oboist Hans Wlach, a colleague of Urbancic's at the Graz Conservatory. It was he who first suggested to Urbancic that exchanging posts might be beneficial to them both.[119] Wlach, Mixa, and Urbancic had all studied musicology with Adler at Vienna University in 1921–1925, but the close friendship of Wlach and Mixa had begun even earlier.[120] Wlach was an amateur poet, and Mixa set some of his texts to music as early as 1918–1919, and he was one of two witnesses at Wlach's wedding in 1932.[121] Furthermore, at a Graz concert devoted to Mixa's songs in July 1936, Wlach gave a pre-performance talk about his development and output as a composer.[122]

Wlach was convinced that, should Mixa return to Austria, his political affiliation would finally enable the career he had long deserved. Wlach's views are clearly expressed in his 1937 review of Mixa's recently published songs from *Des Knaben Wunderhorn*, in the *Zeitschrift für Musik*—a somewhat suspect undertaking given their close friendship. The parlance in Wlach's review is unmistakably influenced by Nazi rhetoric.[123] He praises the "purity" of Mixa's songs, which he claims can restore Germany's "ancient honor" by conquering the "listless, heavy, and often sickly emotional life of the pre-war era." He is also blatantly anti-Semitic, contending that Jews had, in recent years, "stolen" jobs from more worthy contenders, and claiming in particular that Mixa had been forced to depart for Iceland because it was "hopeless to find a suitable job in his homeland, overflowing with Jews." In conclusion, Wlach strongly advocates his friend's return from voluntary exile: "It is high time that the talented musician Franz Mixa, who treads new and lofty paths in his work, be brought back from the North."[124]

A year after writing these words, Wlach saw an opportunity to realize his plan. At his instigation, Urbancic wrote to Mixa in Reykjavík, asking if he might consider an exchange of positions. Mixa happily agreed, returning to Austria in spring 1938, only a few weeks after its annexation by Germany.[125] At around the same time, the Reykjavík Music Society's board resolved to hire Urbancic, after Mixa had presented them, as one board member put it, with "many fine credentials" in his name.[126] In Graz, Urbancic also arranged for most of his own positions at the conservatory and university to be taken over by Mixa.[127]

In Austria, remarkably, Mixa presented the entire case so that high-ranking local Nazi officials were under the impression that they had a mandate for appointing his successor in Iceland. This of course was far from true, and the Reykjavík Music Society's board was blissfully unaware of any such maneuver. Perhaps Mixa saw in this a chance to further bolster his position within the Nazi cultural hierarchy, but in any case Robert Ernst, the director of the Nazi's Vienna Culture Bureau, was happy to comply; after all, Urbancic was the only contender for the position.[128] Seen in another light, by involving the Nazi Party in the exchange, Mixa ensured that Urbancic's exit from Austria was carried out legally, with the consent and approval of the Reich Music Chamber. This might have had future implications, in the unlikely event that Urbancic should decide to return to Austria under Nazi rule. In any case, on July 22, 1938, Mixa received a letter from Ludwig Kelbetz, on behalf of the Steiermark Music Association, thanking him for having facilitated the exchange with Urbancic, "whom we value as an extraordinarily skilled employee."[129]

As could be expected for a long-standing member, Mixa quickly rose to prominence within the Nazi Party following his return to Graz. He was a member of the SA (*Sturmabteilung*) from 1940–1942, and the regional leader (*Gauleiter*) of the Reich Music Chamber until his conscription in 1943. At the end of the war, he was captured by the French army and spent two years as a prisoner of war in Mulsanne, France.[130] He later returned to teach at the Graz Conservatory, serving as its director from 1952–1957, and later taught at the *Hochschule für Musik* in Munich, along with his second wife, renowned Austrian contralto Hertha Töpper.[131]

It may seem bizarre that Franz Mixa, a member of the Nazi Party, should have been willing to save the Urbancic family by facilitating their move to Iceland at such a dire moment. He was certainly an opportunist, like countless others, but he was no fanatical villain. Nothing suggests he took part in the activities of Iceland's fledgling Nazi movement during his years in Reykjavík, and as a critic he wrote enthusiastic reviews of Jewish performers who concertized there, such as violinist Ernst Drucker.[132] Having returned to Austria, he heard that Czech musician Jan Morávek, whose partner was an Icelandic soprano with whom Mixa had worked in Reykjavík, was being mistreated by the Nazis, and used his connections to obtain an orchestra position for him at the Graz Opera.[133] Later in life, Mixa restored his reputation as a composer and teacher, and the Urbancic family remembers him with gratitude to the present day. Without his assistance, their fate might have been far different.

For several years, Melitta Urbancic had considered converting to the Roman Catholic faith. She had no illusions this would spare her from Nazi persecution, since she was a *Volljüdin* by birth. Rather, she held a genuine interest in religion, and she wished for her and her husband to be able to join together in raising their children as Roman Catholics. She had delayed her decision to avoid upsetting her father, a devout Jew, but Alfred Grünbaum had died in Vienna, apparently of heart failure, in April 1938, only a few weeks after the Nazis annexed Austria. For his family, it seemed as though he simply could not bear to witness the collapse of the country he loved.[134] Just over two months later, on July 31, 1938, Melitta Urbancic was baptized into the Catholic faith in St. Peter's, the family's parish church in Graz, and she and her husband also used the opportunity to confirm their marriage vows in a simple ceremony before two witnesses.[135]

In summer 1938, Victor Urbancic fled the Nazis for the second time in his career, leaving a satisfying position in Graz to begin life anew in an unknown country. Like so many others in a similar predicament, he believed the dire situation would not last long, and regarded the family's move to Iceland a temporary solution.[136] In mid-August, he traveled to Iceland alone, taking a train via Copenhagen to Bergen, Norway, and sailing from there on the SS *Lyra* to Reykjavík. He wanted to settle there before his wife and children would join him, and he undertook the trip earlier than originally

Figure 2.8. Victor and Melitta Urbancic (right) with Melitta's parents, Ilma and Alfred Grünbaum, ca. 1936. Ruth and Peter Urbancic are seated at the small table. *Source:* © Sibyl Urbancic, private collection. Used with permission.

planned, as the leaders of the Reykjavík Music Society wished to begin rehearsals for their autumn concert as soon as possible.[137] Urbancic intended for Melitta and the children to join him in Reykjavík in October, and in Graz they had already begun to organize the shipping of their belongings, such as large furniture and their Steinway grand piano.[138]

Melitta and the children made the journey to Reykjavík sooner than planned, however. Daily life in Graz was fast becoming unbearable for people of Jewish descent, who were in constant danger of being reported to the authorities. In September 1938, only a few weeks after her husband departed for Iceland, Melitta was ordered to appear at the Gestapo headquarters for questioning. The officer in charge was boorish and crude, screaming all kinds of obscenities at her, but toward the end, when his colleagues were out of earshot, he whispered to her that she should try to get out of the country as soon as possible.[139] Once released, Melitta decided she would not spend another night in Graz. She grabbed only a few essentials at their house before heading to the train station with one-year-old Sibyl; she even left the front door unlocked so as not to raise suspicion.[140]

Melitta had a long and taxing journey ahead of her. Her first stop was Vienna, where seven-year-old Peter and five-year-old Ruth were already staying with their grandparents. Having bid her mother and parents-in-law an emotional farewell, Melitta and the three children embarked on a train to Copenhagen via Berlin. Peter recalls that his mother was on pins and needles during the journey, particularly on the train from Berlin, which was filled with refugees. The Danish border officials examined all passports intently and expelled dozens of people due to insufficient documentation, but fortunately Melitta's paperwork was impeccable; it was clear she was only passing through Denmark and would not stay long.[141] Years later, she wrote a short story about a woman on a precarious journey similar to her own, across a border with a young child. While she altered many of the details, it contains a powerful passage undoubtedly based on her own experience, about a passport's value in the mind of someone who fears that its validity might be challenged:

> On this journey, I have seen many people bring out their passports with indifference, as if producing just another train ticket or a banknote. I have glanced timidly at these strangers' passports, so carelessly presented; timid because of the thin booklet in my own hand. Who knows what it means, outside of our borders: a passport. For as long as you don't possess one, it seems an

inconceivable wonder; and when it nonetheless materializes, this booklet with its few pages becomes an undeserved mercy, a stroke of good fortune never to be fully justified.[142]

Even after arriving in Copenhagen, their ordeal was far from over. Melitta had assumed that ships departed to Iceland almost daily, and thus had not made plans to stay longer than twenty-four hours. But it turned out they had to wait a few days, and soon she found herself penniless, relying on assistance from complete strangers, until they were able to board the SS *Dronning Alexandrine* on September 20.[143] During their wait, the autumn sun was shining, and she took the children to the nearby Ørsted Park, where they were able to play in a sandbox and enjoy their newfound freedom. The Urbancic children recall that their mother tried to make the journey as enjoyable as possible and that both their parents purposely concealed from the children the precariousness of their situation, both before and after they arrived in Iceland.[144]

Melitta Urbancic and her children were fortunate to have escaped only weeks before the horrors of the *Kristallnacht* were unleashed throughout the Third Reich. In their hometown of Graz, the synagogue went up in flames; approximately three hundred Jews were taken from their homes in the middle of the night and shipped to the Dachau concentration camp. Other Jews were molested and tortured; some were left on the streets in their own blood, whereas others were forced to jump into the river Mur.[145] A year later, the Graz authorities declared, with a depraved sense of pride, that they had reached their long-awaited goal. The city, they proclaimed, was now *judenrein*, "cleansed" of all people of Jewish heritage.[146]

3

World's End

For talented musicians trained in Europe's cultural centers, moving to a remote location such as Iceland proved a challenge in many respects. In terms of its topography, Iceland is a notably barren country, and it could seem strangely uninhabitable for those who had lived near the Vienna Woods or Germany's Black Forest. Located just a few degrees south of the Arctic circle, Iceland can also be an exceptionally dark and cold place. Both Robert Abraham and Heinz Edelstein arrived there late in the year and had to endure an entire Arctic winter before they experienced firsthand the near-perpetual light of its summer nights. The capital, Reykjavík, had only around 38,000 inhabitants in the 1930s, but expanded rapidly as more people relocated from the countryside to start a new, modern life. Its townscape was largely made up of modest wooden houses covered with corrugated iron, which, locals had discovered a few decades before, provided excellent shelter from the wind and rain. A few recent, more substantial buildings made of stone were testaments to the local ambition for Reykjavík to assume the role of a capital: a national hospital, a neo-gothic cathedral for its Roman-Catholic minority, and a state-of-the-art hotel, recently opened, facing the town's central square. Streets were mostly unpaved, and the majority of the population lived in poverty; the financial crisis of the early 1930s had led to widespread unemployment, a housing market in crisis, and a weak local currency, the króna.[1]

The local music scene was still in its infancy, and only a few musicians had received substantial professional training. Among the most prominent Icelandic performers were violinist Þórarinn Guðmundsson, who had trained in Copenhagen, and organist Páll Ísólfsson, a former student of Karl Straube at the Leipzig Conservatory. The country's leading pianist was Árni Kristjánsson, who had recently returned from advanced studies in Berlin and Copenhagen. Another promising talent was violinist Björn Ólafsson, who studied in Vienna, returning home in summer 1939 for what was intended as a short holiday. The outbreak of World War II prevented him from returning to the continent, and instead he became a key player in Iceland's music scene for decades, both as violinist and teacher.

Quality instruments were few and far between, although the situation was slowly improving. A new 26-stop pipe organ was inaugurated in Reykjavík Cathedral in 1934, and adequate grand pianos were at last becoming more common.[2] The first recital on a grand piano ever given in Reykjavík was by U.S. pianist Arthur Shattuck in 1910, but he brought his own instrument, lent by the Danish Hindsberg manufacturers, and it was shipped back to Denmark soon afterward.[3] When Haraldur Sigurðsson, a prominent Icelandic pianist based in Copenhagen, gave a solo recital in the Old Cinema (*Gamla bíó*) in 1914, he had to make do with an upright piano even though the program included substantial works such as Beethoven's *Appassionata* sonata. One critic remarked that it was "a considerable disgrace for the country's capital" to be unable to provide a grand piano for such a worthy occasion.[4] Another colleague was even more outspoken: "This lack of instruments is an outrage and brings shame to our town."[5]

Concerts were most commonly held in venues built for other purposes, such as Reykjavík Cathedral and the Free Church (*Fríkirkjan*), the Old Cinema, Iðnó Theater, or *Báran*, a venue at the northwest corner of Reykjavík's central lake, where its City Hall now stands. Lighter music was daily fare at the town's hotels. The largest ones, City Hotel (*Hótel Borg*) and Hotel Iceland (*Hótel Ísland*), employed dance bands that enjoyed great popularity. Two stores catered to local music lovers, providing sheet music, gramophone records, and instruments: the prosaically named "The Instrument House" (*Hljóðfærahúsið*), situated in Bankastræti, and "Katrín Viðar's Music Store," in Lækjargata 2, only a few yards away.

Orchestral performances were a distinct novelty. The Reykjavík Orchestra (*Hljómsveit Reykjavíkur*) was established in 1925, but consisted of a small group of twenty or so instrumentalists, most of them amateurs. It gave up to seven concerts a year, usually conducted by Sigfús Einarsson, the cathedral organist, and its programs featured works or individual movements by composers like Haydn, Mozart, Beethoven, and Schubert. A significant hurdle was that not all the necessary symphonic instruments or adequate players could be found in the entire country, for example oboe and bassoon. Thus, the Reykjavík Orchestra usually had to resort to playing salon band arrangements, with piano and harmonium taking the missing parts.[6] Artistically speaking, it was far from an ideal situation.

Mixed choirs were also rare in the country until the 1930s. Several male choirs had been active there for over a decade: the YMCA (KFUM) Men's Choir was established in 1916 and the Reykjavík Men's Chorus (*Karlakór Reykjavíkur*) a decade later, and even a few rural towns could boast of male vocal ensembles of adequate quality.[7] But for men and women to join together in a choir was largely unheard of, and met with widespread skepticism. The talented organist Páll Ísólfsson had attempted to form a mixed vocal ensemble upon his return from Leipzig in 1920, giving local premieres of works by Bach, Handel, and Brahms, among others, but this effort petered out after a few years. The most ambitious attempt to form a mixed ensemble was the so-called "Þingvellir Choir," a group of one hundred singers formed especially to perform a newly composed cantata at the 1930 national festival celebrating the millennium of the Icelandic parliament. The audition process confirmed the reluctance of Iceland's male population to be involved with mixed-choir singing; 138 women auditioned, of whom sixty were selected, but only three men out of thirty-five were judged to be at all "usable." Thus, it was only by persuading the YMCA Men's Choir to join the female ensemble *in toto*—and under their own name—that the project could be brought to fruition.[8] The 1930 Festival Choir was by far the largest mixed choir in the nation's history, and its performance was deemed a success, but the group was formed with only one specific event in mind, after which it disbanded. Further progress in the field would take place only in the ensuing decades.

Although circumstances were in many ways less than optimal, local audiences were both enthusiastic and discerning when it came to classical music. Foreign artists who appeared in Reykjavík often expressed their surprise at how intently locals listened to their music-making, and how fervently they expressed their delight through applause. For example, when the Hamburg Philharmonic Orchestra toured in Iceland in 1926, it was the largest musical event in the country's history—the first time locals had the chance to hear a full symphony orchestra perform. At the conclusion of the first concert, a crowded auditorium let forth, according to one critic, "such a tremendous roar of jubilation, that old Iðnó trembled under the impact."[9] Four years later, the ovation for French violinist Henri Marteau, who concertized in

Reykjavík in spring 1930, was described by one critic as "uncontrollable," culminating in a "frenzy of hurrahs" that elicited a string of encores.[10] In a newspaper interview, Marteau expressed his delight at the reception he had received, noting he had "not at all expected such understanding in a country where the art of music is as young as it is here."[11]

After a few short-lived attempts, a comprehensive music school (*Tónlistarskólinn í Reykjavík*) was founded in 1930 under the leadership of Páll Ísólfsson. At first, the school was based in a small octagonal pavilion built in 1922 by the Reykjavík Brass Band, which was for decades the only building in Iceland purposely built for music (see fig. 3.1). The school initially had about thirty students, although enrollment increased each year. The faculty consisted of only a handful of teachers; Ísólfsson and Austrian pianist-composer Franz Mixa taught piano and music theory, while another Viennese musician, Hans Stepanek, taught violin. By 1940, both Mixa and Stepanek had returned to Austria, but two other émigrés had joined the faculty, Heinz Edelstein and Victor Urbancic, as had two outstanding local musicians, pianist Árni Kristjánsson and violinist Björn Ólafsson.[12]

Figure 3.1. The Hljómskálinn Pavilion in central Reykjavík, ca. 1935. The pavilion was home to the Reykjavík School of Music from 1930 to 1944. *Source:* Photo: Karl Christian Nielsen. Public domain, provided courtesy of Reykjavík Museum of Photography.

The Reykjavík Music School was initially run by the Reykjavík Orchestra, but this soon proved to be an unsatisfactory arrangement. In 1932, the nonprofit Reykjavík Music Society (*Tónlistarfélag Reykjavíkur*) was established with the purpose of running both the school and the orchestra, and it soon also began organizing an annual subscription series of solo, chamber, and orchestra concerts, which would become the backbone of the town's musical life for decades.[13] The society was spearheaded by twelve local businessmen and lawyers, so fervent in their mission to spread the "gospel" of classical music among the local population that they became affectionately known as "the twelve apostles." Promoting classical music in Iceland was hardly a lucrative enterprise, and the "apostles" paid any losses incurred out of their own pockets—which happened frequently, particularly in the society's initial years.[14]

The group's leader was Ragnar Jónsson, also known as Ragnar í Smára (Ragnar of Smári) because he owned a successful margarine factory by that name (see fig. 3.2). He was a devoted art lover and cultural patron who later also went into the book-publishing business, issuing the works

Figure 3.2. Ragnar Jónsson, chairman of the Reykjavík Music Society. *Source:* Photo: Ólafur K. Magnússon. © Morgunblaðið. Used with permission.

of Iceland's Nobel Laureate author, Halldór Laxness, among others. Other key members on the society's board were Björn Jónsson, a local merchant who assumed the role of financial officer, and Ólafur Þorgrímsson, a lawyer whose expertise proved invaluable when applying for work permits for foreign faculty.[15] Most of the "apostles" had some musical training; for example, Jónsson played clarinet with the Reykjavík Orchestra and Þorgrímsson composed songs and piano pieces in his free time. What united them all was the urge to improve standards in the capital's musical life, through music education as well as opportunities to hear outstanding musicians perform live. In 1943, noting that a lack of access to instruments was impeding students' progress at the music school, they promptly launched their own instrument store, with newspaper ads calling for "An Instrument in Every Icelandic Home."[16] The "apostles" also dreamed of building a concert hall in Reykjavík, though this proved too ambitious even for such an ardent group. Still, they collected funds for a new building by programming popular operettas as part of the Reykjavík Orchestra's season, and by publishing the much-loved seventeenth-century Icelandic *Hymns of the Passion* in a special collector's edition.[17]

Ragnar Jónsson was an impulsive, even fanatic, trailblazer who lived according to his conviction that wealthy individuals had a moral duty to support culture and the arts.[18] The organist Páll Ísólfsson once remarked that Jónsson had been among the first people in Iceland ever to recognize "that artists also have to eat, just like everyone else."[19] In fact, even devoted professionals sometimes found Jónsson's enthusiasm rather excessive. Stefán Edelstein described what he called a typical visit to Jónsson's home, a place where, since he was also a patron of all of the country's most distinguished painters, the walls were covered with valuable artwork from floor to ceiling. When a guest arrived, Jónsson was likely to put on a gramophone record, for example a Brahms symphony, "and while that was playing on full blast he would utter something like 'Say, did I ever read you this passage from *World Light?*' [a novel by Laxness] and then he began reciting it aloud in a thundering voice, trying to drown out the blaring sound of Brahms."[20]

Another key cultural institution, the Icelandic National Radio (*Ríkisútvarpið*) was also founded in 1930, and like the music school, its music department was spearheded by Páll Ísólfsson. The radio program included classical music from imported gramophone records as well as live performances by local musicians, as recording equipment became available only later, in the early 1940s. A few instrumentalists were contracted to perform twice weekly: violinist Þórarinn Guðmundsson and pianist Emil Thoroddsen, as well as a larger ensemble of four to twelve musicians known as the Radio Orchestra. Music lovers were initially less than impressed by these performances; even a Radio staff member described the orchestra's playing, in a private letter, as "usually poor in quality, imprecise and muddy."[21] Even worse, many Icelanders still had no experience listening to classical music and detested what was often referred to as the "symphonic noise" (*symfóníugarg*) on the program, preferring accordion music and light dance songs instead.[22]

By the 1930s, the citizens of Reykjavík had become accustomed to foreign musicians who came there to work, whether for long or short periods of time. These people had all been drawn to the country for conventional reasons: because they needed work, or yearned for adventure in a distant, exotic land. The Viennese Fritz Weisshappel arrived in Reykjavík in 1928 at only nineteen years of age, initially working as a cellist, though he quickly became one of the town's most sought-after collaborative pianists. Other Viennese musicians in Reykjavík included pianist Carl Billich and violinist Josef Felzmann, both of whom arrived in 1933 to work at Hotel Iceland, where they performed classical music in the afternoon and dance music in the evenings.[23] The Reykjavík Music Society also procured excellent faculty members, such as Franz Mixa and Hans Stepanek, both of whom were also Viennese.[24] These and many other musicians did not arrive under threat, and could return home whenever they desired. No musician had ever come to Iceland because his life was in danger until Robert Abraham arrived there in 1935, joined a few years later by Heinz Edelstein and Victor Urbancic. Like the other foreign musicians before them, they became pioneers on the local scene, establishing a "classical" Western music culture where none had been before.

Abraham: A "Darned Parasite" in Akureyri

In late October 1935, Robert Abraham arrived in Reykjavík from Copenhagen. He later recalled that his first impression of the town was dreadful. As the ship entered the harbor in late evening, Reykjavík seemed a terribly dark and dreary place, lashed with winds and heavy rain. He spent his first night at the Salvation Army but then moved to the university dormitory (*Garður*), where he became acquainted with several local students around his age.[25]

Initially, it was highly doubtful that Abraham would be able to obtain a residence and work permit. His situation differed from that of Edelstein and Urbancic a few years later, as they arrived as employees of the Reykjavík

School of Music and also had full access to legal counsel through the "twelve apostles." Abraham, on the other hand, knew no one in Iceland, and the chances of an unemployed refugee of Jewish heritage being allowed to settle there were minimal. He was granted a permit for only two months, after which time, he was informed in a letter from the Justice Department, he would have to leave the country.[26] But Abraham soon befriended several local students at the university dormitory who were willing to pledge themselves on his behalf. A few days after he received notification of his short-term permit, twenty students wrote a joint letter to Prime Minister Hermann Jónasson, requesting that Abraham "not be denied permission to stay this winter," since he had "come here in good faith that this was still a land open to foreigners."[27] It speaks volumes of Abraham's intellect and charisma that in only a few days he should have been able to gain the trust and support of so many people in a new, remote country.

Abraham followed the latest news from Germany, and thus knew of the Nuremberg Laws the Nazis had passed only a month earlier (see chapter 2). In his initial application to the Justice Department, he cited his engagement to Emmy Schulz as one of the main reasons for his exile to Iceland. His acquaintances at the university also drew attention to this in their letter: "He is unable to return to Germany, since he has been engaged to a German girl, and his return home would, according to the latest laws, put him and his family in grave danger."[28] This may have been only a ruse to increase his chances of being allowed to stay, since his relationship with Emmy Schulz had already ended. In any case, both Abraham and his new friends soon realized that government officials were unlikely to sympathize with that particular situation. Thus, his fiancée was never again mentioned in his correspondence with the Justice Department; instead, Abraham and his supporters emphasized his prodigious musical talents and how he could contribute to cultural life in Iceland.

In presenting his case to the authorities, Abraham also relied on friends and acquaintances in Copenhagen. His indefatigable patron, Lis Jacobsen, wrote her own letter to the Justice Department, recommending him highly "both as a person and as an artist."[29] Still, a recommendation from one of her colleagues may have carried even more weight. Erik Arup, professor of history at Copenhagen University, was at the time collaborating with Jacobsen on the publication of Danish medieval documents, and while their working relationship has been described as volatile, he was a valuable ally. Arup was on friendly terms with leading Icelandic politicians, having served on the joint committee charged with settling the terms of Iceland's independence from Denmark in 1918.[30] Thus, any proposal from him was bound to carry weight on the government level. On November 7, 1935, Prime Minister Jónasson received a telegram from Arup in which he "warmly" recommended a work permit for Robert Abraham, "at least until conditions are clarified elsewhere."[31] The next day, Arup received the reply that Abraham had permission until next spring—a decision Jónasson had already made a week earlier, upon receiving the petition from Abraham's university friends.[32] The minister's quick response, after a group of local students and highly regarded Danish intellectuals had pledged their support, shows that applications from exiled foreigners were not always summarily dismissed, and that personal connections could be immensely valuable. Nevertheless, during Abraham's first years in Iceland he was granted permission to stay for only six months at a time. When his permit expired in May 1937, government officials were slow to respond to his request for renewal, and he found himself without a valid permit for nearly a month.[33] Only in January 1938 was he granted a permanent visa, which of course gave him added security.[34] Just a few months later, Icelandic authorities expelled several German Jews who had resided in the country for several years.[35]

Abraham did not remain in Iceland's capital for long. Soon after his arrival, he met with organist and music school dean Páll Ísólfsson, who suggested that he settle in Akureyri, a town in Northern Iceland with at the time roughly five thousand inhabitants. There, he advised, a talented musician like Abraham was bound to find worthwhile opportunities.[36] Given the circumstances, this was undoubtedly a sound proposal. Akureyri was a town large enough for Abraham to find work as a musician, but he would be less conspicuous to both the police and the leaders of the newly established Icelandic Musicians' Union than by staying in the capital. In Akureyri, Abraham found a small apartment and quickly made local friends, not least students roughly his age who frequented a popular cafeteria near his new home.[37] In an interview decades later, when asked about his early years in Akureyri, he remarked: "Everything was so pure and clean and wonderful there. I immediately felt like a local."[38]

In Akureyri, Abraham made two lifelong friends who helped him adapt to life in a new country. Halldór Halldórsson and Þórarinn Björnsson were both teachers at the local junior college, and Abraham later reminisced that they were "the best company I could have imagined. Halldór proved an invaluable teacher of Icelandic, and Þórarinn would read with me poems by Einar Benediktsson and other masters of the Icelandic language."[39] For the first few months, Abraham relied on his knowledge of Danish, a language widely understood in Iceland, but he was also remarkably quick to master Icelandic. Halldórsson later recalled that he had become largely fluent by Christmas 1935, only two months after his arrival, and many of Abraham's acquaintances would later testify to his impressive command of the Icelandic language.[40]

Having arrived in Akureyri, Abraham began giving piano and music theory lessons—privately, because as yet the town had no music school. He had no practical experience as a teacher; after all, he was only twenty-three years old and had not been allowed to teach in Denmark during his year there. In an interview later in life, he recalled how much he had learned from his first students: "They taught me how to teach."[41] He took on various small jobs, such as playing piano for guests at the local hotel, but a more ambitious undertaking was a solo recital at the Akureyri Town Hall in February 1936, including works by Mozart, Brahms, Schubert, and Schumann. A local critic wrote that "rarely, if ever," had a piano recital given him such satisfaction.[42] In June that year he again gave a recital, this time consisting of a Haydn Piano Sonata in F major and Beethoven's sonatas opp. 109 and 110. This recital was also well received, with a local critic enthusing that Abraham was "one of those truly noble interpreters who care more for their art itself and a genuine understanding of it, than bringing attention to their own talent. Such a thoroughly trained musician could be of immense benefit here, if his talents were allowed to flourish and people valued him according to his worth."[43]

Abraham also found another outlet for his talent: as a choral conductor. In September 1936, he advertised in local newspapers for singers interested in forming a chamber choir of sixteen. The auditions were so successful that "Robert Abraham's Mixed Choir" (*Samkór Róberts Abraham*) began rehearsals later in the autumn and gave its first public performance in April 1937 (see fig. 3.3).[44] The program was far more ambitious than usual for a choir in a small Icelandic town, including selections from large choral works by Bach, Haydn, Gluck, and Brahms, with all the texts translated and sung in Icelandic. Abraham appreciated the challenge of performing choral repertoire that had rarely or never been heard in Iceland, let alone in the small town of Akureyri. The result was described as "extraordinarily refined and tasteful," and "a wonder" given that it was the group's first performance.[45] At another concert in May 1938, the program included movements from Verdi's Requiem and Brahms's *German Requiem*. The choir's programs also included another novelty: symphonic works such as Schubert's *Unfinished* symphony and Beethoven's *Coriolan* and *Egmont* overtures, performed by

Figure 3.3. Robert Abraham's choir at a concert in the New Cinema (*Nýja bíó*), Akureyri, in March 1939. *Source:* © Akureyri Museum. Used with permission.

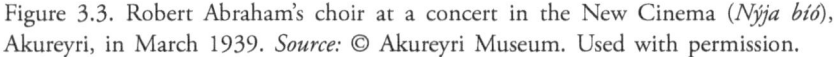

Abraham and Jórunn Norðmann, the ensemble's accompanist, in four-hand piano transcriptions.

Some locals greeted Abraham's intention to form the choir with skepticism. Akureyri already had three well-established vocal ensembles: the Akureyri Cantata Choir (*Kantötukór Akureyrar*, a mixed choir), the Akureyri Men's Choir, and the Geysir Men's Choir, and thus the town's finest singers, particularly the men, already belonged to other groups. But "Robert Abraham's Mixed Choir" was remarkably successful from the start. Demand from singers was so great that the ensemble soon grew to twice the size originally planned, a total of thirty-two singers, and their popularity among the townsfolk was unquestioned. Most of the ensemble's concerts had to be repeated, and often nearly every piece was encored; the group also performed on National Radio, and was accepted into the National Association of Icelandic Choirs.[46] "There is not a single choir that has been given a better reception here," noted one local newspaper, and after its concert in spring 1938 a critic enthused about Abraham's talents: "Other choir conductors could learn much from him."[47]

Abraham also became a sought-after accompanist for singers, both locals from Akureyri and more established artists who came from Reykjavík to concertize there. His contribution was generally well received, yet one particular concert sparked a fierce debate. In October 1936, Abraham gave a joint recital with local soprano Guðrún Þorsteinsdóttir; apart from songs, the substantial program also included solo piano works by Handel, Mozart, Beethoven, Schubert, and Brahms, as well as Abraham's improvised fantasy on three well-known Icelandic songs. The audience reception was enthusiastic, and the pianist even had to repeat one of his solo numbers. The editor of the local newspaper *Dagur* found the evening to have been "wonderful in every way" and that it was clear to everyone that Abraham was "consumed by music." His only criticism was directed toward his fellow townspeople, as he wondered why the talents of such a "magician" had not been put to better use "in the service of musical culture in this town?"[48] Áskell Snorrason seconded this opinion in another local paper, noting that Abraham had made a deep impression as a "more emotional, temperamental, and more substantial artist than when I have heard him previously."[49]

Not everyone agreed. Tómas Björnsson, a local building supply merchant who was also a devoted member of the right-wing Independence Party and on the editorial board of the conservative weekly *Icelander* (*Íslendingur*), wrote an article in that paper criticizing how Abraham's performance had been "terribly overpraised." Björnsson found his playing imprecise, rough, and unrefined. In the rare moments when he played softly enough, Björnsson complained, the outcome was uneven and some notes didn't sound at all. Abraham was at his best, he claimed, in loud and fast movements, such as a Scherzo from an unnamed Brahms sonata, yet he still complained that the effect had been "like he was hitting the piano with iron hammers." Overall, he found in Abraham's playing "nothing of the spiritual dignity and humility that is inherent in all true artists."[50]

Björnsson's critique sparked heated controversy, and many came to the pianist's defense. A medical doctor, Valdimar Steffensen, condemned the article as ignorant and misleading, citing, among others, a glowing recommendation that renowned pianist Ignaz Friedman had written on

Abraham's behalf after making his acquaintance in Paris in 1934.[51] Another, anonymous writer began by gently poking fun of Björnsson, calling him a failed "prophet" who knew far less about music than building supplies, but soon struck a more serious tone:

> Yet we also must agree with the prophet, and indeed emphatically, that it was terribly negligent of Mr. Abraham to hit the piano so loosely with his "iron hammers," given that he uses such powerful tools when playing the piano in the first place, that some of the notes were completely lost and God only knows if they will ever be found again. If Mr. Abraham doesn't have strong enough hammers, then he should be able to get them—and at a good price, too—from Tómas [Björnsson], for at least he is no damned Jew or "darned parasite," which is what composer Björgvin [Guðmundsson] called Abraham the other day.[52]

Here the anonymous writer has reached the crux of his argument: the xenophobic Björnsson only wished to defame Abraham because of his Jewish origin. He further laments that this was not an isolated case, as Akureyri had recently witnessed "a never-ending barrage of attacks" on Abraham, an artist who had received nothing but admiration elsewhere:

> And the muck in this cesspool has not diminished with the new prophet's Nazi judgment. It will be the greatest dishonor for the citizens of this town if they aren't soon able to stop the flow of this sewer, and to dry it up completely. I hope that Mr. Robert Abraham will give another recital here before long, so that locals will be able to hear him play with his iron hammers and respond to Tómas Björnsson's attack in an appropriate manner.

Indeed, Abraham and Þorsteinsdóttir repeated their concert on October 25, and Abraham specifically noted in one newspaper report that this was done "so that as many as possible can judge for themselves the validity of [Björnsson's] review."[53] While no reviews appeared of the repeat concert, the overall turmoil had caught the attention of the Reykjavík papers. On November 3, the socialist daily *Þjóðviljinn* carried an article headed "Persecution of Jews in Akureyri," claiming that Björnsson's review had been written "in the style of the German barbarians," and that its "disgusting, fascist" tone had been generally condemned both in Akureyri and in the capital.[54]

The public debate gradually subsided, but the underlying animosity remained. The author of the anonymous article quoted above had mentioned Björnsson's name in conjunction with that of Björgvin Guðmundsson, a local composer and choral director, who had become a sworn enemy of Abraham and his choir. Guðmundsson had for many years conducted the Akureyri Cantata Choir, the town's only mixed choir until Abraham arrived. It was an ensemble whose main purpose was to perform the conductor's own music, mostly large choral works in traditional Romantic style, such as the cantata *Iceland's Thousand Years* (*Íslands þúsund ár*) and the oratorio *Peace on Earth* (*Friður á jörðu*). Despite his talents, Guðmundsson battled alcoholism and depression that to some extent undermined his career. He also seems to have been highly sensitive, even paranoid, when it came to competition. In an undated letter to his own choir members, he railed against the "animosity and resentment that the choir's enemies, and my own, have constantly stirred up against me here in town."[55]

Guðmundsson, who had been skeptical of Abraham's talents from the start, was convinced that he intended to destroy the Akureyri Cantata Choir by "stealing" its members for his own ensemble. In fact, Abraham had specifically made an appointment with Guðmundsson shortly after arriving in Akureyri. At that meeting, Guðmundsson encouraged him to seek piano students and possibly reestablish the town's brass band, but of course made no mention of starting a choir. Abraham, on the other hand, included one of Guðmundsson's piano works, *Three Chorales and a Fugue*, at his debut concert, framed by works by Schubert and Schumann.[56] This, it turned out, did not suffice to gain the composer's support.

Guðmundsson's true sentiments are revealed in an undated manuscript draft for a history of the Cantata Choir, where he complains bitterly of the "mistreatment" that he endured in Akureyri, and which he traced back to Abraham's arrival in town. His account of the story is as follows:

> But then, in autumn 1936, he gets the idea to start a mixed choir, and it seems clear that Áskell [Snorrason, conductor of the Akureyri Male Choir], Valdimar [Steffensen, a local doctor], and Hallgrímur [Valdemarsson, a cultural patron] played a large role in this. At least Áskell allowed him to pick singers from his ensemble, which is quite a different response to the one we received when we were establishing the Cantata Choir. Then, the Jew and his agents went scouting for collaborators. They managed to entice Fanney Guðmundsdóttir, the Cantata

Choir's pianist, and a few girls from the choir to join his new project, on the condition that it would be short-lived, just a single concert. But this "short while" lasted until mid-April, when Abraham gave two sold-out concerts right before the Cantata Choir traveled to Reykjavík to present concerts there. And now the local newspapers got their voices back; they had no words strong enough to praise this great artist's cultural contribution, but when the Cantata Choir returned from its tour soon afterwards, they were silent like dogs, and of course so was the crowd that had barked so unrelentingly over Abraham's genius. It also became clear that this was no temporary project, for already in September, Abraham's agents made repeated, impudent attempts to steal people from the Cantata Choir, but thankfully these were largely unsuccessful. And then, Sigurður Guðmundsson [dean of the Akureyri secondary school] offered him the school's main hall for rehearsals, "because," he said, "it is such an extremely important cultural enterprise." [. . .] Thus, it is obvious that this was all premeditated from the start. They were going to use this Jew, whose programs of course only consist of foreign music, to ruin the Cantata Choir and destroy its efforts.[57]

Although Guðmundsson's anti-Semitic remarks are certainly appalling, his outburst seems to have been provoked not only by Abraham himself. He lashes out at a prominent local musician for encouraging Abraham and proposing singers from his own ensemble, at the local papers for lavishing attention on Abraham's choir, and at the dean of the secondary school for offering free rehearsal space. While Guðmundsson does not specifically criticize Abraham's talent or his artistic results, he disapproves of his choice of repertoire, which, in contrast to the Cantata Choir, consisted only of "foreign music." A friend of his in Reykjavík was more outspoken about the artistic side in their correspondence. In a letter in October 1940, Sigurður Þórðarson, a composer and office manager of the National Radio, grumbled that he had heard a recent performance of "Abraham's Mixed Choir" on the radio "and it was one of the worst things I have ever heard."[58]

For a talented musician such as Robert Abraham, such humiliation could hardly be endured for long. His patience had already been severely tested in 1936 by the commotion around his recital, as he revealed to his friend Halldór Halldórsson, who had moved to Reykjavík to complete his master's thesis at the university: "I'm not sure what the impact of these attacks has been on my popularity here," he confessed, adding that "at least the 'publicity' that undoubtedly followed these articles was not enough to make me a wealthy man."[59] Abraham hoped that a series of well-attended concerts might improve his financial condition somewhat, but his long-term prospects were a cause of great concern: "If I don't get an office job here in addition to my musical activities, then I think my only choice is to move to Reykjavík—or kill myself!"[60] While this may have been only a flippant comment in a letter to a close friend, it is also a reminder of the hardship Abraham had to endure during his first years in Iceland. He could barely make ends meet, had no institutional support as Edelstein and Urbancic did, and had made bitter enemies in a small town near the Arctic circle, while his closest friend there had moved to Reykjavík. If Abraham was indeed suggesting that his mental strength had begun to waver, it should have hardly come as a surprise.

Despite the adversity he had to face in Akureyri, later in life Abraham always spoke fondly of his time there. "I will always remember these years with gratitude to the people of Akureyri for how kind they were to me," he said in a 1951 interview, further remarking: "I have many fond memories from these years." Yet he could not help but mention an incident that

Figure 3.4. Robert Abraham conducting his choir at a Spring Festival in Svarfaðardalur, a valley in Northern Iceland, June 1939. *Source:* © Elín Þ. Ólafsdóttir, private collection. Used with permission.

remained lodged in his memory: "It is nonetheless a strange coincidence that I was personally never disparaged because of my heritage, until I had arrived in Akureyri. There, two drunk men once shouted towards me that I was a 'damned Jew.' "[61]

Edelstein: The Winter of the Margarine Crates

Although Heinz Edelstein's employment with the Jewish Culture League's orchestra and string quartet in Frankfurt had saved him from the humiliation of working as a door-to-door salesman, by 1937 it had become clear to him that he had to leave Germany as soon as possible. He tried to obtain a position with the symphony orchestra in Bogotá, Columbia, but this failed to materialize, as did his attempts to acquire a visa to the United States.[62] His friends and colleagues were also on the lookout should opportunities arise. Ultimately, it was Ernst Drucker, the League orchestra's concertmaster and the leader of Edelstein's quartet, who introduced him to a man from Iceland who offered to save his life.

In October 1937, Ragnar Jónsson, the margarine magnate and chairman of the Reykjavík Music Society, traveled to Berlin to find musicians to concertize in Iceland in the upcoming season. Most urgently, he wished to engage a violinist and a chamber orchestra for a short-term residency in Reykjavík, but he also hoped to find a cellist who might be persuaded to settle there for a longer period.[63] Iceland had only a handful of local cellists, none of them of truly professional caliber. The Viennese cellist Friedrich Fleischmann had taught a few students at the Reykjavík Music School in 1930–1931 but had returned to the continent at the end of that school year. The school was then without a cello teacher until Hans Quiquerez took the post in 1936–1937, again for only a year.[64] Thus, the need for a resident cello teacher and performer had become fairly urgent.

Jónsson's first choice for a short-term violinist-in-residence was Ernst Drucker, and in order to meet him face to face, he took a train from Berlin to Chemnitz, where Drucker was performing with his quartet.[65] During their meeting, he asked if Drucker knew of any cellists who might consider a more permanent job in Iceland, and Drucker immediately suggested Edelstein. The two arranged a meeting, which must have gone splendidly, as Jónsson wrote to Icelandic composer Jón Leifs on October 7: "[Drucker] has a fine cellist if we would like, Edelstein, who plays in his quartet. I like him very much."[66] A few days later, Edelstein came to Berlin to further discuss the practicalities of his upcoming move.[67] Jónsson wasted no time in informing his fellow "apostles" in the Reykjavík Music Society of this auspicious development. At the Society's meeting in Reykjavík on October 11, it was noted that "a telegram has arrived from Ragnar Jónsson and he has hired a violinist and a cellist to perform here this winter."[68] Thus, Heinz Edelstein's destiny was decided.

Jónsson may have wished to finalize the agreement in more detail, but he stayed only a few days in Germany before continuing by airplane to Russia. A few weeks later, Edelstein performed with the Jewish Culture League orchestra in Hamburg, and it so happened that a friend of Jónsson's, Lúðvíg Guðmundsson, later dean of the Reykjavík School of Visual Arts, was in the city at the same time. He had previously studied medicine in Germany, spoke German fluently, and was also knowledgeable in music; his wife was a pianist and piano teacher.[69] It seems that Guðmundsson regarded Edelstein's hiring as a pure formality but that Edelstein himself expected to undergo some kind of audition, as Jónsson had most likely never heard him play. Edelstein later told his son Stefán that he had been quite nervous as he arrived at the Icelander's hotel with his cello and a copy of his dissertation, ready to demonstrate both his artistic and academic qualifications. After their initial handshake, Guðmundsson scrutinized him closely from top to toe, and then remarked without having heard him play so much as a single note: "All right! It's agreed!"[70]

Since the school year had already begun, the Reykjavík Music Society had to act swiftly to procure Edelstein's residence and work permits. In November, the Icelandic Justice Department approved a work permit for one year, with the proviso that "the Music Society ensure that this man leaves the country before his permit expires, at no cost to the authorities."[71] Edelstein sailed from Hamburg to Iceland in early December 1937, and the northward journey was difficult, with heavy seas that caused him terrible seasickness. A few of the Music Society's "apostles" had come to the pier in Reykjavík to welcome him, and immediately took him to Hotel Iceland, where he stayed the first few nights. Edelstein later recalled that this group made a strange impression; the men were surprisingly awkward and taciturn, leaving him to wonder where on earth he had landed.[72] Edelstein also did not intend to remain in Iceland for long. As his initial contract was only for a year, he hoped to be able to continue his journey to America—or return to Germany should the situation there improve.

During Edelstein's first winter in Iceland, his wife Charlotte remained in Freiburg with their two sons (see fig. 3.5). The marriage had been troubled

Figure 3.5. Charlotte Edelstein with her son Wolfgang, ca. 1933. *Source:* © Benjamin Edelstein, private collection. Used with permission.

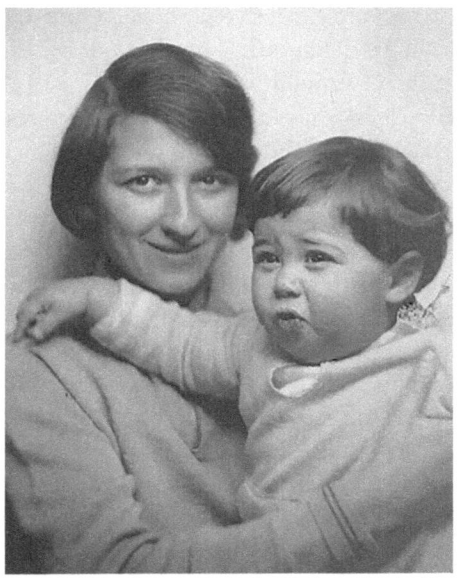

for some time, at least since Edelstein joined the Frankfurt orchestra. He had already suggested a divorce, and encouraged Charlotte to attempt to immigrate to the United States with the two boys. She hoped to obtain a university position there, and corresponded with Helen Froelicher of Ridgewood, New Jersey, herself a Swiss immigrant who along with her husband worked with Roman-Catholic relief organizations in Europe to help hundreds of Jews escape Germany.[73] Mrs. Froelicher did all she could to obtain a local sponsor for her visa application, but this involved considerable bureaucratic hurdles so success seemed increasingly unlikely.[74]

Charlotte Edelstein's life in Freiburg during the winter 1937–1938 was dominated by fear and despair. She immersed herself in her Roman Catholic faith, in the hope that fervent prayers might stop the insanity that had turned her life upside down. She was also frustrated by her husband's indifference to her precarious situation, as she recalled decades later: "He said that my fear of concentration camps, and all the terrors that soon proved to be real, was only an exaggeration. There I was, alone in Germany with two small boys, attempting somehow to make ends meet, and thankful for each day that passed without something even worse happening to us."⁷⁵ Desperate to get away, she suggested taking the boys to Iceland for a holiday, but her husband found this a far too expensive proposal; a four-week journey would cost 1,200 to 1,500 Icelandic krónur—nearly a quarter of his annual salary. Instead, he suggested, they should wait and see.⁷⁶

The two boys, eight-year-old Wolfgang and six-year-old Stefan, had begun attending school. Although the Nazis did not enjoy particularly strong support in Freiburg, it was considered important to teach schoolchildren the "correct" way of thinking. Wolfgang later recalled that as a young boy he had felt "unfit to be a real German" since he belonged to an "inferior" race. He described his first-grade teacher, Herr Kiefer, as a "crazed Nazi" who, each time something went amiss in the classroom, blamed the Jewish boy for everything.⁷⁷ In a 2008 interview, Wolfgang, who later became a renowned education researcher, attributed his interest in the field to his distressing childhood experience in Freiburg:

> I had a very hostile teacher when I was in the first grade, at age six. I had some difficulties writing because I was left-handed, and left-handedness was considered inappropriate maladjustment. And because I had difficulties writing, I was beaten, very often, by this teacher, with a metal ruler across my fingertips. Thus, my early school memories are rather negative, and full of fears of that teacher. In the second grade, that was different. The teacher was a very nice and humane man who treated me well, and so I recovered from the first traumatic experiences quite easily. In the third grade, there was still a Nazi teacher, but she was a woman, and she dealt with me quite decently. So, I had these mixed experiences, and I dwell on these, because I think they probably had a relatively intensive influence on my later orientations, my interest in schools and school reform, and education.⁷⁸

Wolfgang Edelstein also recalled that the taunting by his first-grade teacher emboldened the children at his school to act in a similar way. "My classmates took part in this Nazi business to a certain extent, abusing the Jewish boy who wasn't even given a chance at school," he reminisced. "I was often derided and beaten up by the other kids."⁷⁹

Upon arriving in Reykjavík, Heinz Edelstein settled into an apartment in the city center, at Hverfisgata 39, and immediately began teaching and giving concerts. The leaders of the Music Society were delighted with his work, as one of them remarked in a letter a few months later: "We like him very much indeed. I'm sure he is an excellent man for us."[80]

But though the Icelanders were elated, Edelstein himself was far from satisfied with his working conditions. The local music scene was less developed than he had expected, and he found the institutions he worked for—the Reykjavík Music School and the National Radio—frustratingly disorganized. In March 1938, he shared his impressions with composer Jón Leifs, who resided in Germany. He was pleased to have organized a chamber music course along with Viennese violinist Hans Stepanek, and he also enjoyed collaborating with pianist Árni Kristjánsson. But Edelstein was convinced that Iceland's musical life had to be fortified both from the bottom up and the top down; the leading institutions needed improving, but the grassroots work, including music education for children as well as amateurs of all ages, required even more attention. Music performance on the National Radio was, according to Edelstein, "completely incompetent" and had to be reorganized in all respects. A first step, he suggested, would be to establish a string quartet as a core ensemble for live broadcasts, and then expand it as necessary to form larger ensembles.[81]

Conditions at the Reykjavík Music School were so inadequate, according to Edelstein, that he could discuss them only "in a satirical manner." Coordination and communication between the teaching staff left much to be desired, and the entire syllabus fell short on ambition: "We need an elementary course in the spirit of the German recorder movement, we need better aural training and theory courses, we need a music history course that is tied to a practical *Collegium musicum*. Without such pedagogical work in its broadest sense, any attempts to improve music-making in Iceland will fail."[82] Even the genuinely enthusiastic and altruistic members of the Music Society would not be able to help, Edelstein asserted, unless the entire organization of the music school and orchestra was reconsidered. Yet, though his judgment was grim, Edelstein noted that if the will could be found to build the Icelandic music scene from the ground up, and not simply leave things as they were, he could hardly think of "anything more wonderful" than taking part in it.

In summer 1938, after seven months in Iceland, Edelstein decided to return to Freiburg to visit his family. This was a risky undertaking, as it was becoming increasingly difficult for Jews to leave Germany. Only a few months later, the German Ministry of the Interior annulled all Jewish passports unless they were marked with the stamp *J*, for *Jude* or Jew.[83] It was also not long before all Jews were forced to add a Jewish middle name so their origin was in no doubt; Israel was the name required of all males, while females had to take the name Sara. But these laws had not yet been ratified, and Heinz Edelstein was able to return to Iceland in August, as planned. His marriage, however, appeared irreparable. Before his departure, he signed a document giving Charlotte his permission to immigrate to the United States with their two sons, should an offer materialize.[84] It seemed possible they might never see each other again.

In the end, things turned out differently. As soon as Edelstein arrived back in Reykjavík, he heard of Hitler's looming annexation of the Sudetenland province of Czechoslovakia, and feared that a catastrophic war might break out before long. He acted swiftly, sending a telegram to Freiburg asking Charlotte to get herself and the boys on a ship to Iceland as soon as possible. His request was "completely unexpected and unforeseen," she later recalled—"it was like a clap of thunder out of a clear blue sky."[85] Charlotte tried to react as quickly as she could, but there were some unforeseen delays. She had submitted her passport to the U.S. consulate, and when she requested it back they were unable to locate it for several days. Little Wolfgang did not fully comprehend the danger they were in. He was particularly excited about the upcoming trip, since he had read children's books by Icelandic author Nonni (Jón Sveinsson), which enjoyed great popularity in Germany at the time. His mother strictly forbade him to mention their impending emigration to his friends, but he couldn't resist: "I went and told people all over the place, but no one snitched," he later recalled.[86]

Charlotte, Wolfgang, and Stefan Edelstein departed for Iceland on the SS *Goðafoss* from Hamburg on September 19, 1938. When a Nazi official examined her papers before departure, she said she was only going for a short visit to her husband, and they were allowed through with no further questions. Later, she recalled her relief that the Icelandic vessel departed from Hamburg, where Hitler was not as popular as in other parts of the country; the control at the Danish border was rumored to be more strict.[87] The date of their journey is also worthy of note. By a remarkable coincidence, Charlotte Edelstein and Melitta Urbancic—two Jewish-born women, both recent converts to Catholicism, and both fleeing Nazi Germany with their children to join their musician-husbands in exile in Iceland—made their respective journeys at nearly precisely the same time: Charlotte Edelstein departed from Hamburg on September 19, while Melitta Urbancic began her voyage from Copenhagen only a day later.[88]

Less than two months after Charlotte Edelstein's departure from Freiburg, the city's Jewish population was also subjected to the horrors of the *Kristallnacht*. There, the local synagogue was burned to the ground and

Figure 3.6. Wolfgang and Stefan Edelstein in Freiburg, probably in 1934. *Source:* © Benjamin Edelstein, private collection. Used with permission.

over one hundred Jews were deported to the Dachau concentration camp.[89] Charlotte's sister, Lilli, was arrested by two SS men but released after a lengthy interrogation.[90] That same evening, the Gestapo arrested Edelstein's brother-in-law, the lawyer Erwin Schepses. He spent two weeks in jail, after which he was released due to his military service in World War I.[91]

On board the ship to Reykjavík, Charlotte Edelstein made the somewhat awkward acquaintance of a young German scholar, W. H. Wolf-Rottkay, a devout Nazi about to take up a visiting lectureship in German at the University of Iceland.[92] He and his wife were delighted by the young Stefan, whose blonde hair and blue eyes had already elicited admiration in Nazi Germany; upon seeing him, many of the Edelsteins' acquaintances—and even perfect strangers—had remarked: "All German children should look just like this!" Charlotte Edelstein's recollection of Wolf-Rottkay continues:

> Through their fondness for little Stefan, this man and his wife had now become friendly towards me, and he even called me onto the deck at the earliest show of northern lights. "You

mustn't miss this magnificent display of nature!" he exclaimed in an affable voice. Later, when our paths would cross on the streets of Reykjavík, he would always look the other way, embarrassed, for he had in the meantime learned to distinguish the despicable exiles from the staunch Nazis—and realized what a dreadful mistake he had made![93]

Charlotte Edelstein also recalled her first sight of what was about to become her new homeland, as the ship landed at the small island of Heimaey, off Iceland's southern shore, early in the morning. She excitedly put on a coat and ran onto the deck, but the vision was hardly what she had expected:

> I literally recoiled at the sight. The huge cliff and the port's murky setting seemed eerie in the autumn twilight; I felt as though I had arrived in a completely foreign part of the world. I would also feel this same sense of discomfort later, when the Icelandic lava landscape spread all around us, as if we were on the moon. I shuddered and tip-toed back into the cabin, silently lamenting that my children should have to live in such an inhospitable land, so remote at the edge of the world, and—it seemed to me then—so far away from all the culture to which we were accustomed. What conditions would await us there? Wouldn't my life be just as miserable as it had been in the now completely estranged Germany—only in a different way?[94]

This is a remarkable confession by a woman who had just managed to save her own life, as well as those of her two sons. Yet it turned out to be prophetic. Charlotte Edelstein was never able to fully adapt to life in Iceland and was the first of the émigrés discussed in this book to return to Germany for good (see chapter 8).

As they began their new life together in Reykjavík, the Edelstein family could hardly have wished for a more loyal benefactor than Ragnar Jónsson, the Music Society's chairman, who gladly took them under his wing. During their first year there, they occupied an apartment that Jónsson owned and provided them at a low price (Bergstaðastræti 48). But it was unfurnished, which proved a substantial challenge, as they had been able to bring only a few small suitcases from Germany and had no money to spare. One day, Jónsson—who had earned his fortune from his margarine factory—appeared in a car filled with wooden margarine crates, which the family then proceeded to arrange inventively in their new home, forming a cupboard, a table, a chest of drawers, and other furniture as needed. Of course this was a temporary solution, and eventually the situation turned out better than they had dared to hope: Charlotte's sister was able to ship their old furniture from Freiburg to Iceland the following spring. Nevertheless, the Edelstein family always jokingly referred to their first few months together in Reykjavík as "the winter of the margarine crates."[95] A year later, they moved to an apartment in a three-story house in the western part of town (Ásvallagata 17), near the Catholic church and school that both the boys attended; this would be their home for the next decade.

Among Wolfgang Edelstein's classmates at the Catholic school was an eight-year-old girl, Vigdís Finnbogadóttir, who would later become the first female president of the Republic of Iceland—and the world's first democratically elected female president. In her autobiography, she recalled that the foreign boy wore highly unusual clothes his first day at school, "leather shorts like we had only seen in photos of yodeling men in Tyrol."[96] On his first school day, Wolfgang had difficulty understanding all the Icelandic words and constantly asked the teacher, the Dutch-born Sister Henrietta, to explain in German. Her response was to ask Vigdís to take the new boy under her wing and teach him the language. "This was the first time that anyone had asked me to take on real responsibility," she later recalled. She took her task seriously, walking Wolfgang back from school each day, and thus began a friendship that would last a lifetime.[97] In her description, Heinz Edelstein was a "very sweet man" and Charlotte a "beautiful woman, with luminous dark hair that she tied in a bun like a ballerina. There was sadness in her eyes, but her smile was warm and broad. She spoke little, less than the other mothers I knew. She often went to the Catholic church and sat there for a long time."[98]

Urbancic: Expectations and Reality

Victor Urbancic was in many ways better informed regarding conditions in Iceland than the other foreign musicians who arrived there. His engagement had been under discussion for several months, and he could rely on his former schoolmate Franz Mixa for advice and insider information. The two initially corresponded by mail, but after Mixa's return to Austria in May 1938, they met in person to discuss the details of their exchange. Mixa assured him that Reykjavík had not only all the comforts of a modern city but that its inhabitants also had a deep thirst for culture and, in his words, for "everything beautiful and precious."[99] It does seem as though Mixa, in their conversations, somewhat exaggerated the city's aesthetic charm; in a letter to his parents shortly after his arrival, Urbancic admitted that Reykjavík had fallen far short of his expectations in this regard.[100] For someone born and raised in Imperial Vienna, this was probably to be expected.

Later in life, Franz Mixa recalled that he had never been requested to sign a written contract with the Reykjavík Music Society during his eight years of employment there. Instead, a handshake with its chairman, Ragnar Jónsson, sufficed.[101] This was not the case with Urbancic. In summer 1938, he and Mixa, acting on behalf of the Music Society, signed a seven-clause contract detailing all of Urbancic's numerous obligations. He was to teach at least fifteen piano students and five music theory students, give radio concerts each month, and conduct at least one orchestra rehearsal a week. During the winter months, he was to conduct performances of one or two operas or operettas, in addition to a large choral work ("an oratorio," the contract stipulated), and one or two concerts with the Reykjavík Orchestra.[102] What the contract did not detail was that each concert required dozens of extra rehearsals compared to what Urbancic might have expected in Austria. For such an extensive list of duties, the salary was quite meager, 5,000 Icelandic krónur in total—including remuneration for all concerts and opera performances, as well as orchestral arrangements, should the need arise. Mixa had received 6,000 krónur for the same job, but Urbancic was hardly in a position to negotiate.[103] Having arrived in Reykjavík, he grew concerned that he had settled for too little; everything was more expensive than he had imagined, and he feared his salary might not suffice when his wife and children joined him there.[104]

In Reykjavík, the Urbancic family took over the apartment formerly occupied by Franz and Katrín Mixa, on the second floor of Hverfisgata 35, near the then-unfinished National Theater, where Urbancic would later be employed. The house belonged to sisters who ran a popular hat store on the ground floor, and lived on the third (top) floor themselves. The cohabitation did not run smoothly. Sibyl Urbancic recalls the sisters' strange habit of playing popular songs on their gramophone at the highest volume throughout the day, as if to disturb their musician neighbor who often practiced and gave lessons at home. They showed remarkable perseverance in their enterprise, not least in that 78 rpm records contained only a few minutes of music on each side, although several records could be stacked up to play consecutively. Whenever the music fell silent for more than a few seconds, one of the sisters would run up the stairs from the store and replenish the stack.[105] It is difficult to say whether their behavior was the result of a xenophobic attitude toward foreigners, or merely a dislike of classical music. In any case, another Jewish couple soon took up lodgings in the house, Karl and Irmgard Kroner from Berlin. He was a respected doctor but was refused permission to practice medicine in Iceland, and thus the couple later continued to the United States along with their young son.[106] In a 1948 interview, Urbancic expressed the hope that his family might soon be able to find acceptable housing, as they had been "severely inconvenienced" in their current home.[107] A year later, they purchased a small house at Kambsvegur 9, then a distant suburb east of the city center, where Urbancic would live until his death.

Although Reykjavík was in many ways a strange place, the exiles were certainly relieved to be free citizens again, and enjoyed the opportunity to do things that were unthinkable for Jews in the Third Reich. Among them was an elegant ball (*árshátíð*, or annual celebration) organized by the Reykjavík Music Society at the town's most elegant hotel, Hótel Borg, in May 1939. For Melitta, it was a delightful experience—the first time in years she had been able to dress up and dance to live music in a refined setting. "At first, one doesn't even believe that one still knows how to do such things!" she wrote to her mother in Vienna the following day. She had enjoyed herself thoroughly, she said, describing the atmosphere as "free from all snobbery, simple and natural and cheerful in a calm way, like everything here in Iceland."[108]

Attending that same ball was Charlotte Edelstein, who later described how the very idea of going to a lavish social event had seemed inconceivable, as if emerging from a distant past. Still, she was able to turn her very presence into a personal victory: "That evening," she later wrote, "I enjoyed my own 'triumph' over Hitler by dancing with so many handsome, 'Germanic'-looking men."[109] Yet, darker emotions resurfaced as well. Charlotte did not own an evening gown and thus wore a short skirt that she found woefully inappropriate once she arrived. "From where should I have been able to get a ball gown? After all, we had been excluded from all social life for years. Yet again, I felt that I didn't belong, that I was an outsider—the old, acute fears resurfaced once more."[110]

As "Aryan" Roman Catholics in Vienna, Urbancic's parents had no immediate concerns, but they were terribly sad to see him and his family leave for such a far-away place. They wrote letters to Reykjavík many times a week and did all they could to make their son's life there more comfortable.

For example, out of concern that fresh fruit might be difficult to obtain, they shipped boxes of apples to Reykjavík while this was still possible, before the outbreak of war. Once, they even dispatched a Viennese Sachertorte via mail, presumably fearing that sweet delicacies might be in short supply in the Arctic north.[111] Their most elaborate gift was a state-of-the-art radio receiver that they shipped to Iceland so their son could at least keep up with music on the continent via radio broadcasts.[112] They acquired an identical model for themselves in Vienna and tuned into "Radio Reykjavík" with great enthusiasm when Urbancic was on the air as pianist or conductor, although the reception quality was usually dismal.[113]

Abraham: A New Life in Reykjavík

Robert Abraham's mother, Lise, was able to escape Germany at the last minute. On September 19, 1939, a few weeks after war had broken out, she traveled from Berlin to Copenhagen with only ten Reichsmarks in cash, as Jews were not allowed to leave the country with more money.[114] She hoped to be able to travel to the United States, and had already applied for a visa at the general consulate in Berlin the previous year, but due to her high entry number she would have to wait another two or three years. In the meantime, her request to stay in Denmark was rejected, and on October 14, 1939, two policemen escorted her on board the SS *Dronning Alexandrine*, which was bound for Iceland, handing her passport over to the ship's captain to ensure she would definitely leave the country.[115] As she arrived in Iceland, Lise Abraham already had an approved residence permit there, although this was no sure thing for a German Jew. Her son's influential friends had wielded their influence. These included Sigurður Guðmundsson, dean of the Akureyri Gymnasium, who several weeks before her arrival had dispatched a telegram to Prime Minister Jónasson pledging that Mrs. Abraham's stay in Iceland would be "of no cost to the Icelandic government."[116] The application was approved the following day, demonstrating yet again how Iceland's otherwise unyielding immigration system could be swayed by the support of well-connected friends and acquaintances.[117]

In Iceland, the fifty-two-year-old Lise Abraham made new friends and acquired a basic grasp of Icelandic, but adjusting to her new life there was a challenge. She arrived with virtually no money, and her son already had difficulty making ends meet on his meager salary. She was a refined, elegant lady, accustomed to a more dignified existence than they could now provide for themselves. In Berlin, the Abraham family had always relied on maids for housework, and her descendants still recall stories about how clumsy she was when mopping the floor of their apartment in Iceland, a task she had never before attempted.[118]

In summer 1940, Robert and Lise Abraham moved from Akureyri to Reykjavík, where they found a small apartment near the center of town (Bjarnarstígur 9). Now he once again had to build a new network of students and colleagues, advertising his availability in local newspapers as a teacher of piano and theory, and as an accompanist and arranger of songs. At first, he found only sporadic work, and to make ends meet he took on menial work for the British Army, which had occupied the island earlier that spring (see chapter 5).[119] In October 1940, Mayor of Reykjavík (and later Prime Minister) Bjarni Benediktsson reported to the Ministry for Social Affairs that Abraham was "unemployed, so to speak, and can only barely provide for himself."[120] During their first years in Reykjavík, Lise Abraham, who is referred to in official documents as "a foreign refugee," received a housing subsidy from the municipal authorities—a total of roughly 2,000 krónur, nearly enough to pay the rent of their small apartment.[121]

But news of Abraham's talent spread quickly, and before long he had found enough opportunities as a musician to abandon his work for the army. Among his piano students was a six-year-old prodigy, Þórunn Jóhannsdóttir, who later studied in London and Moscow and eventually married Russian piano legend Vladimir Ashkenazy.[122] Abraham reviewed concerts for *Morgunblaðið*, and appeared on the National Radio both as a pianist and lecturer, speaking on topics such as "The Origins of Opera" and "The Development of Instruments and Their Use Until the Seventeenth Century." He also translated into Icelandic an account of Mozart's last days (original title: *Der Tod eines Unsterblichen*) by Rudolph Genée, and for a local magazine he penned a series of short articles on music from the Ancient Greeks to the late Middle Ages, subjects he had studied with Curt Sachs in Berlin more than a decade earlier.[123]

During his first two years in Reykjavík, Abraham also conducted the choir of the Reykjavík Gymnasium (*Menntaskólinn í Reykjavík*), a secondary school for students from the ages of around sixteen to twenty. Up to that point, the school had only had a male choir under the direction of the town's cathedral organist, who had passed away in 1939. Under Abraham's direction, the school for the first time offered its students the opportunity to sing in a mixed ensemble, something gradually becoming feasible with increasing attendance by female students. The choir gave its first concert in

April 1941, where they performed pieces such as Mozart's *Ave verum corpus*, Schumann's *Brautgesang* op. 146, and a new work by Abraham himself, *Ride to Þingvellir* (*Þingvallareið*), to a text by Kristín Sigfúsdóttir, a female poet whose acquaintance he had made during his time in Akureyri. After the concert, a critic described the new composition as "unusual and enjoyable."[124]

Despite their meager finances, Abraham and his mother had a strong social network among local intellectuals in Reykjavík. Among them was Iceland's leading literary scholar, Sigurður Nordal, who was professor at the University of Iceland and enjoyed an international reputation; for example, he was the Norton Professor of Poetry at Harvard University in 1931–1932. His son, Jón, later one of Iceland's leading composers, was already taking music lessons with Victor Urbancic when Abraham arrived in town. In December 1940, Lise Abraham appeared on Nordal's doorstep with a full score of Beethoven's Ninth Symphony, which was due to be broadcast on National Radio on New Year's Day. Robert wished to encourage fourteen-year-old Jón Nordal to study the score and follow along during the broadcast, and in a letter to friends in Akureyri, Lise Abraham noted how "wonderful" it had been to witness his joy at receiving the unexpected gift.[125]

In Reykjavík, Robert Abraham found love again. Guðríður Magnúsdóttir was six years younger than he, born on a farm on the Snæfellsnes peninsula in western Iceland in 1918 (see fig. 3.7). She had studied in Reykjavík and Denmark, and completed her teacher's exam in 1940, after which she taught at an elementary school. Since she both lived and worked in downtown Reykjavík, she had occasionally seen Abraham around town, but they met for the first time when she asked him to play the piano at an entertainment at her school.[126] They were married on Abraham's thirtieth birthday, May 17, 1942, and found an apartment on Hringbraut, just west of the city center, near the site of today's National Library.

Abraham and Guðríður were blessed with a loving relationship, based on mutual respect and admiration, but in many ways they were opposites. She was determined and strong-willed, and, fortunately for Abraham, willing to take on the day-to-day chores of running the household, allowing him to focus on making music. Since Abraham had a tendency to overspend on books, sheet music, and works of art, Guðríður eventually took full control of their finances and allocated her husband a fixed monthly amount.[127] She even managed the construction of their new house on Hjarðarhagi 29, into which they moved in 1957 along with her parents, who occupied a separate apartment on the ground floor. By then, they had become a family of three.

Figure 3.7. Robert Abraham and Guðríður Magnúsdóttir on their wedding day, May 17, 1942. *Source:* © Elín Þ. Ólafsdóttir, private collection. Used with permission.

Their son, Grétar Ottó, born in 1953, was named after Abraham's paternal aunt Grete, and his father, Otto.

Lise Abraham lived in Iceland for eight years, after which she moved to California to be near her younger son, Peter; her brother and sister-in-law had also immigrated to Los Angeles (see chapter 4). In Iceland, she had become fascinated by the local landscape and began painting landscapes in her free time. Shortly after arriving in California, she gave an exhibit at Raymond and Raymond Galleries in Beverly Hills and was praised by a critic of the New York exile journal *Aufbau* as "a kind of West-Coast Grandma Moses."[128] She never returned to Iceland, and passed away in Berkeley, California, in 1950.

From 1940 onward, Robert Abraham, Heinz Edelstein, and Victor Urbancic all resided in Reykjavík. They became friends and close colleagues, and their contributions to music were invaluable in the small town. But they must soon have realized they were a tiny minority in what was a remarkably homogeneous country, and that, apart from them, few exiles had been admitted into Iceland, despite the horrendous situation on the continent. In the 1930s and 1940s, the local government had a harsh anti-immigration policy, particularly when it came to Jewish refugees. This story has not been widely known until recent years, as scholars have begun to study its treatment of immigrants and asylum seekers. Thus, it is worth briefly suspending the individual narratives of the three musicians to examine more broadly the phenomenon of Icelandic xenophobia and the fates of those who experienced it firsthand—or never even made it there to begin with.

4

"A Country Free of Jews . . ."

Iceland was hardly a welcoming place for foreign immigrants in the 1930s. The great economic depression had hit the country hard and unemployment was high. The few foreigners who resided there were often regarded with suspicion, and many locals vehemently opposed "citizens of other countries taking work from our own countrymen," to quote a petition from the right-wing Independence Party's youth movement to the Justice Minister in 1933.[1] For foreign musicians, the difficulties were even more pronounced, since opposition came from two sides. The government, led by the xenophobic Hermann Jónasson (see fig. 4.1), who became both Prime Minister and Justice Minister in 1934, ran a hardline policy against all immigrants, but especially Jews. In addition, the Icelandic Musicians' Union (FÍH, or *Félag íslenskra hljómlistarmanna*), was founded in 1932 with the primary goal of ensuring that local musicians were given priority over foreigners in hiring.[2]

While the exclusion of Jews was never official government policy, by the second half of the 1930s it was clear that only in rare cases would they be granted permission to reside in Iceland. Evidence for this comes primarily in the form of internal government documents and recollections of private conversations. In 1937, Prime Minister Jónasson insisted, in a conversation with the chargé d'affaires of the local Danish Embassy, that "Iceland has always been a pure, Nordic country, free of Jews, and those who have made it in in the last few years shall be sent back out."[3] The following year, the Ministry of Justice emphasized in a memorandum to the Icelandic ambassador in Copenhagen, who had inquired whether a change in policy was imminent in the wake of the horrifying *Kristallnacht* pogroms, that the government was "in principle opposed" to Jews settling in the country.⁴ Two weeks later, an attaché at the Danish embassy in Berlin was instructed by the Icelandic Ministry of Justice that German Jews should be "discouraged from coming because of the constant vacillation regarding those that are already here."⁵ Despite this uncompromising stance, Icelandic authorities received a considerable number of requests from German Jews hoping to relocate there. Most of these were reviewed by Jónasson himself, who scribbled the same marking on many of them: "No. HJ."⁶ A total of 406 Jews applied for residence in Iceland in 1935–1940, in addition to a group application made on behalf of 130 Czech Jews in 1939. Only about twenty-five were granted permission to stay.⁷ A further sixteen Jews were deported from Iceland between 1936 and 1939; eleven further deportations were planned but never executed.⁸

Despite the gloomy economic outlook, which underpinned this xenophobic response, more and more Icelanders received a musical education as the 1930s progressed, not least thanks to the newly established Reykjavík School of Music. While some pursued music as a cultured hobby, others aimed for a professional career. As the number of local musicians increased, many found it intolerable that foreign musicians—most of them from Germany,

Figure 4.1. Hermann Jónasson, Iceland's Prime Minister and Minister of Justice from 1934–1942. *Source:* © National Museum of Iceland. Used with permission.

Austria, Hungary, and Great Britain—were still being imported to perform at local cafés and dance halls. A key impetus for the founding of FÍH was the demand by local musicians that "competent Icelandic instrumentalists should enjoy all the employment that is available." The newly minted union expressed particular concern that, as of March 1932, Reykjavík was home to at least thirteen foreign instrumentalists, "employed for many months at a high salary."[9] FÍH's founding meeting, a month earlier, was attended by fourteen musicians, most of whom were—understandably—Icelanders, yet foreign musicians could also be considered full members, given certain conditions. Among the founders were two foreigners who had lived in Reykjavík for several years: Viennese pianist Fritz Weisshappel, and Hungarian violinist Georg Takács, who performed at the establishment of restaurateur Alfred Rosenberg and also accompanied silent films at the Old Cinema. However, their membership within the society was noticeably less certain than that of born-and-bred locals. For example, at a meeting in 1936, composer-trumpeter Karl O. Runólfsson expressed his opinion that it was "inappropriate" that Weisshappel should be a member at all, let alone that he should be "rewarded" with "the two best positions in town," that is, as a pianist at the National Radio and City Hotel.[10]

FÍH's strategy was to gradually secure employment for more local musicians at the town's largest and most lucrative hotels, City Hotel and Hotel Iceland, since these provided live music daily and their bands were at the time largely made up of foreign musicians. At the union's founding meeting, the following statement was approved: "Since foreign musicians have until now taken so much work from locals, the society herewith forbids its members to perform with foreigners except for a full fee according to the society's rate."[11] In 1934, FÍH chairman Bjarni Böðvarsson requested that the Justice Department investigate whether three German musicians living in Reykjavík all had the necessary work permits. If not, he insisted, they should be immediately deported, as the union's members were always to be given priority and thus it was "intolerable that these men be allowed to remain in the country."[12] FÍH also took a proactive approach, requesting from their sister organization in Denmark that they not send any more musicians to work in Iceland.[13] The society's concerns were not limited to Iceland's capital. They attempted to prevent foreign musicians from working anywhere in the sparsely populated country, with a petition to the Ministry of Labor requesting that "no foreign instrumentalist be granted employment in the countryside."[14] This was a pedantic attitude fueled in part by xenophobic sentiments, yet given the particular historical situation, it is also understandable to a degree. Local musicians had gone to great trouble and expense in establishing a music school in Reykjavík with the goal of training a new generation of talented local instrumentalists. If no jobs would be available to them upon graduation, the entire project might simply collapse.

Unwanted Foreigners: Klahn and Stepanek

The FÍH union's most urgent cause was for more local players to gain lucrative employment in the town's dance bands, yet it also opposed the hiring of foreign classical musicians, especially ones who were considered too prominent or had won coveted positions. Among those FÍH petitioned against was Albert Klahn, a German musician who immigrated to Reykjavík in 1936 (see fig. 4.2). Born in Schleswig-Holstein in 1885, he was nearly fifty years old when he arrived, considerably older than the three musicians who are the main subjects of the present study. Klahn's father and grandfather were both musicians, and little Albert, who began learning violin at six and trumpet at eight, followed in their footsteps.[15] Upon completing his studies, Klahn was employed as a musician by the German royal navy, traveling all over the world, including China and Japan, India, and the Pacific Islands. Later, he conducted orchestras on board a cruise ship, again traveling widely in Africa and the Americas. Klahn was a renowned raconteur, happy to tell exotic tales from his years of navigating the globe, and he proudly declared that he had visited nearly every settlement on the planet, with two notable exceptions: San Francisco and Greenland.[16]

Having fought for Germany in World War I, Klahn settled in Hamburg, where he worked for the esteemed UFA film company, selecting and conducting music for silent movies at the resplendent 1,200-seat Millerntor cinema. It was there he made the acquaintance of an Icelandic musician, the cellist Þórhallur Árnason, who resided in Hamburg and found a job in Klahn's orchestra. They became fast friends, and Árnason later recalled he had been much impressed by Klahn's intelligence, his dynamic energy, and his prodigious musical skills.[17] With the advent of talkies in 1929, however, the Millerntor orchestra was dispersed, and Klahn once again found himself conducting music on a cruise vessel, this time journeying to North and South America.[18]

As far as the Nazis were concerned, Albert Klahn's racial heritage was impeccable, that is, fully "Aryan," but the same was not true of his wife.

In 1930, he married pianist Fanny Kartz, whose background was a mystery in that the identity of both her blood parents was completely unknown. All that was known of her mother was that she was a young girl heading for America, and, not wanting to bring her infant daughter along, she gave her up for adoption. As it happened, Fanny Kartz was brought up in Hamburg by a wealthy Jewish couple who saw to it she received a first-class education.[19] According to her friends, Fanny was "an unusually kind and intelligent woman," and she had already made her mark as a pianist in Hamburg when the Nazis took power.[20] Since no records existed of her blood parents, the Nazis classified her according to her Jewish foster parents. Thus, she found herself blacklisted by the *Reichsmusikkammer*, after which she was forbidden to teach or play in public. Her husband also lost his job in 1934, as no one wished to hire a musician who was married to a Jew.[21] For the next two years, Fanny and Albert Klahn lived in increasing poverty in Hamburg, gradually relocating to ever-smaller apartments until they inhabited only a single room. They had to sell Fanny's grand piano in order to make ends meet, and made do with a small upright instead.[22] Albert and Fanny Klahn were already planning to start a new life in Brazil when they received an unexpected letter from their old friend Árnason, who in the meantime had moved back to Reykjavík. He persuaded them to abandon their plans for South America and to relocate to Iceland instead.

Upon arriving in Reykjavík in April 1936, Albert Klahn was employed as a conductor of the evening dance band at the City Hotel. A few months later, he also replaced Páll Ísólfsson as conductor of the Reykjavík Concert Band (*Lúðrasveit Reykjavíkur*), where he immediately made his mark by expanding the group, adding wind instruments to what had previously been only a brass ensemble.[23] Klahn was much respected for his work with the Reykjavík band and was described as a "cheerful and dauntless" conductor.[24] Their debut performance in September 1936 was a conspicuous one, as they provided music for a funeral procession for forty crew members of the French Antarctic exploration ship *Pourquoi Pas?*, lost in a violent storm off the coast of Iceland a few days earlier. The solemn ceremony drew a sizable crowd of onlookers, and by all accounts Klahn's direction had already improved the band's playing noticeably. Since he had also implemented a new band uniform, with white pants instead of black ones, many of those assembled for the funeral procession did not recognize the group as local, assuming instead that it was a French band especially dispatched for the occasion. The following day, one of the instrumentalists ran into an acquaintance who had been present and who enthused about the performance, remarking: "You should have seen the French band yesterday! Then you could have seen how a *real* band performs."²⁵

While FÍH did not initially object to Klahn's work with the Reykjavík Concert Band, they changed their tune when he was appointed band director at the Good Templars Hall (*Góðtemplarahúsið*), one of Reykjavík's popular dance venues, in autumn 1937. This provoked the ire of leading FÍH members and, in the following weeks, no less than five union meetings were largely devoted to "the Klahn case," as it was called. The result was unequivocal, a complete ban on FÍH members performing under his direction.²⁶ Soon afterward, the union also objected to Klahn's employment with the Reykjavík Concert Band, on the grounds that local composer-trumpeter Karl O. Runólfsson also possessed the required skills for the job. In turn, band members retorted that it was "crucial" for them to retain Klahn, since his work had already been immensely beneficial.²⁷ He was allowed to keep his position, but even for such a coveted job, the salary was miserable. In one

Figure 4.2. Albert Klahn at his home in Reykjavík, ca. 1950. *Source:* © Reykjavík Museum of Photography. Used with permission.

of the few interviews published with Klahn in Iceland, he recalled that in 1941 he had to temporarily give up his position "because I was too poorly paid, yes, I just couldn't make ends meet from it."[28]

Klahn eventually became a highly respected musician in Iceland—even among his former foes at FÍH. Not only was he allowed to join the union in 1948, but, remarkably, he was elected its first honorary member a decade later.[29] In a book on FÍH's history, published to mark its fiftieth anniversary in 1982, the authors expressed regret at the entire "Klahn case," calling the dispute "an unfortunate matter that people later tried to forget."[30] Klahn took on various jobs on the Icelandic music scene; he was among the founders of the Hafnarfjörður Wind Band in 1950, and the same year he became timpanist for the newly founded Iceland Symphony Orchestra. He died in 1960, having devoted himself to Icelandic musical life for nearly a quarter of a decade. Among his students in the 1930s was Jón Múli Árnason, later a much-loved local songwriter and radio host, who reminisced that Klahn was "the embodiment of kindness" with not "the slightest hint of arrogance."[31] His wife Fanny suffered from an unspecified illness and rarely appeared in public after their arrival in Iceland. Her only documented solo performance was at the City Hotel in December 1936, but she died in 1940.[32]

Albert Klahn was not the only classically trained musician that FÍH found objectionable. The case of Austrian violinist Hans Stepanek is unusual in that he had strong connections to Iceland, had a history of previous employment there, and had an Icelandic wife. Born in 1907, Stepanek began his career in his native Vienna, also working for a while as concertmaster at the Grand Théâtre in Geneva, Switzerland. In 1931, he arrived in Reykjavík, where he joined the faculty of the Music School and became a member of its piano trio (see fig. 4.3), as well as leading the Reykjavík Orchestra. According to a school report, he was said to be "very popular with students and others."[33]

After eight years in Iceland, Stepanek returned to Vienna in 1939, along with his Icelandic wife, Elín Sigurðardóttir. Since he was fully "Aryan," the Nazis had no objection to his employment, and he began his tenure with the Vienna Symphony Orchestra on September 1, 1939—the very day Nazi troops invaded Poland.[34] In light of the circumstances, he attempted to return to Iceland, with assistance from the Reykjavík Music Society, which was prepared to offer him his former position at the school. Still, this plan failed to materialize. Once the Viennese authorities had given their consent, the Icelandic Ministry of Justice requested that FÍH evaluate the Music Society's application for a non-native teacher. FÍH's board concluded that, since the Reykjavík Music School had "been in operation for nearly a decade and has already graduated three violinists, and two [local violinists] are graduates of the Royal Conservatory in Copenhagen, all of whom are FÍH members with poorly paid jobs, we are not at present in need of a foreign violinist."[35] Even with a positive evaluation from the Federation of Icelandic Artists, usually more favorably disposed toward foreigners, the matter was effectively settled and the application was denied.[36]

Stepanek thus remained in Vienna along with his wife and their two young children. He was himself conscripted in 1944, when the Nazi war effort looked increasingly futile. The family survived the last years of the war in dire circumstances, which did not improve when Vienna was captured by Soviet troops. They were able to survive in large part thanks to Red Cross packages containing food and warm clothing from friends and family in Iceland. In a letter published in the Reykjavík daily *Morgunblaðið* in 1946, the Stepanek family expressed their gratitude, "for in these difficult times of shortage and hardship, we would certainly have suffered injury to our health and lives, had we not been fortunate enough to benefit from your

Figure 4.3. The Reykjavík Music School Trio in November 1938: Heinz Edelstein, Árni Kristjánsson, and Hans Stepanek. *Source:* © National Museum of Iceland. Used with permission.

assistance."[37] Stepanek was finally allowed to return to Iceland in 1947. He taught at the Reykjavík Music School for several years before once again relocating to Vienna, where he played with his former orchestra until his retirement in 1971.[38]

The Ones Who Were Rejected

Since Icelandic authorities were willing to reject an application from an outstanding musician who was not only "Aryan" but also had an Icelandic wife and had previously worked there, there was little hope for those of Jewish heritage with no personal connections to the place. Five musicians of Jewish descent are known to have applied for or enquired into the possibility of emigrating to Iceland in 1937–1939, all to no avail. One of them made it to Iceland but was deported, two were denied residence permits, one secured another destination while in the process of applying, whereas the fifth musician made only an informal enquiry to a colleague and was later murdered in a Nazi extermination camp.

The one who made it into the country, Fritz Dehnow (1889–1960), was an attorney by profession, but he also loved music; he played piano and violin and was a talented arranger. Born in Breslau, he completed his doctorate in law after serving in the army during World War I, and then made a career in Hamburg. He fled Germany in 1936 for São Paolo, Brazil, but a year later he arrived in Iceland, hoping to win back his ex-wife, Ilse, who had settled there in the meantime. In this endeavor he had no success; she married an Icelander and remained in Iceland until her death in 2004.[39] Dehnow resided in Reykjavík in autumn 1937, advertising in newspapers for students in German, French, and math, as well as piano, violin, and music theory.[40] He was deported a few months later, but he made it to Argentina and worked as a musician in Buenos Aires. Among his projects there was preparing editions for the music publishing house Ricordi, which included a collection of songs from Scandinavia and Iceland in his own arrangements.[41] Dehnow returned to Germany in 1956 and remained there until his death four years later.

Two musicians requested to immigrate to Iceland but were denied entry. Paul Erdensohn (1889–1956) was a violinist and composer from Dortmund, of Jewish heritage but a baptized Christian. He had studied at the Berlin Academy of Music with such luminaries as Joseph Joachim and Henri Marteau, was considered an excellent string pedagogue, and composed several books of études for aspiring violinists.⁴² In December 1938, he applied for a residence permit in Iceland along with his wife and brother Caesar, a lawyer, but they were all rejected soon afterward.⁴³ Instead, they sailed to China, still an open country with no visa requirements and therefore a popular destination; over 18,000 refugees made it to Shanghai until more restrictive rules came into effect in autumn 1939.⁴⁴ Circumstances there were nothing short of terrible; Shanghai was still in ruins after the Japanese invasion of 1937, and soon Japanese troops took over the city. In 1943, all refugees were gathered in the ghetto of Hongkou in deplorable conditions, plagued by poverty and hunger.⁴⁵ It was only after the war that Erdensohn found a permanent job there, being appointed professor in violin and viola at Shanghai University. He remigrated to Germany in 1951 and died there five years later.⁴⁶

In January 1939, the Icelandic Ministry of Justice received an application for a residence and work permit from Ludwig Misch (1887–1967), a Jewish musician residing in Berlin (see fig. 4.4). As to Misch's talent and

Figure 4.4. Ludwig Misch in Bonn, ca. 1965. *Source:* © Beethoven-Haus, Bonn. Used with permission.

versatility as a musician, there could be no doubt. From the early 1920s until 1933, he was on the faculty of the distinguished Stern Conservatory, where he taught choral conducting, composition, and music education. He was also a classical music critic for the local *Berliner Lokalanzeiger* and wrote program notes for the Berlin Philharmonic Orchestra. Once the Nazis seized power, he was removed from all his posts but was instead allowed to teach music at two Jewish private schools. For a while, he also directed a mixed choir under the auspices of Berlin's Jewish Culture League. Misch initially tried to immigrate to Paris along with his "Aryan" wife, but when this proved impossible, they decided to remain in Berlin, at least for a while.[47] The horrors of the *Kristallnacht*, however, led them to explore all options, including Iceland. Supplementing his application was a glowing recommendation from the conductor Wilhelm Furtwängler, who asserted that Misch, widely known in Berlin for his "outstanding talent," would be an asset to any musical organization. In his own letter to the Ministry of Justice, Misch expressed the hope that his "talent, expertise, and experience" might be of benefit to Iceland's burgeoning musical life.[48] A month later, his application was rejected and all supplementary materials returned to him by mail.[49] Amazingly, Misch managed to survive the entirety of the war in Berlin, although he was obliged to do forced labor and was also mistreated by Russian soldiers once the war had ended. In 1947, Misch and his wife moved to New York, where he established himself as a noted musicologist, largely focusing on Beethoven and his music.[50]

Another musician who considered emigrating to Iceland was Alphons Silbermann (1909–2000), a printer's son from Cologne. He had begun piano studies at the age of nine, but when his talents became clear, his father objected to him pursuing a career in music. The two agreed that he would continue making music alongside his law studies, and although Silbermann completed a doctorate in law, he always worked as a musician on the side, including a stint as rehearsal pianist at the Cologne Opera. Once the Nazis took power, it was clear that Silbermann would have to escape: he was not only Jewish but homosexual as well. His first destination was Paris, where he worked as a bar pianist and served tables at restaurants.[51] He hoped to get to Australia, but his parents objected; they considered it a far too remote destination. Instead, they encouraged him to apply for a residence permit in Iceland, which at least was on the edge of Europe. In his autobiography, Silbermann recalls standing in line alternately at the Australian and Icelandic consulates (presumably the Danish consulate in Paris, since Denmark still managed Iceland's foreign affairs), in the hope of getting to whichever place was first to accept him.⁵² Not surprisingly, given Iceland's strict immigration policy, his Australian papers came through first. Silbermann arrived in Sydney in autumn 1938 and began a career as a musicologist, teaching at the Sydney Conservatory. After the war, he returned to Germany and became a professor at the Cologne Conservatory of Music. He made an important contribution to the sociology of music, and in the last decades of his long life he became a popular interlocutor on German television, widely admired for his intellect and humor.⁵³

At least one other musician hoped to immigrate to Iceland, but without success; he was the only one of this group to be killed in a Nazi extermination camp. Viktor Ullmann (1898–1944) was an outstanding composer and pianist, having studied with Arnold Schoenberg in Vienna before settling in Prague. When Hitler annexed the Sudetenland in autumn 1938, Ullmann pursued every possible means to get out. For example, he repeatedly wrote to a former schoolmate in South Africa, asking if there was any possibility for him to immigrate there, but this turned out to be hopeless.⁵⁴ As Nazi troops marched into Prague in spring 1939, the danger became even more palpable. In June that year, Ullmann penned a letter to Victor Urbancic in Iceland, asking if he saw any possibility for him to obtain work there. Although they were not personally acquainted, Ullmann had heard of his successful emigration through a friend who worked for the Rudolf Steiner Institute in London. Ullmann's letter is brief, only a few lines on a single page, yet his despair is palpable. He asks Urbancic if there might be any possibility for him to find work as a pianist in one of Reykjavík's cafés, since he would gladly take such work in order to escape the Nazi regime.⁵⁵ Urbancic's reply has not survived, but he presumably gave a realistic assessment, that by 1939 it was completely impossible for a Jewish refugee to obtain residence and work permits in Iceland. Thus, apparently, the matter ended, since no correspondence or applications from Ullmann can be found in the Icelandic National Archives.

Three years after Ullmann wrote his letter to Urbancic, he was arrested and transported to the Terezín (Theresienstadt) prison camp in northern Bohemia. The Terezín camp was unique in that its inmates were encouraged to participate in artistic pursuits—concerts, poetry readings, and art exhibits—which the Nazis in turn employed as propaganda, producing documentary films intended to show that their camps were filled with happy inmates. But the realities of life in Terezín were horrifying; in September 1942, the month of Ullmann's arrival there, 3,900 prisoners died out of a total of 58,000 inmates.⁵⁶ Despite the deplorable conditions, Ullmann showed remarkable perseverance, composing and organizing musical performances, including the one-act opera *Der Kaiser von Atlantis*. In October 1944, he was deported to Auschwitz and murdered there along with his wife.

Although a critical re-examination of 1930s immigration policies has taken place in Iceland during the last decade, the stories of these musicians' attempted immigration to Iceland were largely forgotten until brought to light in the Icelandic iteration of this book. In retrospect, it was a substantial loss to Icelandic culture that such distinguished musicians as Erdensohn, Misch, and Ullmann should not have been able to immigrate there. It is nevertheless tempting to speculate what their contributions might have been. Might there have been more excellent choirs, a slew of talented young violinists, a more decisive cultivation of musicology in Iceland? Might we have dozens of additional works by Viktor Ullmann, perhaps inspired by Icelandic vernacular music, or the mountains, geysers, and volcanos of his new homeland? Furthermore, it cannot be ruled out that still more musicians contemplated exile in Iceland, even though sources no longer exist. The government files at the Icelandic National Archives may not be complete, while other musicians may not, in the end, have made formal contact with the authorities—as was the case with both Silbermann and Ullmann. Given the xenophobia and antagonism of leading politicians as well as the musicians' union, Iceland was unlikely to have accepted more exiled musicians than it did, even as the situation on the continent deteriorated. This was, of course, Iceland's loss but also serves as a reminder that the exiles of Abraham, Edelstein, and Urbancic were a remarkable and unexpected stroke of good fortune—for all concerned.

Families in Flight

For most of the exiles who escaped Nazi Germany, not a day passed without worry and anguish over the fates of relatives who might not have been as fortunate. Some had been captured and sent to prison camps, while others were hiding from the authorities at great risk, or had successfully reached safety. Often, the émigrés' gratitude for their own fortune was tinged with guilt at not having done more to save those left behind. All the main protagonists of this volume attempted to bring a parent or parent-in-law to Iceland after the war broke out, although only Robert Abraham did so successfully. They all lost close relatives in the Holocaust, and, in some cases, only a small number of family members survived.

Sometimes, the chance to save a close relative's life was frustratingly close at hand. In January 1939, with a letter to the Icelandic Justice Department, Heinz Edelstein applied for a residence permit for his mother, Ida, noting she intended to "visit me and stay here at my home for a while."[57] Only four days later, she was granted permission to reside in the country for six months, with the proviso that her son guarantee that she "leave the country before the permit expires."[58] But Ida Edelstein never came to Iceland, for reasons that remain unclear. She had moved from Bonn to Berlin in 1936, perhaps to be closer to her daughter Ruth who resided there for a while with her husband and their young daughter. One possible explanation for Ida Edelstein's hesitation regarding her journey to Iceland was that she hoped to be able to immigrate to the United States with Ruth and her family. In any event, things turned out differently than she had hoped. Ruth and Erwin Schepses, along with their daughter, departed on the SS *Washington* from Hamburg on May 4, 1939, and began a new life in Queens, New York, but her mother was not part of their entourage.[59]

A devastating turn of fate appears to have prevented Ida Edelstein from joining her daughter and son-in-law on their journey to New York. When Ruth and Erwin Schepses applied for a U.S. visa, all quota slots available to immigrants from Germany had already been filled. However, since Erwin had been born in Mexico, a country exempted from such quotas by the U.S. Immigration Act, he was allowed entry along with his wife and daughter.[60] As his mother-in-law, however, Ida Edelstein did not qualify for an exemption. Nine days later, she was able to board the SS *St. Louis*, which departed Hamburg for Havana, Cuba, with 937 passengers, most of them German Jews. The story of the ship's ill-fated journey is well known. At around the time of the ship's departure, Cuban authorities altered the existing immigration rules, thereby effectively nullifying the landing permits held by most of those aboard the *St. Louis*. Panic ensued when it became clear that passengers would be refused entry unless they paid a bond of 500 U.S. dollars, a substantial amount beyond the means of nearly all aboard. The ship's captain showed remarkable resilience in dealing with a catastrophic situation. As the journey began, he had taken the unprecedented step of removing a large formal portrait of Hitler from the vessel's ballroom to create a more comfortable atmosphere for his passengers, and he now categorically refused to return to Germany on a ship filled with Jews. Despite repeated attempts, U.S. and Canadian governments refused entry to such a large group of refugees without the necessary visas, and so the *St. Louis* began its uncertain journey back to Europe. After nearly a month at sea, the remaining 908 passengers were finally allowed to disembark in Antwerp, Belgium. Along with Belgium, three other countries agreed to secure entry visas for the passengers: Great Britain, Holland, and France.[61]

Having been assigned to Holland by the authorities, the sixty-year-old Ida Edelstein arrived in Amsterdam in June 1939. This proved to be only a temporary refuge, as the Nazis invaded Holland eleven months later. After the invasion, Mrs. Edelstein appears to have led a nomadic, destitute life; over the next three years, official records list her as living at six different addresses.[62] Amsterdam is a densely populated city, and it proved particularly difficult for Jews to hide there from Nazi authorities. It is believed that 75 percent of Jews in Holland were murdered in the Holocaust, a higher percentage than in other countries.[63] In summer 1942, Ida disappears from public records in Amsterdam, and she probably met her death in Auschwitz. Even late in life, her grandson, Stefán Edelstein, wondered why his father didn't do even more to convince her to join the family in Iceland since she already had permission to come. "I think he was probably plagued by a guilty conscience over this later in life," he said.[64]

Heinz Edelstein's wife, Charlotte, also lost many relatives in the Holocaust. In October 1940, her sister Lilli was among the nearly four hundred Jews arrested in Freiburg and deported to the prison camp in Gurs in southern France. This was a well-organized raid that eliminated nearly all Jews from the city, and the Gurs camp was a miserable destination; flooded with prisoners, it had neither food nor beds for everyone.[65] Lilli was later deported to Auschwitz and murdered there.[66] In 1942, their seventy-eight-year-old mother Jenny was transported from her hometown of Lauban, Silesia, to Terezín, where she later died. For the duration of the war, Charlotte was consumed by worries for her mother and sister, and tried desperately to learn more about their situation. Her husband also attempted to send letters to them with the assistance of the Icelandic embassy in Lisbon, but with no success.[67]

Thus, understandably, the daily life of the Edelstein household in Reykjavík was marked by sorrow and sadness. Like others who had escaped the Nazi terror, they did not have the opportunity to properly work through the mental and emotional challenges they had faced, both prior to and after their emigration. Of the musicians and their families discussed here, the Edelsteins had to endure life in Nazi Germany for the longest period—Heinz for four and a half years, and Charlotte and their sons a year longer. Robert Abraham was a citizen of the Third Reich for a year, as was the Urbancic family, although their ordeal was divided in two:

several months in 1933 followed by another short period in 1938. (Nevertheless, life for "non-Aryans" in Austria was fraught with difficulties even before the *Anschluss*.) Thus it is understandable that post-traumatic stress should have marked the daily existence of the Edelstein family, a situation not alleviated by Charlotte's social isolation and periods of depression (see chapter 5). When Vigdís Finnbogadóttir recalled her childhood memories of the household, Mrs. Edelstein's demeanor was fixed in her mind: "She sometimes looked so desperately sad."[68] Heinz Edelstein also internalized his sorrow and guilt, with mental and physical effects that would take their toll later (see chapter 8).

Victor and Melitta Urbancic did all they could to save their relatives in the dire situation they faced. As Victor's parents were "Aryan" Roman Catholics, they were in no danger in Vienna. All of Melitta's relatives, on the other hand, were Jewish, and their situation soon became desperate. Her mother, Ilma Grünbaum, had remained in Vienna, as did Ilma's sister-in-law, Valerie Neumann, a widow in her sixties. Once the war broke out, Victor and Melitta applied for permission for Valerie to travel to Iceland. In his application for a residence permit in November 1939, Urbancic pledged he would provide her with both room and board, while she would assist with housework and look after the children.[69]

Although Prime Minister Jónasson approved this request on behalf of his government, he was vehemently opposed to it on a personal level. Unusually for him, he added to his signature a note declaring that the application was granted "by the cabinet majority."[70] In April 1939, Jónasson's Progressive Party, which for two years had led a single-party minority government, was joined by the Independence Party and Social Democrats to form a three-party coalition. While Jónasson retained his posts as both Prime Minister and Minister of Justice, he no longer had unilateral control over the country's immigration policy. Nevertheless, it was in his power to delay the Neumann case for months, and when the paperwork was finally sorted, it had become virtually impossible for Jewish citizens to escape Austria. At first, the Urbancic family hoped that "Tante Vali," as they affectionately called her, could journey via Copenhagen in April 1940. This became hopeless when Danish authorities denied her a transit visa, probably bowing to pressure from the Icelandic Steamship Company (*Eimskipafélag Íslands*), who feared their vessel would be forced to land in the British Isles should authorities discover a refugee was on board.[71] With a journey through Denmark out of the question, Urbancic purchased a fare for her on the Icelandic SS *Edda*, which sailed from Genoa to Reykjavík in May. Yet Neumann never made it aboard that ship, either. Perhaps she unsuccessfully tried to cross the border to Italy; perhaps she never received the letter in which her niece informed her of their new plan.[72]

In spring 1942, Victor and Melitta Urbancic made one final attempt, but this time they applied for—and obtained—residence permits for both Valerie Neumann and Ilma Grünbaum, Melitta's mother (see fig. 4.5). Once again, the journey itself proved an insoluble dilemma. As Helgi Briem, the Icelandic chargé d'affaires in Lisbon, explained to Victor Urbancic, no one was allowed to enter Portugal—by that time the only continental port from which ships could set sail to Iceland—without authorization from the respective citizen's home embassy, which in this case was Germany.[73] Since the German government denied all Jews permission to leave the country, the situation was hopeless. In early 1943, the family stopped receiving news from Ilma altogether; they later discovered that she had been transported to Terezín on January 11 and died there three weeks later. By that time, her sister-in-law Valerie was already held in Terezín; her death was recorded on August 9, 1944. Their tragic fates weighed heavily on Melitta, who was

Figure 4.5. Ilma Grünbaum in Vienna, ca. 1937. *Source:* © Sibyl Urbancic, private collection. Used with permission.

beside herself with worries about her family throughout the war. As her daughter Sibyl recalls: "She blamed herself all her life, for not bringing her mother along when we went to Iceland."[74]

The Urbancic family's petitions on behalf of Ilma and Valerie also triggered a more immediately precarious situation for themselves. In his monograph on refugees in Iceland, historian Snorri G. Bergsson notes that local authorities often tried to deport Jews when they felt they had become too visible in the community, or when they were bold enough to apply for residence permits for other family members.[75] While Prime Minister Jónasson had succumbed to government pressure in the case of Ilma Grünbaum and Valerie Neumann, it seems that his pride was wounded and he wanted revenge. At this time, Urbancic still had only a temporary residence and work permit in Iceland, and thus Jónasson, on his own accord, appears to have begun a private campaign to have the entire Urbancic family deported. His plan was, in fact, so secretive that no official documents pertaining to it have survived; the only evidence is oral testimony from an emeritus history professor at the University of Iceland, whose source was a reliable, high-ranking government official with firsthand knowledge of the case.[76] Apparently, the leaders of the other two parties in government, Labor Minister Ólafur Thors and Foreign Minister Stefán Jóhann Stefánsson, worked together to prevent this spiteful scheme.

Although this entire situation caused tremendous anxiety for Victor and Melitta Urbancic, they took great care to prevent their children from feeling anything was amiss. "They never told us about it," says daughter Sibyl, who only learned that Iceland's prime minister had tried to deport her family in 2017, when historian Bergsson published his study on the reception of immigrants in Iceland. In a radio interview four years later, she described the discovery as a complete shock: "I have always felt like Iceland was home to me, and—once I was old enough to comprehend the circumstances under which we arrived—have been grateful for being accepted here as an Icelander and being allowed to live here. But reading this account, 80 years later, it was as if the earth fell out from under my feet. I felt like I was falling into an abyss. It was such a devastating thought."[77]

Most of Robert Abraham's close relatives managed to escape Nazi Germany in time. As already noted, his brother Peter was the first to leave the country. In spring 1933, he immigrated to Copenhagen, where he studied natural science and geography at Copenhagen University, and became a protégé of physicist Niels Bohr (see fig. 4.6).[78] After five years in Denmark, Peter continued on to the United States, in September 1938. He settled

Figure 4.6. Robert and Peter Abraham with (from left) Margrethe and Niels Bohr, Rigmor Adler (Bohr's cousin), and Hans Bohr, in Copenhagen, ca. 1937. *Source:* © Elín Þ. Ólafsdóttir, private collection. Used with permission.

in California and studied music at UCLA, where Arnold Schoenberg was among his teachers. After a stint in the U.S. army during the war, Peter began graduate work in ethnomusicology at UC Berkeley, researching the music of California Native Americans.[79] Due to ill health, Peter Abraham was never able to complete his doctorate. Shortly after 1950 he began to suffer from what was eventually diagnosed as Parkinson's disease, then a largely unknown ailment for which no effective treatment was available. He died in California in 1960, at only forty-five years old.

All four of Lise Abraham's siblings were also able to immigrate to the United States. The oldest of the group, Ernest Golm, had practiced law in Berlin, but in California he and his wife Lisa made a modest living playing bit roles in various Hollywood films, such as the 1944 film *The Hitler Gang*, which depicted the rise of Nazism.[80] Another brother, Gerhard, ran a medical clinic in New Hampshire; Rudolf, a former lawyer, settled in Colorado, while their sister, Emmy Mathias, resided in Wisconsin with her husband.[81]

Robert Abraham's paternal aunt, Grete, had been a librarian at the Berlin University Library but was forced to retire when the Nazis took power. She made it to Denmark in 1939 and lived there until her death.[82] Grete Abraham had three sisters, all of whom died in Nazi concentration camps, including the oldest of the Abraham siblings, Clara Henriette Simon, who died in Terezín in 1944. Her son, Walter Simon, immigrated to England in 1936 and eventually became Professor of Chinese at the University of London. While Professor Simon was a prodigious linguist—he once boasted he could read a newspaper in virtually any European language—he chose to express his contempt for his native land by refusing to speak a single word of German for the remainder of his life.[83] Whenever he and his musically accomplished cousin were reunited after the war, Robert Abraham spoke German while Simon replied in English.[84]

Every life brutally cut short by the Nazis deserves to be remembered for its own sake. Yet the tragic fates of these family members, as well as those of the Jewish musicians discussed earlier, also serve as a reminder that the main protagonists of the present book were in real and present danger while still living in Germany. Had they not been able to leave before it was too late, Robert Abraham, Heinz and Charlotte Edelstein, and Melitta Urbancic—along with the Edelstein and Urbancic children—would likely have been forced to undergo the harrowing journey to Terezín or Auschwitz.[85]

5

New Realities

Adapting to life in Iceland, where local customs were in many ways so different from their own, proved a considerable challenge for the émigré musicians and their families. It is worth remembering that Iceland had never been their destination of choice; they had all initially attempted to immigrate to other areas, such as North and South America, Denmark, and Switzerland. But at least they were free from Nazi oppression, and as time passed they were all able, in their own ways, to negotiate their multiple identities in their process of acculturation, which has been defined as "accepting certain cultural norms while retaining an ethnic content in familial and communal life."[1] They all learned Icelandic, not by any means an easily acquired language, and they were granted citizenship roughly a decade after arriving in the country, as usually granted by Icelandic law at the time (see below). They grew to love the country itself, despite its often brutal weather, strangely barren nature, and lunar-looking lava fields. They also developed an appreciation of Icelandic literature and other art forms. The musicians showed remarkable patience and humility when confronted with less-than-ideal working conditions, including lack of training, the lack of punctuality of their colleagues and ensemble members, and the nepotism that could sometimes be observed in the small, tightly knit society (see chapter 7). They were also genuinely curious about the music of Iceland and its history. Both Abraham and Urbancic arranged and composed works inspired by traditional music, and Abraham also undertook groundbreaking research on the surviving sources of medieval music in Iceland (see chapter 8).

At first, local reaction to the newly arrived exiles was mixed. Iceland had already seen in 1933 the founding of a small Nationalist Party (*Flokkur þjóðernissinna*) that soon became officially affiliated with the German Nazis. In those days, some right-wing nationalists hoped that Germany might support Iceland's claim for full independence from Denmark, but this was never a realistic scenario. After all, the Nazis never encouraged the self-determination of smaller countries; instead, they hoped to bring them into their own fold. The Icelandic Nationalist Party had no real influence on the political scene and never achieved representation in Parliament, but its objectives sometimes received support in local newspapers, not least the right-wing *Morgunblaðið*.

More problematic for Jewish immigrants in Iceland was that the general population's overall attitude toward immigrants was often negative, fueled by chauvinistic nationalism and further incited by a weak economy and high unemployment.² Since immigrants of Jewish origin were seen as belonging to a religion that, while virtually unknown in Iceland, was nonetheless aligned with negative preconceptions, they found themselves on the lowest rung of the ladder. Until the twentieth century, Iceland had seen few Jews among its population, a situation that fueled prejudice and resentment. Even today, practicing Jews remain rare in the predominantly Christian community; remarkably, Judaism was not officially registered as a religious community in Iceland until 2021.³ "There was a lot of prejudice and many Jews were poorly received here," recalls Vigdís Finnbogadóttir, the close friend and next-door neighbor of the Edelstein family. In her biography, published in 2009, she recalled an incident that she and Wolfgang Edelstein experienced when they were in their teens:

> I will never forget one time when I was walking across Parliament Square (*Austurvöllur*) with Wolfgang, late on a winter's day. Behind us were two boys who began to jeer, exclaiming that all those damned Jews should be impaled and roasted alive, and disparaging them using the foulest words imaginable. I remember trying to press closer to Wolli to show my support, as I quickened my pace. Who knows what goes through the minds of people who hear such drivel about themselves? Let alone teenagers?⁴

The exiles could also encounter hostility and distrust in a professional context, since local musicians had diverse opinions on immigrants and the overall situation on the continent. The well-known Icelandic songwriter Jón Múli Árnason was a member of the men's choir *Kátir félagar* (Gleeful Mates), recruited to perform with the Reykjavík Orchestra at Urbancic's first large-scale concert in December 1938. The group was comprised of relatively young singers, and Urbancic had especially requested their participation because the program featured new works by young Icelandic composers. As Árnason recalls in his memoirs:

> Most members of the ensemble were delighted by the offer, although a few nationalists declared that they weren't eager to let refugees from the continent tell them what to do. It would be more apt, they said, to send them back home again, since the German authorities apparently still had some issues to settle with them. Others in the choir balked at such talk and wanted nothing to do with such political nonsense. Our conductor, Hallur [Þorleifsson], agreed and said he looked forward to working with Urbancic, that such outstanding talent was rare, and that he didn't care one iota about politics.[5]

Antagonism toward the musicians discussed here was generally implicit and unspoken; only once, during Abraham's years in Akureyri, were such negative remarks expressed publicly. Firsthand accounts are rare, and the families themselves made little fuss of what they regarded as minor incidents. If Urbancic and Edelstein, or their wives, met with local hostility, they likely did not want to cause further anguish by discussing such matters in front of the children. In terms of the small, insular community, at least the situation was ameliorated by the fact that none of the exiles was a practicing Jew: Robert Abraham was a Protestant, Edelstein an atheist, and the Urbancic family was Roman Catholic, as was Charlotte Edelstein and her two sons.

The Urbancic and Edelstein children did their best to ignore local animosity and tried not to dwell on negative situations. Instead, they emphasized the positive aspects of their early years in Iceland, that they were met with a degree of kindness and tolerance they hadn't known before. From age thirteen to eighteen, Wolfgang Edelstein spent his summers as a helper at Giljá, a farm in northern Iceland, and said he was "extremely proud" of how the local farmers treated him:

> I experienced what had for centuries been a German Jewish boy's dream: that people who weren't Jews would come and offer you some positive opportunities in life. It helped me to get away from the negativity I had experienced before. In Germany, you had to accept not being equal, always being set apart. I came

to the farmers at Giljá and immediately they accepted me as an equal, so I became a dedicated student and a passionate Icelandic farmer! In fact, I became so devoted to the country life that I was convinced that Icelandic farmers were the best people in the world! Being on a fine horse near Hofsjökull glacier and rounding up sheep and bringing them down the mountain—in my mind, this was the ultimate manifestation of finally being equal.[6]

For Edelstein, the farm experience had such a strong effect in part because it gave him "knowledge of a social scene where children were important members of society because they worked. To an extent they worked independently; they were trusted to look after the animals. Children had responsibilities and children enjoyed recognition. For me, this probably was a saving grace; it was extremely important. As I see it, this experience had a deep and lasting influence on my uses of psychology and why—much later—I went into child psychology."[7]

While the three musicians and their families were all eventually granted Icelandic citizenship, this was never easily achieved. Each application had to be approved by the Parliament, which in general took a restrictive stance in such matters in the late 1940s. In each of the three cases, special intervention was required by individual MPs, justified by the exiled musicians' specific contributions and personal qualities. Robert Abraham applied for citizenship in 1946, as he had every right to, since he had resided in the country for more than a decade. Still, as the Parliament moved toward a vote in December that year, its general committee failed to reach a consensus on citizenship applications. The majority wished to "not at present grant citizenship to others than those who are born in Iceland or have lived here since childhood." An MP of the Progressive Party defended this position, noting that special care had to be taken, since "the times are much changed from before, and we now have more foreigners than ever, and more applications than ever."[8] The committee's minority, however, wished to follow a previously established rule that all applicants who had resided in the country for at least ten years should be granted citizenship, regardless of their background. A member of the Socialist Party defended this view, noting in particular that Robert Abraham was a "well-known conductor and a fine man." In the end, the minority was able to sway the vote, and Abraham became an Icelandic citizen in 1947.[9] Yet this was achieved with the smallest of margins: fourteen MPs voted for Abraham's citizenship, while thirteen voted against.[10] Of the six new citizens brought up for a vote on an individual basis, Abraham was the closest to being rejected. Much later, his wife Guðríður confessed to her nephew that she could never bring herself to tell her husband how close the vote actually was—it would have broken his heart.[11]

A year later, the Parliament took a harder stance, and no exceptions were allowed. Thus, Heinz Edelstein was refused citizenship on the grounds that he was not born in Iceland or another Nordic country (i.e., Denmark, Norway, Sweden, or Finland), nor did he have an Icelandic wife.[12] In 1949, it appeared this stance would again prevail and that all applications not meeting this specific requirement would be rejected. Finally, a member of the Independence Party, Jóhann Hafstein, came to the rescue and proposed an amendment that would allow citizenship to Edelstein, Urbancic, and Viennese pianist Carl Billich. Hafstein explained that several MPs had encouraged him to take the step, not least because Edelstein had done "excellent work for the Music School" and Urbancic was "well known to most people here for his contribution to music in this town." Another MP proposed a special amendment for Wolfgang Edelstein, who in the meantime had turned eighteen and thus was no longer eligible for citizenship through his father. The MP noted that he "knew the boy quite well," as Wolfgang had worked on a nearby farm and shown himself to be an "especially hard-working and reliable young man." In this case, the amendments were approved with eighteen votes to five.[13]

New Language, New Names

Countless things can make immigrants stand out in new surroundings. They are likely to speak their newly acquired language with a notable accent, they bear uncommon names, their habitual clothing, manners, and cuisine all differ from local custom. In a small, insular community like Iceland, such differences were particularly pronounced and presented various challenges—some predictable, others unexpected.

This was especially true of the children, who were often painfully aware of their status as foreigners. Peter Urbancic—who immediately adopted the Icelandic form of his name, Pétur—attended the local Catholic school, but it was their next-door neighbor, the fellow exile Irmgard Kroner, who helped him to learn Icelandic. In particular, she drilled him on the rolled R that is characteristic of spoken Icelandic but often proves difficult for foreigners, including native German speakers who employ a guttural R in their language.[14] A few years later, it was Peter's turn to teach his younger sister, Sibyl, how to roll her R before her first day at school. She recalls that language skills were not her only concern as she began first grade. "I wore clothes that were unlike the ones that local kids wore. I had been given my siblings' old hand-me-downs, and that felt terrible. And my schoolbag was different than all the other schoolbags; I found all of this deeply uncomfortable."[15] She emphasizes that she wasn't made fun of, but that, internally, she was keenly aware of being a foreigner. Sibyl even forbade her father to speak to her in public, wherever locals might hear them. She was ashamed, she recalls, because of his pronunciation: "When he spoke Icelandic you could tell that he was a foreigner."[16]

While Victor Urbancic soon acquired a solid grasp of the Icelandic language, he was often likely to fumble with grammar or vocabulary.[17] His occasional gaffes at rehearsals became legendary amongst local musicians. For example, when bringing to a close the penultimate rehearsal of the Reykjavík Orchestra and the Music Society Choir for a performance of a Baroque oratorio, he wished to emphasize punctuality so that the general rehearsal could begin on time. Everyone had to be there at the scheduled

Figure 5.1. Melitta Urbancic with her three children in downtown Reykjavík shortly after arriving in Iceland: Pétur, Ruth, and infant Sibyl in a stroller. *Source:* © Sibyl Urbancic, private collection. Used with permission.

start time, he insisted, "but if you have to come late, please walk in backwards"—by which he meant "through the back entrance," confusing the Icelandic words *afturábak* and *bakdyramegin*.[18] Once, as a choir rehearsal was reaching its conclusion, he announced that the tenors and basses were free to leave but that the sopranos and altos should stay a bit longer, as he was going to "impregnate" them—when he intended only to "improve" their singing (*batna þær*, which in pronunciation is nearly indistinguishable from *barna þær*).[19] While such stories may be amusing, their currency among the local population also tells a tale; they confirmed upon Urbancic a certain outsider status that immigrants could not easily get rid of.[20]

The Icelandic language came fairly easily to Heinz Edelstein, who was an intense perfectionist and already had an impressive knowledge of many languages, including Latin and Greek, before arriving in Reykjavík. His surviving letters show an astoundingly good grasp of both vocabulary and grammar.[21] Edelstein's only cause for regret was the difficulty he had mastering the rolled R, which meant he could never be mistaken for a local. He was finally able to remedy this in 1951, during an extended study trip to West Germany (see chapter 7). From Detmold, he wrote to one of the leaders of the Reykjavík Music Society that he had found a speech therapist who "has taught me the tongue-tip-R, that I have so desired all my years in Iceland. I hope that my pronunciation of Icelandic will be better now than before."[22] Even having lived in Iceland for fifteen years and mastered virtually every aspect of the language, he still wished to improve his pronunciation—although it is certainly amusing that it took a speech therapist in Germany to eliminate this German feature of his diction.

For Robert Abraham's friends and colleagues, his mastery of Icelandic was a source of genuine admiration. His fluency was probably due in part to his having arrived in Iceland at such a young age—he was only twenty-three, a full decade younger than Edelstein and Urbancic—and he had also learned Danish, a language lexically close to Icelandic, before his arrival. As he had an Icelandic wife, Abraham spoke Icelandic at home, and through his marriage he had easier access to Icelandic cultural and social life than most foreigners at the time.

A person's name is yet another distinctive feature of their self-image. Iceland's naming tradition is unusual in that it employs patronymics; instead of family names, a person's last name is the name of the father (or, in recent years, mother) in the genitive case, followed by the suffix *-son* for males and *-dóttir* for females (or, in recent years, *-bur* for non-binary individuals). Wolfgang Edelstein recalled later in life that the first thing he had noticed as a child arriving in Iceland was that all the names seemed to end in -*sohn*, which implied to him that, as he put it, "they were all Jews!"[23] Being accustomed to Jewish last names like Aronsohn, Jacobsohn, or Mendelssohn, his first instinct was that he had now finally arrived in a country were Jews were the majority. In fact, nothing could have been further from the truth.

In response to the growing number of foreigners residing in Iceland in the 1940s, the Parliament passed controversial legislation that required all foreign-born nationals to adapt their names to the local tradition. These laws were ratified only in 1952, after all the people discussed here had already received their citizenship, and thus they did not apply to them—they were all allowed to retain their foreign names if they wished.[24] This legislation was in effect until the early 1970s, when growing resistance led to its repeal. The turning point was an application for Icelandic citizenship by the legendary Russian pianist Vladimir Ashkenazy in 1972; had the law still been in effect, he would have been required to take the name Valdimar Davíðsson.[25]

Because of its multiple adjacent consonants, the family name Urbantschitsch caused considerable confusion with locals. In an otherwise glowing review of Handel's *Messiah* in 1940, novelist Halldór Laxness chose to Icelandify the conductor's name as "Dr. Viktor Úrbansson," adding, in a footnote: "I apologize to him, that I am unable to write his name except in Icelandic."[26] In the years 1941–1942, Urbancic was occasionally referred to in local newspapers as "Viktor Úrbansson," and the socialist daily *Þjóðviljinn* grumbled about his difficult name as late as 1948: "Why can't we just say Úrbansson?"[27] While it is true that the suffix -*čič* in Slavic languages (or -*tschitsch* in German spelling) has the same function as -*son* in Icelandic, Urbantschitsch had long ago become an ordinary family name, and thus "Úrbansson" was not in accordance with the local tradition. As Urbancic's father's name was Ernst, the correct form of the patronymic would be "Ernstsson." Nevertheless, such microaggression prompted Urbancic, upon receiving citizenship in 1949, to formally adopt a different spelling of his last name, derived from the Slovenian *Urbančič*.

Although not required to by law, Robert Abraham chose to adopt an Icelandic form of his name: Róbert Abraham Ottósson. This was a relatively straightforward transformation, since Ottó was already a common name in Iceland and easily takes the patronymic form, while Abraham can function both as a first and last name; in this particular case, many locals took it to be a second given name.[28] He was delighted with his new name and found it corresponded with his own image of his adult self. When invited to conduct in Berlin in 1955, he hadn't returned to his city of birth for twenty-one years and had to decide under which name he would appear there. His German colleague Hermann Hildebrandt suggested his "old" name, but he firmly rejected the idea, insisting that the Icelandic form corresponded to "my new fatherland, the land of my wife and son."[29] Thus, he was listed in the programs of the Berlin Symphony Orchestra as no less than "Róbert A. Ottósson (Reykjavík)," and German critics referred to him as an "Icelandic guest conductor."[30]

"What Shall I Cook?"

The émigrés' culinary traditions differed in many ways from traditional Icelandic custom. They did their best to prepare some of their old favorite foods, but the right ingredients weren't always available, and they had to adjust their recipes accordingly. In her obituary of Charlotte Edelstein, former President Vigdís Finnbogadóttir recalled that food in the Edelstein household was noticeably different from that at the homes of her other schoolmates: "The cookies had a different flavor and the haddock wasn't served with just potatoes and lard, but bathed in cleverly prepared sauces made from Icelandic herbs, so that even the pickiest eaters amongst us kids thought the food there was fit for royalty."[31] To this day, the Edelstein family recalls how Charlotte would herself go out and pick sheep's sorrel—a common weed in Iceland—and she also frequented the harbor area to obtain freshly caught shellfish and other delicacies that most locals had not yet discovered at the time.[32] Since money was in short supply, the émigrés had to be thrifty when it came to food, but this was a lesson they had learned well before arriving in Iceland.

Although Charlotte Edelstein was creative in the kitchen, she found it exasperating to live in a country where so many food items were simply not available, whether due to the harsh climate, geographic isolation, or currency restrictions. She was reminded of this during a trip to England in autumn 1949, even though food rationing was still in force there after the war. Shortly after her return to Reykjavík, she wrote to her friend Lotte Zier, herself a Jewish exile who had remigrated to Germany: "Everything here is even more miserable than last year. Each day, I stand in front of my stove, wringing my hands and sighing: 'What shall I cook?' Even the food rationing in England seemed like paradise compared to here, and—the fruit! You can't buy anything here and if you want to avoid depression it's best not to go into town at all. I feel fine as long as I just stay in my room."³³ She found the food shortages in Iceland nothing short of "catastrophic," and was further outraged when coffee was unavailable for nearly a month in November 1949 due to a drought in Brazil and soaring prices on the international market. "No coffee in the entire country for weeks! And even *this* doesn't lead to a revolution!"³⁴

In the Urbancic household, Melitta conjured forth memories of Austria by baking their favorite desserts from the old home country. Apfelstrudel was relatively easy to make, as long as apples were available, but another delicacy posed a particular problem: Topfenkuchen, which requires quark, an ingredient then not available in Iceland. Instead, she used skyr, a local dairy product that is noticeably more sour, but this convergence of Austrian and Icelandic cuisines became a household staple and was promptly named "Topfenbabies."³⁵ Other culinary pursuits of the Urbancic family were regarded with general bewilderment, such as when Victor would lead them on mushroom-collecting expeditions in the lava fields east of Reykjavík. In those days, mushrooms were rarely seen in stores, and few thought to pick

Figure 5.2. Proud siblings: Ruth, Sibyl, and Pétur Urbancic with their newborn sister. Eiríka Urbancic was born on May 9, 1945, and was the first baby girl born in Reykjavík after the European war ended. *Source:* © Sibyl Urbancic, private collection. Used with permission.

the ones that grew locally. "I think people believed we were preparing some kind of witchcraft," Sibyl Urbancic says when recalling the local reaction to such unusual endeavors.[36]

The Urbancic family came to love skyr, the local dairy product, often consuming it with wild Icelandic berries. They also became accustomed to haddock, which Melitta would often cook for them, and Victor Urbancic even enjoyed more unusual local delicacies, such as blood pudding and liver sausage.[37] But some foods were simply not to be found on the island; for example, fresh fruit was hardly imported at all. One of Victor Urbancic's greatest delights on the Music Society Choir's concert tour to Copenhagen in 1948 was to be able to buy freshly picked strawberries at a farmer's market—a delicacy he had not tasted for an entire decade.[38]

As was to be expected, the German-speaking exiles living in Reykjavík in the 1930s and 1940s formed close bonds both personally and professionally. Edelstein and Abraham were good friends and later worked closely together in music education. Their relations with Urbancic were always cordial and respectful, although not as intimate. They all interacted in German and were thus able to retain their use of their native language in a professional setting. The families were also connected through the education of their children: Stefán Edelstein studied piano with Robert Abraham, who became his long-standing mentor, while Pétur Urbancic studied cello with Heinz Edelstein. The exiles also made friends with German and Austrian musicians who performed in Iceland in the postwar years. When preparing for concerts in Reykjavík in 1946, violinist Adolf Busch and his son-in-law, pianist Rudolf Serkin, practiced in Edelstein's apartment, and Serkin even gave the teenaged Stefán Edelstein a memorable piano lesson.[39] German conductor Hermann Hildebrandt, who appeared with the Iceland Symphony Orchestra in the 1950s, became a good friend of Robert Abraham and recommended him for concerts with his own orchestra in Berlin (see chapter 7).

Wars Near and Far

Iceland was an uncommonly peaceful country, but with war ravaging the continent and no local defense force in place, it was only a matter of time before the war's effects would be felt there. On April 9, 1940, Nazi troops occupied Denmark and invaded Norway, which caused great consternation in Iceland, a country still in union with the Danish king. Iceland had maintained neutrality in the war and still had a German diplomatic presence, but on May 10, British troops occupied the island, meeting with no resistance. The arrival of British, Canadian, and, eventually, U.S. forces had a significant impact on the country's daily life and culture; in some years, foreign troop members equaled 25 percent of the population.[40]

For Iceland, the war years were a time of vigorous economic revival. The high unemployment rate of the 1930s evaporated virtually overnight, as the occupation called for building an extensive network of roads, hospitals, airfields, and bridges across the country. Robert Abraham was among the hundreds of locals who found employment in the lucrative "Brit work" (*Bretavinna*), as did Edelstein, who supplemented his income during the summer months by digging trenches for hot water pipes.[41] Urbancic, on the other hand, turned out to be particularly adept in finding troop members who were trained instrumentalists or singers, inviting them to concertize with him.[42] The greatest boon in this regard was Roy Hickman, a trained baritone who worked for the Royal Air Force. In 1945, he gave a Lieder recital in Reykjavík with Urbancic at the piano, and a year later he performed the bass solos in Handel's *Messiah* under Urbancic's direction. Hickman later became Professor of Voice at the Guildhall School of Music and Drama in London, teaching a number of prominent singers, including tenor Ian Partridge.[43]

No less important for the overall scene were the hundreds of musically inclined troop members who were responsible for notably improved attendance at the town's classical concerts.[44] Among them was American composer Leroy Anderson, of *Sleigh Ride* and *The Typewriter* fame, who had studied Old Norse during his time as a graduate student at Harvard in the early 1930s, and was thus sent to Iceland in 1942 as a member of the Counter Intelligence Corps. Living in Nissen hut barracks near the center of Reykjavík (now the site of Hallgrímskirkja church), he was tasked with translating local newspaper items that might be of interest to the Army command, as well as censoring news on the radio to prevent the distribution of sensitive military information. Anderson lived in Reykjavík only for a year, but in his reminiscences of his time there, written in 1947, he recalled attending two large-scale concerts: Bach's *St John Passion* conducted by Urbancic, and Haydn's *The Seasons* under Abraham's direction.[45]

Throughout the war, Germany would occasionally send reconnaissance aircraft to Iceland, usually from air bases in Norway. When the Nazis were believed to be planning air raids on Reykjavík, citizens were required to take appropriate measures. Sibyl Urbancic's earliest childhood memory is when Reykjavík's air raid sirens began to wail late at night, and her mother carried her, in her pajamas, to a bomb shelter in a nearby basement.[46] In spring 1941, unconfirmed reports suggested that the Germans might attack at any moment. Like many other local children, Pétur and Ruth Urbancic, aged ten and eight, were sent for a temporary stay on a farm in southern Iceland, for their safety.[47] Their parents closely followed the course of the war each day through the BBC Home Service, and spent much of their free time writing letters to friends and relatives, eager to know whether they had been able to leave Austria and find a new home.

It was not entirely obvious that Abraham, Edelstein, and Urbancic would be allowed to remain in Iceland once British troops had occupied the country. When war was declared in 1939, some 70,000 Germans and Austrians residing in the United Kingdom were classified as enemy aliens, and those listed as Category A were interned in camps set up across the UK, the largest settlement of which was on the Isle of Man.[48] Absurd though it may seem, even Jewish refugees could belong to Category A, which in turn led to them being imprisoned along with, in some cases, Nazi enthusiasts. Among the imprisoned Jewish immigrants was Hans Gál, Urbancic's former director at the Mainz Conservatory, who had settled in Edinburgh in 1938 but was captured in 1940 and interned at the Isle of Man for five months. In Iceland, however, these rules were less strictly enforced, and thus Germans and Austrians fleeing racial or political persecution were allowed to remain in safety.[49]

Other German and Austrian citizens were deported soon after the occupation, however. Two of them were professional musicians: German trumpeter Rudolf Camphausen and Viennese pianist Carl Billich, both of whom were held at the Isle of Man camp for four years.[50] There, they were able to continue making music, putting together a small orchestra that performed, among other works, Haydn's "Drumroll" symphony. Billich even wrote an operetta for his fellow campmates titled *A Thousand Days without a Woman* (*Tausend Tage ohne Frau*).[51] Both were released in exchange in 1944 and allowed to return to Austria; Camphausen never returned to Iceland, but Billich made it back in 1947 and lived there until his death in 1989.[52]

During the early years of the occupation, all those with German passports who had been allowed to remain in Reykjavík were kept under close supervision and made to register once a week at the occupying forces' office. Heinz Edelstein had no patience for such tiresome bureaucracy, so he devised another solution. He rented a spare room in the family's apartment to a British intelligence officer, historian Allan Merson, for a modest fee, but instead Merson took care of the weekly registration—and Edelstein could focus on making music as before.[53]

Edelstein: Mountaineering Adventures

When Heinz Edelstein first arrived in Iceland in December 1937, he was less than impressed with the peculiar Icelandic landscape. He was accustomed to the lush, colorful forests of southwestern Germany, and his wife later told their sons that he had initially described Iceland as a country that was "barren, cold, and rough." One of the reasons he chose to return to Germany in summer 1938, she said, was because he so missed seeing "real" trees.[54]

However, Edelstein soon grew to appreciate his new surroundings. According to his son Stefán, he became a "fanatical nature lover" who preferred to spend his holidays in the Icelandic mountains (see fig. 5.3).[55] Today, journeys into the Icelandic highlands are a common pastime of both locals and tourists, but in the 1930s and 1940s such behavior was considered strange and eccentric. Edelstein's fellow émigrés were particularly baffled by such endeavors. Arnold Zeisel, a Viennese Jew who was among the few non-artistic refugees granted permission to stay in Iceland during World War II, was appalled, remarking to a fellow immigrant: "One of our men has gone completely mad! Now he's running around in the wilderness!"[56]

Figure 5.3. Heinz Edelstein in the Icelandic highlands, ca. 1948. *Source:* © Elín Þ. Ólafsdóttir, private collection. Used with permission.

Organist Páll Ísólfsson was more sympathetic, and later recalled that hearing Edelstein's stories of camping in the highlands had been "akin to listening to a fairy tale, and a majestic smile came over his face as he described the Icelandic summer night or the shimmering colors of the mountains and their lively shades of blue."[57]

Despite the occasional complaint about the lack of forests and trees, Edelstein had already become fascinated by the Icelandic wilderness during his first summer in Iceland. In June 1938, a few weeks before departing for Freiburg to be reunited with Charlotte and the boys, he undertook a two-week journey through southern Iceland, alternately on foot and horseback. He detailed his experience in an eleven-page diary, where he recounts his delight at journeying from the picturesque Gullfoss waterfall northward to Langjökull glacier. He was deeply moved by the "vivid silence" that embraced him and his travel partner, the glowing light of Botnssúlur mountains, and the sincere hospitality of local farmers. Upon returning to Reykjavík by bus late at night, however, his delight gave way to frustration. He found the town "ugly, stilted, and chaotic," and saw it as a "difficult, unsolved but pressing task" for local architects to connect the town itself with the historic traditions of the farms he had just visited.[58]

Edelstein soon made local friends who shared his passion for nature, including Páll Arason, a pioneer in organizing highland trips in Iceland. Together, the two traveled widely through the country's remotest parts, including the area in northeast Iceland around Askja, an active volcano situated in the central highlands. A chain-smoker with a sedentary job, Edelstein was never athletic or physically robust, and at least once his ambition got the better of him. In summer 1942, he traveled into the highlands along with two partners, intending to hike a substantial distance into Herðubreiðarlindir, a colorful oasis near the vast Vatnajökull glacier. There, they had arranged for a fourth person to pick them up in a jeep, but through some misunderstanding no one was there when they arrived. By then, Edelstein was too exhausted to continue, while his two hiking partners walked forty-five miles with no food until they reached the next highland farm, from where they arranged for Edelstein to be picked up. When help arrived, he was waiting at the same place in rather poor condition, having subsisted on only leftover tea and All-Bran cereal. This perilous endeavor even made the Reykjavík newspapers, while Edelstein himself recalled that the most challenging aspect of the whole experience wasn't the lack of food but the absolute, deafening silence on the barren highlands.[59]

Melitta and Charlotte: Talent Overlooked

As professional musicians, Victor Urbancic and Heinz Edelstein were able to adapt to daily life in their new country with relative ease. They interacted with locals on a daily basis—students, instrumentalists, singers, and composers—and were widely admired for their skills. However, their respective wives led very different, more isolated lives. Melitta Urbancic and Charlotte Edelstein were both highly talented, holding doctorates in literature (Melitta) and economics (Charlotte), and could certainly have made an important contribution in their fields. Yet their talents were tragically overlooked in a society still dominated by males. At the time, it was virtually unheard of for women to have academic careers: when they arrived in Iceland, only two local women had ever completed a doctorate, and only in 1969 was a female promoted to the rank of professor at the university.[60] As foreign women, they faced a double disadvantage; professionally, they stood no chance.

Thus, Melitta Urbancic and Charlotte Edelstein took on domestic roles. Like thousands of women fleeing Nazism, they shouldered the responsibility of keeping their families together in new and unforeseen circumstances. While their husbands enjoyed successful public careers, earned money, and practiced a new language with local colleagues, they quietly created something no less valuable: a place to call home. With imagination and fortitude, they were able to create a sense of normalcy in their own households, a place of solace and comfort in a setting that seemed so strange and unusual. Thus, they made the pressures of exile less severe, giving their husbands and children the chance to flourish that they themselves were denied.[61] Both Melitta Urbancic and Charlotte Edelstein had difficulty coming to terms with their new lives in Reykjavík. As both had taken the Roman Catholic faith before arriving in Iceland, they frequently attended the local Catholic church but were otherwise socially isolated. They also both gave private lessons in German, English, and French to Icelandic students. Although this never earned them much money, they were nevertheless able to contribute to the family finances, where every króna mattered.

In addition to her earlier work as a literary scholar, Melitta Urbancic was a trained actress—a profession even less likely to gain her employment in Iceland, as she did not fully master the language. She had always been a passionate lover of poetry; on her own estimate, she knew more than two thousand German poems by heart.[62] While this might have provided some opportunities for work in Germany or Austria, Melitta gave only one public appearance in Iceland. In November 1945, she organized her own poetry reading in the main hall of the Reykjavík Gymnasium, reciting poems by her favorite authors: Goethe, Schiller, and Rilke. A local critic found her performance outstanding: "at once lyrical and vigorous, filled with subtle nuances yet always in good taste."[63]

Melitta was also a notable poet herself, and after arriving in Iceland she wrote hundreds of poems depicting life in exile. Only a few of her poems were published during her lifetime, for example in *Zeitspiegel*, the weekly newspaper of Austrian exiles in Great Britain.[64] In 2014, a complete book of poems, *Vom Rande der Welt* (From World's End), was published for the first time, both in the original German and in Icelandic translation.[65] She wrote the volume during her first years in Iceland, and its main topic is her conviction, which differed from many other exiled poets, that in a new country it was each person's duty to try to adapt to a new life, rather than merely waiting to return and continue one's earlier existence. In an afterword to the 2014 edition, Icelandic scholar Gauti Kristmannsson argues that her writings were "self-therapeutic" and that, through writing poetry, she was able to work through the trauma of exile.[66] While the earlier poems in the book express loneliness and sorrow, their tone gradually becomes lighter and more optimistic, as if she had conquered the worst ordeal. Toward the end, the poems are a paean to her new homeland and the strange, rugged beauty of the Icelandic landscape.[67]

Melitta Urbancic was a woman of many talents. In addition to her literary work, she was an impressive sculptor, and for several years she had an art studio in the then-unfinished National Theater building. She left behind several works, including a bust of her husband, now displayed in the National Theater's foyer (see fig. 8.7). Even more unusually, she was a pioneer of beekeeping in Iceland. She had kept bees during the family's years in Graz, and in 1951 she again purchased and installed beekeeping equipment in the family garden. She imported the colonies from Norway and Scotland, and proved remarkably resourceful when adapting their surroundings to the harsh climate.[68] She also taught beekeeping to others, and eventually played a major part in establishing a society of Icelandic beekeepers.[69] Melitta was a strong-willed woman who did not hesitate to speak her mind, and she was always ready to defend her husband when she thought his employers or other musicians were taking advantage of his kindness and humility.[70]

Charlotte Edelstein led a life even more reclusive than Melitta's (see fig. 5.4). She had few friends and usually spent her days reading and praying, attending the nearby Catholic church daily. According to Vigdís Finnbogadóttir, she learned Icelandic quite well, and spoke it "softly, slowly and deliberately, never saying much but always managing to contribute

Figure 5.4. Charlotte Edelstein in Reykjavík, 1947. *Source:* © Benjamin Edelstein, private collection. Used with permission.

something witty yet sensible in just a few sentences. She was such a good teacher that even scatterbrains found themselves getting excellent grades in German because of her determination."[71] In those days, Reykjavík was a city largely without trees, but Finnbogadóttir recalls that in the backyard of the house was a solitary rowan tree that reached above the window of the Edelstein family's apartment, and in springtime and summer Lotte Edelstein would sit by this window, either reading a book or looking silently at the tree: "I always imagined that she was thinking about cherry trees and apple trees, and about how much she missed all the flowers and greenery back in Germany."[72]

Charlotte Edelstein also wrote poetry, though not of the caliber of Melitta Urbancic. Her poems are all religious, fervent prayers to God and the saints for protection and mercy. She also translated sacred verse from other languages into German, including the medieval English carol "Of One That Is so Fair and Bright," best known today through Benjamin Britten's choral setting, *A Hymn to the Virgin*.[73]

After the war, Charlotte found her calling in voluntary humanitarian work, supporting her countrymen in their hour of need. Through the Caritas

Foundation, she collected enough funds to feed one hundred kindergarteners in Freiburg for several years, and she also organized a clothing drive for the city's inhabitants.[74] But her situation in Iceland was far from enviable. Melitta Urbancic was fortunate in having a soulmate in her devoted husband, but for Charlotte Edelstein, the solitude of exile was compounded by the frustration and despair of a broken marriage. She lived in Iceland until 1951, when she returned to Germany—alone.

6

Work to Be Done

The few professional musicians working in Iceland in the 1930s and '40s certainly had their work cut out for them. The country's musical scene was still in its infancy, and Victor Urbancic, Heinz Edelstein, and Robert Abraham approached their task with ambition and grit that soon won them many admirers. While circumstances in Iceland were far from ideal, at least they knew their work was important and appreciated both by their fellow musicians and society at large. In certain other countries—particularly the United States, where competition was harsh—émigrés had difficulty finding suitable work and gaining a footing in society, which could lead to a lack of confidence, and even depression.[1]

Among them, Urbancic, Edelstein, and Abraham presented the first Icelandic performances of many of the classical canon's masterworks, whether symphonic, choral, solo, or chamber music, and they also garnered top respect as teachers at both beginning and advanced levels. While it can be argued that, on the whole, they reinforced Austro-German musical hierarchies through their focus on highbrow classical culture and the established musical canon, this had been, so to speak, their passport into Iceland in the first place. In fact, their musical interests were uncommonly broad, including music from the Renaissance and Baroque eras, which in turn led to a wider repertoire being performed in Iceland than was the case before they arrived. For example, in the 1940s and '50s they gave the local premieres not only of canonic works by Bach and Handel but also of many composers whose works had never been heard in Iceland, such as Tomás Luis de Victoria, Giovanni Pierluigi da Palestrina, Jacques Arcadelt, and Heinrich I. F. von Biber. They were also pioneers in introducing contemporary music, including local premieres of works by Igor Stravinsky, Benjamin Britten, Paul Hindemith, and Arthur Honegger. But the path to such achievements was anything but easy. Before they could introduce demanding works to local audiences, they first had to establish and diligently train the performing forces required: choirs, chamber ensembles, and a symphony orchestra. In this, they had to begin virtually from scratch.

Urbancic: The Music Society Choir

One of the main goals of the Reykjavík Music Society was to invigorate the music scene by presenting the masterworks of the Western canon to local audiences in diligently prepared live performances. The Society sponsored several concerts by the Reykjavík Orchestra each season, but its leaders wished to go even further, thus expanding the repertoire to include chamber music, operettas, and large-scale choral works. In the mid-1930s, the Society established a subscription system for its benefactors, the success of which made such ambitious programming financially viable.[2] At around the same time, it initiated its own mixed choral ensemble, the Music Society Choir (*Kór Tónlistarfélagsins* or *Tónlistarfélagskórinn*), whose main objective was to present at least one large work for chorus and orchestra annually. The ensemble's first concert, in December 1937, was conducted by Franz Mixa—his only appearance with the group since he would soon return to his native Austria. That program consisted of Schubert's Mass in G major, and the as yet unnamed choir was referred to only as "a select group of 26 men and women."[3]

Victor Urbancic's first project upon arriving in Reykjavík was to prepare the group's next concert. In two months, he had to rehearse the choir, which in the meantime had grown to a fifty-member ensemble, as well as a thirty-strong orchestra in a program of works by local composers to be performed on December 1, 1938—the twentieth anniversary of Iceland's independence from the Danish state. This proved easier said than done. After the concert, one local critic remarked that the choir had been "only a mishmash of people from here and there, some of them quite untrained," and that the orchestra was far from being a well-coordinated ensemble. Still, the critic praised Urbancic, giving him full credit for the outcome having nevertheless been "as good and solid as it turned out to be." He was, the critic said, a confident and talented conductor, and "we should consider ourselves especially fortunate that we have gotten such a skilled man to take on this job."⁴

The choir's next project was conducted not by Urbancic but by organist and Music School dean Páll Ísólfsson, since the idea to perform Haydn's *The Creation* had been his initially. The performance, in December 1939, took place in what was known as "Steindór's Automobile Pavilion" (*Bifreiðaskáli Steindórs*), a large shed owned by automobile magnate Steindór Einarsson, and the largest edifice available for a musical performance anywhere in Reykjavík. Einarsson kindly agreed to move his car fleet elsewhere for a few days, and *The Creation* was performed to great acclaim to an audience of nearly two thousand—the largest concert that had ever been held in Iceland. Yet the performance itself perhaps left much to be desired. A remarkable evaluation of it has survived, written by Werner Gerlach, the Nazi consul in Reykjavík, whose private documents were seized by British forces immediately after the occupation in May 1940. In his private notes, he mentions having attended the Music Society Choir's performance of *The Creation*, which clearly left him unimpressed: "Absolutely terrible, from our point of view."⁵

In 1940, Urbancic again took charge of the Music Society Choir, leading the ensemble's concerts for more than a decade. Each year, the choir performed one of the major choral works in collaboration with the Reykjavík Orchestra: Handel's *Messiah* (1940 and 1946) and *Judas Maccabeus* (1947), Mozart's Requiem (1942 and 1949), Bach's *St John Passion* (1943 and 1950) and *Christmas Oratorio* (1944)—a remarkable achievement, especially since none of the works had ever been heard in Iceland. The members of the Music Society Choir were on friendly terms with Mr. and Mrs. Urbancic, as well as their children; it was a "large, warm group of friends," says Sibyl Urbancic.⁶ Besides the conductor, other members of the Urbancic family also contributed to the concerts. Melitta joined the choir in *Messiah*, one of her favorite works. For the performance of *Judas Maccabeus* in 1947, fourteen-year-old Ruth Urbancic performed in the violin section, and her fifteen-year-old brother Pétur was one of three cellists in a group led by his teacher Heinz Edelstein.⁷

Most of Bach's great choral works were, of course, in German, which begged the question of how to ensure the text could be properly understood by locals. For Urbancic, the answer was clear: these works must be sung in Icelandic. For the *St John Passion*, he created a remarkable new version, pairing Bach's genius with the finest Icelandic literature of the era. For most of the chorales, he chose suitable verses from the *Hymns of the Passion*

(*Passíusálmar*), a fifty-hymn cycle by seventeenth-century pastor Hallgrímur Pétursson, the country's most revered poet of the Protestant Baroque era, who died eleven years before Bach was born. Urbancic admired Pétursson's poetry and was convinced that, artistically speaking, it was of higher quality than the original German hymn texts. In a newspaper interview preceding the 1943 concerts, he enthused: "I have now discovered Bach's equivalent in Hallgrímur Pétursson. His *Hymns of the Passion* contain the same magic of literary genius, the same dignity, and the same glorious splendor as the composition itself—the very qualities that many have found lacking in the original German text."[8] Excerpts from the *Hymns of the Passion* were not Urbancic's only source for texts. He also found suitable hymns by other Icelandic poets of the seventeenth century, such as the priest Sigurður Jónsson (1590–1661), and for the aria texts he commissioned new translations from two local poets, Þorsteinn Valdimarsson and Jakob Smári.

Training a group with limited musical skill or experience to perform a large and demanding work like the *St John Passion* was an enormous challenge. The entire performing ensemble—soloists, choir, and orchestra—was approaching the work for the first time, except for Páll Ísólfsson, who had performed the organ part during his years studying in Leipzig, and perhaps Edelstein, though no evidence has survived of his taking part in passion performances in Germany. The evangelist was sung by Þorsteinn Hannesson, a young tenor who went to London later that year to study at the Royal College of Music. From 1947 to 1954, he was an ensemble member at the Royal Opera Covent Garden, singing roles such as the Drum Major in Berg's *Wozzeck* under Erich Kleiber, but the Reykjavík performance of the *St John Passion* was his first major role as soloist. Hannesson later recalled how he would rehearse at Urbancic's home nearly every day for weeks, with Urbancic at the piano and Edelstein on cello, as they taught him, measure by measure, all of the work's recitative:

> Looking back on it now, it boggles my mind that these men should even have considered performing this work here. Still, at no point in my life have I learned more from anyone than from being in the company of these two incredibly talented men and seeing how they worked. And never, ever did I feel that they patronized me in any way. They trusted me to do this job, and they treated me like a professional singer. It was a privilege to work with these two highly educated, brilliant men—they really

were incredible. What an effort it must have been for them to put this all together.⁹

Among those who followed Urbancic's rehearsals with the choir and orchestra was his seventeen-year-old pupil, Jón Nordal, who later described the effect it had on him: "I was there at virtually every rehearsal, whenever I could, and this was maybe the deepest education I received."¹⁰ Another of Urbancic's young students, Jón Ásgeirsson, was charged with writing out the music to the *St John Passion* for each member of the choir. This was long before the days of photocopiers and, due to currency restrictions during the war, the purchase of printed scores from abroad was virtually impossible. All the parts thus had to be copied by hand, and each choir member received only their own line, instead of a piano/vocal score.¹¹

Figure 6.1. Victor Urbancic, the Music Society Choir, and the Reykjavík Orchestra at their performance of Bach's *St John Passion* at Reykjavík's Free Church in 1943. The harpsichord used for the performances was the only such instrument in the country, belonging to Kurt Zier, an exile from Germany. *Source:* © Gunnar G. Vigfússon, private collection. Used with permission.

In April 1943, the Reykjavík Orchestra and the Music Society Choir performed Bach's *St John Passion* at three concerts in Reykjavík's Free Church, the first-ever performance in Iceland of a musical passion setting (see fig. 6.1). The final performance, on Good Friday, was broadcast live on the radio, and among those listening was Eyþór Stefánsson, a voice teacher and composer who lived in the small village of Sauðárkrókur in northern Iceland. The next day, he wrote a letter to Urbancic expressing his thanks:

> One cannot but admire and be carried away by the incredible courage and perseverance that you've shown in presenting such a work of genius, and under the conditions that you have had to accept. . . . My wife and I sat, two alone, in our small, quiet living room;—we imagined that we were there in person at your concert,—we opened all the doors and windows of our souls to enjoy the musical performance as best we could. . . . I will always remember this evening with deep respect and gratitude.[12]

The performance of the *St John Passion* was widely praised as a significant milestone in Iceland's musical development, but not everyone agreed with Urbancic's decision to present the work in Icelandic. Pianist Árni Kristjánsson found that both the work and the old hymns had suffered "too much disruption" in the adaptation, yet he admitted that the Icelandic texts had in part contributed to "the hearts of Icelandic audiences" having been opened "to this magnificent work of music, and so the damage has perhaps been at least partially reversed."[13] For his performance, in June 1944, Urbancic was awarded the Knight's Cross of the Icelandic Order of the Falcon, becoming the first foreign musician to receive the country's highest civilian honor.

Urbancic also performed another of Bach's great choral works in Icelandic. In December 1944, he conducted the *Christmas Oratorio* using the Icelandic translation of the Nativity story, this time adapting local Christmas hymns to Bach's chorales. In a newspaper interview, he emphasized that such an adaptation was "very much in Bach's spirit," since, after all, the composer had intended for the entire congregation to join in singing the chorales.[14] An even larger project sadly remained unrealized. Urbancic was never able to summon the support from the Reykjavík Music Society to perform the *St Matthew Passion*, Bach's longest and most elaborate work, which he also hoped to present in an Icelandic version (see chapter 7).

Galvanizing his local group of amateur singers was not always an easy task, and sometimes even the mild-mannered Urbancic grew frustrated. At the choir's general meeting in 1946, he complained of an overall lack of commitment and punctuality, adding that under such circumstances he was hesitant to begin rehearsing Handel's *Messiah*, that year's big project.[15] Eventually, Urbancic found ways to motivate his singers, and the performance went on as scheduled. Critics agreed that the choir's 1946 performance of *Messiah* was "so powerful and full of character that it was a pure delight," and a clear improvement on their performances of the same work six years earlier.[16]

In June 1948, the Music Society Choir embarked on its only concert tour abroad, appearing at a Nordic Choral Festival in Copenhagen. Approximately one thousand singers from all the Nordic countries took part, and the Icelandic ensemble acquitted itself quite well; several Danish critics noted the choir was among the festival's finest.[17] They presented an all-Icelandic program, including a remarkable work that Jón Leifs, one of Iceland's leading composers, had written a year earlier and now was given its first public performance: *Requiem*, composed in memory of his seventeen-year-old daughter, who had tragically drowned while swimming off the coast of Sweden.[18] While the delicate, moving work, which has received a notable renaissance in recent years, is made up of the simplest of musical elements, its musical language was highly unusual for its time and Urbancic himself said he had been "very close to giving up" while rehearsing the piece. In the end, he was delighted with the performance and the audience's enthusiastic reception. Danish critics were also positive, praising the work as one of the festival's highlights.[19] Upon the choir's return to Reykjavík, they performed the entire program in Austurbæjarbíó cinema, with one critic enthusing that it had been "one of the finest concerts that the capital's inhabitants have had the chance to hear in the last few years."[20] It should also be noted that only a handful of mixed choirs were active in Reykjavík at this time, far outweighed both in prestige and number of performances by the city's male choirs. As one critic noted after their 1948 *a cappella* concert: "It is such a delightful and welcome change to hear a mixed choir."[21]

The Music Society Choir also toured locally in Iceland, giving inhabitants in smaller towns a rare chance to hear mixed choral singing of such caliber. For example, a nine-day trip in autumn 1951 included concerts at the Westman Islands, as well as Akureyri and Húsavík in the north, and Eskifjörður in the east.[22] Shortly afterward, the choir was disbanded, and most of its members followed Urbancic as he established a new choral ensemble at the National Theater (see chapter 7).

Edelstein: Cellist and Teacher

Within a few weeks of Heinz Edelstein's arrival in Reykjavík, the town's inhabitants were able to hear him live, performing chamber music with an old colleague and a new one. In February and March 1938, violinist Ernst Drucker, the leader of the Jewish Culture League's string quartet, presented five concerts in Reykjavík on behalf of the Music Society, performing, along with Edelstein and pianist Árni Kristjánsson, trios by Mozart, Beethoven, Schubert, and Tchaikovsky, to great acclaim. Reviews were unanimously positive, both for the ensemble and, in particular, the town's new resident cellist; organist Páll Ísólfsson, who was also music critic for *Morgunblaðið*, described Edelstein's playing as "excellent and mature," and his tone as "smooth and attractive."[23] A critic for the Reykjavík daily *Alþýðublaðið* noted that Edelstein's cello sound was "unusually mellow and beautiful; combined with a secure technique, he proved to be a dynamic and purposeful artist."[24] The same performance prompted the critic of the socialist *Þjóðviljinn* to assert that "in this country we have rarely heard a more perfect cello performance than Edelstein's." In a rare public mention of Edelstein's situation as an exiled musician, the same critic expressed his wish that the cellist might prove "a greater prophet among Icelanders than he was allowed to become in his German fatherland."[25]

Edelstein soon joined the Reykjavík Music School Trio, a group that had been active on and off for eight years. Its original members were Franz Mixa (piano), Karl Heller (violin), and Friedrich Fleischmann (cello), but they had all returned to Austria, and the trio thus appeared with an all-new membership. Alongside Edelstein were pianist Árni Kristjánsson and violinist Hans Stepanek, who was replaced by Björn Ólafsson in 1939 (see fig. 6.2). Edelstein was a member of this trio for a decade, introducing key works of chamber music to local audiences. Their repertoire centered mostly on the Austro-German masters, but they also occasionally performed more recent works, such as the Piano Trio (1914) by Maurice Ravel, then a virtually unknown composer in Iceland.[26] Apart from performing at the Reykjavík Music Society's subscription concerts, they appeared regularly on National Radio. As reported in the *Radio News* in 1939, listeners were "unanimous in their agreement that we cannot afford to lose such excellent artists from our small group of professional musicians"—presumably a reference to Stepanek's impending return to Austria.[27] Edelstein also performed with the short-lived Music Society String Quartet, whose inaugural concert in April 1945 was the first live string quartet concert in Iceland since a much-lauded

Figure 6.2. The Reykjavík Music School Trio, ca. 1942: Heinz Edelstein, Árni Kristjánsson, and Björn Ólafsson. *Source:* © National and University Library of Iceland. Used with permission.

guest appearance in 1936 by the Prague String Quartet. The local group's repertoire included quartets by Haydn and Beethoven as well as the Icelandic premiere of Shostakovich's String Quartet no. 1.[28] Edelstein also performed live on National Radio in partnership with Urbancic, including sonatas by Beethoven, Brahms, and Chopin, and led the Reykjavík Orchestra's cello section. As the only truly professional cellist in Iceland, he certainly had his hands full.

At the Reykjavík Music School, Edelstein taught cello and chamber music, but he also launched a special preschool course where young pupils could learn to play recorder and to sing, along with elementary music theory. This gradually became one of the school's most popular offerings, which in turn led to conflict between Edelstein and the Music Society, since he believed he should be paid extra for the course in addition to his base salary for teaching older students. In spring 1945, as the school's teachers received a pay raise, Edelstein objected to the Music Society's calculations, which in turn rejected his claims. In a letter to Edelstein, its financial officer noted that his combined salary in the 1944–1945 school year was higher than that of any other teacher.[29] Edelstein was unappeased, as he regarded his salary for the children's courses as "additional pay for additional work" that did not justify a lower annual base salary than his colleagues. He put forth his demands in an eight-page letter, written in immaculate Icelandic, accusing the Music Society of taking advantage of its position, whereas it had a "duty of fairness and justice, to give me proportionally the same pay raise as the other teachers."[30] Be that as it may, his popular children's course meant that Edelstein was for many years the Music School's highest-earning teacher. In 1947, for example, his annual salary was 36,846 krónur, while Urbancic made roughly 32,000, and other teachers received 30,000 each.[31]

While Edelstein was an intelligent and inspired musician, he was also a reticent introvert. "He was a bit dry and it was difficult to get to know him," reminisced Þórarinn Óskarsson, who played trombone with the Iceland Symphony Orchestra in its first season.[32] Edelstein also placed little importance in worldly goods. He went everywhere on foot, and sometimes reminded his friends in jest that he had never in his life owned an apartment, an automobile, or even, after moving to Iceland, a bicycle.[33] In the early 1950s, once his wife Charlotte had remigrated to Germany and their sons both attended university abroad, he lived in a small, spartanly furnished one-room apartment in the western part of Reykjavík, at Hringbraut 111. Perhaps due to his frugal lifestyle, as well as his own remigration to Germany in the 1950s (see chapter 8), Edelstein left behind only a small collection of letters and other documents, making him a somewhat more inscrutable character than Abraham and Urbancic.

Playing the cello and teaching music was Edelstein's life; when at home he largely kept to himself, reading or practicing for an upcoming concert.[34] "My father could be a little fanatical," said his son Stefán. At home, Edelstein would practice behind closed doors, and Stefán later recalled sitting on the other side of the door to his bedroom listening to the Bach suites that his father played so often: "I knew all the Bach cello suites long before I knew anything at all about music."[35] Among Edelstein's few close friends was the German-Jewish artist and teacher Kurt Zier, who had arrived in Iceland in 1939 and became influential as a teacher and later director of the Reykjavík School of Visual Arts (*Myndlistar- og handíðaskólinn*). After Zier's remigration to Germany a decade later, Edelstein mostly socialized with Robert Abraham and his wife Guðríður, but overall he led something of a monkish existence.[36]

Edelstein had a reputation as a strict and demanding teacher. Among his chamber music pupils at the Reykjavík Music School was Haukur Guðlaugsson, an organist who also studied piano and was coached by Edelstein on Mozart's *Kegelstatt* trio in the 1940s. He recalls Edelstein being very precise and disciplined in his approach: "He just let you hear it if you weren't playing well."[37] Stefán Edelstein concurs: "He was very demanding and could be harsh."[38] Gunnar Kvaran, a well-known Icelandic cellist and cello teacher, studied with Edelstein in 1953–1954 and describes him as a "passionate man, with a strong temper; my respect for him was tinged with fear."[39] Edelstein would occasionally make jokes to his students that not everyone found appropriate. Composer Þorkell Sigurbjörnsson attended Edelstein's preschool class, and later in life recalled how Edelstein would instill terror in his students by issuing dire warnings: "If you haven't all learned this song by our next lesson, I'll take you and fry you alive on a pan." After one such episode, one student's mother phoned Edelstein, furious at his "revolting" teaching methods. "But my dear madam," he replied remorsefully, "I was only trying to be funny!"[40] Nevertheless, Edelstein was certainly a dedicated teacher who went above and beyond what could be expected of him. During the war years, when all "unnecessary" imports to Iceland were limited due to currency restrictions, obtaining printed scores for his pupils became all but impossible. Determined not to let this impede his teaching, Edelstein would sometimes sit for days copying cello sonatas by hand so his students would have something suitable to play.[41]

His Icelandic students, colleagues, and local music lovers in general had immense respect for "Doktor Edelstein," as he was always addressed. Sigrún Löve, who studied with him in 1950–1951, recalls that she admired him not only for his musicianship but also for his dapper clothing, the beautiful suits and shining shoes, and his habit of wearing a black beret whenever he was outdoors (see fig. 6.3). "He was so completely different from all the Icelandic men," she recalls.[42] Pétur Urbancic, who was Edelstein's cello student for many years, adds that he has only fond memories of him: "He was an outstanding man, noble and cultured."[43]

Abraham: A Choral Pioneer

During his first years in Reykjavík, Robert Abraham's most prominent role was as conductor of the Harpa Choral Society, a mixed choir that had been active for several years. This was an ensemble with a social mission, providing access to music to lower- and middle-class amateurs, and supported by the

Figure 6.3. Heinz Edelstein, ca. 1950. *Source:* © Elín Þ. Ólafsdóttir, private collection. Used with permission.

local Social Democratic Party. Until Abraham took over, it was a small and rather poorly balanced group, whose performances were largely limited to the Social Democratic Party's own events. Abraham, on the other hand, recruited more singers and had remarkably ambitious plans in terms of repertoire. In March 1943, the choir gave the Icelandic premiere of Haydn's oratorio *The Seasons*, along with the Reykjavík Orchestra. This was Abraham's first appearance conducting an orchestra in Iceland, and the performance was an important milestone for him and his singers. "He is a temperamental and decisive conductor who knows what he wants," one critic remarked.[44]

Following this success, Abraham became increasingly prominent on the Reykjavík concert stage. He conducted the Icelandic Musicians' Society Orchestra in spring 1944 (see chapter 7), and two years later the Harpa Choral Society collaborated with the Reykjavík Orchestra in a program including Brahms's *Schicksalslied* and Bach's Cantata no. 79, both in Icelandic translation. One critic noted that the concert had had a "cultivated, cultural flair" and that the orchestra had never been in better form. Still, he wondered if the choir had perhaps chosen an overly difficult assignment with the Cantata, particularly in the dull acoustics of the Trípólí Cinema, a barracks built for film and theater by the U.S. army and the latest addition to Reykjavík's makeshift concert venues.[45]

Just as he had done in Akureyri, Abraham wished to expand the concert repertoire of the ensembles he worked with in Reykjavík, with local premieres by composers whose works were virtually unknown in Iceland. Among first Icelandic performances given by the Harpa Choral Society under his direction were Jacques Arcadelt's *Ave Maria*, Modest Musorgsky's *Ode to the Sun* for men's chorus, and Paul Hindemith's *Frau Musica*, a "cantata for amateur musicians" based on texts by Martin Luther.[46] Abraham was so proud of the choir's performance of the latter, in spring 1945, that he penned a letter to Hindemith telling him how the work had resonated strongly for a large audience who had "never heard anything like it before."[47] Under Abraham's direction, Harpa also participated in a festival of Nordic amateur choirs in Copenhagen in summer 1946, to positive reception.[48]

With his contagious enthusiasm and talent, Abraham could coax impressive results even from ensembles that hardly seemed destined for success. The Craftsmen's Choir (*Karlakór iðnaðarmanna*) was a male choir based in Reykjavík, founded in 1932 by a group of students at the local technical school. Initially, it had been directed by local organist Páll Halldórsson, and was considered one of Reykjavík's lesser male choirs. Once Abraham took over in 1943, it became noted for the quality of its singing, as well as for its novel and ambitious programs. Their first concert together prompted one critic to remark that Abraham had "in a short time been able to turn the Craftsmen's Choir into an ensemble that can perform even very demanding works brilliantly, and yet this seemed to be a choir with only modest potential for development."[49] As before, Abraham's programs contained works introduced to Reykjavík audiences for the first time, such as Brahms's *Alto Rhapsody* and the Prisoners' Chorus from Beethoven's *Fidelio*. The program at a concert in the Old Cinema in spring 1947 was no less ambitious: it included Sibelius's cantata *The Origin of Fire* (*Tulen synty*) as well as the opening chorus from Stravinsky's opera-oratorio *Oedipus Rex*, the first live performance of any work by Stravinsky in Iceland (see fig. 6.4).[50] This chorus was so well received that it had to be immediately repeated, and organist-critic Páll Ísólfsson gave a vivid depiction in his review:

> Then Abraham appeared and seemed to be in a combative mood, as if he wished to say: "Farewell, ye ancient virtues!" Or was it the name *Stravinsky* that electrified the mind? This composer's

works have long been debated and for many his name has the effect of a red cloth on a bull. But there was little time for such reflection. With lightning speed, the conductor raised his hands, and the inconceivable happened: Stravinsky's music was heard for the first time in concert in Iceland, performed by the Craftsmen's Choir![51]

It took more than a little talent and optimism to train Icelandic carpenters, plumbers, and electricians to perform such demanding music, even more so when no recordings were available. But Abraham was up to the challenge, and during rehearsals he sometimes used colorful language to invigorate his singers. Once, he likened Stravinsky's score to a traditional "delicacy" of Icelandic cuisine, exclaiming, "This music is like rotten shark and *brennivín* [acquavit]!"[52]

For Abraham, a more prestigious conducting opportunity would soon present itself. In the spring of 1947, the board of the Icelandic National

Figure 6.4. Robert Abraham at a concert with the Craftsmen's Choir in 1947, with pianist Anna Pjeturss. *Source:* © Elín Þ. Ólafsdóttir, private collection. Used with permission.

Radio began discussing the possibility of establishing a radio choir, modeled after such ensembles in Denmark, Sweden, England, and other countries. In October that year, Robert Abraham was engaged to conduct the choir, which would consist of twenty-four semiprofessional singers. The board chairman at the time was philologist Jakob Benediktsson, who had recently moved back to Iceland from Copenhagen, where, more than a decade earlier, he had been one of the main instigators of Abraham's move to Iceland. Benediktsson later remarked that, of all the decisions made during his tenure on the Radio's board, establishing the National Radio Choir and selecting Abraham as its conductor was the one of which he was most proud.[53]

The Radio Choir (*Útvarpskórinn*) was a milestone in the development of Iceland's choral scene. This was the country's first choral ensemble where members were paid for their work; the choir rehearsed three times a week, and each member received 400 krónur monthly for their participation. Among the choir members was a young soprano, Þuríður Pálsdóttir, who would soon become one of Iceland's leading professional singers, but the group also included skilled semiprofessionals and amateurs, such as Abraham's wife, Guðríður. Every other week, an entire evening was devoted to recording a new program of roughly twenty to thirty minutes' duration on 78-rpm shellac records. Preparing the programs was a substantial undertaking, especially since much of the music had to be copied by hand, due to currency restrictions that prohibited large-scale purchases of scores from abroad. The backbone of the choir's programs consisted of traditional fare, including Bach, Haydn, Mendelssohn, and Brahms, but they also performed newer works, such as by Hindemith and Jón Leifs. In larger compositions, Abraham could occasionally draw on members of the Radio Orchestra, for example when performing Bach's Cantata no. 161 (*Komm, du süße Todesstunde*) on Maundy Thursday 1948, and the opening and closing movements of Cantata no. 6 (*Bleib bei uns, denn es will Abend werden*) on Good Friday 1949. As their first season came to a close, Abraham was justifiably proud of his achievement: of the forty-nine works the choir had recorded for the Radio, twenty-five were Icelandic premieres.[54] Abraham also made his own arrangements for the ensemble. The choir's first program, in autumn 1947, included three of his arrangements of Icelandic folk songs, two of which have become repertoire classics in Iceland: the sorrowful lament *Meyjarmissir*, and the vivacious *Vínaspegill*.

The National Radio's choral initiative was not without opponents. Some found it outrageous for such an undertaking to be fully funded by a state organization, particularly at a time of economic woes, for the local economy was contracting after the wartime boom. In a newspaper interview, composer Jón Þórarinsson, who was also employed at the Radio's Music Division, defended the decision, noting that the choir demonstrated the Radio's commitment to culture. This was, he emphasized, the first Icelandic choir to reach such a level of professionalism, performing a new program at a high artistic level every two weeks, and thus the Radio's budget was well spent: "All good things are costly," he remarked.[55] Not everyone agreed, even within the walls of the National Radio itself. Another composer, Sigurður Þórðarsson, was the Radio's Executive Secretary, but in his free time he conducted the Reykjavík Men's Choir. In a newspaper article, he denounced the decision to form the choir, which he claimed had led to fewer opportunities for other choirs to perform on National Radio. As for Þórarinsson's praise for the choir's artistic achievements, he retorted that performing a well-rehearsed program every two weeks was "precisely what the choir has not yet been able to do."[56] Although Þórðarson did not specifically attack Abraham, he had long disapproved of his conducting (see chapter 3). The Radio's executive board replied that their refusal to contract the Reykjavík Men's Choir had nothing to do with the Radio Choir but rather was due to Þórðarson's "unreasonable demand" for a fee of 10,000 krónur, far more than any other choir had been paid for radio broadcasts. Nevertheless, such criticism, coming from a high-ranking Radio official, was certainly embarrassing.[57]

In some cases, public criticism of the Radio Choir was directed toward Abraham himself. In the right-wing *Morgunblaðið*, an anonymous reader expressed his astonishment that a foreigner had been chosen as the group's conductor.[58] Benediktsson, as the Radio board chairman, responded that Abraham was, "according to the judgment of those locals who have the finest taste in music, considered the best-educated and most talented choral director available here." In addition, he noted that Abraham had already been granted Icelandic citizenship, "and thus it does not matter at all where he was born, and it would be nothing but absurd narrow-mindedness to take more notice of a man's place of birth than of his talents and education."[59]

Although the Radio Choir was intended as a studio ensemble, it gave two public concerts during its brief existence. A concert in Reykjavík Cathedral in February 1949 included Haydn's *Missa brevis* in B-flat (the "Kleine Orgelmesse") and Brahms's *Begräbnisgesang* (see fig. 6.5); a year later, the program contained Bach's Cantata no. 80 (*Ein feste Burg ist unser Gott*) and the Offertorium from Verdi's Requiem. Both programs also demonstrated Abraham's growing interest in Icelandic church music, since they included

Figure 6.5. Robert Abraham with the National Radio Choir and string orchestra in the Reykjavík Cathedral, 1949. On the left-hand side can be seen, among others, concertmaster Björn Ólafsson, organist Páll Ísólfsson, and cellist Heinz Edelstein. Source: © Elín Þ. Ólafsdóttir, private collection. Used with permission.

his own arrangements of Kyrie-, Credo-, and Sanctus-chants from *Graduale*, the missal of the Icelandic Lutheran church, first issued in 1594.[60] While the Radio Choir was a landmark ensemble, setting a higher standard for choral singing than Iceland had previously known, it proved to be short-lived. After little more than two years of activity, the choir was disbanded in spring 1950 as the Iceland Symphony Orchestra began rehearsals for its inaugural concert. The orchestra was also funded in part by the National Radio, the financial resources of which were limited, and the choir was therefore discontinued as a money-saving measure.

Despite its brief lifespan, the National Radio Choir was an important milestone for Abraham's career. Its biweekly broadcasts established his reputation throughout the country, and he had an opportunity to refine his skills in wide-ranging repertoire with some of the finest choral singers available. He had arrived in Iceland at just twenty-three years old, with only two years of university study behind him and little professional experience to speak of. With the founding of the Radio Choir in 1947 and the Iceland Symphony Orchestra in 1950 (see chapter 7), Abraham was finally able to work with highly trained musicians on a professional level. It was an opportunity he fully deserved.[61]

"Abraham's Outrage"

In his early years in Iceland, Abraham gained a reputation as a temperamental conductor. The limited training and experience of most Icelandic musicians, sometimes combined with a notable lack of discipline, certainly required unrelenting patience and perseverance. If things went awry, Abraham was liable to erupt and storm out in a frenzy, only to return as soon as his anger had subsided. At one rehearsal of his choir in Akureyri, in the late 1930s, the singers had difficulty with a movement from Brahms's *Liebeslieder Waltzes*, causing Abraham to make a tempestuous exit. During his absence, one of the choir members, well-known poet Kristján frá Djúpalæk, composed a humorous verse about the conductor's temper. Tossing off improvised quatrains, known as *ferskeytlur*, often in a witty or sarcastic tone, was a popular pastime in nineteenth- and twentieth-century Iceland. The verse might be rendered as follows, in a loose translation (the original, with the requisite end-rhymes and vowel alliteration, is also shown for comparison):

> Here resound the songs of Brahms,
> with their wondrous dreamy air,
> accompanied by Abraham's
> outrage up to the stratosphere.
>
> [Óma lögin eftir Brahms,
> undurþýð og dreymin,
> ásamt skömmum Abrahams
> úti himingeiminn.]

The quatrain appears to have amused and delighted Abraham, at least as time passed, as he quoted it himself in a 1951 interview.[62]

Several accounts have also survived of Abraham's podium behavior during his early years in Reykjavík. He had no qualms about cutting off and starting again if performers went astray, even at a live concert. At the performance of Haydn's *The Seasons* in 1943, the bass soloist entered on the wrong beat after a long rest in one of his arias; when the Radio Choir performed Bach's Cantata no. 80 at the Reykjavík Cathedral in 1950, strings and winds drifted apart during the opening ritornello. In both cases, Abraham cut off abruptly, exclaiming with a stern grimace: "Again!"[63]

More unexpectedly, in one case the musicians continued despite Abraham's injunction to stop. During a performance of Gian Carlo Menotti's *The Medium* in 1952, a small mistake in the orchestra led Abraham to cut off, but the lead singer, Guðmunda Elíasdóttir, was so engrossed in her performance that she continued as if nothing had happened. The concertmaster eventually took charge and steered the orchestra through the rest of Act I while Abraham stared down at the podium, transfixed with rage. At intermission, he threw away his baton and stormed outside; Elíasdóttir later recalled the backstage horror of not knowing whether they would have a conductor for the second act. A few minutes later, someone knocked on her dressing room door to inform her that Abraham had returned: "He ran a few laps around the Lake (*Tjörnin*, in central Reykjavík), but he's fine now!"[64] In her autobiography, soprano Þuríður Pálsdóttir recalls another "typical Abraham scene," as she puts it, at a performance of Rossini's *The Barber of Seville*. Apparently, she hadn't held a specific note, presumably a fermata, as long as they had rehearsed, and Abraham was so incensed that he refused to bow with the singers at the end.[65]

While some locals interpreted Abraham's outbursts as a sign of arrogance, these episodes may have been provoked primarily by his ambition to give the music full justice. One of Abraham's closest friends, linguist Halldór Halldórsson, said he always found Abraham's attitude to music to be somewhat spiritual: "Music was divine to him in the same way that God is divine to those who are religious."[66] Abraham clearly found it difficult to adjust his artistic expectations to local standards, especially in the beginning. In a newspaper interview in 1960, he explained how Icelanders seemed to have a completely different notion of discipline than Germans: "Sometimes one gets a little angry—feels that perhaps there is a lack of discipline here. In many ways, Icelanders have a different attitude than in many foreign countries—here people aren't very familiar with the 'outer' discipline, so to speak. So you have to try to build on the 'inner' discipline that people have in themselves. This can, of course, vary from person to person, but usually this can be successfully achieved."[67]

Abraham's volatile temper may also have been provoked in part by worries outside of music. Until the end of World War II, he was understandably concerned about the fates of many of his relatives, while at the same time having to work through his own trauma of exile. In any case,

Abraham gradually learned to control his temper as the years went by. His wife, Guðríður, often assumed the role of peacemaker, mitigating potentially turbulent situations. Composer Jón Þórarinsson noted that without her "insight into problems and intuitive understanding for the perspectives of both sides," there might have been "more disagreements, and their solutions more arduous."[68] After nine years of marriage, Abraham joyfully noted in an interview: "I hardly ever get angry anymore."[69]

That said, Abraham was known to occasionally lose his patience in his later years. At a rehearsal of Beethoven's Ninth Symphony with the Philharmonia Choir in 1966, the choir had to master a small but important detail: how to rise simultaneously at a specific moment in the finale. This proved an unexpected challenge, as one choir member recalled six years later, in a speech given at Abraham's sixtieth birthday celebration:

> We had spent roughly half a rehearsal repeating this utterly non-musical exercise, again and again, without success. It seemed that the choir was completely incapable of rising all at once; the outcome was more akin to a tempestuous ocean wave. Time and again, the conductor spurred us on, but some choir members took a bit of extra time to blow their noses before standing, while others sprung up like a coil spring, so enthusiastically that nearby chairs tumbled over. In the end, Róbert [Abraham] pulled his hair out and, in exasperation, stormed off backstage. I don't recall how long he stayed there, and I don't know what prayers he recited, but when he returned, he calmly addressed us with words to this effect: "I come from a country that has a lot on its conscience, including two world wars. Whereas this country of yours, it is truly a blessed country—you have no army, no war, no military discipline. Here there are no trains that depart on the dot, and the ships sail whenever the wind blows. But this also means that there is nothing here called *Präzision* [precision].—Well, my friends, let's try it once again." And, lo and behold, we were finally able to rise from our seats in striking simultaneity—so much so, in fact, that this became, according to many a novice concertgoer, the most memorable detail of "seeing" the Ninth, as it was often called.[70]

The extremes of Abraham's disposition could go both ways. When things went better than expected, he became so overjoyed he would put down his baton and wipe away a tear. His tempi were liable to fluctuate accordingly; the Icelandic baritone Guðmundur Jónsson recalled that once, when recording the song *King Sverrir* (*Sverrir konungur*) by nineteenth-century composer Sveinbjörn Sveinbjörnsson, Abraham found the music "so sublime, that the song, which usually takes around four minutes and ten seconds to perform, lasts a whole six minutes and fifteen seconds on this recording."[71] At another rehearsal, an orchestra member was mightily displeased when Abraham asked them to play through a certain movement once more, since they were starting to play it so well. "As if we're doing this just for fun," the player remarked haughtily.[72]

Yet the majority of Abraham's colleagues appreciated his enthusiasm and talent for creating an inspired atmosphere. At the first joint *Messiah* rehearsal with the Philharmonia Choir and Iceland Symphony Orchestra in November 1973, a reporter noted his encouraging approach as he addressed his ensemble: "My darlings, now please sing this playfully, with rejoicing, as if all the problems of the world had been solved."[73] As he welcomed Guðmundur Jónsson to a rehearsal as the baritone soloist for Dvořák's Te Deum, Abraham turned to the choir with a glint in his eyes, saying: "My friends, did you know that Dvořák composed this part especially for Guðmundur?"[74]

While Abraham was widely admired in Iceland for his musical talent and charisma, to some extent he remained an enigma even to his closest friends. Linguist Halldór Halldórsson, who knew Abraham since his arrival in Akureyri in 1935, made the following remarks in Abraham's obituary, nearly forty years later:

> The contrasts in Róbert's inner life were revealed in various ways. Sometimes he could be like a child—almost naive—but he also emanated deep wisdom and lived experience. He had a fierce temper, but at the same time he was warmhearted and gentle. He was a hard worker, often hardly resting at all, yet no man was more at ease playing and enjoying himself in the company of good friends. He was ambitious in his life and work, yet it would be hard to find a more humble person. He tamed his inner beast and let each element of his inner nature come into its own according to the circumstances. His personality was not just a symphony in major or minor. It consisted of many other tonalities, some of them exceedingly rare.[75]

Abraham had a lively, energetic presence on the podium; he typically finished a concert soaking wet with perspiration.[76] At home, he usually wore a maroon silk coat over his daily clothing, and his signature pipe was always kept near.[77] His family still fondly recalls his aversion to all practical, day-to-day projects; these were without exception carried out by his wife, Guðríður. Once, she had hired workers to redo the bathroom in their house while he was abroad, but when he returned home the work remained incomplete. The next day, Abraham, incensed to be unable to take his daily bath, took a taxi in his nightgown to the nearest public swimming pool. In winter, he would sometimes swim in the Atlantic Ocean. This was a rare undertaking in those days, and one that highly amused his neighbors, who could see him walking in his robe to the coast, roughly three hundred yards from his home, scrambling among the large rocks before he dipped into the frigid ocean.[78]

Abraham delighted in giving nicknames to people and objects. He referred to himself as "Úddi," but also sometimes "Hróbjartur" (an old Icelandic form of Robert) when writing to friends within Icelandic academia.[79] His wife, Guðríður, was nicknamed "Gríður," or "Grieschen," their son, Grétar Ottó, was "Tumi" (his nickname throughout his life), and even the family cars were "Mikosch" (a Czech Tatra model) and, later, "Úddínó" (a Volkswagen beetle). Guðríður was the designated driver in their marriage, while her husband sat in the passenger seat with his bulging briefcase, filled with music scores and pipes.[80] Abraham was known for reading a book while walking from one destination to another; anything else, he felt, was a waste of time. During his research, he would make copious annotations in a plethora of spiral notebooks now preserved at the Icelandic National Archives, providing valuable insight into his scholarly mind.

According to Abraham's students, he was a devoted and passionate teacher with a special talent for explaining complex topics so that they seemed easy. They also recall that he had limitless patience and that lessons could easily stretch an extra hour when the music made him lose track of time.[81] His family adds that he took particular delight in explaining the wonders of classical music to people who had never before had the chance to experience it. For example, he would occasionally invite the mailman, or the shoemaker who ran a workshop nearby, into his living room and play for them passages from Wagner's *Die Meistersinger von Nürnberg* or some other masterwork he felt they absolutely had to hear.[82]

Abraham had a lively imagination and could put himself in children's shoes with ease. The choir director Þorgerður Ingólfsdóttir, who was Abraham's piano student as a child and later became his protégé in musicology and liturgical studies, recalls that on her ninth birthday, a large and unusually colorful envelope arrived in the mail. On the cover, her name had been flamboyantly written in multicolored pencils, but the sender's name and address on the flip side was far more unexpected: "George Frideric Handel / Heaven." As it turned out, the envelope contained a book of easy keyboard pieces by the Baroque master, who, it appeared, followed the young girl's progress with enthusiasm—even from beyond the grave.[83]

Urbancic: A Versatile Musician

Victor Urbancic was a mild-mannered, amicable man, both on and off the podium. In 1939, after one of his first orchestral concerts in Iceland, one of the "apostles" of the Reykjavík Music Society noted that although Urbancic was "a calm man and somewhat reserved in his day-to-day demeanor, it is as if he becomes emboldened as soon as he lifts his baton."[84] Þorsteinn Sveinsson, Chairman of the Music Society Choir (and later the National Theater Chorus), remarked that Urbancic worked "quietly, with modesty and humility, and it is not least this approach that earns him the love and admiration of all those who know him and work under his direction."[85] Pianist Rögnvaldur Sigurjónsson, who appeared as soloist with Urbancic in Beethoven's Piano Concerto no. 4 in 1948, believed that Urbancic's gentle approach was the key to his success. He described Urbancic as "a unique personality and a very fine man, through and through. He was just so gentle and kind, people felt an affinity with him at once because everyone liked him. That's why they did as he asked."[86]

Some, however, saw Urbancic's humility as a possible drawback. In his autobiography, Ævar Kvaran, an actor at the National Theater during Urbancic's tenure there in the 1950s, remarked: "Victor was such a kind spirit, so warmhearted and sincere, that I have never met a finer man. Perhaps his only fault was that he was too kind. He lacked toughness in the right places, and this is why he wasn't always appreciated as he should have been."[87] Soprano Þuríður Pálsdóttir found Urbancic's temperament best suited to music that was gentle, in harmony with his personality. When Mozart's *Magic Flute* was produced at the National Theater in 1956, she recalled decades later, he lent the music a heavenly beauty and calm: "He was never in a rush, his tempi were always so good and well grounded. He always gave you time to sing very beautifully."[88]

Urbancic was also a dedicated and admired teacher. Among his first piano students in Iceland was Magnús Blöndal Jóhannsson, who later studied composition at Juilliard and became Iceland's first serial composer. Urbancic's pupils in music theory included several other future composers:

Figure 6.6. Victor Urbancic with two of his children, Ruth and Pétur, in Reykjavík, ca. 1944. *Source:* © Sibyl Urbancic, private collection. Used with permission.

Árni Björnsson, Jón Ásgeirsson, and Jón Þórarinsson, as well as pianist-conductor Jóhann Tryggvason, whose daughter Þórunn would later marry pianist Vladimir Ashkenazy. Yet another theory student, who began his lessons only a few weeks after Urbancic's arrival, was twelve-year-old Jón Nordal, later a renowned composer (see chapter 3). The boy suffered from illness and was unable to attend school on a regular basis, so Urbancic came to the family home and gave him lessons there instead. Shortly thereafter, the young Nordal began to show him original compositions, and thus Urbancic also became his composition teacher. Pianist Jórunn Viðar studied privately with Urbancic after returning from studies at the Berlin *Hochschule für Musik* in 1939. She admired his many talents and later claimed that she had begun to compose largely because of his encouragement: "One could say that that's where I really got going [with composition], because he gave me such interesting assignments."[89]

Many of Urbancic's students admired his talent for making even the most complex topics seem easy. Clarinetist Gunnar Egilson recalled how he had already attempted to learn music theory for two years, with little success, but as soon as he began lessons with Urbancic, it all seemed much clearer than before. "He was such an animated and engaged teacher that it was inevitable—you were just bound to learn from him."[90] Another theory pupil, Ragnar Björnsson, later Cathedral organist in Reykjavík, found it memorable to witness him explain what had previously been, in the student's mind, "something akin to magic runes. Finding the right approach to each student seemed to come incredibly easily to him, and in addition one had the feeling that imparting his immense knowledge to us was something that gave him incalculable pleasure."[91]

Urbancic was also a pianist of rare talent. He seldom appeared in public as solo pianist, though he did occasionally perform solo sonatas on National Radio, such as Schubert's Piano Sonata in B-Flat, D. 960 in January 1949.[92] He was far better known as a collaborative pianist, appearing regularly with the most talented Icelandic singers and instrumentalists. His sight-reading skills were legendary, and as a vocal accompanist he was able to transpose any piano part at sight. Ragnar Björnsson later recalled that "no matter how poorly written out were the so-called 'compositions' that we, his students, brought to our lessons, he played everything at sight as if it were fully practiced."[93] Regarding Urbancic's conducting skills, clarinetist Gunnar Egilson noted that his baton technique was among the most beautiful of all conductors he had worked with. "His beat was so smooth, yet also decisive and rewarding; it was impossible to misread it."[94]

As a performer, Urbancic was particularly fond of music from the Baroque era. In addition to performing the large choral works of Bach and Handel with the Music Society Choir, he premiered other key works through his own efforts with singers at the Roman Catholic church. At a concert there in spring 1941, for example, he gave the Icelandic premieres of Pergolesi's *Stabat mater*, along with works by Alessandro Stradella and Tomás Luis de Victoria.[95] In December of that same year, he premiered several movements from Bach's Mass in B minor and Handel's complete setting of Psalm 112, *Laudate pueri*. In his review of the concert, composer Emil Thoroddsen wrote that although the choir was rather small and still needed better coordination, Urbancic was "a fine conductor, who has a good talent for stimulating his people to give their best."[96]

Urbancic also introduced important works of the Baroque as an organist, conductor, and editor. He performed one of Heinrich I. F. Biber's *Rosary Sonatas* with a local violinist in 1955, apparently the first performance in Iceland of any of Biber's works, and conducted the Reykjavík Orchestra's string ensemble in Bach's *The Art of Fugue* in spring 1945. "Few in the audience will forget this evening," wrote Robert Abraham in the role of music critic for *Morgunblaðið*, noting that the interpretation had been "restrained and convincing."[97] In 1952, Urbancic published a volume of ten songs by (or attributed to) J. S. Bach, and commissioned Icelandic translations from Margrét Jónsdóttir, a local poet (see fig. 6.7). The book was intended

Figure 6.7. The cover page of *Ten Songs by Johann Sebastian Bach*, edited by Victor Urbancic in 1952. *Source:* Private collection of the author.

for domestic use, with easy-to-play arrangements and a brief afterword by Urbancic himself, in which he traced the composer's life and career. His selections included four movements from Bach's *Peasant Cantata* BWV 212, songs from the Schemelli and Anna Magdalena Bach collections, as well as the familiar keyboard minuet now attributed to the Dresden organist Christian Petzold. While the volume itself does not appear to have had a wide or lasting influence, its final item, *Ó Jesúbarn blítt* (*O Jesulein süß*), in Jónsdóttir's translation, remains a staple of Icelandic choirs during Advent and Christmas to the present day.[98]

The limited resources available in Reykjavík meant that for the players of the Reykjavík Orchestra, even standard orchestral repertoire presented a nearly insurmountable challenge. In December 1941, the Music Society devoted an entire concert to W. A. Mozart in commemoration of the 150th anniversary of his death, a program that included his Symphony no. 39. Prior to this, the Reykjavík Orchestra had always employed a supplementary piano and/or harmonium to fill in instrumental parts for which no players could be found. The 1941 concert was a significant milestone, as Urbancic noted in an interview, for it was the first time that the orchestra, as he put it, "dares to take on the challenge of performing a large and well-known Mozart symphony according to the original score. Such an effort demands all our energy and we are ourselves looking forward to seeing how we'll do."[99] From this point on, the orchestra made no use of filler instruments, and *Morgunblaðið*'s critic praised Urbancic's convincing performance on the podium: "He conducted the symphony with fiery passion, bringing each and every theme to life."[100]

In addition to conducting the Reykjavík Orchestra at concerts produced by the Music Society for their subscription season, Urbancic and the orchestra also participated in Reykjavík's music theater scene. The Music Society itself produced an operetta annually from 1938–1944, with profits used to underwrite the costs of running the orchestra and music school. In 1939, Urbancic conducted the operetta *Das Dreimäderlhaus* with music by Schubert, and a production of Lehár's *The Land of Smiles* followed a year later—a welcome diversion in what was by then a country occupied by British soldiers. Urbancic also conducted the premiere of the first Icelandic operetta, Sigurður Þórðarson's *Spellbound* (*Í álögum*) in spring 1944. The Viennese operetta style came naturally to Urbancic, and his extensive theater experience was highly valued in these collaborations. The most popular production of the war years was Hervé's operetta *Mam'zelle Nitouche*, performed well over one hundred times both in Reykjavík and in smaller towns around the country in 1941. On Urbancic's contribution to that show, a local critic remarked: "We have received many fine musicians from abroad in recent years, but, with all due respect, it must be said that he is probably the finest of them all. What he has accomplished in the short time that he has worked here, is, truth be told, so immense that one hopes the Reykjavík Music Society will be able to keep him as long as possible."[101]

By the time the Urbancic family arrived in Iceland, they all belonged to the Roman Catholic faith, as Melitta had been baptized just a few weeks before leaving Austria (see chapter 2). Iceland's Catholic congregation was a small minority, less than two hundred individuals, in a country where the Evangelical Lutheran church enjoyed the status of official state religion. Reykjavík's neo-gothic Catholic cathedral had been built as recently as 1929, and many considered it unnecessarily large for such a small congregation.[102] When Urbancic arrived in Iceland, he discovered the church had no organist. He thus volunteered to take on the post himself without pay, a post he held until his death. In lieu of payment, the Catholic bishop would bring the family a box of apples and oranges every Christmas. These were rare delicacies, as fresh fruit was rarely available except in the holiday season.[103]

Urbancic was an ambitious servant of the Catholic church and eventually convinced the bishop and congregation that a proper organ was needed instead of the small harmonium used since the cathedral's inauguration. The Danish organ firm Frobenius was chosen to build a quality instrument with thirty-six stops and 2,170 pipes, the first fully mechanical organ in Iceland—and one that also required the expansion of the organ loft. Raising the necessary funds took an entire decade, and was a significant achievement for the small congregation. The organ was finally inaugurated in November 1950, on the 400th anniversary of the death of Jón Arason, Iceland's last Roman Catholic bishop before the Reformation.[104] As for the question of why a musician with Urbancic's daunting workload should have assumed the additional, voluntary task of organist, his daughter Sibyl claims that he wished to give thanks to the almighty powers for saving him and his family from a horrible fate. Thus, he never regretted the time he spent playing organ at church services in Reykjavík—even if apples and oranges were his only material reward.[105]

Urbancic's talents as an organist were enjoyed not only by the Catholic congregation. He recorded many organ works for the National Radio, including first performances of works by local composers such as Björgvin Guðmundsson and Sigurður Þórðarson. He rarely gave solo organ recitals but naturally performed more frequently once a first-class instrument was at his disposal. After the war, he also had delivered from Vienna a beautiful chamber organ with pedals, built in 1754, that his uncle had obtained from a small village church in Tyrol when Urbancic was a child, so that the prodigious boy could practice organ at home. This instrument was a welcome addition to the Urbancic family's collection. For years after it arrived at their house in Reykjavík, the family had the habit of beginning each day with a Bach chorale: Urbancic played the organ, and his wife and children sang along in four parts.[106]

Urbancic also showed genuine interest in performing new Icelandic works, knowing that local composers could hone their craft only if given opportunities to hear their own music. Among the local works he premiered are many that have since been nearly forgotten. In 1940 he conducted a full program of Icelandic music with the Reykjavík Orchestra, including two new works: an *Icelandic Suite* by Árni Björnsson and *On Crossroads* (*Á krossgötum*) by Karl O. Runólfsson. The concert was considered an important milestone, as it was the first performance of full-size orchestral works written by former composition students at the Music School. One critic said the concert had proved that "such things can well be studied in Iceland," and that Urbancic had conducted with "unusual sensitivity and confidence."[107] When critic-composer Emil Thoroddsen died in 1944, at the age of forty-six, his largest unperformed work was a nearly complete draft for a festival cantata, submitted for the Alþing Festival Competition in 1930; even in its unfinished state, it had won second prize.[108] In 1954, at a concert to mark the tenth anniversary of Thoroddsen's passing, Urbancic conducted the National Theater Choir and Iceland Symphony Orchestra in his own completion of the work. In a review of the concert, the critic of the socialist daily *Þjóðviljinn* had particular praise for "the contribution of the conductor, who, with his artistic vision and multiple talents, put the final touches on this incredibly beautiful and enchanting work."[109]

Urbancic was also an ardent supporter of Jórunn Viðar, at the time Iceland's only female composer. She took lessons from him in the early 1940s, having been forced to return to Iceland from piano studies in Berlin because of the war. Urbancic was among the first to recognize her talent as a composer. In 1945, when she had moved to New York and was studying with Vittorio Giannini at Juilliard, he wrote to her, asking for works he could perform in public. "The darling guy has always been so kind to me," she wrote to her mother, "and I'm quite surprised that he should remember me, since I'm not at all used to being highly regarded in the music scene back home."[110] Viðar complied by sending Urbancic a score of her variations for solo piano on an Icelandic folk tune, *Sortnar þú ský*, which he duly performed on National Radio in September 1946.[111] Four years later, he conducted her score to the film *The Last Farm in the Valley* (*Síðasti bærinn í dalnum*), the first feature film score by an Icelandic composer (see fig. 6.8). In 1955, he also premiered Viðar's delightful, folk-inspired choral work, *Rhymes of*

Figure 6.8. Victor Urbancic conducting the recording of Jórunn Viðar's score for the film *The Last Farm in the Valley* (*Síðasti bærinn í dalnum*) in January 1950. The orchestra was a pickup ensemble led by violinist Þórarinn Guðmundsson. *Source:* © Sibyl Urbancic, private collection. Used with permission.

Ólafur the Greenlander (*Mansöngur fyrir Ólafs rímu Grænlendings*), with the National Theater Choir and strings from the Iceland Symphony Orchestra.[112]

In addition to his work on behalf of local composers at home, Urbancic was committed to promoting Icelandic music abroad. After the aforementioned Nordic choral festival in Copenhagen in 1948, where the Music Society Choir sang a program of Icelandic works, Urbancic traveled to Vienna—his first visit there after the war. There, he gave two radio talks on Icelandic music, and, equipped with 78-rpm records supplied by the National Radio, was able to play examples of works by contemporary Icelandic composers. His other stops on the tour were Graz, where he discussed and played piano works by Páll Ísólfsson on the radio, and Salzburg, where he lectured on Icelandic traditional music.[113]

Urbancic: Composer and Folk Song Arranger

While Urbancic was a remarkably versatile musician, his main career in Iceland was as an orchestral and choral conductor, along with collaborative piano and teaching. Despite being a fairly prolific composer, particularly before emigrating, he was reluctant to promote his own works, and after his death they were all but forgotten for more than half a century. Urbancic's compositional output consists of over seventy works, most of them written between 1918 and 1938 during his years of study and employment in Austria and Germany. The oldest surviving works were written in 1918 and were presumably performed at the family home in Vienna: a Cello Sonata, *Three Movements* for Cello and Piano, and ten songs with piano accompaniment. Four of the latter are to poems by his paternal aunt, Minna Despić, who was a talented writer and issued several books of poetry during her lifetime.

All in all, Urbancic composed over fifty songs to German poetry, writing the majority over seven years (1918–1924) while a student in Vienna—likely inspired by his lessons with Joseph Marx, a notable Lieder composer. Urbancic's love for literature found a natural outlet in his settings, which show the influence both of Hugo Wolf and Gustav Mahler; among his literary sources were *Des Knaben Wunderhorn* and Hans Bethge's *Die Chinesische Flöte*, both of which had already been mined by Mahler a few years earlier. The songs are usually fairly brief, colorful depictions of the texts in question, as suggested by the titles themselves, such as *Spring Rain* (*Der Frühlingsregen*), *Falling Leaves* (*Fallendes Laub*), *Winter Evening* (*Winterabend*), and *Glowing Stars* (*Sternenglanz*). Urbancic also set to music a poem by his wife Melitta, *Ebene im Vorfrühling*, just a few weeks after they began dating in spring 1924. A few years later, their collaboration took a different turn when Melitta composed a melody to her poem *Ist alles zu lernen*, to which her husband provided the piano part. Urbancic's last setting of German poetry was the song cycle *Elisabeth*, to poems by Hermann Hesse, composed in Graz in 1936.

During his university years, Urbancic also wrote several substantial instrumental works, including a Sonata for Violin and Piano op. 3 and a *Fantasy-Sonata* for clarinet and piano op. 4, both composed in 1924. His output from the 1920s is colorful and often remarkably virtuosic, not least the piano parts, likely intended for himself. But overall, Urbancic was no revolutionary in his music, which, despite a high degree of chromaticism, relies on a broad tonal framework.

During his employment in Mainz, Urbancic's daunting workload prevented him from composing as much as before. His worklist contains only three works written between 1926 and 1933, all of them incidental music for the theater, including an overture to Hugo von Hoffmansthal's drama *Death and the Fool* (*Der Tor und der Tod*). The most substantial of Urbancic's compositions from his years in Graz are Sonata no. 2 for Violin and Piano

(1934); a *Hymn* (*Hymnus*, 1937) for the feast of Saint Francis of Assisi for tenor, choir, orchestra, and organ; and a Concerto for Orchestra, completed in January 1938, only a few months before his departure from Austria. A large-scale work written in 1937 appears not to have survived: the cantata *Call of Spring* (*Frühlingsruf*) for narrator, tenor solo, choir, "people's choir" (*Volkschor*), and orchestra. It seems likely that this was an occasional work, perhaps even written at his colleague Kelbetz's request for his not-so-covert Nazi gatherings at the Graz Conservatory (see chapter 2).

Having settled in Iceland, Urbancic seldom found time to compose. He did, however, complete a handful of original works as well as arrangements; the latter include songs from a seventeenth-century Icelandic music manuscript, *Melódía*, for men's chorus (1942), as well as several folk-song arrangements for SATB chorus (see below). On a larger scale are a *Concertino* for three saxophones and string orchestra (1945) and *Missa in honorem Jesu Christi regis* (1946; also known as *Christkönigsmesse* in German), a setting of the mass ordinary written for the choir of the Roman Catholic cathedral in Reykjavík. In the latter, he took care to write music within the limits of the small, amateur ensemble, scoring the work for three-part SABar choir with organ accompaniment. The mass, which shows his mastery of modal counterpoint, was often performed at church services during his tenure there. Urbancic also wrote an *Overture to a Comedy* (*Ouvertüre zu einer Komödie*) for orchestra in 1952, a short, lively work dedicated to the Iceland Symphony Orchestra in the midst of the unpleasant dispute regarding the hiring of Olav Kielland as the orchestra's chief conductor (see chapter 7).

Urbancic wrote his most substantial work, *Ode to Skálholt* (*Óður Skálholts*), in 1956, two years before his death. The fifty-minute work, scored for mixed choir, narrator, and wind ensemble, was his submission to a cantata competition to celebrate the 900-year anniversary of the Cathedral of Skálholt, a key site for Icelandic religious practice and history. The competition was modeled on one held in 1930 for the millennium celebrations of the Icelandic Parliament: first, a literary competition was held to determine the work's text, and, in this case, the winner was a poetically inclined priest, Sigurður Einarsson. Then, composers were invited to set his lyrics to music, with a deadline of March 15, 1956. Eight works were submitted, and a month later it was announced that Páll Ísólfsson, the doyen of Icelandic musicians, had won first prize. Urbancic took second place, which came with a smaller cash prize of 7,000 krónur.[114] Since Ísólfsson's work was the sole piece performed at the Skálholt ceremony, Urbancic's cantata lay dormant for forty years. The score resurfaced only in the 1990s and was premiered in Reykjavík in 1996 by the Langholt Church Choir and a twenty-three-member wind ensemble.

Ode to Skálholt is a large and ambitious work, consisting of seven substantial choral movements, with two interludes for wind ensemble, both of which are based on sixteenth-century Icelandic hymn melodies. The choral movements also have a distinctly "Icelandic" flavor, not least through Urbancic's use of parallel fifths—characteristic of the Icelandic tradition of *tvísöngur*—as well as using themes from the fourteenth-century Roman Catholic liturgy of Saint Thorlak.[115] By coincidence, Robert Abraham was writing his doctoral dissertation on the origins of this liturgy at precisely the same time, thus again demonstrating the exiled musicians' genuine interest in Iceland's musical patrimony (see chapter 8).

The original works and arrangements that Urbancic wrote in Iceland do not share all of the stylistic traits of his earlier works. One notable characteristic is their light, jovial spirit, seen for example in the *Overture to a Comedy* as well as the *Concertino* for three saxophones, the latter a fusion of neoclassic and jazz influence. In that work, composed in summer 1945, Urbancic may have been inspired by lighter styles of music that had become prominent as the United States occupied Iceland in 1941. In comparison to his earlier output, Urbancic's Icelandic works often employ more conventional formal structures and are less technically demanding to perform—which, considering the local resources, is certainly understandable.

In Iceland, Urbancic also became a passionate arranger of local folk songs, something that remained a novelty there. When pastor and amateur composer Bjarni Þorsteinsson published his massive tome of nearly a thousand pages titled *Icelandic Folk Songs* (*Íslenzk þjóðlög*) in 1906–1909, many of his countrymen failed to see the point of such an enterprise. On the brink of independence, Icelanders longed for progress and wished to adapt what were regarded as more "civilized" customs of other nations; the old styles of vernacular music were considered "primitive" and "stagnated" in comparison with the esteemed Austro-German tradition.[116] In the early decades of the twentieth century, local composers largely avoided using folk song as a basis for their work. The handful of Icelandic composers who wrote in the Western "classical" tradition, such as Sveinbjörn Sveinbjörnsson (author of the national anthem) and Cathedral organist Sigfús Einarsson, adopted a Danish-German Romantic style, influenced by composers such as Mendelssohn and Grieg. The only composer fully engaged in writing "national" music based on indigenous song in the 1920s was Jón Leifs, a major figure in Icelandic music history, but given that he lived in Germany until 1944, his local influence during this time was negligible.

Instead, it was the foreign composition teachers active in Iceland in the 1930s and 1940s—Franz Mixa and Victor Urbancic—who encouraged a national school of composition based on vernacular song. They were both deeply familiar with folk-inspired music from other European countries, and saw indigenous songs as fascinating material that deserved cultivation and respect.[117] Through their enterprise and commitment, they were able to convince Icelanders that the material was worth preserving and that well-crafted arrangements were an ideal way of keeping the tradition alive.

Franz Mixa, who was Iceland's first real teacher of composition, was particularly fascinated by the country's traditional songs, seeing in them a perfect expression of the harsh natural environment.[118] During his years there, Mixa even composed a nationally inspired opera, *Eyvind of the Mountains* (*Fjalla-Eyvindur*), to a libretto he had written with his Icelandic wife, Katrín.[119] In 1937, Mixa also penned a detailed article in *Morgunblaðið* about Jón Leifs and his position as Iceland's foremost nationalist composer. There, Mixa writes approvingly of Þorsteinsson's folk song volume, noting that he "provided Icelandic musicians with a treasure that was only waiting for them to discover it." He was also impressed with Leifs's national style, adding that the Icelandic folk songs, with their unusual melodic and modal characteristics, required an equally atypical treatment "if they are not to lose any of their strangeness, yet also have something to say to a modern audience."[120]

Among Mixa's composition students at the Reykjavík Music School was Karl O. Runólfsson, a trumpeter who would soon become a talented composer. Among the works he wrote under Mixa's tutelage were *Three Icelandic Folk Songs* for orchestra, premiered at the Nordic Composers' Festival in Copenhagen in 1938. That evening was a major landmark in itself, for it was the first time that an entire orchestra concert was devoted to Icelandic music. When Mixa returned to Austria that same year, Runólfsson continued his studies with Urbancic, who also had a deep interest for local traditional music and was remarkably knowledgeable about it even before arriving in Iceland. A few years earlier, Urbancic had spotted, in the window of a music shop in Graz, Jón Leifs's volume of simple arrangements of Icelandic folk songs for piano. He purchased a copy and was immediately fascinated by it, as he later described on the occasion of Leifs's fiftieth birthday: "These songs enchanted me and from that day I could not stop thinking about

Iceland, such was the magical beauty and pungent force that emanated from these old songs. Soon I knew all of them by heart."[121]

Thus, it was only natural that Urbancic should transmit his enthusiasm for Iceland's native music to his students, not only Runólfsson but also Jórunn Viðar and Jón Ásgeirsson, who became two of the country's most devoted folk-inspired composers of their generation. Another of Urbancic's students, Jón Nordal, composed in this vein under his tutelage as a teenager. Among the projects Urbancic assigned him was to arrange a suite of songs from Þorsteinsson's collection for two violins and cello; his arrangements were premiered at a student concert in spring 1942, by Urbancic's children, Ruth and Pétur, on violin and cello, along with another violinist schoolmate.[122] Toward the end of his long life, Nordal expressed his gratitude to his former teacher for introducing him to the world of Icelandic folk music: "It was Urbancic who led me in this direction, asking me to study and arrange these songs—not the Icelandic teachers."[123] Nordal's involvement with such material reached its climax in 1982, when his orchestral work *Choralis*, based on an ancient Icelandic hymn tune, was given its first performance by the National Symphony Orchestra in Washington, DC, under the baton of Mstislav Rostropovich.[124]

Urbancic's interest in old Icelandic music also led him to create a substantial corpus of arrangements himself. Many were performed in public and even recorded during his lifetime, while others were intended only for teaching purposes and remain unpublished. Soon after arriving in Iceland, Urbancic began mining Þorsteinsson's anthology for songs from local manuscripts and hymnals dating from the fifteenth to the seventeenth centuries. He arranged fifteen of these for voice and piano/organ in a simple, unassuming style, and many of them were given their first public outing in summer 1941, when Urbancic accompanied tenor Eggert Stefánsson on a concert tour in Northern Iceland.[125] In an interview upon their return to Reykjavík, Stefánsson noted the positive reception accorded these settings and that many audience members had thanked him specifically for "the cultural work that I am doing, by bringing the people back their old hymns." The idea, he acknowledged, came from Urbancic, who had "done the nation a great service by bringing these very beautiful songs back to light."[126] A local critic agreed, writing after their concert in Akureyri Church: "His arrangements are in precisely the same spirit as the songs themselves. It is as if the settings grow from the melodies themselves, and that melody and accompaniment are one living unity, simple and yet so wondrously beautiful."[127] During his early years in Iceland, Urbancic also assembled a volume of twelve simple folk song arrangements, which he used to introduce Icelandic folk songs to his piano students.[128] His arrangements are testimony to his dedication to the vernacular tradition, as well as his eagerness to make his students and local audiences more aware of their own musical heritage.

Urbancic's main contribution in this regard was a series of arrangements of Icelandic folk songs for SATB chorus, intended for and premiered by the Reykjavík Music Society Choir under his direction. In all, he arranged more than twenty folk songs for mixed choir. While he could count on his own ensemble to perform them, he was convinced the local tradition deserved a much wider audience, and should become part of the international choral repertoire. With this in mind, he compiled a set of fifty choral arrangements by various authors, a broad compendium of Icelandic folk songs intended for worldwide publication. Seventeen of the arrangements were Urbancic's own, while the rest were by colleagues such as Robert Abraham, Emil Thoroddsen, and Karl O. Runólfsson.

Figure 6.9. Victor and Melitta Urbancic with their children and son-in-law, 1952. From left: James Erb, Ruth, Sibyl, and Pétur Urbancic, and Eiríka between her parents. *Source:* © Sibyl Urbancic, private collection. Used with permission.

The intended folk song compendium was a collaborative project between Urbancic and his wife Melitta, who painstakingly made singing translations of all the lyrics into English and German. In 1956, the Icelandic Federation of Mixed Choirs agreed to support and subsidize the project, paving the way for publication. After Urbancic's death two years later, Melitta attended to final revisions and arranged for the collection to be issued by a globally renowned publishing house.[129] An agreement was made with Universal Edition in Vienna, whose director was a former classmate of Urbancic and happy to support a publication in his memory. In Iceland, composer Sigursveinn Kristinsson, Urbancic's former student, worked for the local Federation of Mixed Choirs and was instrumental in garnering support for the project, but when he left Reykjavík in 1958 to lead a music school in the countryside, the project was taken over by another local musician, Hallgrímur Helgason. It soon became apparent that he had serious doubts about the entire enterprise, asserting that rights had not been secured—a claim Melitta contested. Eventually, he was able to prevent the volume's publication altogether, and even refused to return the original manuscript despite Melitta's strenuous objections. She was devastated that her ambitious collaboration with her late husband never saw the light of day, and even considered filing a law suit to redress her claims, but she was advised that a foreign woman would never win a case against several of Iceland's prominent cultural figures.[130] In hindsight, the entire dispute appears to have been motivated at least in part by xenophobia. Locals believed that Iceland's vernacular songs belonged to Icelanders alone, and were determined to prevent a "foreign" musician from earning acclaim for bringing them onto the international stage—even if he was, by that time, long deceased. Urbancic's arrangements were finally published by the Icelandic Music Information Center in 1998, on the fortieth anniversary of his death.

7

Conflict and Controversy

A decisive cultural turning point of twentieth-century Iceland was when in March 1950 the Iceland Symphony Orchestra gave its inaugural concert, followed only weeks later by the opening of the National Theater. By investing in culture on a large scale, the young republic was showing its ambition to become a "nation among nations," to shape its cultural identity not only through its widely admired literary heritage but through all forms of art. As far as the new orchestra was concerned, its achievements were made possible by the groundbreaking work already undertaken by Victor Urbancic, Heinz Edelstein, and Robert Abraham for more than a decade. Thus, understandably, all three were prominent in the new orchestra's first season. Edelstein led the cello section of four, a straightforward choice since he was by far the most experienced cellist available. Urbancic and Abraham were the finest conductors Iceland had to offer, indeed the only ones in the entire country who had significant experience in the field of orchestral conducting. Thus, it seemed self-evident the three would be among the leading figures of the newly formed orchestra for a long time to come.

This, however, was not to be. As far as Abraham, Edelstein, and Urbancic were concerned, the early 1950s were years of disagreement, frustration, and rejection. Positions they believed they had earned through their hard work were given to others; they had difficulty competing with younger local musicians, as well as with talented foreigners who made their careers in Iceland with the support of the Reykjavík Music Society. Thus, Abraham, Edelstein, and Urbancic all bid farewell to the orchestra, either temporarily or for good, finding other means of employment instead. Abraham became a self-educated scholar of plainchant and liturgy, Edelstein established his own music school for young children, and Urbancic took a new position as Music Director at the National Theater, which soon led to a startling and unpleasant showdown with his former employers.

A Symphony Orchestra for Iceland

In the early 1940s, the number of proficient local players was slowly increasing, yet the Reykjavík Orchestra presented fewer concerts than it had at the outset, as it had become but one component of the Reykjavík Music Society's subscription concerts. The leaders of the Musicians' Union (FÍH) found this situation deeply unsatisfactory, and accused the Music Society's board of lacking interest in building a competent orchestra.[1] In 1944, this dismay led FÍH to establish its own ensemble, "The Icelandic Musicians' Union Orchestra," in direct competition with the Reykjavík Orchestra. Its first and only concert was led by Robert Abraham, a choice that may at first seem surprising since he was not a member of FÍH, a union that had largely excluded foreign musicians since its inception. But few musicians in Reykjavík were equal to such a task, and Abraham's independence from the Music Society, and thus the Reykjavík Orchestra, was considered an asset. In fact, FÍH's first choice for conductor was Páll Ísólfsson, who declined because his wife was dying of cancer. In addition, Ísólfsson was less than suitable since he was the dean of the Music School and thus employed by the Music Society. The same was true of Urbancic, whose contract with the Society stipulated he could not be employed by ensembles other than the Reykjavík Orchestra.[2] At a preparatory meeting for the FÍH orchestra's concerts, Abraham noted that "in no way" did he wish to "shove in front of Dr. Urbancic." Abraham's greatest concern was recruiting talented players; he warned that the orchestra could hardly survive without Edelstein and the Reykjavík Orchestra concertmaster Björn Ólafsson, both of whom were employees of the Music Society and thus not allowed to take part.[3]

The Icelandic Musicians' Union Orchestra was a thirty-six-member ensemble that rehearsed twice weekly and gave a concert in Lake Cinema (*Tjarnarbíó*), a small cinema in the center of town, in May 1944 (see fig. 7.1). The concert, which was so well received that it had to be repeated no fewer than four times, included Schubert's Symphony no. 5 and several smaller works for choir and orchestra, with the choral part taken by Abraham's own ensemble, the Harpa Choral Society. While the group lacked some of the Reykjavík Orchestra's key members, it reflected FÍH's objectives in

Figure 7.1. Robert Abraham with the Icelandic Musician's Union Orchestra and the Harpa Choral Society in Tjarnarbíó, May 1944. *Source:* © Elín Þ. Ólafsdóttir, private collection. Used with permission.

that it was comprised virtually of only native Icelanders: Fritz Weisshappel, a founding member of FÍH, played double bass, but Edelstein and Albert Klahn did not take part. Critics noted that Abraham had demonstrated "great talent" as a conductor, and that the results were "always good, when he is on the podium."[4] A second project was planned for autumn 1944 but never materialized because the Reykjavík Orchestra resumed rehearsals after being inactive for an entire year.

Still, in the long run it proved an excessive burden for the Reykjavík Music Society, which after all was a nonprofit organization run by a few amateurs, to manage an orchestra, choir, and music school. While most earlier seasons had included at least one purely orchestral concert under Urbancic's direction, in 1945 and 1946 the orchestra accompanied only the Music Society Choir, performing the oratorio *Peace on Earth* (*Friður á jörðu*) by Björgvin Guðmundsson in spring 1945—a fitting project as peace in Europe was finally on the horizon—and Handel's *Messiah* in 1946. Thus, once again, frustration grew among the players themselves, who craved more decisive opportunities for the orchestra to improve as an ensemble.

As the future of the Reykjavík Orchestra appeared increasingly uncertain, leading performers took the initiative. In autumn 1947, a group of musicians began making plans for an independent orchestra that would rehearse twice weekly and perform a full concert later that season. Almost forty players signed up for the project, even though their work would be unpaid, at least at the beginning. This time, Urbancic conducted the first concert of the Reykjavík Symphony Orchestra, as it was called.[5] The concert took place on January 20, 1948, in the newly built East Town Cinema (*Austurbæjarbíó*), which became Reykjavík's main concert venue until the opening of the National Theater in 1950. The program consisted of Haydn's Symphony no. 100 and Beethoven's *Coriolan* overture, as well as his Piano Concerto no. 4 with Rögnvaldur Sigurjónsson, a young pianist who had recently returned from studies with Sascha Gorodnitzki in New York. This was Reykjavík's first "pure" orchestra concert in three years, and reviews were positive, although Páll Ísólfsson, writing for *Morgunblaðið*, admitted that some challenges were simply too demanding for the young ensemble.[6]

Urbancic was among those who found the haphazard organization of orchestral playing in Iceland unacceptable. In a newspaper interview in 1942, he pointed out that the Reykjavík Orchestra had two kinds of players: amateurs who worked day jobs unrelated to music and were thus able to rehearse only in the evenings, and professional musicians who played in dance bands at night but were happy to rehearse classical music in the daytime. Thus it was nearly impossible to assemble both groups for rehearsals, and it also proved an exhausting arrangement for the professional players, who were expected to rehearse for no pay during their valuable time off, as Urbancic explained: "It takes considerable discipline and stamina, after having played jazz for five or six hours each evening, to keep a seventh hour free for Beethoven and Mozart."[7] Six years later, Urbancic still faced the same problem: "Recently, we have had to bring together people who work all kinds of jobs at all hours, day and night, and you can imagine what difficulties this entails. This is why a real professional orchestra is our first and greatest demand."[8]

The Reykjavík Symphony's next concert, in March 1948, was an all-Mozart program directed by Robert Abraham. While attendance was not as good as the orchestra's leaders had hoped, the performance was considered a great success artistically. In a review, composer Jón Þórarinsson declared that no orchestra in Iceland had ever played "a more enjoyable and flawless concert," and that it had been testimony to the conductor's "precision, dedication, and good taste."[9]

The ensemble's third concert proved more difficult to arrange, not least because the Musicians' Union continued to oppose work permits for foreign musicians. Páll Ísólfsson had agreed to lead a concert in spring 1949, and the orchestra's board had invited Jan Morávek, an Austrian-Czech musician who had recently settled in Reykjavík with his Icelandic wife, to join them on bassoon—one of the instruments that local musicians had not yet fully mastered.[10] The Musicians' Union had already protested Morávek being granted a work permit and encouraged members not to play with him.[11] The orchestra's direction requested an exemption, so that Morávek might be able to perform at "one or two of the orchestra's concerts this spring."[12] This was rejected on the grounds it would create "additional discomfort and chaos," according to a member at the Musicians' Union meeting at which the matter was decided.[13] Eventually, the concert was postponed until December, by which time the conflict had been successfully resolved and Morávek given permission to play as long as he had a valid work permit.[14] It appears he gave a stellar performance. In his review of the concert, Robert Abraham, this time in the role of music critic, expressed his particular delight in the bassoon part having been dispatched with great confidence "for the first time after many years of waiting!"[15]

After much deliberation, a professional ensemble called the Iceland Symphony Orchestra was founded in 1950, with financial support from both the state and city of Reykjavík. It was a group of only forty members, largely the core players of the Reykjavík Symphony Orchestra, but with the addition of five professional wind and brass players hired especially from the Federal Republic of Germany. Robert Abraham conducted the group's inaugural concert in March 1950, with a program consisting of Beethoven's *Egmont* overture, Schubert's *Unfinished* symphony, and Bartók's *Romanian Folk Dances*; in addition, four of the newly arrived German musicians joined a local clarinetist in a performance of Haydn's B-flat Divertimento for woodwind quintet. "The audience's delight was immense," *Morgunblaðið* reported the next morning, though one critic complained that the strings had seemed uncomfortable playing less than *forte*, and that the Bartók dances lacked rhythmic vitality: "Rome wasn't built in a single day," he acknowledged.[16] Urbancic conducted the orchestra's next concert, two weeks later, a program that included Beethoven's Symphony no. 1.

The Iceland Symphony Orchestra was a young and inexperienced ensemble, and its small size limited its repertoire options. Abraham, for one, was frustrated by the need to focus so extensively on music from the Classical period: "You can't play Mozart and Haydn forever!," he bemoaned in a letter to his German-Swedish colleague Kurt Bendix.[17] He was also displeased with the orchestra's management, which tended to leave important programming decisions to the last minute.[18] Nevertheless, Abraham and Urbancic enthusiastically trained the new orchestra and conducted most of its concerts during its first two seasons; Abraham led seven concerts and Urbancic six. In addition, German conductor Hermann Hildebrandt directed three concerts in December 1950, and Jussi Jalas devoted an entire program to works by his father-in-law, Jean Sibelius.[19]

Urbancic and Abraham were both widely praised for their performances with the new ensemble. In December 1951, one critic lauded Urbancic's "confident and inspired" conducting of a program that included Handel's *Water Music* and Prokofiev's *Classical Symphony*.[20] Although Abraham had less experience as an orchestra conductor, his results appear to have been no less distinguished. After the orchestra's first performance of Beethoven's Symphony no. 5 in November 1950, critic and poet Þorsteinn Valdimarsson declared Abraham had achieved "a major victory as a conductor, and deservedly so, for this tempest of destiny, that raged in the strings during Beethoven's symphony, can only be conjured forth by someone who has carefully honed his craft for years."[21]

While audiences and critics were impressed by Abraham and Urbancic as orchestra conductors, the same was not true of the leaders of the Icelandic music scene, particularly Ragnar Jónsson, head of the Reykjavík Music Society. In a 1953 article, he asserted that "those interested in orchestral matters" had already during the Symphony's inaugural season become aware of the "flaws" of "the two men, who were primarily active here as conductors." Urbancic, he maintained, had plenty of experience but lacked the "fortitude, authority, and vigor" required of the orchestra's future leader. Abraham, on the other hand, was a more forceful personality but had far less experience as an orchestral conductor, "and—perhaps only because of this—has never been able to establish full authority over the orchestra or win the sympathy and trust of its musicians."[22]

Jónsson's article was an attempt to defend a controversial decision that would shape the orchestra's development for years to come. In early 1952, the Norwegian Olav Kielland was appointed the Iceland Symphony's first Chief Conductor. He was fifty years old, a tall, heavyset man with a big, sometimes bullish temper. Kielland had led the Oslo Philharmonic from 1933–1945 but was rumored to have been sympathetic to the German cause during World War II, which in turn curtailed his possibilities for work in Norway in the postwar era.[23] This seems to have been small cause for concern in Iceland, and his month-long stay in Reykjavík in autumn 1951 was deemed so successful that the orchestra's board offered him a permanent position.

Many locals considered Kielland's hire an undeserved snub toward Abraham and Urbancic. Soon after the hire was officially announced, Urbancic himself penned a short open letter that was printed in the local media, noting the orchestra's leadership had ignored him so completely that he only read about this new development in the Reykjavík newspapers.[24] For the next few days, local newspapers were full of support for the snubbed conductor. One reader asserted that it had been a long time since a short article had received "so much attention as the humble open letter by Victor Urbancic" and found the orchestra board's behavior to be disgraceful, not least because it was impossible to "name a single person who has been of more value to them for a very long time."[25] Another reader expressed his outrage that the leaders of the Reykjavík Music Society, "so full of arrogance and intellectual smugness, believe themselves to be the only real authority in musical matters, and treat those, whom Icelandic musical culture has the most to thank, with utter humiliation."[26]

Defeats and Setbacks

The controversy surrounding Olav Kielland's appointment marked the beginning of an acrimonious conflict that would affect Reykjavík's musical scene for several years. Some of its key players had been among the country's leading musicians for decades, while others were of a younger generation just beginning to make its mark. Among the latter was composer Jón Þórarinsson. Born on a farm in Eastern Iceland in 1917, he arrived in Reykjavík in his late teens to study at the Music School, including composition lessons with Franz Mixa—and, following his departure, with Urbancic. He soon began working for the National Radio, and in 1944 went on to study composition with Paul Hindemith at Yale University, completing his master's degree there in 1947. Most unusually, the National Radio paid part of his Yale tuition expenses, with the proviso that he return to work there after completing his studies.[27]

Initially, the young Þórarinsson was an eager supporter of his teacher Urbancic. For example, he wrote a glowing review about the *St John Passion* in 1943, declaring it "the most remarkable event in Reykjavík's musical life" that season, and a colossal victory for Urbancic.[28] Upon his return from Yale in 1947, things took an unexpected turn: Þórarinsson was appointed Head of Music Theory at the Reykjavík Music School, where he enjoyed the support of the dean, Páll Ísólfsson. With this appointment, all of Urbancic's theory and composition students were automatically transferred to Þórarinsson, which in turn led to fewer teaching hours and a lower salary for Urbancic. Among the students who unwillingly had to change teachers was composer Jón Nordal, who later became director of the Reykjavík Music School himself. He remarked in 2016: "That's when I left Urbancic, just like everyone else did. It was just horrible, the way he was treated."[29] As a result, relations between Urbancic and Þórarinsson were understandably strained, and this dispute would culminate in the fierce controversy concerning Urbancic's employment at the National Theater a few years later (see below).

Jón Þórarinsson also led an initiative to establish a string quartet under the auspices of the National Radio in 1947, led by violinist Björn Ólafsson. Remarkably, when appointments were made for the ensemble, the Radio snubbed Heinz Edelstein, who was without doubt Iceland's most experienced cellist and had for years expressed his wish to form a permanent string quartet. Instead, the position went to Edelstein's former student, Einar Vigfússon, who had recently returned from advanced studies in London. When Edelstein pressed Ólafsson to justify the decision, he insisted it had been at Þórarinsson's suggestion. Edelstein reacted by writing a lengthy letter to Þórarinsson, although he made it clear he was reluctant to protest a matter in which he himself was closely involved. Still, his position was unequivocal:

> I will not waste many words on the disparagement that I have been shown; I was not even spoken to, let alone asked for advice on this matter. Yet I must emphasize that all those who know me are well aware that my main passion as a performer is, and always has been, string quartet playing, and that I have fought for the creation of a quartet ever since I arrived in this country. I have already demonstrated my ability in this field during the time when the "Music School String Quartet" was active, and have received recognition for my skills both by local and foreign musicians.[30]

Edelstein acknowledged that his former student Vigfússon was "a fine cellist" and found it self-evident that he should be offered a suitable job in Reykjavík, for example in the new orchestra. But he insisted that little was known of Vigfússon's talent for chamber music, "and he must have had little experience in the field thus far." It was crucial, Edelstein asserted, that the best available players be selected for such a significant ensemble, since "music, which still has such weak roots in this country, will only be able to thrive, if it is carefully nurtured. Everything that is done should be done as well as possible, and that which cannot be done well at present, should await a more opportune time." Vigfússon's appointment was, Edelstein lamented, yet another example of the corruption he had begun to find characteristic of Iceland in general: "This idea of 'coterie,' which I would rather call by its less pleasant but more candid name [i.e., corruption], has been a harmful enough influence in all areas of Icelandic society, but to the fragile plant that is Icelandic musical life it will prove nothing less than fatal. If the Radio, which should set a good example in such matters, allows itself to be swayed by biased judgment, then it is a true stab in the back."[31] It is not certain that Edelstein ever delivered his strongly worded letter to Þórarinsson. A handwritten copy remains in the possession of Edelstein's family, but no trace of it can be found in Þórarinsson's archive at the National Library of Iceland, or in the Radio's collection at the National Archives.

Yet there can be no doubt that Edelstein never forgave Þórarinsson for the perceived slight, which only compounded his displeasure with Þórarinsson's work for the Symphony Orchestra in the early 1950s (see below). In any case, thinking back on their relationship, Stefán Edelstein did not mince words: "He couldn't stand Jón Þórarinsson. He hated him! Once my father and I were walking across Parliament Square (*Austurvöllur*) and then he suddenly saw Þórarinsson walking towards us from the opposite direction. 'Da kommt der Teufel!' he said—'There comes the devil!' "[32] Edelstein led the Iceland Symphony Orchestra's cello section from its inaugural concert in March 1950 until spring 1951. Later that year, he went to Germany on an extended study trip and did not return to the orchestra as a permanent member. While he did subsequently join the cello section occasionally on a temporary basis, he never again assumed the leading position he had held during the orchestra's first season.[33]

It is, of course, understandable that the new generation of Icelandic musicians who began their careers in the late 1940s and early 1950s should have sought appropriate work in their field, even if it meant challenging the foreign musicians who had worked so tirelessly there for over a decade. After all, this had also been the older generation's goal: to train local musicians so they could contribute to the music scene in turn. It was probably unavoidable that Edelstein and Urbancic would in some way be affected by this influx of young musicians, since they had been so prominent for more than a decade and had taken on many different tasks. It may also be that it was relatively easy for locals to obtain work that had earlier been given to "foreigners" and that, in such cases, colleagues tended to turn a blind eye. Robert Abraham had experienced his share of jealousy while living in Akureyri (see chapter 3), but he may have been less affected by such incidents after moving to Reykjavík, since he had an Icelandic wife and was generally considered "more of an Icelander" than other foreign-born musicians. Practically speaking, his situation was also different in that his wife, Guðríður, had a full-time job as a primary school teacher. Thus, she could assume the role of breadwinner while her husband delved into work that demanded extensive preparation and was underpaid or even unpaid, such as his research in the 1950s into Icelandic music history (see chapter 8).

Urbancic had directed the Music Society Choir for more than a decade (see fig. 7.2), but his relationship with the Society's board members was

Figure 7.2. Victor Urbancic conducts the Music Society Choir in rain and wind on Iceland's Independence Day, June 17, 1949. *Source:* © Reykjavík Museum of Photography. Used with permission.

becoming increasingly strained. Both Urbancic and the choir members felt the board had shown their work "the greatest negligence and indifference," including delayed payments to soloists who had performed at their concerts.[34] In 1952, matters came to a head after Urbancic had for months tried to contact chairman Ragnar Jónsson, as well as key board members Björn Jónsson, the Society's financial manager, and lawyer Ólafur Þorgrímsson.[35] On September 29, Urbancic announced to the boards of the Music Society and the Music School that he would no longer conduct the choir, adding that he had already guaranteed its continued existence in another form, with no connection to the Music Society.[36]

The following evening, choir members gathered at an impassioned general meeting that lasted past midnight. Urbancic explained his decision to leave, blaming the Music Society's negligence, but also made it clear he would continue his other work for the Society, such as teaching at the Music School. The choir declared unanimous support for its conductor, who they saw, as one member remarked, as the choir's "creative force." Then Þorgrímsson spoke on behalf of the Music Society, asserting that Urbancic had been too impulsive in his decision and the Society had every intention of continuing with the choir. Yet he also added a more unpleasant remark: should Urbancic resign as choir director, this would also nullify his contract with the Music School, as the two were part of the same agreement.[37] Of course, Urbancic could not risk losing his job at the Music School, through which he earned most of his income. A week later, Urbancic and the Music Society agreed, thanks to a special arbitration committee initiated by and made up of choir members, that he would continue working with the choir. Still, he noted this would be for a trial period only, as certain issues had not yet been fully resolved.[38]

Urbancic's final concert with the Music Society Choir was a performance of Arthur Honegger's "symphonic psalm" *Le Roi David*, performed at the National Theater in December 1952, with instrumentalists from the Symphony Orchestra. Although the music was novel for both the ensemble and its Icelandic audiences, the performance was deemed a success, "earning the musicians the greatest honor, and to the audience's unreserved delight," according to one critic.[39] But Urbancic's trial period had come to an end; he left his position after this concert, having already received permission to establish a new choir at the National Theater. Most members of the Music Society Choir followed him there, and thus it was obvious the ensemble had run its course.[40] Yet Urbancic's move to the National Theater was hardly without controversy; in fact, it threatened to completely derail Reykjavík's fragile music scene for months on end.

Urbancic: War at the National Theater

When the Iceland Symphony Orchestra and the National Theater began their existence in spring 1950, the intention was for the two to enjoy a symbiotic relationship. Since the orchestra's concert schedule in its first seasons was sparse, the plan was for it also to contribute to operas, musicals, and even incidental music at the theater. Aside from being financially feasible, this would enhance the orchestra's visibility and public image, which was of vital importance as the notion of tax payers funding a full-time orchestra was controversial to say the least. The two institutions were also linked in that the National Theater was the orchestra's main performing venue until the opening of the University Cinema (*Háskólabíó*) in 1961. It seemed clear that Victor Urbancic, who conducted the National Theater's inaugural performance, the Icelandic play *New Year's Eve* (*Nýársnóttin*), would take on some kind of leading role in music at the theater. After all, he had directed more concerts with the Reykjavík Orchestra than anyone else, and already had extensive experience as an opera conductor in Germany and Austria.

During the orchestra's initial seasons, the leaders of the Reykjavík Music Society wielded considerable power in its organization, particularly Jón Þórarinsson, who became its chairman, and Ragnar Jónsson, who had been a leading figure in the town's artistic life for decades. But, with the inauguration of the National Theater, a major new institution had been established, and its director, Guðlaugur Rósinkranz, wished to remain independent from both the orchestra and the Music Society. Initially, he appointed Þórarinsson as music advisor to the theater, but the two never got on well. Their relationship came to a head in 1952, after the premiere of a new Icelandic play, *Tyrkja-Gudda*, with music by Urbancic, that received fairly negative reviews. Þórarinsson maintained he hadn't even known that the play required music, to which Rósinkranz replied he had no use for people who "didn't do their jobs properly," and eliminated the position of music advisor entirely.[41] This was the opening gambit in an extended tug of war between the Theater and the Music Society/Iceland Symphony, which would become the decade's most dramatic conflict on the local artistic scene.

As Rósinkranz's relationship with the Reykjavík Music Society deteriorated, he considered the benefits of having his own, independent theater orchestra. Following a triumphant run of Verdi's *Rigoletto* in 1951, under Urbancic's direction, he developed plans for presenting operas annually on his own, and hired Urbancic, whom he found to be "outstandingly alert, sympathetic, and resourceful," as a full-time conductor and artistic advisor.[42]

The leaders of the Music Society were outraged by Rósinkranz's intentions, accusing him of attempting to "boycott" the Symphony Orchestra and destroy its business model, since income from the theater was crucial to its financial survival.[43] It was obvious that Reykjavík would not be able to support two symphony orchestras; even with its collaboration with the National Theater, the Iceland Symphony was run on a shoestring budget. In autumn 1952, the conflict reached a fever pitch when the Symphony and National Theater each planned to stage an opera independent of the other. Jón Þórarinsson had negotiated with the Royal Swedish Opera that it would provide singers for the Symphony's production of *Tosca*—a thinly veiled declaration of war against the theater, which had announced its own production of *La traviata*, with local singers in all roles. In the end, nothing came of the intended *Tosca* production; that opera was first staged in the National Theater a few years later, under Urbancic's direction.

In January 1953, Guðlaugur Rósinkranz declared that negotiations with the Iceland Symphony Orchestra had broken down, and that the National Theater would establish its own orchestra and choir with Urbancic as the permanent music director. Ragnar Jónsson responded with a furious open letter in *Morgunblaðið*, where he criticized that the position had not been advertised and asked whether "any responsible musicians" had been consulted in advance.[44]

The situation became notably more embarrassing as the personal enmity between key cultural players played out in public. An enraged Ragnar Jónsson decided to publicly "withdraw" a greeting he had sent to Rósinkranz only shortly before, on the latter's fiftieth birthday. In yet another disparaging letter, printed in a leading newspaper, he likened the theater director's decision to start his own orchestra to nothing less than the Japanese attack on Pearl Harbor, calling it "one of the most disgusting cultural attacks I have ever witnessed."[45] Rósinkranz in turn responded by returning to Jónsson the latter's birthday present to him, the Music Society's exquisitely bound edition of Hallgrímur Pétursson's classic *Hymns of the Passion*.[46]

This squabble made daily local headlines in early 1953, and newspapers had a field day describing the "cold war" and "guerilla warfare" taking place between Reykjavík's cultural leaders.[47] Iceland's newspapers were at the time all politically affiliated, and both *Tíminn*, issued by the Progressive Party, and the socialist *Þjóðviljinn* supported the National Theater against the conservative-leaning Music Society. An op-ed in *Tíminn* asserted that the nation's music scene was "collapsing due to egomania and fanaticism, which poses a threat to our true musical culture."[48] *Þjóðviljinn* expressed the wish that the music itself should "not be forgotten in the furor and acrimony of the very people who should be its servants."⁴⁹ The right-wing *Morgunblaðið*, on the other hand, ran an extensive interview with Þórarinsson, attempting to explain the Music Society's standpoint.⁵⁰

In their negotiations with Rósinkranz, the leaders of the Iceland Symphony Orchestra demanded that the National Theater should establish its own advisory music committee, to ensure that artistic decisions regarding music be made with "determination and expertise."⁵¹ The wording implies, yet again, distrust toward Urbancic and his artistic judgment. In August 1953, the Minister of Culture appointed a three-member music committee, consisting of Rósinkranz, Páll Ísólfsson, and the Iceland Symphony's concertmaster, Björn Ólafsson, thus giving the Music Society a majority in all its decisions.⁵² Shortly afterward, Urbancic resigned as music director, on the grounds that the new committee would *de facto* impede his authority as music director. Newspapers claimed that Urbancic was planning to move abroad and that he was being "chased out of the country" by harassment and aggression, but he repudiated such rumors and said he would prefer to

Figure 7.3. Victor Urbancic in Reykjavík, ca. 1950. *Source:* © Sibyl Urbancic, private collection. Used with permission.

continue working in Iceland.⁵³ In fact, Urbancic did inquire about available positions at several U.S. universities in spring 1954, which shows that his patience had indeed run out and he did consider leaving Iceland for good.⁵⁴

In the end, a compromise solution was found: Urbancic would continue his work at the National Theater but had to accept working with the advisory committee. He could at least draw strength from the overwhelming support expressed for him in local newspapers. One weekly journal suggested that Þórarinsson's efforts to produce operas with the Iceland Symphony was direct proof of his vindictiveness toward Urbancic.⁵⁵ Composer Jón Leifs, who had for years been skeptical of the Music Society and its control of the local music scene, also came to Urbancic's defense. In his view, the cause of the dispute was that "those very few men who have had complete authority in musical matters here in recent years and who certainly did commendable work early on, view the music scene as their own private matter and wish to control everything themselves, without the nation itself having any say in the matter."⁵⁶ A similar tone was struck by an anonymous writer in *Tíminn*, who observed that at the core of the debate was "a small group of men," that is, the Music Society, who seemed "to fear losing their grip on dictatorial power, and therefore all their opponents are blacklisted."⁵⁷

While the "War in the National Theater" played out as a conflict between the two main powers in Icelandic cultural life, Ragnar Jónsson and Guðlaugur Rósinkranz, it soon became clear that the Music Society's leaders lacked all faith in Urbancic's talent as an opera conductor. Jón Þórarinsson put it bluntly in a newspaper interview, insisting that while Urbancic had "some good qualities," he was not at all suitable for a music directorship. "This opinion is not at all a new one, as it has been expressed repeatedly, for at least the last five years, when discussing possible candidates for leading the Symphony Orchestra."⁵⁸

Ragnar Jónsson agreed. He was himself a larger-than-life personality and wished to see another vibrant, dynamic character at the helm of the orchestra he had fought tirelessly to establish. He found Urbancic a dull and uninspiring conductor, lacking decisiveness and persistence. He even expressed his distasteful view that Urbancic's success in Iceland was due only to local sympathy toward his plight as an exile, asserting in a newspaper article that "this hospitable nation has championed him more than any other foreigner who sought refuge here from the late Hitler."⁵⁹ In a blunt letter to Urbancic in spring 1952, Jónsson admitted having for years expressed his "displeasure" with his work at the Music School, and that he had "warned" his colleagues about Urbancic's lack of talent:

It is in no way an underestimating of your qualities and talent for me to assert that no Icelander who wants to be taken seriously will even entertain the notion that you might be capable of being the artistic leader of an orchestra that is intended to be the backbone of our national musical culture. [. . .] You lack all the main qualities that such a man must have. You are such a well-educated and intelligent man that you must see there is no reason for you to take offense at me for saying this. You must know that I have never considered you a great conductor; on the contrary, it has become eminently clear that you lack all the main qualities that a good conductor must have, even though the Reykjavík audience only fully grasped this once they had heard the orchestra under Hildebrandt and Kielland.[60]

Jónsson was convinced that his decision to hire Olav Kielland (see fig. 7.4) as the orchestra's Chief Conductor had been fully justified. In his letter to Urbancic, he asserted that Kielland was "precisely the man we need, a bril-

Figure 7.4. Olav Kielland, Chief Conductor of the Iceland Symphony Orchestra, 1952–1955. *Source:* © National and University Library of Iceland. Used with permission.

liant, solid, well-educated man of his word, a man with varied experience. An inspired genius, who never yields to damned indecisiveness or to local politics. He has precisely the qualities that you lack—qualities that most of even the finest men do not possess."

Urbancic replied with a lengthy letter in which he examines his fifteen years of working for Jónsson and the Music Society, his hopes and disappointments. His response is a remarkably candid document of his state of mind, as he puts all the cards on the table, judging both his pros and cons with rare honesty, even ruthlessness toward himself:

> I am fully aware of what I am capable, and what I am not. I know, for example, that I am only an average piano soloist due to lack of practice, somewhat better as an organist, but an excellent chamber musician and a world-class accompanist. I have absolutely no ambition as a piano teacher and have pointed this out from the very start. But in all the other subjects that I have taught at the Music School, I am the finest teacher available—perhaps with the sole exception of Robert Abraham in music theory for children, but certainly *not* Jón Þórarinsson. [. . .]
>
> I also know myself as a conductor. I have made this my life's work fully aware of what I am lacking: a fiery temperament as well as a certain amount of grandiosity and ruthlessness that any conductor needs. Still, my choice has been a fortunate one, for example during my seven years as a permanent conductor at the Mainz theater, and then in Iceland, where it has been precisely my temperament that has made it possible for me to achieve unimaginable results, given the very challenging circumstances. There are two ways to lead people: by force, or by gracefully encouraging them to cooperate. I find the latter more suited to Icelanders. You can have your own opinion on this, but you have no right to speak in the name of all who are "taken seriously." On the contrary: no one who is taken seriously can find it objectionable that a man with my experience, both here and abroad, should at least be consulted in all artistic matters, such as hiring players and even permanent or guest conductors—except if he has a personal interest in keeping the one man, aside from Robert Abraham, who has professional expertise in this field, away from such decisions, either because of some frustrated ambition, or for other, mysterious reasons.[61]

Next, Urbancic turns to the matter of Kielland's appointment. He feels spurned, he says, not because Kielland lacks skill as a conductor but because he is being offered such different working conditions that there can be no comparison of their work. Here, Urbancic expresses his frustration with the conditions under which he had labored in Iceland for fifteen years. The Music Society, he says, paid him a measly salary for a demanding job, made him a deal with all kinds of practical matters a conductor shouldn't have to worry about, and yet never fully trusted him to undertake all of his ambitious projects:

> If he [Kielland] had been offered the same working conditions as I was, he would certainly have banged his fist on the table. He would have banged with such force that he would have awakened you and your friends in the Music School from your dreams of the amateur having full control over the creative artist.
>
> I haven't banged my fist on the table. I believed what I was told: that Iceland was a poor country, the Music Society a poor organization that couldn't afford any of the extravagances of culture that other countries can offer. Still, I was determined to devote all my energy to Icelandic musical life. I showed up to orchestra rehearsals in the evening weary and exhausted after having taught for many hours earlier in the day; I put up with having far fewer rehearsals than what I thought was absolutely necessary; did all the sectionals myself, to save money; I spent each free evening for months copying and pasting the Icelandic text into the score of the *St John Passion*; copied by hand all the orchestral parts to the two Chopin concertos; all the parts to two operettas—and after the 75th performance of *Mam'zelle Nitouche* I had to request legal advice from our friend Ólafur Þorgrímsson to enforce the provision that I should be paid at least *the same* salary as each orchestra member for a performance, when I had prepared for months before the orchestra even began rehearsals.
>
> O[lav] K[ielland] doesn't have to do any of this. He can focus on just one of my many tasks, gets all the rehearsals he asks for, and no one would even think of making him load instruments and chairs onto a truck. He only needs to raise his magic wand, and even then he is rewarded by a spotlight. And immediately, people say: This must be an excellent conductor.[62]

As for Kielland's talents, local opinion was certainly divided. Most agreed he was a decisive and demanding orchestra leader, and that his results were often impressive. Ragnar Jónsson sang his praises as an "outstanding spiritual leader" and a comrade in a "holy defensive war against ignorance and sloth."[63] Others were more critical. In a letter to literary scholar Sigurður Nordal, Páll Ísólfsson admitted that Kielland was an "amazingly hard worker, and a true Viking when he rehearses our young orchestra," but he found his personality so disagreeable that he thought it unwise to renew his contract: "He succumbs to sudden fits of rage, resulting in total pandemonium. One moment he believes himself to be the greatest of all living conductors, then he collapses like a wet whip. I don't appreciate such people, and most of this is the result of poor upbringing and boorishness."[64] In 1953, having recently performed Mozart's Piano Concerto no. 24 with Kielland, composer Jón Nordal confessed to Ísólfsson that he was unimpressed by the conductor, who "gushes out the most obvious facts and the simplest truths with his thundering voice, in such an aggravating manner that one is completely unnerved."[65]

Among the orchestra members who had little patience for Kielland was Heinz Edelstein. His son, Stefán, recalled that his father "hated the smugness and arrogance; he found him to be an intolerable show-off."[66] In a letter in autumn 1952, Heinz Edelstein himself described Kielland as a "wild Romantic" who only knew how to make music by "screaming at the orchestra and through distorted *espressivo* gestures."[67] At one rehearsal, Edelstein had had enough and decided he would never again look directly at Kielland on the podium, even when he specifically cued or instructed the cello section; instead, he would fix his eyes on his music stand or glance sideways. It didn't take long before Kielland noticed and, predictably, lost his temper. A special mediation session was required with Edelstein and the orchestra's general manager, who—unfortunately for the cellist—happened to be his other nemesis, Jón Þórarinsson. In the end, Edelstein had to promise to shape up and look at the conductor as needed.[68]

Victor Urbancic and Robert Abraham also had their doubts regarding Kielland's musicianship, although they never expressed their opinion publicly. In his copy of a program book in November 1952, Urbancic wrote that Kielland's performance of Beethoven's Symphony no. 2 had been "dull and imprecise."[69] Three years later, writing to a friend in Germany, Abraham described his interpretation of Tchaikovsky's Fifth Symphony as "a world record in symphonic noise."[70] In a letter to Þórarinsson, he complained that the "nearly insufferable" *fortissimo* brass had made a caricature of the final movement of Beethoven's Seventh.[71] While Abraham and Urbancic were hardly impartial observers, their judgment was decisive and cannot be overlooked.

Ragnar Jónsson, who for decades had been one of the leading decision makers and financial sponsors of the Reykjavík music scene, was severely disgruntled by Urbancic's appointment at the National Theater. Even more than in his candid letter to Urbancic, quoted above, he vented his rage in a private correspondence in September 1953 to Bjarni Benediktsson, former mayor of Reykjavík, who had, just two days earlier, been appointed culture minister. In his letter, Jónsson describes Urbancic as a "cunning man, deferential, very greedy for money," and claims to have never seen anything remarkable in him other than his negative qualities. "Dr. Urbancic doesn't do a single thing well. But Icelanders are uncommonly hospitable and, because he was a refugee, he enjoyed much sympathy here."[72] While Urbancic certainly felt, on occasion, underpaid and undervalued, nothing in Jónsson's description is supported by other contemporary accounts. Yet it was Melitta Urbancic who bore the full brunt of Jónsson's rage: "The woman is simply insane. I cannot in any way consent to being an anti-Semite, although I have in my experience of doing business with Jews learned to be especially careful in dealing with them."[73] Jónsson's offensive comments certainly show the least appealing side of this cultural mogul, who felt his command slipping away and used all available means to regain control.

In hindsight, the controversy surrounding the National Theater's music directorship seems hardly more than a tempest in a teapot. More than anything else, it showed how the boundaries between Iceland's cultural institutions and main power brokers were still in the process of being drawn. In this case, both the National Theater director and the leaders of the Symphony Orchestra wished to be able to make important decisions regarding opera performance without the other's consent. The "War in the National Theater" rattled the Symphony Orchestra's existence for only a short while, and had no lasting consequences—except for Victor Urbancic. When push came to shove, foreign musicians found themselves in an unpleasant position vis-à-vis local cultural moguls, who could respond to their demands with arrogance and contempt, even xenophobic attacks. Sibyl Urbancic recalls that her usually calm and amiable father was deeply upset by the treatment he received from the Music Society in the early 1950s. "This was the only time in my life that I saw him angry and frustrated, he found it all so terribly unjust. He was really very deeply hurt."[74]

Once the orchestra dispute had been settled, Ragnar Jónsson and Guðlaugur Rósinkranz made peace with one another. "Neither of us has ever borne a grudge for the words spoken in the heat of this war," Rósinkranz recalled in his 1977 memoirs.[75] But Jónsson always held a grudge against Urbancic, who was only rarely invited to conduct the Iceland Symphony Orchestra again. Moreover, his performances at the National Theater were sometimes reviewed by Jónsson, in an arts magazine that he himself published—a rather underhanded act of revenge. When Lehár's *The Merry Widow* was staged in 1956, he found the interpretation sluggish; Urbancic, he said, was "notably lacking in stamina, and he doesn't have the wide perspective that demands perfect discipline."[76] A year later, *The Magic Flute* was equally dismal in Jónsson's opinion, with conducting that was "dull, imprecise, and hesitant," while Urbancic himself seemed "somehow disoriented."[77]

Remarkably, Jónsson also reviewed Urbancic's return to the Iceland Symphony in September 1954—his first subscription concert in nearly three years. Of course Jónsson was far from impartial, but his review in *Morgunblaðið* verges on the risible. He describes how Urbancic was greeted with an enthusiastic welcome, "just like the Prodigal Son, and given flowers like in the old days when he was the town's big mover and shaker," implying that the warm welcome was less than deserved.[78] According to Jónsson, the performance verged on disaster, with Urbancic's interpretation of Smetana's overture to *The Bartered Bride* no more than "meaningless gibberish," while the soloist, a young, little-known Soviet cellist playing Dvořák's Cello Concerto, seemed to have completely misunderstood the work. His name was Mstislav Rostropovich.

While the turmoil at the National Theater was an unexpected footnote in Icelandic music history, it should not divert attention from the true achievements of Urbancic's tenure there. With the theater's inauguration, Icelandic singers for the first time had the opportunity to perform staged operas in their native country. There had been several outstanding Icelandic opera singers in the first half of the century, including tenors Pétur Jónsson and Stefán Íslandi and soprano María Markan, but due to lack of local opportunities they all made their careers abroad, in Denmark, Germany, and the United States, respectively. With the opening of the National Theater, the path was clear for a new generation of opera singers who would assume leading roles in local performances for decades to come, the most prominent of which were sopranos Þuríður Pálsdóttir and Guðrún Á. Símonar, tenor Magnús Jónsson, and bass-baritones Guðmundur Jónsson and Kristinn Hallsson.[79] Through Rósinkranz's support in the 1950s, opera finally had a professional base in Iceland, which led to a transformation of the local music scene.

The Icelandic premiere of Verdi's *Rigoletto* in 1951 was a watershed moment, and the following seasons nearly always included a major opera production under Urbancic's direction: *La traviata* (1953), *Cavalleria rusticana* and *Pagliacci* (1954), *The Magic Flute* on the bicentenary of Mozart's birth (1956), and *Tosca* (1957). These performances were unanimously well received. Of the 1957 production of *Tosca*, one critic enthused: "In no opera that has been performed here has the singing been as uniformly good and outstanding in every way as in *Tosca*."[80]

Urbancic's repertoire at the National Theater went beyond serious opera. He also conducted lighter operettas, such as *Die Fledermaus* (1952), *The Merry Widow* (1956), and *The White Horse Inn* (1957), works which, as a native Viennese, he knew as well as anyone. Incidental music performed under his direction included Mendelssohn's score to *A Midsummer Night's Dream* (1955) as well as Páll Ísólfsson's score to Davíð Stefánsson's folklore-inspired *The Golden Gate* (*Gullna hliðið*, 1951 and 1955). He also contributed his own original music to two productions: Jakob Jónsson's *Tyrkja-Gudda* (1952) and Klabund's *The Chalk Circle* (1955). Thus, Urbancic's contribution to opera and theater in Iceland during the last years of his life was remarkable both in quality and quantity. In total, he conducted the music for over 550 performances in the years 1950–1957, his performances setting a high standard not to be surpassed for decades.

Edelstein: Teaching the Joy of Music

For Heinz Edelstein, teaching music to children had been a particular interest ever since his student years in Freiburg. At the Reykjavík Music School, he immediately saw an opportunity to make an impact in the field, in addition to his cello and chamber music lessons. During his first year in Iceland, he began instructing "several groups of children and teenagers how to play recorder," as reported by the local *Radio News* in January 1939.[81] Prior to Edelstein's arrival, recorders had been completely unheard of in the country, but he was convinced of their utility in introducing music to young children. Soon afterward, he received permission to establish a special children's division at the school, which was still based in the small octagonal Pavilion. In 1944, the school moved into several rooms in the National Theater, construction of which had been halted during the war. Among the children who attended lessons with Edelstein were two eight-year-old boys who later became prominent in Icelandic cultural life: composer Atli Heimir Sveinsson, and Styrmir Gunnarsson, the influential editor of the *Morgunblaðið*.[82]

After only a few months in Iceland, Edelstein wrote a five-page article in which he defined his views of music education for the *Reykjavík Music Society Journal*, a publication issued from 1938 to 1941. Edelstein was convinced that music carried the "fundamental potential of each human being," and that focusing only on students' technical abilities with the goal of a professional career was a sign of cultural decline. Teaching young children how to sing and play an instrument, as effortlessly as possible, could awaken in them a joy of music that might benefit them even if they never became professionals.[83] The recorder, he argued, was an ideal instrument for young children because it was cheap and did not require extensive technical facility. By learning an instrument at an earlier age than had previously been common in Iceland, children were allowed to incorporate music "organically, and thus it becomes a natural way of life instead of a trained skill, as often is the case."[84] Edelstein added that he was generally unimpressed by child prodigies in music; he found them to be "usually the result of an abnormal training, something akin to a talking parrot."[85]

A prerequisite of introducing simple, pedagogically useful songs to the local children was having appropriate texts in the Icelandic language to which they could be sung. Among Edelstein's acquaintances in Iceland was poet Þorsteinn Valdimarsson, who provided him with many texts and translations, such as the well-known German children's song *Fuchs, du hast die Gans gestohlen*, which in its Icelandic rendering became *Refur, þú ert ræningi (Fox, You Are a Thief)*. In addition to their recorder playing and singing, the children learned the Tonic sol-fa method, with its accompanying hand signals for each note.[86]

Edelstein also wanted his students to have the opportunity to perform music that was recently composed, although of course it had to be within their capabilities. With this in mind, he asked composer Jón Þórarinsson—about a year before their relationship soured dramatically—to write a few easy songs for his students. He requested they be in "a new style," fairly short and to texts of his own choice, "as long as they are suitable for children."[87] The result was *Six Old Folk Poems with New Songs for Children*, first performed at a student concert in spring 1950, under Edelstein's direction, and issued by Ragnar Jónsson's publishing house a few months later.[88] Edelstein was particularly pleased with his advanced class that year, and although he had for a while considered remigrating to the Federal Republic of Germany, he decided to stay, at least for a while. As he explained to his friend Kurt Zier, he had come to realize that "feelings of fulfillment or emptiness in life have nothing to do with one's geographical location, or even one's cultural environment. And to abandon this work, which no one else can take over, would be ill-advised, even though I must accept my long-standing bouts of depression as a bonus."[89]

Edelstein's teaching methods were widely admired, and he was even asked to demonstrate them to eminent visitors from abroad. In March 1951, Armenian composer Aram Khachaturian visited Iceland along with four other Soviet artists on behalf of MÍR, the Society for Artistic Relations between Iceland and the Soviet Union, which wielded considerable influence on the local cultural scene during the Cold War. Khachaturian directed the Iceland Symphony Orchestra in a concert of his own works, and along with other members of his cultural delegation he visited the Reykjavík Music School. There, they attended one of Edelstein's classes and heard his pupils play recorders and sing (see fig. 7.5).[90]

Figure 7.5. Aram Khachaturian (second from left) with Heinz Edelstein and his students at the Reykjavík Music School in 1951. The woman with the fur hat is soprano Nadezhda Kazantseva, who was also part of the Soviet delegation and appeared in concert with the Iceland Symphony Orchestra. *Source:* © National and University Library of Iceland. Used with permission.

The Children's Division of the Reykjavík Music School had enjoyed great popularity since it was initiated in the late 1930s. After years of disagreement over his remuneration for this part of his work (see chapter 6), Edelstein and the school's principal decided the time had come for Edelstein to establish his own private music school for young children. This was in spring 1951, a time when Edelstein had also become disillusioned with his position at the Symphony Orchestra (see above). Therefore, he decided to devote himself entirely to teaching and largely retired as a cellist. This transition was made in full cooperation with the Music School, and Edelstein's most loyal supporter in the new enterprise was Ragnar Jónsson, chairman of the Music Society.

As he prepared to launch the new school, Edelstein spent the school year 1951–1952 in West Germany, where, through a generous grant from Jónsson, he was able to study the latest innovations in music education. Edelstein observed a course for string players at the Odenwaldschule, a progressive rural boarding school where his friend Kurt Zier had assumed the position of dean, having remigrated from Iceland in 1949. Edelstein also visited an institute for music pedagogy in Detmold, and in a small town in Westphalia he encountered an outstanding music instructor who had specialized in teaching refugee children, reporting back to Iceland that "the musical accomplishments of these children are so astonishing, that no one would have been able to convince me they were possible, if I hadn't seen them with my own eyes."[91] The teacher used a method Edelstein had not seen before, the Orff-Schulwerk developed by composer Carl Orff in the 1930s. Upon his return to Iceland, Edelstein introduced this method in his own teaching, and it became prominent in music education there for decades.

Still, after fourteen years in Iceland, Edelstein did not fully enjoy returning to his old fatherland. Germany was completely transformed from what he knew before, the destruction of the war remained visible, and the country had been divided into two. He was fully comfortable in neither East nor West Germany, as he explained in a letter to Björn Jónsson, the Reykjavík Music Society's financial officer:

> Yet I wouldn't want to stay here for long. This place has the same problems as anywhere else, but here they are more pronounced because the borders between the two worlds run through the middle of the country. And both worlds are, it seems to me, fundamentally flawed. In the West, you have an appalling lack

of social responsibility, with luxury and opulence thriving in the midst of hardship and despair, like some caricature of capitalism in a Communist propaganda pamphlet. On the other hand, in the East, where many good things happen in the social and cultural realms, you find the same oppression that I recall from the Hitler era. And they're not on speaking terms, West and East Germans. If this situation continues for a generation, I'm sure that there will be two languages here, and no one will be able to translate one into the other. It is as if these people have been consumed by a contagious insanity.[92]

During Edelstein's stay in Germany, he was granted reparations from the German state for having had to flee the Third Reich. Remarkably, he chose to spend most of the total sum of 7,200 German marks on instruments and sheet music for his new school in Iceland. With additional funding from Ragnar Jónsson, the school had all the instruments and equipment it required.[93] This is primarily a testament to Edelstein's strong dedication to his work, but may also suggest a resentful attitude toward the entire notion and process of reparation. In any case, he preferred to use the German government's money to purchase instruments for Icelandic children instead of spending it for his own personal benefit.

Nonetheless, Edelstein did appreciate how in Germany he was received "with open arms and hearts" everywhere. He sensed a comradeship with others who shared his goals in music education, and this in turn fueled his enthusiasm. This was something he had often found lacking in his work with Icelandic colleagues, as he mentioned in one of his letters. In Reykjavík, he said, music teachers were often at odds with each other and lacked solidarity: "To have to fight with people because of my goals, instead of having true colleagues, makes me cheerless and unproductive. My work with the Icelandic children themselves has always been the opposite: positive and enchanting. But with adults, I have never experienced this will to cooperate," except, he noted, with his colleague Ingólfur Guðbrandsson, a music teacher and pioneer in choral work with children, who was the recipient of the lines quoted above.[94]

Edelstein returned from Germany with solid ideas for a new school, and the Children's Music School (*Barnamúsíkskólinn*) was established in autumn 1952. In its first year, it had an enrollment of approximately one hundred children, most of whom were aged from eight to thirteen, but in 1955 even younger children were admitted, aged five to seven, with enrollment growing to 250.⁹⁵ Students attended group lessons twice a week and were taught to play recorders and simple percussion instruments, encouraging them to make music together from the very start.⁹⁶ They were given elementary instruction in music theory, and also joined together in a choir.⁹⁷

The school's purpose, according to Edelstein, was to "encourage interest in music among children and teenagers, and to get them to spend their free time in an ennobling manner."⁹⁸ As before, he was convinced music should not be reserved only for trained professionals, but that it was not least a social activity; his new school should not only aim to polish the "best diamonds" but to give everyone an opportunity to experience the joy of making music. Having completed three years of pre-school, the most talented students were selected and invited to begin learning violin, cello, or piano.⁹⁹ In addition to Edelstein, Robert Abraham taught piano to the older pupils, and in autumn 1955 a third teacher was added to teach Dalcroze eurhythmics. Abraham was no less of an ambitious and inventive educator than Edelstein. Among the larger projects he devised for his students was *Wir bauen eine Stadt*, a 1930 children's song cycle by Paul Hindemith about an imaginary city built and ruled by children alone, which in Icelandic translation became *We'll Build a New Reykjavik* (*Við reisum nýja Reykjavík*). He also formed an ensemble to perform the *Toy Symphony* sometimes attributed to either Leopold Mozart or Edmund Angerer, which students played under his direction both at a concert and on National Radio (see fig. 7.6).¹⁰⁰

Edelstein was deeply interested in music of the Baroque, and during his year studying in West Germany in 1951–1952 he had frequented German libraries to copy sonatas and other works he could use in his teaching. He knew that many Baroque and early Classical works were well suited to beginners, and purchased for his new school many instruments for such music that had rarely been seen in Iceland before, including a Sperrhake "revival" harpsichord. Only Edelstein's friend Kurt Zier had previously owned a harpsichord in Iceland, but he had taken it back with him to Germany in 1949.¹⁰¹ Edelstein also purchased recorders and several teaching instruments called *Fiedel*, a kind of viola da gamba with five or six strings and fretted fingerboards, built in varying sizes from soprano to bass. Edelstein created an ensemble of Fiedel students that appeared annually at the Children's Music School's spring concert, and after the concert he invited all ensemble members to join him at a local coffee house for hot chocolate and waffles. Even today, some of his former students recall their joy and surprise that a demanding teacher like Edelstein should reward them with such an outing to celebrate their achievements.¹⁰²

Figure 7.6. Students from the Children's Music School rehearse under the direction of Robert Abraham, spring 1961. *Source:* © Elín Þ. Ólafsdóttir, private collection. Used with permission.

While teaching at the music school gave Edelstein a sense of purpose, his daily life in Reykjavík was monotonous and solitary, not least after Charlotte and the two boys had left Iceland (see chapter 8). In spring 1953, he found the insular atmosphere in Reykjavík to have a "paralyzing" effect on him, both personally and professionally. In a conversation with Guðríður, Robert Abraham's wife, he complained he was "wasting away," and he confessed, in a letter to Kurt Zier, that, although he was an introvert by nature, his new lifestyle might be too much of a good thing.[103] He wondered, he said, how long the pleasure of working with children at his music school could outweigh "a lack of all human connection and spiritual harmony."[104]

The school's annual spring concert in May 1955 was a somewhat more public affair than in preceding years. At a well-attended concert in the so-called Independence House (*Sjálfstæðishúsið*) by Parliament Square in central Reykjavík, the children played recorders, Fiedel, xylophones, and drums; they also formed a choir that performed *a cappella* and with instrumental accompaniment (see fig. 7.7). Older pupils played piano and violin, and a few piano students played their own compositions, which were met with great enthusiasm from the audience. By way of introduction, Edelstein explained the school's mission in a kind of personal manifesto:

> Whoever is unable to express himself in any way with music is unable to fully come into his own. Music needs to be a valued part of general education, and perhaps nothing is better suited to solving the problems we now face in raising a new generation. Whoever makes music with others is able to enjoy two things: he enjoys the freedom experienced when expressing oneself through singing or playing an instrument, but is at the same time bound to the laws of the whole, to which he belongs. I cannot imagine a better preparation for participating in life in a free country.[105]

Figure 7.7. Heinz Edelstein conducts students from the Children's Music School at a public concert in May 1955. *Source:* © Tónmenntaskóli Reykjavíkur. Used with permission.

Unusually, two local publications carried "reviews" of the concert, but of course both were flattering and kind to the young students. A critic for *Tíminn* wrote that "the children's singing and playing was usually very good and they were enthusiastically received by a packed house of listeners."[106] Another critic noted that "it was enjoyable to see how serious and immersed they were in their short, simple songs, despite the large crowd. They were well-behaved and lovely children, appropriately shy. And all this transpired in such an unpretentious and informal manner, just like at a regular rehearsal; there was no stiff concert atmosphere, and of course there is nothing more natural, if you make a mistake at a rehearsal, than to begin again!"[107]

Only a few days later, a group of Edelstein's students was invited to record their program for National Radio. The recording still exists and is an impressive testimony to the thoroughness of Edelstein's training; the singing is pure and in tune, and the instrumental performances are clean and charming in their simplicity. The repertoire was, presumably, typical for his student programs: Baroque dances, duets by Georg Philipp Telemann, simple canons such as Michael Praetorius's *Viva la musica*, and an arrangement of Brahms's *Lullaby* for piano three hands and percussion.[108] "It was very enjoyable to hear the young instrumentalists and Dr. Edelstein has certainly obtained remarkably good results in a short period of time," *Morgunblaðið*'s critic wrote of the children's radio debut.[109]

Abraham: Return to Berlin

Like his colleagues in exile, Robert Abraham was vexed by Olav Kielland's appointment as chief conductor of the Iceland Symphony. Although he continued to conduct the orchestra, with three concerts in the 1953–1954 season and five in 1954–1955, he spent most of his time on an ambitious research project that would eventually become his doctoral dissertation (see chapter 8). He also began exploring possibilities for a conducting career outside Iceland. While his application for a position with the Freiburg Symphony Orchestra in autumn 1955 was unsuccessful, his friendship with German conductor Hermann Hildebrandt, who had conducted in Reykjavík in 1950 and 1953, led to an offer to conduct a Mozart program with the Städtisches Berliner Sinfonieorchester, now the Konzerthausorchester Berlin.[110] This was among East Berlin's finest orchestras, founded just four years earlier as the eastern part's answer to the West's Berlin Philharmonic. Their concert with

Abraham was so successful that he was offered a position as guest conductor for the 1956–1957 season.

Abraham enjoyed returning to the city of his birth even though it was radically changed, and, though the Berlin Wall had not yet been built, the political division between east and west was becoming ever more ingrained. His wife Guðríður accompanied him and was able to experience Berlin for the first time, but their young son stayed in Iceland with his grandparents. When he wasn't rehearsing or directing concerts, Abraham spent his days at the Berlin State Library, researching medieval plainchant and preparing what would become his dissertation (see Chapter 8).

Abraham conducted a wide range of programs during his season in Berlin, from Mozart to contemporary works. Critics praised the "outstandingly good influence" his work had had on the orchestra, with his energy and admirable musicianship.[111] As his time in Berlin came to a close, he was offered an extension of his contract, but he refused, choosing instead to return to Iceland to resume his career. A few years later, Abraham was

Figure 7.8. Robert Abraham with his wife Guðríður Magnúsdóttir and their son Grétar Ottó Róbertsson, May 1959. *Source:* © Elín Þ. Ólafsdóttir, private collection. Used with permission.

offered to conduct in the Holy Land. In November 1962, he conducted the Israel Radio Orchestra in Jerusalem and Beersheba, with a program of Haydn, Mozart, and Schumann, as well as Nordic music by Carl Nielsen and Jón Leifs, and received excellent reviews.[112]

Abraham's concert programs in Iceland further testify to the breadth of his musical talent. In his first years in Reykjavík, he had conducted ad-hoc ensembles in works by Mozart, Schubert, and others, but with the founding of the Iceland Symphony, his orchestral repertoire expanded rapidly. Among the local premieres conducted by Abraham in the early 1950s were Brahms's Symphony no. 2 and Beethoven's *Pastoral* Symphony (both 1951), Dvořák's Cello Concerto (1952), Musorgsky's *Night on Bald Mountain* (1953), and Schumann's Symphony no. 1 (1954), as well as new Icelandic works such as Karl O. Runólfsson's *Fjalla-Eyvindur* overture and Jón Þórarinsson's *Of Love and Death*, a song cycle for baritone and orchestra.[113] As orchestra conductor, he also appeared with renowned soloists, including violinist Isaac Stern and pianists Friedrich Gulda, Shura Cherkassky, and Vladimir Ashkenazy.

Abraham also conducted operas, though this was never a primary focus of his career. He conducted Gian Carlo Menotti's *The Medium* in a double-bill with the premiere of Jórunn Viðar's folktale-inspired ballet *Olaf Lily-Rose* (*Ólafur liljurós*) at the Reykjavík Theater in October 1952, and Rossini's *The Barber of Seville* at the National Theater in 1958—the first opera performance there with a fully Icelandic cast. It was a resounding success, as one critic noted: "I don't think the Symphony Orchestra has ever performed dramatic music as well or better than now, and Róbert Abraham Ottósson was cheered more than any other performer at the premiere, which is an honor he fully deserves."[114] Two years later, he conducted Donizetti's *Don Pasquale*, but he never had the opportunity to conduct Weber's *Der Freischütz* or Offenbach's *The Tales of Hoffmann*, two operas he himself suggested for the National Theater—let alone his favorite works of all: Mozart's *The Magic Flute* and Beethoven's *Fidelio*.[115]

By the year 1955, it seemed as if the storms and conflicts of the preceding years had calmed. Victor Urbancic was enjoying his position at the National Theater, Heinz Edelstein had established a music school for young children, and Robert Abraham had conducting engagements abroad and also devoted much of his time to musicological research. They were all in their prime, but none was to enjoy a long life. Each of them passed away long before his life's work was complete.

8

Endings

"Was it because of the anxiety suffered by refugees from the Nazi state that their life's energy was spent so quickly?"[1] This question was raised by Stefán Edelstein in a 1969 eulogy for his family friend Kurt Zier, another German who sought refuge in Iceland shortly before World War II. It also applies to Victor Urbancic, Heinz Edelstein, and Robert Abraham, all of whom passed away in their prime: Urbancic was fifty-four years old when he died, Edelstein fifty-seven, and Abraham two months shy of his sixty-second birthday. In the 1960s, it should be noted, the average life expectancy of an Icelandic male was seventy-one years.[2] Of course, their untimely deaths cannot be reduced to a single cause, but they had all experienced hardship and anxiety, even direct danger, after Hitler's rise to power. Later in life, they did not have the necessary tools or support to process their earlier traumas, and their lives in Iceland were marked by a different kind of tension: working long hours under inadequate conditions, often for demeaningly low pay, while having to endure professional quarrels and even public humiliation. While their premature deaths were most painfully felt by their families and friends, they were also an unexpected and deeply felt blow to musical life in Iceland.

Urbancic: Requiem aeternam . . .

Victor Urbancic had always had a strong constitution and rarely became ill, even with the flu. His ailment began in earnest on June 4, 1957—his daughter Sibyl's twentieth birthday. She had just completed an English exam at the Reykjavík Gymnasium, and by coincidence she found herself on the same bus home as her father. He seemed disoriented and confused, repeatedly asking her where she was coming from, and it soon became clear that he had suffered a stroke. For the next three days, Urbancic experienced severe cognitive impairment, but his condition gradually improved and he regained his former strength. Later that summer, he was well enough to visit Austria for the last time, along with his wife and daughter Eiríka.[3] In January 1958, he made what was to be his last trip abroad, spending two months in the United States on a grant from the U.S. Department of State, to examine music and theater throughout the country. In New York, he was particularly delighted by a new musical, Leonard Bernstein's *West Side Story*, as well as by Bernstein's rendition of Stravinsky's *Rite of Spring* with the Philharmonic at Carnegie Hall.[4] Two other Broadway musicals, *The Music Man* and *My Fair Lady*, also left a favorable impression, but he was disappointed by a lackluster performance of Verdi's *La forza del destino* at the Metropolitan Opera.[5] He heard the Cleveland Orchestra under Szell and the Philadelphia Orchestra under Ormandy, both of which impressed him greatly, met with renowned organist E. Power Biggs in Boston, and lectured on Icelandic music in no fewer than five cities, including Boston, New York, Chicago, and Bloomington, Indiana.[6] He thoroughly enjoyed the tour, but the flight back to Iceland was long and taxing, with a protracted layover in frigid temperatures in Newfoundland, and in retrospect it proved too demanding for his fragile health.

The day after his return in late February, Urbancic lost his balance and fell twice, first on the steps of the Reykjavík Music School, and again that evening at a rehearsal at the National Theater; after the second fall, he was unable to regain his equilibrium and, though he tried to brush it off, it gradually became clear that he had again suffered a stroke. While his illness appeared to worsen, the convalescent Urbancic seemed unable to grasp the situation properly. He would sit in his bed for hours studying the score to Cole Porter's *Kiss Me, Kate*, which he was scheduled to conduct at the National Theater later that year. Once, when his doctor paid him a house call, he decided to test Urbancic's alertness by enquiring how many actors and singers would be taking part in the production. Urbancic replied that there would be at least two thousand people on stage, which of course was a wild exaggeration. By mid-March, he was suffering from aphasia; bedridden, he was unable to speak at all.[7]

As there were no neurosurgeons in Iceland in the 1950s, prospects for Urbancic's recovery seemed bleak. But Melitta was determined not to

Figure 8.1. Victor Urbancic with his mother Hildegard in Vienna in summer 1954, four years before his death. *Source:* © Sibyl Urbancic, private collection. Used with permission.

give up, and managed to arrange for her husband to be operated on by a skilled specialist in Vienna. She had booked a flight via Hamburg on Maundy Thursday, but as they arrived by ambulance at the Reykjavík airport, Urbancic's local doctor showed up to inform them there would be no room for a stretcher on their connecting flight and that everything would have to be postponed until after the Easter weekend. They had no option but to return home, where Urbancic died the following day, on Good Friday, 1958, at fifty-four years of age.[8] His funeral was held at Reykjavík's Catholic Church, where the National Theater Choir bid its conductor farewell with movements from Brahms's *German Requiem*, conducted by Robert Abraham.

Victor Urbancic's career in Iceland spanned just short of twenty years, during which he achieved an incredible amount of groundbreaking work. He was an uncommonly dedicated and devoted musician, whose life revolved around his teaching and conducting duties. There is no doubt that the conflicts in the National Theater and his strained relations with the leaders of the Iceland Symphony Orchestra and Reykjavík Music Society made his last years difficult and took a toll on his health. In a speech at a memorial concert for Urbancic, given by the Icelandic Composers' Society at the National Theater in November 1958, composer Jón Leifs remarked:

> His kindness and conscientiousness are well known to all. He was willing to help everyone and take on virtually every role that was assigned to him, even when it was hardly possible to pull off satisfactorily, and he always did his best. He wasn't the only one in this country who had to settle for unfulfilled ambitions, inadequate conditions, and poor preparations. When your environment demands too much of you, and you work unrelentingly without imagining that you'll ever be able to reach your goal—that's when the body fails. That's how Urbancic went.[9]

To be fair, it should be noted that Leifs himself liked to assume the role of a martyr, and his words should be interpreted in that context; he was also implying that his own working conditions were no less inadequate than Urbancic's. Even so, his words ring true.

Melitta Urbancic later recalled that during his final illness, before he was no longer able to speak, her husband repeatedly said: "When I am no longer ill, please collect money for Icelandic doctors to specialize abroad, so that no one should have to suffer here without help, or have to go abroad for treatment."[10] After Urbancic's death, the National Theater Choir established a memorial fund in gratitude for his work. Its income, free donations as well as receipts from an annual memorial concert, was used to support a local neurology specialist to study abroad. Iceland's first two neurologists received student fellowships from the Urbancic Fund, and on the occasion of Urbancic's seventy-fifth birthday in 1978, a substantial grant from the fund was used to help purchase Iceland's first CT scanner.[11] Thus, even though Urbancic's untimely death was devastating, it did, in the end, lead to considerable medical advances in his memory.

Home, Near and Far

Only a small minority of those who fled the Nazi regime returned permanently to their native land after the war. Worldwide, it has been estimated that 6 percent of émigrés made their way back for good, while many more returned for visits of varying duration.[12] The hesitation felt by exiles to return is understandable. They had already spent considerable effort adjusting to their new country, and its culture and language, making friends and professional connections along the way. In most cases, they had navigated such challenges successfully and were reluctant to uproot themselves yet again. The old homeland, on the other hand, had in many ways become a foreign place, and the wounds inflicted there were not easily healed after the war. Many émigrés were averse to returning to a country where only a few years earlier they had been made to suffer humiliation and barbarous treatment, to say nothing of having to face former colleagues and acquaintances who had stood silently by in their hour of need—or had even taken part in the atrocities themselves. For those who did consider remigration, finding work in the old homeland was no easy task, as other musicians had already filled their positions, whether at orchestras, conservatories, or universities.[13] In addition, Germany and Austria faced serious economic difficulties, and living conditions were hard in cities that had been devastated by bombing, cold, and hunger. Local authorities were remarkably unwelcoming and hesitant to address the grievances of returning exiles, while, on the individual level, those who returned were often met with suspicion, even jealousy.[14]

Victor and Melitta Urbancic visited Urbancic's family in Vienna several times after the war (see fig. 8.1), but their daughter Sibyl says that her mother had no desire to move back permanently, as it would have been too painful after all she had endured. Melitta was well aware that Nazism had not been fully eradicated, but was only lying dormant in Austrian society. She also found Vienna a markedly different place without all the Jews who earlier had put such a distinctive mark on the city's cultural and intellectual life.[15] More than anything, though, it was her husband's work in Iceland that made both of them want to stay. "Iceland is my workplace," Victor Urbancic stated in an interview three years after the war ended, affirming that he was "deeply moved by the warmth that I am met with everywhere, even by people who have nothing to do with music. This is the reason why I feel at home here."[16]

Melitta Urbancic lived in Iceland until her death in 1984 but was buried in Purkersdorf, just west of Vienna; her husband, on the other hand, is buried in the old cemetery (*Hólavallakirkjugarður*) in Reykjavík.[17] The older Urbancic children, Pétur, Ruth, and Sibyl, all spent time in Vienna in the 1950s and '60s. Their grandmother Hildegard was by then a widow and resided in the old family home together with her younger son Erich, a lawyer. She wished to get to know her grandchildren better and share with them the city's rich culture, and thus she invited each of them to live with her for a while. In Vienna, where she studied violin at the Conservatory,

Ruth met her future husband, an American music student named James Erb. They were married in 1952 and made their home in the United States; he had an esteemed career as a choir director and musicologist, while she was active as a violinist and violist, and was among the founders of the Richmond Symphony Orchestra. Sibyl studied organ and church music in Vienna and has resided there continuously since 1959. The oldest and youngest Urbancic children made their homes in Reykjavík: Pétur had a career as a musician, guide, and translator, while Eiríka was a medical secretary at the National University Hospital.

Robert Abraham had a somewhat different connection to Iceland than Edelstein and Urbancic; he was younger when he arrived there, and had an Icelandic wife and in-laws. He regarded himself as Icelandic through and through, and so did others, which led to him occasionally being offered opportunities reserved for local musicians. For example, at the Independence Festival at Þingvellir in 1944, at which Iceland was formally declared a republic, Abraham conducted, along with four Iceland-born conductors, a specially formed Festival Choir of the Society of Icelandic Male Choirs.[18] He was delighted to be able to take part in the festival "just like any other Icelander," as he put it.[19] A few days later, he was the toast of a party held by fellow émigrés Kurt and Lotte Zier to celebrate Iceland's independence. He accompanied a few songs on their harpsichord—the only such instrument in Iceland at the time—including two new patriotic songs especially composed for the Independence Festival and a staple of nationalist sentiment ever since: Emil Thoroddsen's *Who has a Fairer Fatherland* (*Hver á sér fegra föðurland*) and Þórarinn Guðmundsson's *My Father's Land* (*Land míns föður*).[20]

Abraham traveled to Germany several times after the war, and as noted in chapter 7, spent a full season guest-conducting in Berlin. When he returned from his first trip there in 1955, he said it had been excruciating to see the devastation of war. "Where I grew up as a child, everything was still in ruins. What once was our house is now a heap of rubble, covered with weeds. Most houses in the neighborhood were unrecognizable, except the church where I was confirmed, the Twelve Apostle Church. I was able to attend a service there one Sunday. The priest was not the same one that I heard give sermons back in the old days, but still I felt as if I had arrived back home."[21] Nevertheless, Abraham's strongest feelings were for Iceland, where by that time he had made his home for twenty years—almost as long as his life in Berlin before emigrating—and where he would reside for nearly another two decades. In 1957, returning from his year abroad, he remarked:

"Although Berlin is my old native city and I had all the best conditions for my work there, I always missed Iceland, the landscape, the climate, the language, and I would not have wished to settle abroad permanently."[22]

Heinz and Charlotte Edelstein both remigrated to the Federal Republic of Germany, but separately. While they never filed for divorce, theirs had been a marriage of convenience for their entire sojourn in Iceland. Charlotte returned to Freiburg in 1951 and lived there for nearly the rest of her life. As a female economist in her late forties with no relevant work experience, she was unable to find work in her field in postwar Germany. Instead, she worked primarily as an author, writing a book on Saint Bridget of Sweden and translating Icelandic short stories into German under a Nordic-sounding pseudonym, Karola Adalsten.[23] She also was an enthusiastic host for Icelandic students, attended concerts and lectures, and was delighted to be able to rebuild her existence in her old hometown. Gunnsteinn Ólafsson, an Icelandic musician who made her acquaintance in Freiburg in the 1980s, recalls her as having had a delightful sense of humor and that "her curiosity and fascination for life all around her seemed limitless."[24] Toward the end of her life, Lotte lived at an elderly care facility in Berlin and died there in 1997, at ninety-three. Although she had been back in Germany for forty-six years, she chose Iceland as her final resting place and was buried in Reykjavík.

Edelstein: Return to Germany

Heinz Edelstein led his newly founded Children's Music School in Reykjavík for only four years. In 1956, due to a cardiovascular ailment, his doctors recommended that he settle in a warmer climate, and he returned to Germany that summer, teaching cello and music theory at the Odenwaldschule, a progressive boarding school near Frankfurt. It was an unusually comfortable situation, since his son Wolfgang was already a faculty member and the school's headmaster was Kurt Zier, Edelstein's closest friend in Iceland during the war years and beyond. Thus, like most remigrants after the war, Edelstein was recruited through personal acquaintance rather than through official channels or public institutions.[25] Yet he left Iceland and his colleagues there with a heavy heart. In a letter to organist Páll Ísólfsson, he wrote: "I do not lightly put an end to a twenty-year period of my life. Even less so, when I have such strong bonds of loyalty to a country that gave me shelter when my life depended on it, and gave me opportunities for work that brought out my best qualities. But no one can choose his own fate."[26]

Edelstein's weak heart was not in fact the main cause of his illness; it was, he reflected, "a symptom rather than the disease itself." He had for years suffered from serious bouts of depression that had, in his own words, made his daily life and work "nearly impossible, while they lasted. Although I may have been able to keep this more or less secret, in recent years my condition has worsened to such an extent that I had no choice but to seek therapy, or else throw in the towel."[27] He attended psychiatric sessions at Heidelberg University Hospital five times a week and viewed the treatment as "a kind of revision of my whole self," as he put it in a letter to music teacher and conductor Ingólfur Guðbrandsson, one of his few friends in Iceland who knew the true nature of his troubles.[28] In May 1957, Edelstein was glad to report some progress, but he said he was afraid to withdraw from therapy too soon for fear that he might regress again. Guðbrandsson took over as headmaster in Edelstein's absence for the 1956–1957 school year, after which Robert Abraham led the music school until 1961.

While Germany's mild climate was beneficial to his health, Edelstein wondered whether he would ever be able to feel fully at home there again. In another letter to Guðbrandsson in Iceland, he openly expressed his internal conflict, admitting it had been "quite a task to overcome my inner resistance to being here." He found work conditions in German public schools inferior to those at his own private school in Reykjavík, and the students themselves less enthusiastic than he had expected. "In addition, I feel little or no attachment to this country that once was my fatherland. It is as if the wounds I received here many years ago are becoming more sensitive, not less."[29] Thus, Edelstein did not dismiss the idea of returning "home," as he put it: "I am still not certain whether I will settle here for good or return home to Iceland. Whatever one can say about the conditions of music education there in general, my work at the Children's Music School was a true delight. There is no such thing as pure happiness in the world, but in my work with children in Iceland I found deep satisfaction, and this is most important."[30] Like many other émigrés, Edelstein found himself in an ambiguous situation once the totalitarian regime had collapsed; he felt completely at home neither in his new country nor the one he had left behind. He did, however, find one unexpected source of joy during his last years in Germany: his cello. "I have begun to love my instrument again, which I had neglected for many years," he enthused, noting he had joined both a string quartet and a trio.[31] Yet, in the end, Edelstein admitted that he saw "no urgent need" for his work in Germany.[32] In Iceland, he had become used to his contribution being virtually indispensable, and had grown

Figure 8.2. Charlotte, Stefán, Heinz, and Wolfgang Edelstein reunited for the last time in Freiburg, Christmas 1958. *Source:* © Benjamin Edelstein, private collection. Used with permission.

fond of his role as a pioneer. With thousands of outstanding musicians in Germany, his efforts there seemed pointless in comparison.

Edelstein visited Iceland in 1957 but returned to his teaching duties at the Odenwaldschule, though only part-time, at doctor's orders. He had been diagnosed with more serious heart muscle damage, which, he told his former colleagues in Iceland, was not life threatening but required him to reduce his activities substantially.[33] When his son Stefán visited the Odenwaldschule in autumn 1958, he was shocked by his father's poor physical condition: "He looked terrible," he wrote to a colleague in Iceland.[34]

In the last year of his life, Edelstein considered relocating once again, this time to Israel. He spent several weeks there in spring 1959 and hoped to return soon for a longer stay, though this was not to be.[35] He visited Iceland once again in May, reuniting with many of his old friends for the last time.[36] Heinz Edelstein died of cardiac failure on October 5, 1959, and was buried in Hambach, Germany, three days later. His sons and wife all made the journey there to be present: Wolfgang came from Hamburg, Stefán from Reykjavík, and Charlotte cut short a holiday in Spain.[37] Heinz Edelstein had, in his own way, become an Icelander long ago. It is emblematic of his love for the country, its language, and its culture that two Icelandic books were on his nightstand when he died: Halldór Laxness's epic novels *Salka Valka* and *Iceland's Bell*.[38]

Shortly after Edelstein's death, his son Wolfgang wrote a card expressing his gratitude to Ragnar Jónsson, the head of the Reykjavík Music Society, who, he declared, had done "more for my father than anyone else." He noted what a "remarkably strong bond" had connected Edelstein to Iceland and its language, even though he had ended up being unable to live there due to poor health.[39] Wolfgang Edelstein completed his doctorate in 1962 and lived for most of his adult life in Berlin, where he was Director of the Max Planck Institute for Human Development. He was also for many years a special advisor to the Icelandic Ministry of Culture and played an important role in the development of Iceland's educational policy. Wolfgang Edelstein passed away in 2020. His brother Stefán studied electrical engineering in England in 1950–1954 but then took up music again, studying at the Freiburg Conservatory. Upon returning to Iceland, he led the music education department at the Reykjavík School of Music, and also appeared widely as pianist. In 1962, Stefán Edelstein took over as headmaster of the school his father had founded, the Children's Music School, a post he held for a remarkable fifty-five years, until his retirement in 2017. He passed away in Reykjavík in 2024. Two of his offspring have also become musicians: his son Kristján Edelstein is a guitarist and grandson Alexander a concert pianist.

Abraham: Iceland's First Musicologist

Robert Abraham was roughly a decade younger than Edelstein and Urbancic, and he also lived longer than his émigré colleagues. When Heinz Edelstein passed away in 1959, Abraham was the only one alive of the three, and he lived for another fifteen years. Thus, his career in Iceland was twice as long as those of the others, and he was the only one of the three who spent his entire career as a musician in Iceland. In fact, the years from 1959 to 1974 were the period of Abraham's greatest success, not only as a musician, but also as a teacher and scholar.

Ever since his arrival in Iceland, Abraham had been fascinated by the music of Iceland and its history. The country had no tradition of musicology, but he soon began his own informal research. In autumn 1937 he returned to Denmark for a short visit, and there he gave a radio talk about Icelandic music, past and present. In Iceland, he gave a series of radio lectures in 1940–1941, including an episode titled "Iceland's Role in Medieval Music." He also arranged movements from the *Graduale*, Iceland's sixteenth-century Lutheran missal, for organ, choir, and solo voices, performing them in concert with the Radio Choir.[40]

Gradually, Abraham's interest in Icelandic music history became more pronounced, particularly after Olav Kielland's appointment at the Symphony Orchestra resulted in fewer conducting opportunities. In particular, he became fascinated with the local history of plainchant. After its Christianization in the year 1000, Iceland followed the Roman Catholic rite of Nidaros (Norway) until the Reformation in the mid–sixteenth century. The zeal of the Reformation, as well as the passage of time and poor conditions for preservation in general, led to the destruction of most of the thousands of medieval liturgical manuscripts that the country once possessed. Not a single Icelandic medieval manuscript of liturgical plainchant has survived complete, but well over a hundred fragments of varying sizes still give some idea of the repertoire. Abraham was particularly fascinated by one of the most substantial of these, the office of Saint Thorlak (Þorlákur Þórhallsson), the twelfth-century Bishop of Skálholt, and Iceland's patron saint. A substantial, though not fully complete, manuscript written ca. 1400 contains most of the music for his office on his feast days, December 23 (the day of his death) and July 20 (the translation of his relics). Since Saint Thorlak is the only Icelander to have been recognized as a saint by the papacy, its contents have a special local significance.[41]

Abraham threw himself into the study of the Saint Thorlak liturgy, and it occupied most of his time in the 1950s. In 1953, he visited Nashdom Abbey in Buckinghamshire, England, receiving guidance from the eminent chant scholar Dom Anselm Hughes. Abraham was fascinated by his stay in the abbey, where he found that the monks lived "completely beyond time itself," as he put it.[42] He would use each trip abroad as an opportunity to research the provenance and context of the Saint Thorlak liturgy in libraries better equipped than those in Iceland, such as the Bibliothèque nationale in Paris, Staatsbibliothek in Berlin, Copenhagen's Royal Library, and London's British Museum. The last provided him with the missing piece in the puzzle of the music's provenance. In a thirteenth-century manuscript of Dominican liturgical items (British Library, Add. 23935), he was able to locate the models for nearly all of the Saint Thorlak chants, whose origins were, until then, unknown. Thus, Abraham could demonstrate that although the texts of the Icelandic liturgy—Latin verse in praise of Saint Thorlak—were the work of an anonymous local poet, the music itself was imported, a sign of a significant link between Iceland and the European traditions of medieval chant.[43]

Having studied the Saint Thorlak liturgy for eight years, Abraham defended his thesis for a doctorate in musicology at the University of Iceland on November 10, 1959 (see fig. 8.3). He wrote his dissertation in German but was delighted that it should be accepted at the local university, not least since its topic was music for an Icelandic saint.[44] His opponents at the defense were Magnús Már Lárusson, a local professor of church history, and Bruno Stäblein, the renowned German musicologist, who became a valued colleague and friend. Abraham's academic achievement was widely noted in Iceland and earned him great acclaim; after this, in accordance

Figure 8.3. From Robert Abraham's doctoral defense at the main hall of the University of Iceland, November 1959. At the podium is German musicologist Bruno Stäblein. *Source:* © Elín Þ. Ólafsdóttir, private collection. Used with permission.

with Icelandic tradition, he was commonly referred to by his friends and colleagues as "doktor Róbert."[45] It was a remarkable accomplishment not least because having had to flee Germany after only two years of university education, the doctorate was Abraham's only academic degree.

Abraham's dissertation on the Saint Thorlak liturgy was his most ambitious scholarly work, but when time allowed he continued his research on Icelandic music history. With assistance from Stäblein, he traced a two-part song from a seventeenth-century Icelandic collection—*Heyr þú oss himnum á*, recently made famous through a poignant choral arrangement by Anna Þorvaldsdóttir—to a *Sanctus* from continental Europe, found in several continental manuscripts from the fifteenth and sixteenth century.[46] He also published essays on a medieval theoretical fragment and the processional singing of the monks at Þingeyrar monastery in Northern Iceland, and contributed to internationally renowned dictionaries, writing four entries for the *Cultural-Historical Encyclopedia of the Nordic Middle Ages* (*Kulturhistorisk leksikon for nordisk middelalder*) and the entry on Iceland for the *New Grove Dictionary of Music and Musicians*.[47] He attended international conferences and symposia, including the International Josquin Conference in New York in 1971, and was widely respected in the international scholarly community for his erudition.

Although Abraham was Iceland's first musicologist of note, he had no direct students or followers in the field.[48] The University of Iceland had no department of musicology, and Abraham's later work there was limited to teaching music and liturgy in the theology department, as part of preparing young priests and theologians for their future work (see below). Thus, a continuation of his musicological work did not really take place until the early 2000s, with the founding of the Iceland University of the Arts and several local musicologists returning home after studies abroad.

Abraham: Ode to Joy

With the demise of the Reykjavík Music Society Choir in 1952, performances in Iceland of large-scale choral works came to a sudden halt. It was a deplorable situation that threatened to undo all of Victor Urbancic's pathbreaking work, yet the leaders of the Iceland Symphony waited until after his death to arrange for a satisfactory alternative. In 1959, board members Ragnar Jónsson and Þorsteinn Hannesson, along with its general manager, Jón Þórarinsson, approached Robert Abraham about leading a new choral society that would operate in conjunction with the orchestra. Þórarinsson later remarked that they had been prompted by the fact that Abraham was, at that moment, "without a choir," a situation they found unacceptable.[49] It was, to be sure, an opportune moment. With his dissertation virtually complete, Abraham had more time on his hands, and the Philharmonia Choral Society (*Söngsveitin Fílharmónía*) was officially established in April 1959, a mixed ensemble of roughly seventy singers, although it grew considerably in size over the ensuing decade.

A full year later, in April 1960, the Philharmonia Choral Society made its debut with the Iceland Symphony, augmented by singers from the National Theater Chorus, in the local premiere of Carl Orff's *Carmina Burana*. From then on, a large concert by the Philharmonia and the symphony, performing one of the masterworks of the choral repertoire, became a major annual event in Reykjavík's cultural life: Brahms's *German Requiem* (1961, see fig. 8.4), Handel's *Messiah* (1963 and 1973), Mozart's Requiem (1964), Bach's Magnificat and Stravinsky's *Symphony of Psalms* (1965), Beethoven's Ninth Symphony (1966 and 1970) and *Missa solemnis*

Figure 8.4. Robert Abraham rehearsing the Philharmonia Choral Society and the Iceland Symphony Orchestra in Brahms's *German Requiem*, November 1961. Photo: Kristján Magnússon. *Source:* © Elín Þ. Ólafsdóttir, private collection. Used with permission.

(1970), Verdi's Requiem (1968), Dvořák's Te Deum (1972), and Haydn's *The Creation* (1973). Through his work with the Philharmonia, Abraham became Iceland's uncontested leader of symphonic choral works, and, in a sense, Urbancic's successor in the field. These were all works close to his heart; once, when a reporter asked Abraham what work he had found most enjoyable to perform with the choir, he replied: "All of them! I'm such a fortunate man that I've always gotten to conduct the music I love."[50]

Nearly all of the Philharmonia's concerts featured music being introduced to Icelandic audiences for the first time. The only works previously heard were *Messiah* and Mozart's Requiem (under Urbancic's direction) and *The Creation* (conducted by Ísólfsson). Abraham also continued Urbancic's efforts of introducing works in Icelandic translation. Earlier performances of *Messiah* had been in English, presumably since more people spoke that language than German, but for both his performances, Abraham used an Icelandic translation by poet Þorsteinn Valdimarsson. Earlier on, when working with the Harpa Choral Society and the Radio Choir, Abraham had also commissioned translations for works in German, including Bach cantatas. His reasoning was the same as Urbancic's: that the music could have its full and desired effect only if both the performers and the audience could fully grasp the meaning of the text.

Abraham's working methods occasionally caused conflict, even publicly. For example, shortly before a performance of Mozart's Requiem in 1964, it was announced that Þuríður Pálsdóttir would not sing the soprano solo, since, as one newspaper reported, "after rehearsals began, she and the conductor disagreed about the work's interpretation."[51] In her autobiography, Pálsdóttir gave her account of the incident: at the first soloist rehearsal, Abraham insisted that she sing more quietly than she found appropriate, and she became so exasperated that she put her score on the piano and left the rehearsal, saying "Get someone else to sing this." Abraham tried to make peace and asked the bass soloist to convey his apologies, but Pálsdóttir would not be budged.[52] She had been a close and valued colleague for years, as one of the leading members in the Radio Choir and later as a soloist in *Carmina Burana*, but this led to a permanent rift in their friendship, and they did not speak again for years.[53]

Each of the Philharmonia's concerts with Robert Abraham were regarded as major events, but one project had greater significance than all the others. In February 1966, the choir performed Beethoven's Ninth Symphony five times to a sold-out audience in Háskólabíó, the university cinema that opened in 1961. The Icelandic premiere of the Ninth Symphony was seen as symbolic of the country's rapid cultural progress since its independence. Shortly before the millennial celebrations of the Icelandic Parliament in 1930, composer Jón Leifs had suggested performing Beethoven's Ninth with a local choir and an orchestra imported from Germany, but even this had proved impossible to arrange.[54] Just over three decades later, the moment had arrived. After the first concert, Jón Þórarinsson wrote in a review: "Now that great moment has arrived when we Icelanders have become co-owners, along with other cultural nations of the world, of one of the greatest gifts mankind has received: Beethoven's Ninth Symphony."[55]

The Ninth was a work of special significance to Abraham, who had sung the finale with the Bruno Kittel choir in Berlin during his student days, and conducted the entire work from memory. Yet, leading up to the Reykjavík performance, even Abraham's colleagues were skeptical of the enterprise, feeling that such a large undertaking was premature and that neither the choir nor the orchestra yet possessed the skills required for such a demanding work. One choir member recalls that, as he put it, many locals were convinced that "now we were attempting something that Icelanders just weren't yet ready to do."[56] Another choir member maintained that even the executives of the Iceland Symphony had their doubts, and that Árni Kristjánsson, the National Radio's head of music, had remarked, referring to Abraham: "Well, I suppose it is best to let him make a fool of himself, for once."[57] The performances proved the skeptics wrong, and the town's most fervent music aficionados were said to have attended all five concerts.[58]

Following up on the Ninth Symphony's success, the orchestra's executives approached the choir for an even more ambitious project: Beethoven's *Missa solemnis*, to be conducted by the orchestra's Polish chief conductor, Bohdan Wodiczko. The members of the Philharmonia held Abraham in high regard and saw this proposal to be "a thinly veiled statement of no confidence" regarding his abilities.[59] Although symphony orchestras around the world rely on choral directors to prepare their ensembles for performances conducted by others, this was not yet common in Iceland; both Urbancic and Abraham had always conducted their own respective ensembles when performing with an orchestra. Rehearsals for *Missa solemnis* began in autumn 1966, but without Abraham, who expressed his doubts that the choir was ready for such a demanding work. Instead, three young local musicians were hired to lead rehearsals, but after only a few weeks, it became clear that choir members were displeased with the arrangement, and the concert was canceled. When local media approached the orchestra's management for an explanation, they were told it had proved impossible to recruit enough male voices for the choir.[60]

Despite his earlier reservations, Abraham himself conducted the Philharmonia Choral Society in Beethoven's *Missa solemnis* in 1970, to mark the choir's tenth anniversary as well as the composer's bicentenary. It was certainly the most challenging project the choir had ever undertaken, and, judging from reviews, the results were mixed. While most critics were courteous, pointing out that the local premiere of such a difficult work was a major achievement in itself, some were more critical; it was the only time that a large-scale concert with Abraham was, at least partly, so poorly received. In one weekly paper, an anonymous reviewer complained that the choir had been "terribly out of tune, particularly the female voices, and a disgrace to its conductor, the nation, and themselves."[61] That critic also dismissed a positive review that the performance had received from Stefán Edelstein, since he and Abraham were on such friendly terms that his review couldn't be taken seriously. It was true that Edelstein was Abraham's former student and trusted colleague, but the anonymous reviewer may also have been insinuating that immigrant musicians formed some kind of loose "immigrant clique" that praised each other in public.

While Abraham continued to appear as conductor with the Iceland Symphony Orchestra, his work there became less frequent in the 1960s. This was largely due to his demanding and varied schedule: teaching at the university, rehearsing the Philharmonia, and supervising music for the Lutheran church (see below). He was also displeased with the orchestra's haphazard scheduling, and its limited size; as late as 1965, he had to rearrange the wind parts of Stravinsky's *Symphony of Psalms*, as the work's demands for five flutes and four oboes could not be met.[62] Still, he conducted at least one orchestra concert each season—apart from his collaborations with the Philharmonia—and his programs often included local premieres. For example, he conducted the first complete Icelandic performance of Stravinsky's *Oedipus Rex* in December 1971, nearly twenty-five years after leading the Craftmen's Choir in its opening chorus (see chapter 6). Other significant local premieres by Abraham in the late 1960s and early 1970s were Anton Bruckner's Symphonies nos. 3 and 4, as well as Gustav Mahler's Symphony no. 1 and *Das Lied von der Erde*. Abraham was particularly delighted to have an opportunity to perform the latter, for since Mahler had died before giving the work's premiere, his assistant, Bruno Walter, who later became Abraham's idol, conducted the first performance in Munich in 1911. Abraham himself had heard Walter conduct *Das Lied von der Erde* on two occasions, first in Berlin as a teenager, and again at the Edinburgh Festival in 1947, with the Vienna Philharmonic and with Kathleen Ferrier and Peter Pears as soloists.

Abraham: Composer and Arranger

As a composer, Robert Abraham was not prolific and never did much to promote his own work in the field. He could even gently poke fun at his efforts, for example when preparing one of his compositions for performance by the Philharmonia Choral Society a few years before his death. When writing out the choral score, he attributed the work to a completely unknown composer by the name of Trebor Maharba—which happens to be Robert Abraham spelled backward.

Abraham's lack of activity as a composer is likely explained by his busy schedule, and composing was hardly the most lucrative profession in Iceland during his lifetime. Several student works from Berlin have survived (see chapter 1), but some of the works he composed in Iceland appear to exist only in part, or have been lost. His overture written for the Icelandic play *The Dance at Hruni* (*Dansinn í Hruna*), produced by the Akureyri Theater in 1937, has survived complete, and orchestral parts exist for an *Overture on Old English Folk Songs*, written for the National Theater's 1950 production of Dickens's *The Cricket on the Hearth*.[63] His *Ride to Þingvellir* (*Þingvallareið*), written for the boys at the Reykjavík Gymnasium choir in 1941, exists in sketch form only. In 1953, he composed a setting of Psalm 148, presumably intended for choir and orchestra, for which only the choral parts have survived.[64]

Another composition from Abraham's years in Akureyri that has survived in full is *The Shrew* (*Svarkurinn*), a four-minute setting for SATB choir and piano of a poem by nineteenth-century author Grímur Thomsen. Abraham composed the piece for his Akureyri choir, and it was premiered at their Easter concert in 1940, after which one enthusiastic critic declared it "nothing less than a masterpiece."[65] This work was performed again by the National Radio Choir in spring 1949, and that performance has been preserved on a shellac record.[66] It does not appear to have been performed since, although a set of performing materials from around 1970 suggests that Abraham intended to revive it with the Philharmonia Choir around that time.[67] The text tells of a shrew who, when approaching the end of her life, is desperate to secure a place in either heaven or hell, although even the demons of the underworld threaten a revolt should she be accepted there. Although its poetic language is complex, the text was likely among the ones Abraham encountered when learning Icelandic in Akureyri; he later reminisced that his friends had studied Thomsen's works with him during his early years there. His setting, which includes an important role for a solo bass who narrates the story, must have been a considerable challenge for his Akureyri singers in 1940.

Two of Abraham's Icelandic works are settings of sacred texts. For Christmas 1943, he gifted his wife his setting for voice and piano of *That Wondrous Night* (*Nóttin var sú ágæt ein*), a Christmas poem by the early modern priest-poet Einar Sigurðsson (1539–1626). In 1967, he wrote an *Icelandic Kyrie* (*Miskunnarbæn*) for SATB choir and piano, to verses from Icelandic religious poetry from the fifteenth and sixteenth centuries. The work was premiered by the Philharmonia Choral Society the following year, under Abraham's direction, at a concert celebrating the thirtieth anniversary of the National Association of Mixed Choirs.[68] The setting is influenced by Abraham's work as a scholar, as its modally inflected themes have a distinctly medieval flair. In a contrasting middle section, he asks the choir to recite a medieval prayer verse, in canon and *sotto voce*.

Figure 8.5. Robert Abraham after an orchestra rehearsal in March 1960. *Source:* © Elín Þ. Ólafsdóttir, private collection. Used with permission.

Abraham was far more active as an arranger, and some of his work in this field remains in the repertoire of Icelandic choral groups. His arrangements always served a practical purpose, filling up his own concert programs or as favors to friends and colleagues. He arranged several Icelandic folk songs for the National Radio Choir in the late 1940s, and for the choir of Hamrahlíð Gymnasium, founded by his student Þorgerður Ingólfsdóttir in 1967, he made excellent arrangements of the student songs *Gaudeamus igitur* and *Du alte Burschenherrlichkeit*, as well as the Bohemian carol *Come, All Ye Shepherds*. His scholarly interest in the Saint Thorlak liturgy also inspired two short fanfares for brass ensemble, both titled *Intrada on Themes from Þorlákstíðir*, intended for graduation ceremonies at the University of Iceland in the 1960s.[69]

Abraham was also noted for his improvisatory skills. His controversial concert in Akureyri in 1936 (see chapter 3) included a piano fantasy on three well-known Icelandic songs; when the concert was repeated soon afterward, he selected different songs, including a well-known lullaby, *Sleep, My Young Love* (*Sofðu, unga ástin mín*). Critic Áskell Snorrason wrote that the former improvisation had been "a distinguished work," while the latter, he said, was "an excellent testament to his outstanding talent and training, along with a lively, creative imagination and understanding of the nature of Icelandic folk song."[70] Abraham would also sometimes display his improvisatory skills at parties, when he would sit down at the piano and play a short theme, before extemporizing in the styles of various composers. According to one eye-witness, he would preface each variation with something along the lines of: "This is how Beethoven would have treated it; here is what Schumann would have done; Mozart might have done something like this."[71]

Abraham: Church Music Director

In an unlikely twist of fate, the "Jew" Robert Abraham came to hold a prestigious position as the music director (*söngmálastjóri*) of the Icelandic National (Lutheran) Church, an official denomination to which, in the mid–twentieth century, around 90 percent of the population belonged. The post of music director, established in 1941, was initially held by a local church musician, Sigurður Birkis (1893–1960). Upon Birkis's death, Abraham, who had recently defended his doctoral thesis, was appointed and assumed the role in 1961. His main objective was to encourage and support music-making in local church parishes, including congregational hymn singing, which at the time was in a state of decline, as local church choirs had improved notably in the postwar years and were largely carrying hymn singing on their own. Abraham was convinced that both factors had to be strong: "It isn't enough to have a good church choir, if the congregation is silent and doesn't sing at all," he said in an interview in 1961.[72]

Abraham held the post of Church Music Director until his death and was an ambitious proponent of church music in various forms. He established a Church Music School (*Tónskóli Þjóðkirkjunnar*) to educate church organists and cantors; in the early years, the school was operated from a single room on the upper floor of Abraham's home. He organized courses for organists and choir directors who lived and worked in the countryside, traveling across Iceland to provide continuing education for church musicians on the local parish level. He also wished to give the younger generation an opportunity to learn more about the church's music traditions, and thus in the 1960s he initiated the Church Choir School, which provided introductory courses in hymn singing, liturgy, and music history to university students and young professionals in Reykjavík and surrounding towns.

Perhaps Abraham's greatest contribution to Icelandic church music was his substantial work as an arranger of hymns for practical use within the service. He published two important collections of his own arrangements: *Seven Hymns* for three equal voices (1964) and *22 Sacred Songs* for mixed choir (1967), where his main source was the *Graduale*, the sixteenth-century missal of the early Lutheran church in Iceland. These arrangements demonstrate his ambition and consummate skill as arranger, and many are still in the repertoire of local choirs in Iceland. Abraham also introduced to Lutheran Iceland a form of the mass ordinary with unaccompanied monophonic chant. Since the 1930s, local parishes had performed choral responses in traditional Romantic style, composed by cathedral organist Sigfús Einarsson, which enjoyed great popularity.[73] Regarded as "popish" and too old-fashioned, the monophonic liturgy met with considerable resistance at first. Yet Abraham was convinced of its value, and it eventually replaced Einarsson's responses in Protestant churches throughout the island.[74]

The church also benefited from Abraham's talents as choral conductor, not least in connection with the consecration of a new cathedral at Skálholt, an important historical site of Christianity in southern Iceland from the eleventh century onward. It also had a connection to Abraham's scholarly work, since Saint Thorlak had been bishop there in the twelfth century. In the eighteenth and nineteenth centuries, as Iceland was ravaged by economic and natural disasters, the large cathedral in Skálholt had been replaced with a much smaller church, but with the new republic a push was made for a substantial modern cathedral to be built in its place.[75] For the consecration ceremony, in July 1963, Abraham formed and rehearsed an ensemble that became known as the Skálholt Choir, consisting of locals from the countryside surrounding the church, most of them untrained in music and with little experience of choral singing. A far easier solution would have been to bring in one of Reykjavík's finest choirs to perform at the ceremony, but Abraham wished instead to create a permanent foundation for music-making in the new church. For three months leading up to the consecration ceremony, he would take a bus to Skálholt—in those days, a three-hour bus ride on dirt roads—where he rehearsed local farmers and housewives on Thursday and Friday evenings, and then took the bus back to Reykjavík on Saturday.[76] In the end, it proved to be worth the effort. Until Abraham's death, the Skálholt Choir performed under his direction once each summer, at the Skálholt Festival held on Saint Thorlak's feast of translation.

Another of Abraham's lasting contributions as church music director was a simple idea that he asked a colleague of his to execute. In 1972, the Icelandic Lutheran Church issued a new hymnal, and the Bishop concurrently formed a five-member editorial committee to supervise an addendum to it. Among its members were Abraham and composer Þorkell Sigurbjörnsson, his former student at the Reykjavík Music School, who would become Iceland's leading composer of sacred choral music. Abraham was particularly fond of a medieval hymn, *Hear, Heaven's Maker* (*Heyr, himna smiður*), by the Icelandic chieftain Kolbeinn Tumason, supposedly written shortly before his violent death in a battle in 1208. While this is the oldest surviving hymn text written by an Icelander in the native language, it had been set to music only once, by an amateur composer in the early twentieth century.[77] That setting had never gained popularity, and Abraham found it a shame that no suitable melody existed for such a beautiful hymn text. He urged Sigurbjörnsson to try his hand at it, and the result came sooner than expected. The composer later recalled that as he was driving back home from the editorial meeting, in a winter storm with treacherous road conditions in the city, the tune began to take form in his mind.[78] He completed his setting soon afterward, and Abraham conducted the first performance with the Skálholt Choir in summer 1973.[79] Sigurbjörnsson's haunting melody, poignantly harmonized, has for decades been one of Iceland's most loved hymns. Internationally, it became widely known in 2013, when members of the Icelandic band *Árstíðir* (Seasons) gave an impromptu performance at a train station in Wuppertal, Germany, which went viral and reached millions of viewers online within a few months.⁸⁰ More recently, it has entered the repertoire of leading choral ensembles such as Voces8, who recorded it in 2021.

Yet another part of Abraham's duties on behalf of the Lutheran Church was his teaching at the University of Iceland's Theology Department. He began work there as an adjunct lecturer in 1961, and five years later was appointed Associate Professor of Liturgical Music. For the first time, music became an important part of the training of theology students, with Abraham teaching theory, music history, and hymnology.⁸¹ The chair of the theology department later recalled that Abraham had been a passionate advocate for music in the curriculum, and that he had insisted that all students take part, even those who described themselves as tone-deaf or unmusical.⁸² Abraham became a much-admired faculty member, and, in 1970, he was the third professor to be presented with the "Student Star," an award given by the Student Union for outstanding teaching and mentorship.⁸³ Originally, it was planned that Abraham would also conduct the University Choir as part of

Figure 8.6. Robert Abraham and his wife, Guðríður Magnúsdóttir, listening to the Philharmonia Choral Society singing on their doorstep on Abraham's sixtieth birthday, May 17, 1972. *Source:* © Elín Þ. Ólafsdóttir, private collection. Used with permission.

his faculty duties, but limited interest among students, along with his busy schedule, led to these plans being shelved.[84] On the other hand, he directed a smaller choral ensemble of theology students at various events, primarily within the department itself.

Abraham: Last Farewell

In March 1974, Abraham traveled to Sweden to attend a conference on Nordic hymnology at Lund University. Shortly after arriving there, he had a serious heart attack and was immediately taken to the local hospital. His wife Guðríður arrived from Iceland soon afterward, and for a few days his condition appeared to be improving. He was due to be discharged the following day when he suffered another, fatal attack. Robert Abraham, or Róbert Abraham Ottósson, as he had been known for twenty-five years, passed away on March 10, 1974, two months short of his sixty-second birthday. His funeral was held at the Reykjavík Cathedral, and he was buried in the city's Fossvogur Cemetery.

Abraham's death came as a massive shock to the cultural community in Iceland. He had been incredibly active in a variety of fields, as a scholar, teacher, arranger, conductor of choirs and orchestras, and many saw him as simply irreplaceable. In a eulogy, one of the leaders of the Icelandic Musicians' Union wrote that "A more devastating void could hardly have been left in Icelandic musical life, and it will never be filled."[85] Pianist Rögnvaldur Sigurjónsson noted that Abraham's arrival in 1935 was "probably one of the greatest blessings that musical life in Iceland has ever received, and his influence will be felt in nearly all its fields for a long time."[86] Gylfi Þ. Gíslason, a former culture minister, emphasized that with his talent, Abraham could have made a career anywhere in the world, and that his countrymen owed him an enormous debt for his wide-ranging contribution:

> His work was not only a source of joy and growth, but also increased the faith of both his audiences and fellow musicians in the future potential of culture in Iceland. When remembering Róbert A. Ottósson, it is understandable that gratitude for his unforgettable moments on the podium should immediately spring to mind. But perhaps even more valuable was the courage that he gave to his country by taking on projects that must have seemed insurmountable, and then commanding them so

thoroughly—the optimism that he, with his energy, expertise, and talent, nurtured and intensified in the minds of all those to whom he brought his message, and those who delivered it with him.[87]

Abraham's wife, Guðríður Magnúsdóttir, died in 1990, after sixteen years of widowhood. Their son, Grétar Ottó Róbertsson, was an orthopedic surgeon, working in both Iceland and Sweden. He passed away in 2021.

Influence and Legacy

Since their deaths, the legacies of Victor Urbancic, Heinz Edelstein, and Robert Abraham have been preserved and passed on to new generations of Icelandic musicians and music lovers. Many of their students were for decades among the country's most prominent musicians, whether as singers, instrumentalists, composers, conductors, or teachers. Institutions they helped establish and nurture remain active today: the Iceland Symphony Orchestra, the National Theater, the Philharmonia Choral Society, and Edelstein's music school.

Abraham's career in Iceland was twice as long as those of Edelstein and Urbancic, and thus it is only natural that of the three, his influence should continue to be felt most strongly. This is particularly true in the field of church music, since many of his students were organists or priests in important parishes for decades after his death. In a more general sense, the Philharmonia Choral Society and the Hamrahlíð School Choir, which was founded by his student Þorgerður Ingólfsdóttir in 1967 through Abraham's influence, have continued his legacy as a choral conductor. After Abraham's death, the Philharmonia took a while to regain its bearings, which it finally did in the 1980s under the direction of Martin Hunger, or, to give his Icelandified name, Marteinn H. Friðriksson—another exiled musician, who arrived from East Germany in 1964 and lived in Iceland until his death in 2010.[88]

It is difficult to fully grasp the musical characteristics of Abraham, Edelstein, and Urbancic as interpreters because their surviving recordings are largely inaccessible. They all recorded substantially for the National Radio, predominantly in the 1940s and 1950s, when Urbancic and Edelstein were employed by the Reykjavík Music Society and Abraham conducted the National Radio Choir. Most of these early recordings, largely on 78-rpm shellac records, are preserved in the National Radio archive; only some have been digitized, and none is publicly accessible. Their later recordings, with the Symphony Orchestra and the Philharmonia Choir, were done on tape and have considerably better sound quality, but these are largely as inaccessible to the public as the older discs.

Only a handful of their recordings were ever released commercially. In 1949, Urbancic and the Music Society Choir made several 78-rpm records on behalf of His Master's Voice and its Icelandic representative (*Fálkinn*); these included Jón Leifs's *Requiem*, works by Björgvin Guðmundsson and Páll Ísólfsson, as well as Urbancic's own folk song arrangements. Selections from Robert Abraham's concerts with the Philharmonia Choir—Brahms's *German Requiem* and Handel's *Messiah*, the latter a recording of his final concert, in December 1973—were released on a single 33-rpm record in 1979. A CD release from 1993, containing archival recordings by pianist Rögnvaldur Sigurjónsson, includes Schumann's Piano Quintet in a live performance from 1948, in collaboration with the Reykjavík Music School quartet, with Heinz Edelstein on cello and Hans Stepanek on violin. The sound engineer in charge of the broadcast serendipitously captured the performance on shellac records. When they were rediscovered more than forty years later, they turned out to be in pristine condition, as they had been broadcast only once since the original performance.[89] While Urbancic's and Abraham's choral and orchestral performances were limited by the available forces, the performance of Schumann's Quintet with Edelstein and friends is truly outstanding, and a worthy memorial to his talent.

In twentieth-century Iceland, it was common for busts to be made of important cultural or political figures, intended to be displayed in appropriate public spaces. Melitta Urbancic herself sculpted a bust of her husband, which was unveiled to mark his seventieth birthday in 1973 (see fig. 8.7). Soon after Abraham's death, the Choir of Skálholt Cathedral and alumni of the Reykjavík School of Music commissioned a bust of him from the Icelandic sculptor Sigurjón Ólafsson, which was unveiled in 1977. No official memorial exists for Heinz Edelstein, but his legacy lives on in the school that he established, now called Tónmenntaskóli Reykjavíkur. There, roughly 170 children aged five to fifteen study music each year.[90] Several former students of the school have achieved considerable success on the international music scene, including singer Björk Guðmundsdóttir, who studied flute there as a child, and pianist Víkingur Ólafsson.

Abraham's choral arrangements were often heard in the years following his death. For example, the Langholtskirkja Church Choir gave a concert

Figure 8.7. Eiríka Urbancic unveils her mother's bust of Victor Urbancic in the National Theater of Iceland on what would have been his seventieth birthday in 1973. *Source:* © Eiríka Urbancic, private collection. Used with permission.

dedicated to his sacred arrangements only a few months after his death in 1974, and released an LP album later that same year.[91] His original compositions have been less frequently performed, although the Hamrahlíð Choir released his *Icelandic Kyrie* on an LP in 1983 and has performed it several times since. A memorial concert held at Skálholt Cathedral in spring 1975, featuring five choirs, soloists, and instrumentalists in a total of two hundred performers, proved influential in another way.[92] Concerts had only rarely been held in the church since its inauguration in 1963, but harpsichordist Helga Ingólfsdóttir was so impressed by the church's acoustics that she soon afterward arranged a summer concert series there. It has continued ever since and has been an important contribution to musical life, not least in the fields of Renaissance and Baroque music.[93]

Urbancic's compositions have occasionally been heard in Iceland since his death. A memorial concert at the National Theater in 1958 included several rarely performed works, such as the *Overture to a Comedy* and the

Concertino for three saxophones, performed by the Iceland Symphony Orchestra, and the Violin Sonata from 1924 performed by Björn Ólafsson and Jórunn Viðar, who also performed the Sonatina for piano and the youthful *Caprices mignons*.[94] The Iceland Symphony has performed the *Overture to a Comedy* several times since, including under Chief Conductor Rumon Gamba in 2003. The *Fantasy-Sonata* was released on CD by clarinetist Kjartan Óskarsson and pianist Hrefna Eggertsdóttir in 1994, and the first performance of *Ode to Skálholt* in 1996 was a significant event. In recent years, Urbancic's music has been featured more frequently in live performance, for example with portrait concerts in the Sigurjón Ólafsson Art Museum in 2019 and 2023.

The artistic work of both Victor and Melitta Urbancic has also received considerable attention in Austria and Germany in recent years. Austrian scholars have examined Urbancic's career there, particularly within the context of institutional histories of the Mainz and Graz conservatories, where he was employed.[95] A more public kind of acknowledgment was seen at the Graz Conservatory in 2019, when the school's choir hall was named the Victor Urbancic Auditorium. His own music was performed at the dedication ceremony, including an arrangement of an Icelandic folk song to Melitta's German translation. In 2022, the Berlin-based *musica reanimata*, a society dedicated to performing works of composers persecuted by the Nazi regime, sponsored an evening of Urbancic's music at the Berlin Konzerthaus. Later that year, a selection of Melitta's poetry was published in German, as was Agneta Hauber's doctoral dissertation on her poetry.[96] In 2023, Austrian soprano Marina Colda, along with pianist Julia Tinhof, released a disc titled *Vorahnung*, containing twenty-three songs by Urbancic, a landmark release and the first album dedicated entirely to his music.

In contrast, the lives and work of Robert Abraham and Heinz Edelstein have received little attention in German or Anglo-American scholarship. This is to some extent understandable: Abraham had no career as a professional musician in Germany except for his tenure in Berlin from 1955–1957, and Edelstein was never a public figure during his years in Freiburg or at the Odenwaldschule. His name is occasionally mentioned in books about Jewish musical life in the Third Reich, particularly for his participation in the Jewish Culture League orchestra.[97] A more recent manifestation of the stories of Heinz and Charlotte Edelstein appeared onstage, in New York City in February 2023. In *Doomsday Scrolling*, a theater work exploring the effects of war on twelve women from various times and places, actress Ylfa

Edelstein took on the role of her grandmother, portraying the story of her earlier life in Germany and flight to Iceland.[98]

Fictional Stories

While the stories of German émigrés in Iceland have most commonly been told by historians, they have also occasionally provided inspiration for fictional works, such as novels that take place during World War II or in the postwar years. The earliest novel of this kind was published in 1989, *The Jew's Street Song* (Icelandic title: *Götuvísa gyðingsins*) by Einar Heimisson, a scholar who also wrote a doctoral thesis on immigration policies in the Nordic countries in the 1930s. He based his novel on the actual story of the Jewish couple Hans and Olga Rottberger, who arrived in Reykjavík in 1935 but were deported three years later along with their two young children. Although the Icelandic authorities had no scruples about sending them back to certain death in Germany, the ship they were on made a landing in Copenhagen, where they were fortunate enough to receive residence permits and survive the war.[99] Heimisson himself met and interviewed Olga Rottberger, and also presented her story in nonfiction form, including an extensive interview for Icelandic television. His novel does not specifically feature music, except for a scene in which the couple visits Reykjavík Cathedral, where an "influential" organist performs a work by Bach for them in the empty church.[100] The model here is Páll Ísólfsson, who according to the Rottberger's later account was kind to them during their stay and once invited them to a private concert at the cathedral.[101]

Böðvar Guðmundsson's 2009 novel, *Morning Continues* (Icelandic title: *Enn er morgunn*), tells the tale of Johannes Kohlhaas, a young German-Jewish musician, whose escape from the Nazi regime is unique and unexpected in that he is entrusted by no less a personage than Heinrich Himmler to journey to Iceland in search of remnants of *Ur*-Germanic culture. The charming and intelligent Kohlhaas soon wins the respect of locals, but when the British occupy Iceland, he is arrested and deported to the United Kingdom. As was pointed out when the book was published, many details of Kohlhaas's story are based on an actual person, German linguist Bruno Kress, who was deported to the Isle of Man in 1940, yet he was neither Jewish nor a professional musician.[102] Rather, in his book Guðmundsson weaves together two stories, those of Kress and Robert Abraham, whose charm and musical talent were legendary. The author himself made Abraham's acquaintance in 1962, when the latter taught students at the Reykjavík Gymnasium a few Icelandic folk songs for a school performance of an Icelandic play, in which Guðmundsson played the leading role.[103] Thus, it is hardly a coincidence that, in the novel, Kohlhaas has the job of conducting that same gymnasium's choir.

In author Sjón's 2019 novella *Red Milk* (Icelandic title: *Korngult hár, grá augu*), which takes place in the postwar years, certain characters correspond directly to actual persons. The main protagonist is Gunnar Kampen, a young Reykjavík man from an affluent family. His future seems bright, but he finds himself aligned with neo-Nazis, and he establishes an anti-Jewish political party. Among other things, the book explores how events and experiences in childhood can direct a person to a dark path later in life. Gunnar's mother sings in the Reykjavík Mixed Choir, as it is called in the book, under the direction of Robert Abraham. One scene takes place at an afternoon tea in the Kampen family home, where Abraham is a guest of honor, surrounded by admirers. The boy, however, finds Abraham "loud and disagreeable," and his presence also annoys another guest, the Nazi occultist Savitri Devi, an actual person who visited Iceland in 1946–1947.[104] On this afternoon, some kind of dispute breaks out between Devi and Abraham, but the other guests side with the musician, and the Nazi thus retreats from the living room. Later, Kampen receives from an anonymous sender a typewritten list of Jews residing in Reykjavík and other Icelandic towns. The list bears the heading "ENEMIES OF ICELAND—1ST CATEGORY, JEWS" and among the names listed are Abraham, Edelstein, and Urbancic, along with other actual exiles, such as Karl Kroner and Kurt Zier.[105] In the end, Kampen's deranged neo-Nazi ideals come to a sudden close, for he is found dead on a train in England.

The Urbancic family story has been a source of inspiration for Austrian writer Rudolf Habringer, who has written not only biographic essays on Urbancic but also a full-length novel, *Island-Passion*, published in 2008. Its protagonist is a young Austrian, Richard Behrend, who travels to Iceland in 1972. There, he hears of the artistic achievements of his compatriot, musician Karl Wallek, who had fled Graz in 1938 because of Nazi persecution—just as Urbancic did. The story of Wallek's fate won't leave Behrend alone, but as he tries to find out more about his life and work, he also realizes how his own life story seems to echo that of the long-deceased musician.[106] *Island-Passion* is the largest work of fiction based specifically on the stories of one of the exiled musicians in Iceland, and most details of Wallek's biography are directly modeled on that of Urbancic and his family.

Postlude

Although their specific achievements have begun to fade from living memory, Heinz Edelstein, Victor Urbancic, and Robert Abraham are still considered among the "founding fathers" of the Icelandic music scene. They certainly had an immense influence on the growth of music in Iceland from 1935 to 1974, and their contribution ensured that the development of choirs, orchestras, music education, and scholarship occurred more rapidly than it would have under other circumstances. In recent decades, their stories have been brought to light and seen as increasingly relevant as the country's immigration policy has come under scrutiny for its lack of procedural fairness and equity. In this context, the lives and careers of these three musicians have been remembered not only for their own sake but also, in a wider context, taken the form of a history lesson for younger generations.

My own involvement with their life stories dates back to spring 2001, when I was working on my doctoral dissertation at Harvard University. One morning, I received an email from Icelandic literary scholar Þröstur Helgason, who was then editor of *Morgunblaðið*'s Saturday culture section. He had heard of my work and asked if I might be interested in contributing a series of articles on the musicians that had fled the Nazi regime to Iceland. As this was a topic completely unrelated to my dissertation, I took a few days to consider it, but the idea proved irresistible. During my summer break that year, I contacted members of the Abraham, Edelstein, and Urbancic families, who graciously shared their stories with me, and the articles appeared, as double-page spreads with large images, on three consecutive Saturdays in July 2001.[1]

At that time, I had been living and studying in the United States for nearly a decade, and had not paid particular attention to Iceland's ongoing debates on immigration policy. It wasn't until the first article appeared that it became clear to me that the original idea for the series had come from *Morgunblaðið*'s chief editor, Styrmir Gunnarsson, who had himself studied music with Heinz Edelstein as an eight-year-old boy and always recalled his former teacher with affection.[2] In the same issue as my article on Edelstein, he wrote an extended editorial in which he drew explicit parallels between the situation of the 1930s and the growing threat of racism and xenophobia in the early twenty-first century. While my objective had simply been to commemorate the artistic achievements of these three musicians, Gunnarsson urged his readers to draw from them a sobering lesson for our own century:

> In our times, when there is much discussion as to whether racism is becoming more prevalent here, it is useful to recall that people who come here from other countries play an important role in creating a more varied and constructive society. It is therefore nothing but narrow-mindedness, rooted in ignorance, to object to people moving here from other countries. On the contrary, we should welcome them with open arms, as the stories of these three aforementioned men demonstrate how valuable they were to our society.[3]

Gunnarsson asserted that Icelanders had a "unique opportunity" to create a "model society" in their country, adding: "A nation that has created for itself such an agreeable existence cannot be known for letting prejudice towards people of foreign background become prevalent."[4]

The stories of foreign musicians in Iceland have been told often and in different guises, both before and after my articles for *Morgunblaðið*. In a groundbreaking radio series, first broadcast on Icelandic National Radio in 1997, Sigríður Stephensen told the stories of the foreign musicians who lived and worked in Iceland in the 1930s and '40s, including the three exiles as well as Franz Mixa, Carl Billich, Jan Morávek, and others. A particularly valuable feature of this series were interviews with the musicians' colleagues and family members, many of whom have since passed away. From a scholarly perspective, in 2013 the Austrian-Icelandic historian Óðinn Melsted wrote a BA thesis devoted to foreign musicians in Iceland from 1930–1960, and his study was later published in book form by the Icelandic Historical Society.[5]

A more unconventional view of history appeared in *Homeland*, an exhibition by the U.S. artist-musician Erik DeLuca in Reykjavík's Marshall House in summer 2021. There, he presented an artist's view of the Icelandic authorities' ruthless response to asylum applications in the 1930s.

DeLuca, whose grandmother was a Holocaust survivor, had photographed all applications and related documents at the Icelandic National Archives, and these were projected on several large screens in a continual loop. On one wall of the exhibition space, Melitta Urbancic's poem *Home By Right* (*Heimatrecht*) could be read in three languages, including a translation by her great-granddaughter, Katherine Caldwell. Another wall showed only the inscrutable abbreviations and logos found in the Justice Department's correspondence, representing the menial process of bureaucracy. Its antithesis could be seen on the floor, which was covered with lyme grass, a reminder that even fragile life can grow to improve its environment under the right conditions. As DeLuca himself explained: "Lyme grass sucks up nitrogen from the air and brings it down to the soil. It rejuvenates damaged soil."[6]

Similar parallels with history continue to be drawn, and the legends of the "founding fathers" of Icelandic music are still evoked in discussions of current immigration policies. For example, in autumn 2021, Iranian musician Elham Fakouri, a recent graduate of the music department of the Iceland University of the Arts, was denied a work permit despite having lived in the country for three years. This decision was widely criticized, and taken up by local media. In *Lestin* (*The Train*), a cultural program on the National Radio, Fríða Björk Ingvarsdóttir, dean of the Iceland University of the Arts, weighed in on the situation. She urged the authorities to take a more open-minded approach regarding immigrants and asylum seekers, declaring that Icelandic society was, sadly, too homogeneous for its own good. Specifically, she cited the stories of the exiled musicians from the Third Reich as proof that immigrants had long had "an invaluable impact on Iceland's cultural heritage, especially in the field of music. And, today," she added, "we simply regard these people as Icelandic."[7] The remonstration was successful, and Fakouri was allowed to stay.

Public discussion of the topic continued in December 2021, when the producers of the radio program *Lestin* examined more closely the stories of exiles and immigrants to Iceland in the 1930s.[8] In a mini-series titled *Heavy Conscience* (*Á samviskunni*), producer Anna Marsibil Clausen interviewed well-known Icelandic musician Benedikt H. Hermannsson, who is also the great-grandson of Prime Minister Hermann Jónasson, about his family history. She also discussed the topic with Sibyl Urbancic, who drew explicit parallels between the current global refugee crisis and Jónasson's attempt to deport her entire family: "We experience such things all the time; once every few months here in Iceland, but every single day in Austria and anywhere in the world. Children are being deported from countries where they've already settled and are in contact with other children and are happy and have friends, and all of a sudden they're not allowed to stay there anymore. In my mind, this is so horrendous; there's hardly anything that I think is a greater crime against children than this."⁹

In Gunnarsson's *Morgunblaðið* editorial, quoted above, as well as other writings both before and after, the lives of Heinz Edelstein, Victor Urbancic, and Robert Abraham have been used to draw a picture of "model refugees" who enriched their host country's culture more than anyone could have imagined. While this is of course true, it must also be noted that they were all in an uncommonly privileged position, as highly educated, white, upper-middle-class, Central European males. Their acceptance into Iceland at that particular time was a rare exception, a result of powerful locals aspiring, on a personal level as well as on behalf of the entire nation, to the cultural capital associated with classical music. In this context, it should also be noted that, in recent decades, many other emigrés have continued to enrich Iceland's musical life. As before, some arrived of their own volition in search of adventure, but others were driven into exile because of conditions in Eastern Europe preceding or immediately following the collapse of communism, for example from Poland, Hungary, and the Baltic States. The contribution of these individuals to music in Iceland has also been invaluable and still remains to be studied in detail.

Through their tireless and ambitious work, Heinz Edelstein, Victor Urbancic, and Robert Abraham made a lasting contribution to culture in Iceland. While their specific efforts may have largely faded from memory, their achievements live on in the institutions they helped to create, and the musicians they trained. They arrived in a country that had virtually no professional music scene, yet now, less than a century later, Iceland is known, to quote a 2023 article in *The Guardian*, as a "seed bed for musical talent" that includes musicians of all genres: Björk and Sigur Rós, Víkingur Ólafsson and Anna Þorvaldsdóttir, Hildur Guðnadóttir and Laufey.¹⁰ Such progress would hardly have been possible without the prodigious talent and ambition of the three exiled musicians discussed here. In today's world, the stories of Edelstein, Urbancic, and Abraham are doubly relevant: worth remembering both for the remarkable success of their achievements, and as a small part of the global phenomenon of exiled musicians able to forge new lives even as their old ones crumble.

Acknowledgments

This book has been a long time in the making. My first publication on these three musicians dates back to 2001, and a more extensive article on Robert Abraham followed on his centenary in 2012. The idea of writing a full-length study came only later, during a month-long stay in Berlin in 2019, when I discovered documents related to Abraham in the Archive of the Academy of Arts. Thanks to a subsequent grant from the Icelandic Research Fund, I was able to devote myself fully to the project for three years and complete the present study.

My profound thanks go to the children and grandchildren of Robert Abraham, Heinz Edelstein, and Victor Urbancic for sharing their stories with me through personal reminiscence, as well as allowing me access to letters, photographs, and other invaluable material. Special thanks go to Sibyl, Pétur, and Eiríka Urbancic, Stefán Edelstein, Monika Keller, Benjamin and Ylfa Edelstein, Elín Þ. Ólafsdóttir, and Ásdís Lovísa Grétarsdóttir. Sadly, Grétar Ottó Róbertsson passed away soon after I began writing this book, but I am thankful he was able to follow its progress in the early stages and share with me many valuable memories. My gratitude to all of them is immense, and I hope it is adequately reflected in the work itself.

Many others have also assisted my research in one way or another. Heide Sommer welcomed me to her home in Wacken, Germany, where she told me about her mother's love for Robert Abraham and showed me dozens of letters he had written to her parents after the war. Ibrahim Assaf, the Ambassador of Lebanon in Austria, generously showed me the Urbancic family home in Vienna, which is now his residence. Aðalheiður Þorsteinsdóttir, Anna Jórunn Stefánsdóttir, Corinne Halter, Gunnar Hrafnsson, Hildigunnur Halldórsdóttir, Kristján Árnason, and Regine Hildebrandt kindly allowed me access to unpublished material. Many others have shared their own recollections, or discussed with me various aspects of the topic. Listing them all (in Icelandic alphabetical order) is in no way an adequate expression of my gratitude, but it will have to do: Árni Björnsson, Bergljót Sigríður Einarsdóttir, Bjarki Sveinbjörnsson, Böðvar Guðmundsson, Erik DeLuca, Albrecht Dümling, Christian Fastl, Gerður G. Bjarklind, Guðfinna Dóra Ólafsdóttir, Gunnar Kvaran, Hanna Kristín Stefánsdóttir, Haukur Guðlaugsson, Helga Kress, Lily E. Hirsch, Hjálmar H. Ragnarsson, Renee Schepses Hoffman, Jón Nordal, Jónas Tómasson, Katrín Fjeldsted, Lilja Árnadóttir, Margarete Froelicher-Grundmann, Mirjana Plath, Rudolf Habringer, Sigríður Ragnarsdóttir, Sigrún Löve, Sigurjón Birgir Sigurðsson, Vigdís Finnbogadóttir, Vilhjálmur Örn Vilhjálmsson, Þorgerður Ingólfsdóttir, and Þórarinn Óskarsson.

I owe an enormous debt to a whole consortium of archivists in Iceland, Germany, and Austria, for their assistance in locating and accessing a plethora of archival documents. In particular, I would like to thank the staff at the National Archives of Iceland and the National and University Library in Reykjavík, who showed admirable patience as I sifted through a seemingly endless stream of boxes and folders in their collections. My thanks also go to the staff of the Staatsbibliothek zu Berlin, where I had the good fortune of doing research during the summer months of 2022 and 2023.

At SUNY Press, Richard Carlin was a model of patience and support. My thanks also go to Eleanor Goodman and John Wentworth for their expert copyediting, and to three anonymous readers for their helpful comments. Also, my sincere thanks to Claudia Macdonald, George Fisher, Hjálmar H. Ragnarsson, and Þorvaldur Kristinsson, all of whom read early drafts of this book and made valuable suggestions.

Last but not least, I am grateful to my family, in particular my parents, Sigrún and Eggert, and sister, Elín, who were the first and most enthusiastic readers of the initial draft, and who have been unfailingly supportive from start to finish.

Notes

Introduction

1. Pamela Potter, "Kunst und Musik in der NS-Zeit: Was wir wissen und was wir zu wissen glauben," in *Stand und Perspektiven der NS-Forschung in der Musik*, eds. Klaus Aringer, Susanne Kogler, and Markus Helmut Lenhart (Graz: Leykam Buchverlag, 2021), 12.

Chapter 1

1. Stefan Zweig, *Die Welt von Gestern. Erinnerungen eines Europäers* (Ditzingen: Reclam, 2023), 15.
2. For more on the history of the house at Gymnasiumstraße 59, see Heidi Brunnbauer, *Im Cottage von Währing/Döbling . . . Interessante Häuser—interessante Menschen* (Gösing/Wagram: Edition Weinviertel, 2003), 125–127.
3. See Mira Delavec Touhamin and Franc Križnar, eds., *Josipina Urbančič Turnograjska* (Preddvor: KD Josipine Turnograjske, 2018).
4. Walter Killy et al., ed., *Dictionary of German Biography* (Munich: K.G. Saur, 2006), 10:173.
5. Ruth Erb (Urbancic), "Æskuminningar" (typewritten memoir), 1–2 (private collection, Sibyl Urbancic).
6. Melitta Urbancic, biographical essay on Victor Urbancic (private collection, Sibyl Urbancic).
7. Sibyl Urbancic, interview with the author, August 18, 2019.
8. Melitta Urbancic, biographical essay on Victor Urbancic (private collection, Sibyl Urbancic).
9. Victor Urbancic, notebooks (private collection, Sibyl Urbancic).
10. Melitta Urbancic, biographical essay on Victor Urbancic (private collection, Sibyl Urbancic).

11. Peter Berger, "Exiles of Eden: Vienna and the Viennese During and After World War I," *1914: Austria-Hungary, the Origins, and the First Year of World War I*, eds. Günter Bischof, Ferdinand Karlhofer, and Samuel R. Williamson Jr. (New Orleans: University of New Orleans Press, 2014), 178.

12. Brigitte Biwald, "Krieg und Gesundheitswesen," in *Im Epizentrum des Zusammenbruchs. Wien im Ersten Weltkrieg*, eds. Alfred Pfoser and Andreas Weigl (Vienna: Metroverlag, 2013), 294–301.

13. Viktor Urbantschitsch, "Die Entwicklung der Sonatenform bei Brahms," *Studien zur Musikwissenschaft* 14 (1927): 265–85; Urbantschitsch, "Die Sonatenform bei Brahms: ein Beitrag zur Geschichte der Instrumentalmusik," dissertation, Universität Wien, 1925. Urbancic's work is still referred to in recent monographs on Brahms's music, see for example Margaret Notley, *Lateness and Brahms: Music and Culture in the Twilight of Viennese Liberalism* (Oxford: Oxford University Press, 2007), 40.

14. Sibyl Urbancic, interview with the author, September 6, 2022.

15. Sibyl Urbancic, interview with the author, September 6, 2022.

16. Sibyl Urbancic, interview with Anna Marsibil Clausen in *Lestin*, Iceland National Radio, first broadcast December 15, 2021.

17. Sibyl Urbancic, interview with the author, August 18, 2019.

18. Ernst Urbantschitsch to Victor Urbancic, Vienna, April 1, 1939 (private collection, Sibyl Urbancic).

19. The exchange of letters between Mitterer and Rilke is published in Rainer Maria Rilke and Erika Mitterer, *Besitzlose Liebe. Der poetische Briefwechsel*, ed. Katrin Kohl (Berlin: Insel, 2018).

20. Gunilla Eschenbach, "Nachwort," in Melitta Grünbaum, *Begegnungen mit Gundolf*, ed. Gunilla Eschenbach (Marbach am Neckar: Deutsche Schillergesellschaft, 2012), 87–88.

21. For more on Melitta Urbancic and her poetry, see Gunilla Eschenbach, "Nachwort," 85–98; Agnete Hauber, *Melitta Urbancic: Lyrik am Rand der Welt. Exil und Integration in Island* (Berlin: Peter Lang: 2022).

22. Robert Stalla, *Theater in der Josefstadt 1788–2030, Architektur, Geschichte, Kultur* (Munich: Hirmer Verlag, 2021), 1:137–38, 263.

23. Dietrich Höroldt, *Bonn. Von einer französischen Bezirksstadt zur Bundeshauptstadt, 1794–1989* (Bonn: Dümmlers Verlag, 1989), 397–99.

24. During Emanuel Edelstein's lifetime, the family lived at Friedrichstraße 16, but after his death, Ida and the children moved to Meckenheimer Straße 58; that house no longer stands, and since 1978 the street has been called Thomas-Mann-Straße; email from Tim Glander (Stadtarchiv Bonn), November 23, 2022; Stadtarchiv Bonn, Emanuel Edelstein, Meldekarte.

25. Dr. Emanuel Edelstein, "Die Aufgabe der jüdischen Turner," *Jüdische Turn-Zeitung* 7 (1900): 73–75; Max Bodenheimer to Edelstein, January 21, 1901, and other letters in the Central Zionist Archives, Jerusalem.

26. Ruth Schepses to German authorities (Entschädigungsbehörde), Hollis, NY, March 28, 1954 (Landesamt für Bürger- und Ordnungsangelegenheiten Berlin,

documents concerning Ida Edelstein); "Aus den Städtischen Nachrichten," *Bonner Zeitung*, January 23, 1917. http://bonn1914-1918.de/chronik-1917/59-januar-1917/980-1917_01_23.html

27. Dr. Emil Cohn, "Dr. Emanuel Edelstein, Worte an seinem Grabe" (private collection, Stefán Edelstein).

28. "Aus den Städtischen Nachrichten," *Bonner Zeitung*, January 25, 1917, http://bonn1914-1918.de/59-chronik-1917/januar-1917/982-1917_01_25.html. Dr. Edelstein's grave is located in the Jewish cemetery of Bonn-Castell.

29. Renee Schepses Hoffman, interview with the author, January 28, 2022.

30. Badische Albert Ludwigs-Universität Freiburg, Abgangszeugnis (private collection, Stefán Edelstein).

31. Abgangszeugnis (Heinz Edelstein), Archiv Humboldt-Universität zu Berlin.

32. Email from Heather Forster, Humboldt-Universität zu Berlin, February 22, 2021; email from Thomas Becker, Universität Bonn, March 19, 2021.

33. Dietrich Höroldt, *Bonn. Von einer französischen Bezirksstadt zur Bundeshauptstadt, 1794–1989*, 486–92.

34. Annette Morreau, *Emanuel Feuermann* (New Haven, CT: Yale University Press, 2002), ix, 268–91.

35. Markus Zepf, "Wilibald Gurlitt," in *Lexikon verfolgter Musiker und Musikerinnen der NS-Zeit*, eds. Claudia Maurer Zenck, Peter Petersen, and Sophie Fetthauer, Hamburg: Universität Hamburg, 2017. www.lexm.uni-hamburg.de/object/lexm_lexmperson_00001984

36. Heinz Edelstein, *Die Musikanschauung Augustins nach seiner Schrift "De musica,"* Ohlau, 1929; Philipp Jeserich, *Musica Naturalis: Speculative Music Theory and Poetics from Saint Augustine, to the Late Middle Ages in France*, trans. Michael J. Curley and Steven Rendall (Baltimore: Johns Hopkins University Press, 2013), 55.

37. Leopoldine Schwalbach, *Zum Bericht über eine Generation*, ed. Thomas Lindemann (Karlsruhe: Info Verlagsgesellschaft, 1997), 182, 193, 208–13.

38. Charlotte Edelstein-Schottländer, "Der Solidarismus als wirtschaftstheoretisches System," dissertation, Albert-Ludwigs-Universität, Freiburg im Breisgau, 1929.

39. Heinz Edelstein to Wiedergutmachungsbehörde, March 10, 1950, Staatsarchiv Freiburg, F 196/1-2465.

40. Stephan Würthle, *Der Birklehof—Ein deutsches Landerziehungsheim in nationalsozialistischer Zeit*, 2nd edition (Freiburg im Breisgau: Albert-Ludwigs-Universität, Historisches Seminar, 1998), 43; Heinz Edelstein, report on Wiedergutmachung, Staatsarchiv Freiburg, F 196/1-2465.

41. Erik Levi, *Music in the Third Reich* (New York: St. Martin's Press, 1994), 1.

42. The house was destroyed in World War II; the house later built in its place is now Genthiner Straße no. 28; see Landesamt für Bürger- und Ordnungsangelegenheiten, Berlin, 258.018, files on Robert, Lise, and Peter Abraham.

43. Otto Abraham, "Über den Erfolg der Künstlichen Frühgeburt," dissertation, Friedrich-Wilhelms-Universität zu Berlin, 1894.

44. "Góðir Íslendingar," *Vísir*, December 14, 1961.

45. Otto Abraham, "Das absolute Tonbewußtsein," *Sammelbände der internationalen Musikgesellschaft* 3 (1901): 1–86; Viktoria Tkaczyk, "The Testing of a Hundred Listeners: Otto Abraham's Studies on 'Absolute Tone Consciousness,'" in *Testing Hearing: The Making of Modern Aurality*, ed. Tkaczyk et al., 49–51.

46. A full list of Abraham's recordings is in Susanne Ziegler, *Die Wachszylinder des Berliner Phonogramm-Archivs* (Berlin: Staatliche Museen zu Berlin—Preußischer Kulturbesitz, 2006), 83–98.

47. George and Eve List, "Translator's Preface," in Otto Abraham and Erich M. von Hornbostel, "Suggested Methods for the Transcription of Exotic Music," *Ethnomusicology* 38 (1994): 425. For a recent, more critical analysis of their research, see Benjamin Steege, "Between Race and Culture: Hearing Japanese Music in Berlin," *History of Humanities* 2 (2017): 361–74.

48. Otto Abraham to Marcus Rubin, Berlin, December 13, 1910, Det kongelige bibliotek, Copenhagen, NKS 4596 4to, I, 1.

49. Robert Abraham, family tree (private collection, Elín Þ. Ólafsdóttir); David Paisey, "Adolphus Asher (1800–1853): Berlin Bookseller, Anglophile, and Friend to Panizzi," *The British Library Journal* 23 (1997): 150. https://de.wikipedia.org/wiki/Moritz_Daniel_Volkmar

50. See the bibliography of articles co-authored with Hornbostel in Erich Moritz von Hornbostel, *Tonart und Ethos. Aufsätze zur Musikethnologie und Musikpsychologie* (Wilhelmshaven: Florian Noetzel, 1999), 369–77.

51. Otto Abraham to Marcus Rubin, Berlin, January 9, 1913, Det kongelige bibliotek, Copenhagen, NKS 4596 4to, I, 1.

52. Abraham, "Das absolute Tonbewußtsein," 69.

53. Gunnar Björnsson, "Sögur og tilvitnanir," http://filharmonia.is/index.php?option=com_content&view=article&id=115&Itemid=115; see also Carl Stumpf, *The Origins of Music*, ed. and trans. David Trippett (Oxford: Oxford University Press, 2012), 35–36.

54. Björn Magnússon and Gunnar Þorsteinsson, "Dr. Róbert Abraham Ottósson heimsóttur," *Stúdentablaðið* 48 (1971): 10.

55. The National Archives of Iceland, Róbert Abraham Ottósson, 2012-002, BA/6, 3.

56. Robert Abraham to the University of Iceland, Reykjavík, October 2, 1958; The National Archives of Iceland, Róbert Abraham Ottósson 2012-002, A/4, 4.

57. Landesamt für Bürger- und Ordnungsangelegenheiten, Berlin, 258.018, files on Robert, Lise, and Peter Abraham; Grétar Ottó Róbertsson, interview with the author, June 30, 2021. A death announcement was printed in *Berliner Tageblatt und Handels-Zeitung* on January 26, 1926, 10.

58. Erich von Hornbostel, "Otto Abraham †," *Psychologische Forschung* 7 (1926): 291–93.

59. Lise Abraham to Lis Jacobsen, Berlin, October 10, 1926, Lis Jacobsen Collection, Det Kongelige Bibliotek, Copenhagen, no. 489.

60. The National Archives of Iceland, Róbert Abraham Ottósson 2012-002, BI/3, 3; BI/4, 1. In 1933, Lise Abraham and her sons resided at Giesebrechtstraße 7 in the Charlottenburg district, a bit further west than their earlier home; they likely moved to a smaller apartment after Otto Abraham's death. By 1936, Lise had moved yet again, and seems to have lived at 33 Nürnberger Straße until she left Germany; see The National Archives of Iceland, Róbert Abraham Ottósson, BI/3, 3; *Amtliches Fernsprechbuch für den Bezirk der Reichspostdirektion Berlin.* https://digital.zlb.de/viewer/image/15849352_1936/45

61. Robert Abraham, curriculum vitae (1961), The National Archives of Iceland, Róbert Abraham Ottósson 2012-002, A/2, 9; Albrecht Dümling, "On the Road to the "Peoples' Community" [Volksgemeinschaft]: The Forced Conformity of the Berlin Academy of Music under Fascism," *The Musical Quarterly* 77 (1993): 459; see also Eta Harich-Schneider, *Charaktere und Katastrophen. Augenzeugenberichte einer reisenden Musikerin* (Berlin: Ullstein, 1978), 89. As a child, Robert also took harpischord lessons with Alice Ehlers, who had been Wanda Landowska's first pupil and who later moved to California; she was a good friend of Lise Abraham, Robert's mother. See Robert Abraham, curriculum vitae [1954], The National Archives of Iceland, Róbert Abraham Ottósson 2012-002, A/2, 9; Lise Abraham to Lis Jacobsen, Berlin, October 10, 1926, Lis Jacobsen Collection, Det Kongelige Bibliotek, Copenhagen, no. 489.

62. Robert Abraham, interviewed by Þorkell Sigurbjörnsson, *Vaka*, Iceland National Radio, first broadcast December 10, 1971.

63. Robert Abraham, "Bruno-Walter-Minning," typewritten radio manuscript in The National Archives of Iceland, Róbert Abraham Ottósson 2012-002, K/4, 3.

64. Newspaper clippings in The National Archives of Iceland, Róbert Abraham Ottósson, K/3, 15.

65. The National Archives of Iceland, Róbert Abraham Ottósson 2012-022, D/2, 2.

66. Róbert A. Ottósson, "Adolf Busch," *Morgunblaðið*, August 25, 1945.

67. Erik Ryding and Rebecca Pechefsky, *Bruno Walter—A World Elsewhere* (New Haven, CT and London: Yale University Press, 2001), 142.

68. Robert Abraham to Bruno Walter, Reykjavík, January 20, 1954; Bruno Walter to Robert Abraham, Beverly Hills, February 16, 1954, The National Archives of Iceland, Róbert Abraham Ottósson 2012-002, A/2.

69. "Flísin er týnd, en núna á hann sprota meistarans," *Mynd*, September 19, 1962.

Chapter 2

1. Michael Schäbitz, "The Flight and Expulsion of German Jews," in *Jews in Nazi Berlin: From Kristallnacht to Liberation*, cited in Snorri G. Bergsson, *Erlendur*

landshornalýður?, Flóttamenn og framandi útlendingar á Íslandi, 1853–1940 (Reykjavík: Almenna bókafélagið, 2017), 160.

2. Kathrin Clausing, *Leben auf Abruf. Zur Geschichte der Freiburger Juden im Nationalsozialismus* (Freiburg: Stadtarchiv Freiburg im Breisgau, 2005), 71.

3. Lily E. Hirsch, *A Jewish Orchestra in Nazi Germany*, 3.

4. Hirsch, *A Jewish Orchestra in Nazi Germany*, 4.

5. See Marion A. Kaplan, *Between Dignity and Despair: Jewish Life in Nazi Germany* (New York: Oxford University Press, 1998), 74–83.

6. Gabriele Fritsch-Vivié, *Gegen alle Widerstände. Der Jüdische Kulturbund 1933–1941* (Berlin: Hentrich & Hentrich Verlag, 2015), 20.

7. Hirsch, *A Jewish Orchestra in Nazi Germany*, 2.

8. Donald Niewyk, *The Jews in Weimar Germany*, 80, quoted in Marion A. Kaplan, *Between Dignity and Despair: Jewish Life in Nazi Germany* (New York: Oxford University Press, 1998), 13.

9. Gabriele Fritsch-Vivié, *Gegen alle Widerstände*, 15.

10. Hirsch, *A Jewish Orchestra in Nazi Germany*, 1.

11. Marion A. Kaplan, *Between Dignity and Despair*, 12.

12. Kaplan, *Between Dignity and Despair*, 5.

13. Hirsch, *A Jewish Orchestra in Nazi Germany*, 32.

14. Jens Malte Fischer, *Richard Wagners Das Judentum in der Musik. Eine kritische Dokumentation als Beitrag zur Geschichte des Antisemitismus* (Würzburg: Königshausen & Neumann, 2015), 19–21; see also Hirsch, *A Jewish Orchestra in Nazi Germany*, 32.

15. Hirsch, *A Jewish Orchestra in Nazi Germany*, 34–35.

16. Hirsch, *A Jewish Orchestra in Nazi Germany*, 133–34.

17. Theo Stengel and Herbert Gerigk, *Lexikon der Juden in der Musik* (Berlin: Bernhard Hahnefeld Verlag, 1940), 57; see also Erik Levi, *Music in the Third Reich*, 64.

18. Levi, *Music in the Third Reich*, 67.

19. Levi, *Music in the Third Reich*, 49.

20. Kaplan, *Between Dignity and Despair*, 70–71.

21. Herbert A. Strauss, "The Movement of People in a Time of Crisis," in *The Muses Flee Hitler: Cultural Transfer and Adaptation, 1930–1945*, eds. Jarrell C. Jackman and Carla M. Borden (Washington, DC: Smithsonian Institution Press, 1983), 49–50; Maren Köster, "Musik-Remigration nach 1945. Konturen eines neuen Forschungsfelds," in *"Man kehrt nie zurück, man geht immer nur fort." Remigration und Musikkultur*, eds. Maren Köster and Dorte Schmidt (Munich: edition text + kritik, 2005), 20.

22. Peter Gay, "'We Miss Our Jews': The Musical Migration from Nazi Germany," in *Driven into Paradise: The Musical Migration from Nazi Germany to the United States*, eds. Reinhold Brinkmann and Christoph Wolff (Berkeley: University of California Press, 1999), 21.

23. Herbert A. Strauss, "The Movement of People in a Time of Crisis," in *The Muses Flee Hitler*, 50–51; Florian Scheding, "'Problematic Tendencies': Émigré

Composers in London, 1933–1945," in *The Impact of Nazism on Twentieth-Century Music*, ed. Erik Levi (Vienna: Böhlau, 2014), 248; Irving Abella and Harold Troper, "Canada and the Refugee Intellectual, 1933–1939," in *The Muses Flee Hitler*, 263–64.

24. Jarrell C. Jackman, "Introduction," in *The Muses Flee Hitler*, 24.

25. Sabine Feisst, *Schoenberg's New World: The American Years* (New York: Oxford University Press, 2011), 331, fn. 327.

26. Claudia Maurer Zenck, "Challenges and Opportunities of Acculturation: Schoenberg, Krenek, and Stravinsky in Exile," in *Driven into Paradise: The Musical Migration from Nazi Germany to the United States*, eds. Reinhold Brinkmann and Christoph Wolff (Berkeley: University of California Press, 1999), 176; Gay, "'We Miss Our Jews,'" 29.

27. Cf. Jarrell C. Jackman, "Introduction," *The Muses Flee Hitler*, 16.

28. Gay, "'We Miss Our Jews,'" 21.

29. Jean Medawar and David Pyke, *Hitler's Gift: The True Story of the Scientists Expelled by the Nazi Regime* (New York: Arcade Publishing, 2000); see also Dorothy Lamb Crawford, *A Windfall of Musicians: Hitler's Émigrés and Exiles in Southern California* (New Haven, CT: Yale University Press, 2009), ix: "Hitler's (unintentional) Gift to American Music."

30. Gay, "'We Miss Our Jews,'" 21.

31. Gay, "'We Miss Our Jews,'" 24; Hanns-Werner Heister, Claudia Maurer Zenck, Peter Petersen, "Einleitung: Vor sechzig Jahren began die Vertreibung," in *Musik im Exil. Folgen des Nazismus für die internationale Musikkultur*, eds. Heister, Zenck, and Petersen (Frankfurt am Main: Fischer, 1993), 18.

32. Pierre Bourdieu, *Distinction: A Social Critique of the Judgement of Taste*, trans. Richard Nice (Cambridge, MA: Harvard University Press, 1987), 18.

33. See Albrecht Riethmüller, "Musik, die "deutscheste" Kunst," in *Verfemte Musik. Komponisten in den Diktaturen unseres Jahrhunderts*, eds. Joachim Braun, Vladimir Karbusický, and Heidi Tamar Hoffmann (Frankfurt am Main: Peter Lang, 1995), 91–103; Celia Applegate and Pamela Potter, "Germans as the "People of Music": Genealogy of an Identity," in *Music and German National Identity*, eds. Celia Applegate and Pamela Potter (Chicago: University of Chicago Press, 2002), 1–3.

34. Paula Berger, report on Heinz Edelstein, August 7, 1950, Staatsarchiv Freiburg, F 196/1-2465.

35. Stefán Edelstein, interviewed by the author, August 23, 2019. The schoolmaster at Birklehof, Wilhelm Kuchenmüller, was said to have been fond of Nazism, but he was also a humanist. It has been suggested that his party membership may have given him more leeway with the Nazis, enabling him to protect Jews at his institution for as long as he did; see Stefan Würthle, *Der Birklehof*, 49–74.

36. Theo Kellner to Heinz Edelstein, Freiburg, June 14, 1934 (private collection, Stefán Edelstein).

37. Charlotte Edelstein, "Aufbruch ins Ungewisse," typewritten manuscript (private collection, Stefán Edelstein).

38. Birklehof school authorities to Nazi officials, November 23, 1935, quoted in Stephan Würthle, *Der Birklehof*, 56.

39. Hans Hinkel (on behalf of the *Reichsmusikkammer*) to Heinz Edelstein, Berlin, July 11, 1936 (private collection, Stefán Edelstein).

40. Heinz Edelstein, Wiedergutmachung report, Staatsarchiv Freiburg, F 196/1-2465.

41. Wolfgang Edelstein, interviewed by Christoph Lindenmayer, Bayerischer Rundfunk, December 12, 2006. www.br.de/fernsehen/ard-alpha/sendungen/alpha-forum/wolfgang-edelstein-gespraech100-attachment.pdf?

42. Charlotte Edelstein, Wiedergutmachung report, Staatsarchiv Freiburg, F 196/1-4371.

43. Charlotte Edelstein was baptized as Roman-Catholic in the St. Liobannunnery near Freiburg on November 30, 1935; her sons were baptized in summer 1937; Archiv des Deutschen Caritasverbandes, Freiburg, 284.1.016 E.

44. Stefán Edelstein, interviewed by the author, August 23, 2019.

45. Deutscher Caritasverband, Freiburg, April 30, 1955; Charlotte Edelstein, Wiedergutmachung report, Staatsarchiv Freiburg, F 196/1-4371.

46. Wolfgang Edelstein, interviewed by Christoph Lindenmayer, Bayerischer Rundfunk, December 12, 2006. www.br.de/fernsehen/ard-alpha/sendungen/alpha-forum/wolfgang-edelstein-gespraech100-attachment.pdf?

47. Hirsch, *A Jewish Orchestra in Nazi Germany*, 9–13; see also Gabriele Fritsch-Vivié, *Gegen alle Widerstände: Der Jüdische Kulturbund 1933–1941*, 29–42.

48. Eva Hanau, *Musikinstitutionen in Frankfurt am Main, 1933 bis 1939* (Cologne: Studio, 1994), 80.

49. For a listing of the activities of the *Jüdischer Kulturbund*, see Stephan Stompor, "Uraufführungen 1933–1941 im Jüdischen Kulturbund und durch weitere jüdische Ensembles in Berlin und anderen Städten," in *Verfemte Musik. Komponisten in den Diktaturen unseres Jahrhunderts*, eds. Joachim Braun, Vladimir Karbusický, and Heidi Tamar Hoffmann (Frankfurt am Main: Peter Lang, 1995), 66–67.

50. Lily E. Hirsch, "Germany's Commemoration of the Jüdischer Kulturbund," in *Dislocated Memories: Jews, Music, and Postwar German Culture*, eds. Tina Frühauf and Lily E. Hirsch (Oxford: Oxford University Press, 2014), 243; see also Hirsch, *A Jewish Orchestra in Nazi Germany*, 27; Kurt Düwell, "Jewish Cultural Centers in Nazi Germany: Expectations and Accomplishments," in *The Jewish Response to German Culture: From the Enlightenment to the Second World War*, eds. Jehuda Reinharz and Walter Schatzberg (Hanover, NH & London: University Press of New England, 1985), 314–15.

51. Hirsch, *A Jewish Orchestra in Nazi Germany*, 29–30; Eike Geisel and Henryk M. Broder, *Premiere und Pogrom. Der Jüdische Kulturbund 1933–1941* (Berlin: Siedler, 1992), 26.

52. Eva Hanau, *Musikinstitutionen in Frankfurt am Main*, 93.

53. Antje Kalcher, "Julius Prüwer," in *Lexikon verfolgter Musiker und Musikerinnen der NS-Zeit*, eds. Claudia Maurer Zenck and Peter Petersen. www.lexm.uni-hamburg.de/object/lexm_lexmperson_00002153

54. Joachim Carlos Martini, *Musik als Form geistigen Widerstandes. Jüdische Musikerinnen und Musiker 1933–1945, Das Beispiel Frankfurt am Main* (Frankfurt am Main: Brandes & Apsel, 2010), 2:310.

55. Herbert Freeden, "Jüdischer Kulturbund ohne jüdische Kultur," quoted in Marion A. Kaplan, *Between Dignity and Despair*, 47.

56. Kurt Michaelis, quoted in Lily E. Hirsch, "Germany's Commemoration," 245.

57. Martha Hirsch, quoted in Hirsch, "Germany's Commemoration," 245.

58. "ff," "Jüdischer Kulturbund Hannover," *Nachrichtenblatt, Amtliches Organ der Synagogen-Gemeinde Hannover*, May 21, 1937, 1–2.

59. Kathrin Massar, "Symphonieorchester des Jüdischen Kulturbunds Rhein-Main/Frankfurt am Main," "Hans Wilhelm Steinberg—In memoriam," https://oper-frankfurt.de/media/pdf/AusstellungWilliamSteinberg.pdf; Levi, *Music in the Third Reich*, 57.

60. "Það er gaman að lifa á þessum þroskaárum íslenzkrar tónlistar," *Heimilispósturinn* 2/3 (1951), 2.

61. Albrecht Dümling, "On the Road to the 'Peoples' Community,'" 464.

62. Dümling, "On the Road" 464, 466; "Vortragsabend," Staatliche akademische Hochschule für Musik, February 8, 1933 (program in Archiv Universität der Künste, Berlin). The program did not include music by Abraham.

63. Dümling, "On the Road," 469 and 477.

64. Robert Abraham to Oskar Fried, Akureyri, July 19, 1936 (private collection, Elín Þ. Ólafsdóttir).

65. See Fred K. Prieberg, *Musik im NS-Staat* (Cologne: Dittrich, 2000), 285; Pamela M. Potter, *Most German of the Arts: Musicology and Society from the Weimar Republic to the End of Hitler's Reich* (New Haven, CT: Yale University Press, 1998), 173. Otto Abraham is listed in the infamous *Lexikon der Juden in der Musik*, eds. Theo Stengel and Herbert Gerigk, 16.

66. "Vierhändiges Klavierstück" (marked "1932—Emmy!"), National Archives of Iceland, Róbert Abraham Ottósson 2012-002, BI/4, 1.

67. Heide Sommer, *Lassen Sie mich mal machen: Fünf Jahrzehnte als Sekretärin berühmter Männer* (Berlin: Ullstein, 2019), 16.

68. Heide Sommer, email to the author, April 5, 2020.

69. Emmy Grenz to Robert Abraham, Bad Kissingen, June 20, 1948; Emmy Grenz to Robert Abraham, Bad Kissingen, February 2, 1949 (private collection, Elín Þ. Ólafsdóttir); Robert Abraham to Emmy Grenz, Reykjavík, December 7. 1948, Robert Abraham to Emmy Grenz, Reykjavík, May 8 and 23, 1964 (private collection, Heide Sommer).

70. Heide Sommer, email to the author, April 5, 2020; see also Robert Abraham's diary, 1966, National Archives of Iceland, Róbert Abraham Ottósson 2012-002, C/1, 4, 71.

71. Archiv der Akademie der Künste, Berlin, Hermann Scherchen-Archiv no. 292 and 293.

72. Robert Abraham, scrapbook, 1934–1953 (private collection, Elín Þ. Ólafsdóttir). While no records document the attendance at the concert, invitations were sent to many of the world's leading musicians in Paris at the time, including Stravinsky, Prokofiev, Ravel, Poulenc, Kurt Weill, Alfred Cortot, Nadia Boulanger, and Wanda Landowska (Archiv Akademie der Künste, Berlin, Hermann Scherchen-Archiv no. 293). Abraham's former teacher, Curt Sachs, was present, and in a later recommendation he praised his performance there as that of "a conductor who is both temperamental and controlled" (Sachs, recommendation for Robert Abraham, Paris, April 11, 1935, copy in National Archives of Iceland, Róbert Abraham Ottósson 2012-002, A/3, 6).

73. Henry Prunières, quoted in David Josephson, "The Exile of European Music: Documentation of Upheaval and Immigration in the *New York Times*," in *Driven into Paradise: The Musical Migration from Nazi Germany to the United States*, 99.

74. Kristian Hvidt, *Forsker, Furie, Frontkæmper. En bog om Lis Jacobsen* (Copenhagen: Gyldendal, 2011), 312, 342–44; Vilhjálmur Örn Vilhjálmsson, *Medaljens bagside. Jødiske flygtningeskæbner i Danmark, 1933–1945* (Copenhagen: Forlaget Vandkunsten, 2005), 225.

75. Abraham and Lis Jacobsen had most likely first met in Berlin during her visits there a few years earlier. She was there for a conference in 1929 and lectured at Berlin University in 1930, and she is known to have met Robert and Peter Abraham at least during the earlier of these visits; see Lis Jacobsen, "Utrykte erindringer," The Royal Library, Copenhagen, Tilg. 489, kaps. 90, p. 112; Lis Jacobsen to Grete Abraham, Copenhagen, March 5, 1929, and January 11, 1930, The Royal Library, Copenhagen, Lis Jacobsen Collection (Lis Jacobsens arkiv). According to a promissory note dated October 17, 1935, Jacobsen had loaned Abraham 4,000 Danish kroner upon his arrival in Copenhagen (roughly $12,000 in current value), which Abraham appears to have not repaid; see Lis Jacobsen to Robert Abraham, Copenhagen, March 11, 1955, Abraham to Jacobsen, Reykjavík, May 17, 1955, The Royal Library, Copenhagen, Lis Jacobsen Collection (Lis Jacobsens arkiv), nr. 489.

76. Lis Jacobsen, "Utrykte erindringer," The Royal Library, nr. 489, kaps. 90, 112–13.

77. Grete Abraham-Nielsen, Sandvig, August 12, 1942; Peter Abraham to Niels and Margrethe Bohr (no place), July 15, 1935; Los Angeles, September 15, 1940; Niels Bohr Archive, Copenhagen; Report on Peter Abraham's residence permit application, September 7, 1934, Danish National Archives, Copenhagen, Udlændingesag nr. 43752.

78. Izabela A. Dahl, "Dänemark als Zufluchtsland für jüdische Flüchtlinge," in *Skandinavien als Zuflucht für jüdische Intellektuelle 1933–1945*, eds. Izabela A. Dahl and Jorunn Sem Fure (Berlin: Metropol, 2014), 216.

79. Det Unge Toneselskabsorkester (Aksel Agerby) to Lis Jacobsen, Copenhagen, October 15, 1934, The Royal Library, Copenhagen, Det Unge Tonekunstnerselskab, Korrespondance 1934.

80. Although the orchestra concerts were arranged through Lis Jacobsen, Robert Abraham already knew at least one of its members. Danish flautist Johan Bentzon, later a member of the Danish Radio Symphony Orchestra, had also taken part in Scherchen's Paris seminar. Bentzon was a board member of Det Unge Tonekunsterselskab orchestra, and may thus have been in a position to facilitate Jacobsen's request; see Aksel Agerby, "Det unge tonekunstnerselskabs orkester gennem 5 sæsoner," *Dansk Musik Tidsskrift* 10 (1935): 62–65.

81. See the promissory note dated October 17, 1935, and signed by Robert Abraham, The Royal Library, Copenhagen, Lis Jacobsen Collection (Lis Jacobsens arkiv) nr. 489.

82. "Tre Orkester-Koncerter i Glyptoteket," *Berlingske Tidende*, January 5, 1935.

83. "F," "Barok-Musik i Glyptoteket," *Berlingske Tidende*, January 15, 1935; "Kris," "Koncert i Glyptoteket," *Ekstrabladet*, January 15, 1935.

84. "Siden sidst," *Dansk Musiktidsskrift* 9 (1935): 33; "Siden sidst," *Dansk Musiktidsskrift* 9 (1935): 79. On Lunn, see Sigurd Berg, "Lunn, Sven," *Dansk biografisk leksikon*, 3rd ed. (Copenhagen: Gyldendal, 1981), 9:210.

85. "Ralf," "Fra Barok til Klassik," *Berlingske Tidende*, February 20, 1935; Erik Abrahamsen, "Fra Barok til Klassik," *Dagens Nyheder*, February 20, 1935.

86. Emmy Schulz to Robert Abraham, Berlin, December 19, 1934 (private collection, Elín Þ. Ólafsdóttir).

87. Emmy Schulz to Robert Abraham, Berlin, May 1, 1935 (private collection, Elín Þ. Ólafsdóttir).

88. Wilhelm Hansen to the Danish Ministry of Justice, Copenhagen, October 23, 1934; president of Dansk Tonekunstner Forening to the Danish Ministry of Justice, October 31 and November 7, 1934, Danish National Archives, Copenhagen, Udlændingesag nr. 45347.

89. Danish Ministry of Justice to Copenhagen Police Chief, March 14, 1935, Danish National Archives, Copenhagen, Udlændingesag nr. 45347.

90. Police reports regarding Robert Abraham's residence permit, March 1–August 31, 1935, Danish National Archives, Copenhagen, Udlændingesag nr. 45357.

91. Jakob Benediktsson, "Sextugur í dag: Dr. Róbert A. Ottósson," *Þjóðviljinn*, May 17, 1972.

92. Guðjón Albertsson, "Ég elska járnbrautina," *Alþýðublaðið*, May 26, 1965.

93. Albertsson, "Ég elska járnbrautina."

94. Gauti Kristmannsson, "Bergmál minninganna," in Melitta Urbancic, *Frá hjara veraldar/Vom Rand der Welt* (Reykjavík: Stofnun Vigdísar Finnbogadóttur í erlendum tungumálum, 2014), 100.

95. Melitta Urbancic to Ilma Grünbaum, Mainz, April 16, 1931 (private collection, Sibyl Urbancic).

96. Victor Urbancic to Joseph Marx, Mainz, June 7, 1933, Austrian National Library, Autogr. 868/15.

97. Melitta Urbancic to Ilma Grünbaum, Mainz, April 16, 1931 (private collection, Sibyl Urbancic).

98. Michael Fend, "Hans Gál," in *Musik im Exil. Folgen des Nazismus für die internationale Musikkultur*, 172.

99. "Die Mainzer Musikhochschule unter jüdischer Herrschaft," *Mainzer Tageszeitung* [no date] 1933 (private collection, Sibyl Urbancic); see also Michael Fend, "Hans Gál," 172.

100. Victor Urbancic to the mayor of Mainz, April 18, 1933; Urbancic to Staatskommissar Jung, Mainz, May 18, 1933; Hilfskommissar to Staatskommissar Jung, Mainz, May 5, 1933; Staatskommissar Jung to Victor Urbancic, Mainz, May 23, 1933; Stadtarchiv Mainz, Personalakte Viktor Urbantschitsch, E12/14.

101. Hilfskommissar to Staatskommissar Jung, Mainz, May 5, 1933, Stadtarchiv Mainz, Personalakte Viktor Urbantschitsch, E12/14.

102. Hilfskommissar to Staatskommissar Jung, Mainz, May 5, 1933, Stadtarchiv Mainz, Personalakte Viktor Urbantschitsch, E12/14.

103. Paul Falk to Staatskommissar Dr. Barth, Mainz, July 13, 1933, Österreichisches Generalkonsulat to Staatskommissar Dr. Barth, Frankfurt am Main, July 20 and August 12, 1933; Staatskommissar Dr. Barth to Austrian General Consul, Mainz, August 14, 1933; Stadtarchiv Mainz, Personalakte Viktor Urbantschitsch, E12/14.

104. Sibyl Urbancic, interviewed by Anna Marsibil Clausen, *Lestin*, Iceland National Radio, first broadcast December 15, 2021.

105. The Urbancic family home at Brunnengasse 11 no longer stands. The street has also been renamed; the building now standing on the site of the Wiesler house is Waldmüllergasse 14.

106. Rudolf Habringer, "In dunklen Zeiten: Über das Wirken des Musikers Victor Urbancic am Grazer Konservatorium," in *Gradus ad musicam: 200 Jahre Johann-Joseph-Fux-Konservatorium*, ed. Eduard Lanner (Graz: Amt der Steiermärkischen Landesregierung, 2016), 49.

107. Alois Kernbauer, *Der Nationalsozialismus im Mikrokosmos. Die Universität Graz 1938: Analyse—Dokumentation—Gedenkbuch* (Graz: Akademische Druck- u. Verlagsanstalt, 2019), 493–96.

108. Sibyl Urbancic, interviewed by Anna Marsibil Clausen, *Lestin*, Iceland National Radio, first broadcast December 15, 2021.

109. "rb.," "Opernfragmente im Musikverein," *Grazer Tagespost*, December 9, 1935.

110. Melitta Urbancic to Alfred Grünbaum, Graz, January 8, 1937 (private collection, Sibyl Urbancic).

111. Helmut Brenner, *Musik als Waffe? Theorie und Praxis der politischen Musikverwendung, dargestellt am Beispiel der Steiermark 1938–1945* (Graz: H. Weishaupt, 1992), 173; Mona Silli, "Chronik des Johann-Joseph-Fux-Konservatoriums. Die musikgeschichtliche Entwicklung der Instrumentalmusikerziehung von 1815 bis zur Gegenwart" (PhD dissertation, Universität für Musik und darstellende Kunst, Graz, 2009), 79.

112. Rudolf Habringer, "Emigration an den Rand der Welt," 93–95; see also Helmut Brenner, *Musik als Waffe?*, 57–65; Mona Silli, "Chronik des Johann-Joseph-Fux-Konservatoriums," 94–97; Markus Helmut Lenhart, "Geschichte ohne Brüche? Das Jahr 1938 und 200 Jahre Kunstuniversität Graz," 144 and 147–48.

113. Habringer, "In dunklen Zeiten," 51; Fritz Redl to Victor Urbancic, New York, March 3 and March 28, 1938; Victor Urbancic to The [American] Musicological Society, Graz, April 30, 1938 (private collection, Sibyl Urbancic); Fritz Redl to Betty Drury, New York, April 20, 1938, Betty Drury to Fritz Redl, New York, May 26, 1938 (New York Public Library, Emergency Committee in Aid of Displaced Foreign Scholars Records).

114. Alfred W. Glogg (Schweizerische Rundspruch-Gesellschaft) to Victor Urbancic, Bern, June 20, 1938 (private collection, Sibyl Urbancic).

115. Ludwig Kelbetz to Robert Ernst, Graz, April 29, 1938 (private collection, Sibyl Urbancic), cited in Habringer, "In dunklen Zeiten," 52.

116. As late as December 1939, Hildegard Urbantschitsch received a phone call from an official representative of the *Reichsmusikkammer*, asking if her son would be returning to the Third Reich soon, and suggesting that, if so, he would easily find a job: "He answered, that you would certainly also find something here (which I doubted)." In this case, the official must have presumed that he would return alone; see Hildegard Urbantschitsch to Victor Urbancic, Vienna, December 13, 1939 (private collection, Sibyl Urbancic).

117. Minutes, board meeting of the Musikverein für Steiermark, Graz, May 17, 1938, quoted in Susanne Windholz, "Franz Mixa: Gesamtwerk, Tätigkeiten und Werkaufführungen in Graz" (MA-thesis, Karl-Franzens-Universität Graz, 2007), 20.

118. Fred K. Prieberg, *Handbuch Deutsche Musiker 1933–1945* (Kiel, 2004); Bundesarchiv Berlin, NSDAP-Mitgliederkartei (Franz Mixa). Mixa's early membership in the Nazi Party has rarely been mentioned in Icelandic writings; for example, there is no mention of it in Óðinn Melsted's book on foreign musicians in Iceland, *Með nótur í farteskinu. Erlendir tónlistarmenn á Íslandi 1930–1960* (Reykjavík: Sögufélag, 2016). The Austrian writer Rudolf Habringer is among those who have criticized the whitewashing of Austrian Nazi musicians after World War II; see "Eine Recherche,

ein Essay, ein Roman. Nachschrift zu meinen Texten über Victor Urbancic," in *Das Unergründliche und das Banale. Essays* (Wels: Mitter Verlag, 2017), 121–28, and "In dunklen Zeiten," 54; see also Markus Helmut Lenhart, "Melitta and Victor Urbancic: Art in Exile in Iceland," in *Cultural Translation and Knowledge Transfer on Alternative Routes of Escape from Nazi Terror*, eds. Susanne Korbel and Philipp Strobl (New York: Routledge, 2022), 236.

119. Rudolf Habringer, "In dunklen Zeiten," 52.

120. For example, Urbancic and Wlach both took the same course on Bach's music in 1924; a year later, Mixa and Urbancic both took a course on Handel's oratorios. Guido Adler advised both Wlach and Urbancic, while Urbancic and Mixa both studied composition with Joseph Marx; see DEMOS—Datenbank zur Erforschung der Musik in Österreich. www.demos.ac.at

121. Susanne Windholz, "Franz Mixa: Gesamtwerk, Tätigkeiten und Werkaufführungen in Graz," 59, 62; Christian Fastl, "Wlach, Johann (Hans) Joseph," *Oesterreichisches Musiklexikon online*, ed. Barbara Boisits. www.musiklexikon.ac.at/ml/musik_W/Wlach_Johann.xml

122. Susanne Windholz, "Franz Mixa: Gesamtwerk, Tätigkeiten und Werkaufführungen in Graz," 102.

123. While Wlach's rhetoric might suggest he had already become a member of the Nazi Party when writing his review, he joined only on May 1, 1938, with party membership number 6.272.166; Bundesarchiv Berlin, NSDAP-Mitgliederkartei (Hans Wlach). Claudia Maurer Zenck has pointed out that Mixa was among those of the younger generation of composers believed to have a special role to play in the "new" Nazi Austria; see "Kein schleichender Übergang," *Die Tonkunst* 3/4 (2009): 424.

124. Hans Wlach, "Franz Mixa. 30 Lieder aus 'Des Knaben Wunderhorn,'" *Zeitschrift für Musik* 104 (1937): 495, 497. In 1939, Wlach wrote again on Mixa's music in the *Zeitschrift für Musik*, asserting it contained a "political power of life." He also surmised whether such music could be composed anywhere else than in the "City of the Popular Uprising," citing Hitler's honorary title of *Stadt der Volkserhebung*, bestowed on Graz a year earlier; see Hans Wlach, "Konzert und Oper," *Zeitschrift für Musik* 106 (1939): 661.

125. Victor Urbancic to Robert Ernst, May 21, 1938, cited in Habringer, "In dunklen Zeiten," 52.

126. Björn Jónsson to Jón Leifs, Reykjavík, July 16, 1938, Jón Leifs Collection, National and University Library, Reykjavík, Lbs 751 NF. Mixa's request was formally approved on the Music Society's meeting on June 24, 1938, see Minutes of the Reykjavík Music Society 1932–1946, National and University Library, Reykjavík, Lbs 1146 NF.

127. Alois Kernbauer, *Der Nationalsozialismus im Mikrokosmos*, 493–94. However, Mixa was not offered the position of substitute Dean, which Urbancic had held, and also did not take Urbancic's position as organ teacher; see Georg Zauner, *Der Komponist Franz Mixa. Leben und Werk* (Tutzing: Hans Schneider, 2002), 31–32.

128. Victor Urbancic to Robert Ernst, St. Peter bei Graz, May 21, 1938; Robert Ernst to Victor Urbancic, Vienna, May 25, 1938 (private collection, Sibyl Urbancic).

129. Erwin von Lauppert and Ludwig Kelbetz to Franz Mixa, Graz, July 22, 1938 (private collection, Hertha Töpper), quoted in Susanne Windholz, "Franz Mixa: Gesamtwerk, Tätigkeiten und Werkaufführungen in Graz" (MA-thesis, Karl-Franzens-Universität Graz, 2007), 21.

130. Markus Helmut Lenhart, "Geschichte ohne Brüche? Das Jahr 1938 und 200 Jahre Kunstuniversität Graz," in *Stand und Perspektiven der NS-Forschung in der Musik*, eds. Klaus Aringer, Susanne Kogler, and Markus Helmut Lenhart (Graz: Leykam, 2021), 151; Susanne Windholz, "Franz Mixa: Gesamtwerk, Tätigkeiten und Werkaufführungen in Graz," 12.

131. Alois Kernbauer, *Der Nationalsozialismus im Mikrokosmos*, 494.

132. Franz Mixa, "Fiðluhljómleikar Ernst Drucker," *Nýja dagblaðið*, March 1, 1938.

133. Guðrún Egilson, *Tvístirni. Saga Svanhvítar Egilsdóttur* (Reykjavík: Almenna bókafélagið, 2002), 51.

134. Markus Helmut Lenhart, "Geschichte ohne Brüche? Das Jahr 1938 und 200 Jahre Kunstuniversität Graz," 149.

135. Habringer, "In dunklen Zeiten," 54.

136. Sibyl Urbancic, interviewed by the author, August 18, 2019.

137. In early August 1938, Urbancic was in Berlin, but had intended to return to Graz for two weeks. It was only while in Berlin, having received a telegram from the Reykjavík Music Society, asking him to come to Iceland sooner so they could begin rehearsals for the Society's autumn concert, that he decided to take a ship from Bergen, Norway, on August 18; Victor Urbancic to Melitta Urbancic, Berlin, August 10, 1938 (private collection, Sibyl Urbancic).

138. Victor Urbancic to Melitta Urbancic, Reykjavík, September 1, 1938 (private collection, Sibyl Urbancic).

139. Sibyl Urbancic, interviewed by the author, August 18, 2019.

140. Sibyl Urbancic, interviewed by Sigríður Stephensen, *Heimsmenning á hjara veraldar*, Iceland National Radio, first broadcast 1997.

141. Pétur Urbancic, interviewed by the author, August 23, 2019; Páll Valsson, *Myndir úr lífshlaupi Péturs Urbancic* (Reykjavík: Nostrum, 2021), 12.

142. Melitta Urbancic, "Überfahrt," typewritten manuscript (private collection, Sibyl Urbancic).

143. Sibyl Urbancic, interviewed by Sigríður Stephensen, *Heimsmenning á hjara veraldar*, Iceland National Radio, first broadcast 1997; Pétur Urbancic, interviewed by the author, August 23, 2019.

144. Sibyl Urbancic, interviewed by the author, August 18, 2019; Pétur Urbancic, interviewed by the author, August 23, 2019.

145. "Bericht über die Ereignisse in Graz am 10. November 1938," The Wiener Library, no. 1375/296. www.pogromnovember1938.co.uk/viewer/image/93983/1

146. www.jewishvirtuallibrary.org/graz; www.geni.com/projects/Jewish-Community-of-Graz-Styria-Austria-Steiermark-%C3%96sterreich/55312

Chapter 3

1. Gauti Kristmannsson, "Bergmál minninganna," in Melitta Urbancic, *Frá hjara veraldar/Vom Rand der Welt* (Reykjavík: Stofnun Vigdísar Finnbogadóttur í erlendum tungumálum, 2014), 89–90.
2. "X," "Dómkirkjuorgelið nýa," *Lesbók Morgunblaðsins*, September 23, 1934.
3. "Hr. Arthur Shattuck um Ísland," *Gjallarhorn*, September 8, 1910; "Arthur Shattuck og 'Politiken,'" *Fjallkonan*, September 27, 1910, 147.
4. Árni Thorsteinson, "Piano-hljómleikar," *Morgunblaðið*, October 25, 1914.
5. S.F., "Hljómleikar Haralds Sigurðssonar," *Vísir*, October 28, 1914.
6. Sigfús Einarsson, "Hljómsveit Reykjavíkur," *Morgunblaðið*, September 22, 1926.
7. Páll Ásgeir Ásgeirsson, *Fóstbræðralag. Saga Karlakórsins Fóstbræðra í níutíu ár* (Reykjavík: Karlakórinn Fóstbræður, 2001), 32.
8. For more on the development of choral singing in early twentieth-century Iceland, see Árni Heimir Ingólfsson, "Starting from Scratch: Nation Building and the Creation of an Icelandic Choral Tradition," in *The Nature of Nordic Music*, ed. Tim Howell (Abingdon: Routledge, 2019), 71–86.
9. H., "Þýska hljómsveitin," *Vísir*, June 3, 1926; see also Árni Heimir Ingólfsson, *Jón Leifs and the Musical Invention of Iceland*, 77–82.
10. Sigfús Einarsson, "Hljómleikarnir í gær," *Morgunblaðið*, April 15, 1930; "Dagbók," *Morgunblaðið*, May 8, 1930.
11. "Hljómleikar," *Vísir*, April 15, 1930.
12. "Starfsemi Tónlistarfél. starfsárið 1940–41," Minutes of the Reykjavík Music Society, 1932–1946, National and University Library, Reykjavík, Lbs 1146 NF.
13. Kristján Sigurðsson, "Tónlistarskólinn 1930–1940," *Tímarit Tónlistarfélagsins* 2 (1940): 13–14.
14. "Tónlistarfélagið," *Tímarit Máls og menningar* 1 (1938): 18–19.
15. See Gunnar Bergmann, "Postulasaga," *Tíminn*, March 22, 1964.
16. *Alþýðublaðið*, November 5, 1943.
17. "Passíusálmar," *Vikan* 7 (1944): 7.
18. Ingólfur Margeirsson, *Ragnar í Smára* (Reykjavík: Listasafn ASÍ, 1982), 62.
19. Matthías Johannessen, *Hundapúfan og hafið* (Reykjavík: Bókfellsútgáfan, 1961), 208.
20. Stefán Edelstein, interview with the author, August 23, 2019.
21. Guðrún Reykholt to Jón Leifs, Reykjavík, December 16, 1935, Jón Leifs Collection, National and University Library, Reykjavík, Lbs 751 NF.
22. Gunnar Stefánsson, *Útvarp Reykjavík. Saga Ríkisútvarpsins 1930–1960*, 72 and 97–98; Kristján Friðriksson, "—höfum aldrei heyrt æðri tónlist!," *Útvarps-*

tíðindi 2 (1940): 330; see also Árni Heimir Ingólfsson, *Jón Leifs and the Musical Invention of Iceland*, 174.

23. Sigurður Pálsson, *Norður í svalann. Viðtöl við aðflutta Íslendinga* (Reykjavík: Bókaútgáfan Salt, 1982), 101, 105.

24. Óðinn Melsted, *Með nótur í farteskinu*, 38.

25. Guðjón Albertsson, "Ég elska járnbrautina," 8; Robert Abraham to the Icelandic Ministry of Justice, Reykjavík, October 25, 1935, National Archives of Iceland, Cabinet of Iceland I, Ministry of Justice, B/498.

26. The Icelandic Ministry of Justice to Robert Abraham, Reykjavík, October 29, 1935, quoted in Snorri G. Bergsson, *Erlendur landshornalýður?*, 258.

27. Friðrik Einarsson, Ólafur Briem, and Jóhann G. Salberg on behalf of twenty students at the University of Iceland to Hermann Jónasson, Reykjavík, October 31, 1935, National Archives of Iceland, Cabinet of Iceland I, Ministry of Justice, B/498-4.

28. Friðrik Einarsson, Ólafur Briem, and Jóhann G. Salberg on behalf of twenty students at the University of Iceland to Hermann Jónasson, Reykjavík, October 31, 1935, National Archives of Iceland, Cabinet of Iceland I, Ministry of Justice, B/498-4.

29. Lis Jacobsen to the Icelandic Ministry of Justice, Copenhagen, November 14, 1935, National Archives of Iceland, Cabinet of Iceland I, Ministry of Justice, B/545-1.

30. Thyge Svenstrup, *Arup: En biografi om den radikale historiker Erik Arup, hans tid og miljø* (Copenhagen: Museum Tusculanums Forlag, 2006), 210–17, 546–52.

31. Erik Arup to Hermann Jónasson, Copenhagen, November 7, 1935, National Archives of Iceland, Cabinet of Iceland I, Ministry of Justice, B/498-4. A week later, Arup sent a letter to Prime Minister Jónasson in which he reiterated his request and included written recommendations from Lis Jacobsen and others; Arup to Hermann Jónasson, November 15, 1935, copy in National Archives of Iceland, Róbert Abraham Ottósson 2012-002, A/3, 6.

32. The Icelandic Ministry of Justice to Robert Abraham, Reykjavík, November 1, 1935; Hermann Jónasson to Erik Arup, Reykjavík, November 8, 1935, National Archives of Iceland, Cabinet of Iceland I, Ministry of Justice, B/498-4.

33. Robert Abraham to Ragnar Bjarkan, April 15 and June 6, 1937, Ministry of Justice to Robert Abraham, June 23, 1937, National Archives of Iceland, Cabinet of Iceland I, Ministry of Justice, B/545-1.

34. The Icelandic Ministry of Justice to Robert Abraham, January 19, 1938, National Archives of Iceland, Cabinet of Iceland I, Ministry of Justice, B/636.

35. These Jews were Olga and Hans Rottberger, along with their two children, and Alfred Kempner; see Vilhjálmur Örn Vilhjálmsson, *Medaljens bagside. Jødiske flygtningeskæbner i Danmark 1933–1945*, 11.

36. "Það er gaman að lifa á þessum þroskaárum íslenzkrar tónlistar," 2–3; Björn Magnússon and Gunnar Þorsteinsson, "Dr. Róbert Abraham Ottósson heimsóttur," 10–11; Guðjón Albertsson, "Ég elska járnbrautina," 8.

37. See "Norðanmaður," "Sesselja Eldjárn sextug," *Morgunblaðið*, July 26, 1953.
38. Guðjón Albertsson, "Ég elska járnbrautina," 8.
39. Guðjón Albertsson, "Ég elska járnbrautina," 8–9.
40. Halldór Halldórsson, "Samkór," *DV*, October 15, 1994.
41. S., " 'Það er gaman að lifa á þessum þroskaárum íslenzkrar tónlistar.' Viðtal við Róbert Abraham Ottósson," *Heimilispósturinn* 3 (1951): 4.
42. "Auditor" [Valdimar Steffensen], "Robert Abraham," *Dagur*, March 5, 1936.
43. Áskell Snorrason, "Robert Abraham," *Verkamaðurinn*, June 16, 1936.
44. No Icelandic choir had until then been named after its conductor, but this was common in Germany, for example the Bruno Kittel-Choir in Berlin, of which Abraham had been a member during his student years.
45. "Konsert," *Dagur*, April 8, 1937.
46. *Alþýðublaðið*, May 21, 1939.
47. "Auditor" [Valdimar Steffensen], "Samkór R. Abrahams," *Dagur*, April 18, 1940; "Blandaður kór," *Verkamaðurinn*, May 14, 1938; *Verkamaðurinn*, May 14, 1938.
48. "X" [Ingimar Eydal, editor of *Dagur*], "Músik-kvöld," *Dagur*, October 8, 1936.
49. Áskell Snorrason, "Hljómleikar," *Verkamaðurinn*, October 10, 1936.
50. Tómas Björnsson, "Konsert," *Íslendingur*, October 16, 1936.
51. Valdimar Steffensen, "Tómas Bjørnsson og tónlistin," *Íslendingur*, October 23, 1936. See also Tómas Björnsson, "V.St. kemur í ljós," *Íslendingur*, October 30, 1936.
52. "Dómur 'aríans,' " *Verkamaðurinn*, October 20, 1936.
53. "Konsert," *Dagur*, October 22, 1936.
54. "Gyðingaofsóknir á Akureyri," *Þjóðviljinn*, November 3, 1936.
55. Björgvin Guðmundsson, "Ávarp," Björgvin Guðmundsson Collection, National and University Library, Reykjavík, Lbs 125 NF; see also Haukur Ágústsson, *Ferill til frama. Ævisaga Björgvins Guðmundssonar tónskálds* (Akureyri: Ásprent, 2011), 81 and 84.
56. "Auditor" [Valdimar Steffensen], "Robert Abraham," *Dagur*, March 5, 1936.
57. Björgvin Guðmundsson, "Kantötukór Akureyrar," manuscript, vol. 1, 77–79, in box marked "Diaries etc.," Björgvin Guðmundsson Collection, National and University Library, Reykjavík, Lbs 125 NF.
58. Sigurður Þórðarson to Björgvin Guðmundsson, Reykjavík, October 30, 1940; see also his letter from June 19, 1940. Björgvin Guðmundsson Collection, National and University Library, Reykjavík, Lbs 125 NF.
59. Robert Abraham to Halldór Halldórsson, Akureyri, March 21, 1937 (private collection, Hildigunnur Halldórsdóttir).
60. Robert Abraham to Halldór Halldórsson, Akureyri, March 21, 1937 (private collection, Hildigunnur Halldórsdóttir).
61. "Það er gaman að lifa á þessum þroskaárum íslenzkrar tónlistar," 2 and 4.

62. Stefán Edelstein, interview with the author, August 23, 2019.
63. Ragnar Jónsson to Jón Leifs, written on board an airplane en route to Sweden, October 7, 1937. Jón Leifs Collection, National and University Library, Reykjavík, Lbs 751 NF.
64. Óðinn Melsted, *Með nótur í farteskinu*, 210, 224.
65. Stephan Stompor, *Jüdisches Musik- und Theaterleben unter dem NS-Staat* (Hannover: Europäisches Zentrum für Jüdische Musik, 2001), 111.
66. Ragnar Jónsson to Jón Leifs, en route to Sweden, October 7, 1937, Jón Leifs Collection, National and University Library, Reykjavík, Lbs 751 NF.
67. Arthúr Björgvin Bollason, "'Svo sú passa þennan strák,'" *Morgunblaðið*, August 16, 2020; Páll Valsson, *Vigdís. Kona verður forseti* (Reykjavík: JPV, 2009), 97–98.
68. The Reykjavík Music Society, meeting minutes, October 11, 1937, Minutes 1932–1946, National and University Library, Reykjavík, Lbs 1146 NF.
69. Einar Magnússon, "Lúðvíg Guðmundsson fyrrv. Skólastjóri—Minningarorð," *Morgunblaðið*, August 31, 1966.
70. Stefán Edelstein, interview with the author, June 15, 2001. Each of the two Edelstein sons told his own version of their father's recruitment to Iceland. According to Wolfgang, it was Ragnar Jónsson who met Edelstein in Berlin, which is corroborated by Jónsson's letters. Stefán, on the other hand, emphasized his father's meeting with Lúðvíg Guðmundsson in Hamburg, a meeting otherwise not corroborated in the sources. I have chosen to make use of both accounts, since they are not necessarily mutually exclusive, and Guðmundsson was verifiably in Germany in autumn 1937 (see Vilhjálmur S. Vilhjálmsson, "Atvinnuleysi unglinga og ráðstafanir gegn því," *Alþýðublaðið*, May 2, 1938).
71. The Ministry of Labor and Transportation to the Reykjavík Music Society, Reykjavík, November 10, 1937, National Archives of Iceland, Cabinet of Iceland I, Ministry of Justice, B/545-1.
72. Stefán Edelstein, interview with the author, August 23, 2019.
73. "In Memoriam Madeleine Stebbins," https://cuf.org/wp-content/uploads/2021/11/39.4-Lay-Witness-Insert.pdf; Victor Conzemius, "Eine Flüchtlingsmutter in den USA," *Neue Zürcher Zeitung*, March 13, 1998.
74. Mrs. Helen E. Froelicher, letter to Charlotte Edelstein, Ridgewood, N.J. (USA), May 9, 1938 (private collection, Stefán Edelstein).
75. Charlotte Edelstein, "Aufbruch ins Ungewisse," typewritten manuscript (private collection, Stefán Edelstein).
76. Heinz Edelstein, letter to Charlotte Edelstein, Reykjavík, May 18, 1938 (private collection, Stefán Edelstein).
77. Bollason, "'Svo sú passa þennan strák,'" *Morgunblaðið*, August 16, 2020; Corinna Halter, "Jüdische Emigration nach Island während des Nationalsozialismus. Fall Wolfgang Edelstein," Cultural studies term paper, Humboldt Universität, Berlin, 2015, 8.

78. Beate Sodian, "SRCD Oral History Interview," Wolfgang Edelstein, Max-Planck-Institute for Human Development, Berlin, Germany Part I: October 17, 2008 and Part 2: March 2, 2009, www.srcd.org/sites/default/files/file-attachments/edelstein_wolfgang_interview.pdf; see also Wolfgang Edelstein, interviewed by Christoph Lindenmeyer, Bayerischer Rundfunk, December 12, 2006.

79. Bollason, "'Svo sú passa þennan strák,'" *Morgunblaðið*, August 16, 2020; Wolfgang Edelstein, interview with Ágúst Þór Árnason, "Lífið og skólinn," Iceland National Radio, first broadcast January 1, 2020.

80. Björn Jónsson, letter to Jón Leifs, Reykjavík, July 16, 1938, Jón Leifs Collection, National and University Library, Reykjavík, Lbs 751 NF.

81. Heinz Edelstein, letter to Jón Leifs, Reykjavík, March 24, 1938, Jón Leifs Collection, National and University Library, Reykjavík, Lbs 751 NF.

82. Heinz Edelstein, letter to Jón Leifs, Reykjavík, March 24, 1938, Jón Leifs Collection, National and University Library, Reykjavík, Lbs 751 NF.

83. Helmut F. Pfanner, "The Role of Switzerland for the Refugees," in *The Muses Flee Hitler*, 237–38.

84. Heinz Edelstein, written statement, Hamburg, August 30, 1938 (private collection, Stefán Edelstein).

85. Charlotte Edelstein, "Aufbruch ins Ungewisse," typewritten manuscript (private collection, Stefán Edelstein).

86. Corinna Halter, "Jüdische Emigration nach Island während des Nationalsozialismus. Fall Wolfgang Edelstein," Cultural Studies paper, Humboldt Universität, Berlin, 2015, 10.

87. Charlotte Edelstein, "Aufbruch ins Ungewisse," typewritten manuscript (private collection, Stefán Edelstein).

88. SS *Goðafoss* (which set sail from Hamburg) had a longer journey than SS *Dronning Alexandrine* (from Copenhagen), and thus Melitta Urbancic arrived in Reykjavík two days before Charlotte Edelstein, despite having left Copenhagen a day later. *Dronning Alexandrine* arrived on the evening of September 25 (*Vísir*, September 24, 1938), but *Goðafoss* arrived on September 27 (*Þjóðviljinn*, September 28, 1938).

89. Ernst Otto Bräunche, "'Die Reichskristallnacht' in Freiburg." *Zeitschrift des Breisgau-Geschichtsvereins ("Schau-ins-Land")* 103 (1984): 150; Kathrin Clausing, *Leben auf Abruf*, 260–62.

90. Police report on Lilli Schottländer, Freiburg, November 10, 1938, Staatsarchiv Freiburg, F 196/1 Nr. 6099.

91. Renee Hoffman (Schepses), interview with Andrew Budris. https://bellport.com/vnews/columns/oral-history/vn_oral-history.htm

92. Wolf Helmuth Wolf-Rottkay was a visiting lecturer at the University of Iceland during the 1938–1939 academic year, see "Nýr þýskur sendikennari," *Morgunblaðið*, October 8, 1938; for more on Wolf-Rottkay, see Vilhjálmur Örn Vilhjálmsson, "Heil Hitler og Hari Krishna." fornleifur.blog.is/blog/fornleifur/entry/1385163

93. Charlotte Edelstein, "Aufbruch ins Ungewisse," typewritten manuscript (private collection, Stefán Edelstein).

94. Charlotte Edelstein, "Aufbruch ins Ungewisse," typewritten manuscript (private collection, Stefán Edelstein).

95. Charlotte Edelstein, "Aufbruch ins Ungewisse," typewritten manuscript (private collection, Stefán Edelstein).

96. Páll Valsson, *Vigdís*, 63.

97. Páll Valsson, *Vigdís*, 63; Vigdís Finnbogadóttir, interview with the author, January 3, 2020.

98. Vigdís Finnbogadóttir, interview with the author, January 3, 2020; Vigdís Finnbogadóttir, "Charlotte Edelstein," *Morgunblaðið*, September 13, 1997.

99. Franz Mixa to Victor Urbancic, Hadersdorf-Weidlingau, June 22, 1938 (private collection, Sibyl Urbancic).

100. Ernst Urbantschitsch to Victor Urbancic, Vienna, September 15, 1938 (private collection, Sibyl Urbancic).

101. Anna Bjarnadóttir, "Þá þyrsti í þekkingu og drukku í sig allt sem ég gat veitt þeim," *Lesbók Morgunblaðsins*, April 4, 1987.

102. "Arbeitsvertrag," contract signed July 14 and 15, 1938 (private collection, Sibyl Urbancic).

103. See "Áætlun um tekjur og gjöld Tónlistarskólans veturinn 1934–35," and minutes from September 23, 1935, Minutes of the Reykjavík Music Society, 1932–1946, National and University Library of Iceland, Lbs 1146 NF.

104. Ernst Urbantschitsch to Victor Urbancic, Vienna, September 15, 1938 (private collection, Sibyl Urbancic).

105. Sibyl Urbancic, interview with the author, August 18, 2019.

106. Þór Whitehead, *Ófriður í aðsigi. Ísland í síðari heimsstyrjöld* (Reykjavík: Almenna bókafélagið, 1980), 87–90.

107. "Ísland er minn starfsvettvangur," *Musica* 1/3 (1948): 6.

108. Melitta Urbancic to Ilma Grünbaum, Reykjavík, May 7, 1939 (private collection, Sibyl Urbancic). See also "Árshátíð Tónlistarfélagsins," *Vísir*, May 5, 1939.

109. Charlotte Edelstein, "Aufbruch ins Ungewisse," typewritten manuscript (private collection, Stefán Edelstein).

110. Charlotte Edelstein, "Aufbruch ins Ungewisse," typewritten manuscript (private collection, Stefán Edelstein).

111. Ernst Urbantschitsch to Victor Urbancic, Vienna, October 22, 1938; February 2, 1939 (private collection, Sibyl Urbancic).

112. Ernst Urbantschitsch to Victor Urbancic, Vienna, September 4, 1938; October 6, 1938 (private collection, Sibyl Urbancic).

113. Ernst Urbantschitsch to Victor Urbancic, Vienna, November 14, 1938 (private collection, Sibyl Urbancic).

114. Robert Abraham, curriculum vitae (1954), National Archives of Iceland, Róbert Abraham Ottósson 2012-002, A/2, 9.

115. Report on Louise Johanna Sara Abraham's request for residence permit in Denmark, Copenhagen, September 29/October 14, 1939, The Danish National Archives, Copenhagen, Udlændingesag nr. 45347. Robert sailed to Copenhagen in the summers of 1937 and 1938 to reunite with his brother and mother, who took a train from Berlin to see them; see Robert Abraham, curriculum vitae (1954), National Archives of Iceland, Róbert Abraham Ottósson 2012-002, A/2, 9.

116. Sigurður Guðmundsson, Þórarinn Björnsson, et al., telegram to Hermann Jónasson, Akureyri, August 31, 1939, National Archives of Iceland, Cabinet of Iceland I, Ministry of Justice, B/636; see also Guðjón Albertsson, "Ég elska járnbrautina."

117. Hermann Jónasson, telegram to Sigurður Guðmundsson, September 1, 1939, National Archives of Iceland, Cabinet of Iceland I, Ministry of Justice, B/636.

118. Ingibjörg Magnúsdóttir, interview with the author, January 11, 2012.

119. "Róbert Abraham," *Dagur*, October 10, 1940.

120. Bjarni Benediktsson to the Ministry of Social Affairs, Reykjavík, October 18, 1940, National Archives of Iceland, Cabinet of Iceland II, Ministry of Labor, B/648-3.

121. The Mayor of Reykjavík (Bjarni Benediktsson) to the Ministry of Social Affairs, February 5, 1942; the Mayor of Reykjavík to the Ministry of Social Affairs, February 9, 1942; the Mayor of Reykjavík to the Ministry of Social Affairs, February 16, 1943, National Archives of Iceland, Cabinet of Iceland II, Ministry of Labor, B/648-3.

122. "Sex ára telpa tekin á erlendan tónlistarskóla," *Vísir*, April 6, 1946.

123. Rudolph Genée, *Síðustu dagar Mozarts. Frásögn eftir heimildum*, trans. Robert Abraham (Reykjavík: Tónlistarfélagið, 1941); Róbert Abraham, "Þættir úr sögu tónlistarinnar," *Samtíðin* 13 (1946), vols. 2–3, 5–7, 10: "Getgátur um uppruna tónlistar," "Tónlist frumþjóða og fornra menningarþjóða," "Upphaf samhljómsins," "Síðari hluti miðalda," "Notkun hljóðfæra," "Um tónlist forn-Grikkja."

124. "Söngskemmtun skólanemenda," *Þjóðviljinn*, April 23, 1941. Only sketches for this work have been preserved, see National Archives of Iceland, Róbert Abraham Ottósson, BA/6, 3.

125. Lise Abraham to Halldór Halldórsson, January 1, 1941 (private collection, Hildigunnur Halldórsdóttir).

126. Ingibjörg Magnúsdóttir, interview with the author, January 11, 2012.

127. Ingibjörg Magnúsdóttir, interview with the author, January 11, 2012; see also "Það er gaman að lifa á þessum þroskaárum íslenzkrar tónlistar," 4; Jón Þórarinsson, "Minning: Guðríður Magnúsdóttir kennari," *Morgunblaðið*, March 16, 1990.

128. Peter Fabrizius, "Brief aus San Francisco," *Aufbau*, June 18, 1948, 33; see also "Vatnslitamyndir frá Íslandi sýndar í Kaliforníu," *Morgunblaðið*, June 17, 1948; Harald St. Björnsson, "Minningarorð: Frú Lise Abraham," *Morgunblaðið*, March 2, 1950.

Chapter 4

1. Jóhann G. Möller (on behalf of Heimdallur, the Young Conservatives Association) to the Icelandic Minister of Justice, Reykjavík, October 3, 1933, National Archives of Iceland, Cabinet of Iceland I, Ministry of Justice, B/0498.

2. Such ideas resonated strongly with government policy. In May 1932, Hermann Jónasson, then Reykjavík's Chief of Police (and later Prime Minister) reminded an official in the Ministry of Justice that he had received "verbal instruction from the Minister of Justice to not allow foreigners to present concerts or other entertainment here" (Reykjavík Police Chief to Ministry of Justice, Reykjavík, May 24, 1932, National Archives of Iceland, Cabinet of Iceland I, Ministry of Justice, B/571-3). This "ban" seems not to have lasted for long, although throughout the 1930s, the Ministry of Justice usually sought the opinion of Páll Ísólfsson, as one of the country's leading professional musicians, before permitting foreign musicians to give concerts in Iceland.

3. Vilhjálmur Örn Vilhjálmsson, *Medaljens bagside*, 11.

4. Hermann Jónasson, telegram to the Icelandic Embassy in Copenhagen, Reykjavík, November 23, 1938, National Archives of Iceland, Foreign Ministry 1967, B/45-21.

5. Icelandic Ministry of Justice to Helgi P. Briem, Danish Embassy in Berlin, December 7, 1938, National Archives of Iceland, Ministry of Justice, Db. 14 nr. 316.

6. See, for example, National Archives of Iceland, B/598-13; B/635-8; B/636-1.

7. "Sagnfræðileg perla komin úr skel fyrir vestan," https://fornleifur.blog.is/blog/fornleifur/entry/2206939; Einar Heimisson, "Die Asylsituation in Island in den dreißiger Jahren im Vergleich mit den anderen nordischen Ländern" (PhD dissertation, Albert-Ludwigs-Universität, Freiburg im Breisgau, 1992), 241.

8. Snorri G. Bergsson, *Erlendur landshornalýður?*, 252, 280.

9. Theodór Árnason, "Kjör hljóðfæraleikara," *Vísir*, March 8, 1932.

10. Minutes of the Icelandic Musicians' Union (FÍH), April 30, 1936, FÍH archives, Reykjavík.

11. Hrafn Pálsson, *Félag íslenzkra hljómlistarmanna 50 ára* (Reykjavík: Félag íslenskra hljómlistarmanna, 1982), 10.

12. Bjarni Böðvarsson (FÍH chairman) to the Icelandic Ministry of Justice, Reykjavík, May 15, 1934, National Archives of Iceland, Cabinet of Iceland I, Ministry of Justice, Db. 10 no. 959. The three musicians in question (Willy Petrick, Fritz Klingbeil, and Erich Benske) performed primarily at Hotel Iceland (*Hótel Ísland*); see *Vísir*, February 13, 1934. Since Benske married an Icelandic woman in Reykjavík in 1936, it seems as though FÍH's demand to have these musicians deported was at best only partially successful; see "Dagbók," *Morgunblaðið*, May 27, 1936.

13. "Engir danskir hljóðfæraleikarar til Íslands fyrst um sinn," *Alþýðublaðið*, February 9, 1938.

14. Hrafn Pálsson, *Félag íslenzkra hljómlistarmanna 50 ára*, 19.

15. Fritz Jaritz, "Albert Klahn 65 ára," *Alþýðublaðið*, August 10, 1950.

16. Bjarni Benediktsson, "Hann hefur leikið um allan heim nema í San Fransiskó og Ivigtút," *Þjóðviljinn*, May 31, 1953.

17. Þórhallur Árnason, "Albert Klahn hljómsveitarstjóri—Minning," *Morgunblaðið*, December 21, 1960.

18. Dr. Jessen to Sozialbehörde Hamburg, Flensburg, October 6, 1955, Staatsarchiv der Freien und Hansestadt Hamburg, 351-11_7891, Entschädigungsakte Albert und Fanny Klahn.

19. "Vinur" (pseudonym), "Minning frú Fanny Klahn," *Þjóðviljinn*, December 8, 1940; Þórhallur Árnason, "Minning Fanny Kartz Klahn," *Morgunblaðið*, November 30, 1940.

20. "Vinur" (pseudonym), "Minning frú Fanny Klahn," *Þjóðviljinn*, December 8, 1940.

21. "Liste der aus der Reichsmusikkammer ausgeschlossenen Juden, jüdischen Mischlinge und jüdisch Versippten," K-L, Bundesarchiv, Berlin, R 55/21303; Dr. Jessen to Entschädigungsbehörde, Flensburg, February 24, 1954, Staatsarchiv der Freien und Hansestadt Hamburg, 351-11_7891, Entschädigungsakte Albert und Fanny Klahn.

22. Dr. Jessen to Entschädigungsbehörde, Flensburg, February 24, 1954, Staatsarchiv der Freien und Hansestadt Hamburg, 351-11_7891, Entschädigungsakte Albert und Fanny Klahn.

23. "Nýr stjórnandi að Hljómsveit Reykjavíkur," *Alþýðublaðið*, September 26, 1936.

24. "Lúðrasveit Reykjavíkur," *Þjóðviljinn*, November 10, 1936.

25. "Minningar rifjaðar upp í Hljómskálanum," *Vísir*, October 18, 1967.

26. Hrafn Pálsson, *Félag íslenzkra hljómlistarmanna 50 ára*, 21–22; Minutes of the Icelandic Musicians' Union (FÍH), October 10, October 11, and October 27, 1937; January 9 and January 12, 1938, FÍH archives, Reykjavík.

27. Minutes of the Icelandic Musicians' Union (FÍH), January 12, 1938, FÍH archives, Reykjavík.

28. "Albert Klahn, Tíu ára starfsafmæli," *Musica* 1/4–5 (1948), 10.

29. "Aðalfundur FÍH: Gunnar Egilsson endurkjörinn formaður," *Alþýðublaðið*, March 26, 1958.

30. Hrafn Pálsson, *Félag íslenzkra hljómlistarmanna 50 ára*, 21.

31. Jón Múli Árnason, *Þjóðsögur Jóns Múla Árnasonar* (Reykjavík: Mál og menning, 1996), 236.

32. "Hljómleikar," *Alþýðublaðið*, December 19, 1936.

33. Kristján Sigurðsson, "Tónlistarskólinn 1930–1940," *Tímarit Tónlistarfélagsins*, May 1, 1940, 7; "Tríó Tónlistarskólans," *Útvarpstíðindi*, January 9, 1939, 188.

34. Ulrike Grandke, email to the author, Historisches Archiv, Wiener Symphoniker, May 10, 2021.

35. Icelandic Musicians' Union (Skafti Sigþórsson, secretary) to the Icelandic Justice Department, Reykjavík, February 16, 1940; see also Páll Ísólfsson to the Icelandic Justice Department, Reykjavík, February 13, 1940, National Archives of Iceland, Cabinet of Iceland I, Ministry of Justice, B/636.

36. The Federation of Icelandic Artists (Karl O. Runólfsson, Friðrik Ásmundsson Brekkan, Ríkarður Jónsson) to the Icelandic Justice Ministry, Reykjavík, February 20, 1940, National Archives of Iceland, Cabinet of Iceland I, Ministry of Justice, B/636.

37. "Þakkir frá Stepanek," *Morgunblaðið*, July 18, 1946.

38. "Hans Stephanek kom hingað aftur í gær," September 27, 1947.

39. Dehnow's stay in Iceland is described in more detail in Snorri G. Bergsson, *Erlendur landshornalýður?*, 225–26; Sigurgeir Jónsson, "Menn hætta bara ekki allt í einu að vinna og sitja með hendur í skauti," *Eyjafréttir*, October 21, 2015.

40. "Dr. Fritz Dehnow," *Vísir*, September 28, 1937.

41. Heiko Morisse, "Fritz Dehnow," in *Lexikon verfolgter Musiker und Musikerinnen der NS-Zeit*, eds. Claudia Maurer Zenck, Peter Petersen and Sophie Fetthauer (Hamburg: Universität Hamburg, 2013), www.lexm.uni-hamburg.de/object/lexm_lexmperson_00005334; "Dehnow Jonsson" (pseudonym), *Aires escandinavos, 33 canciones islandesas, noruegas, suecas y dinamarquesas* (Buenos Aires: Ricordi americana, 1957). The Nordic volume begins with two Icelandic songs arranged by Dehnow, the well-known *Ísland, farsælda frón* and *Amma gamla*, which is in fact not a folk song but rather written by Ingunn Bjarnadóttir (1905–1972).

42. Sophie Fetthauer, *Musiker und Musikerinnen im Shanghaier Exil, 1938–1949* (Neumünster: von Bockel Verlag, 2021), 635, 659.

43. Kongelig Dansk Gesandskab to the Icelandic Justice Ministry, Berlin, December 17, 1938, National Archives of Iceland, Cabinet of Iceland I, Ministry of Justice, B/598-13.

44. Sophie Fetthauer, *Musiker und Musikerinnen im Shanghaier Exil*, 40.

45. Sophie Fetthauer, *Musiker und Musikerinnen im Shanghaier Exil*, 35–45. Caesar Erdensohn's description of the deplorable conditions in Hongkou is reproduced in Werner Himmelmann, *Das Schicksal der jüdischen Rechtsanwälte und Notare während der Zeit des Nationalsozialismus: am Beispiel Dortmund* (Dortmund: Anwalt- und Notarverein 1993).

46. Sophie Fetthauer, *Musiker und Musikerinnen im Shanghaier Exil*, 636; Sophie Fetthauer, "Paul Erdensohn," in *Lexikon verfolgter Musiker und Musikerinnen der NS-Zeit*, eds. Claudia Maurer Zenck and Peter Petersen. www.lexm.uni-hamburg.de/object/lexm_lexmperson_00003288

47. Ludwig Misch, "Berufsverbot als Musikkritiker," in *Sie durften nicht mehr Deutsche sein. Jüdischer Alltag in Selbstzeugnissen 1933–1938*, eds. Margarete Limberg and Hubert Rübsaat (Frankfurt am Main: Campus Verlag, 1990), 241–44.

48. Ludwig Misch to the Icelandic Ministry of Justice, Berlin-Wilmersdorf, January 14, 1939, National Archives of Iceland, Foreign Ministry 1967-003, B/75.

49. The Prime Minister's Office to Ludwig Misch, Reykjavík, February 14, 1939, National Archives of Iceland, Foreign Ministry, 1967-003, B/75. Furtwängler's letter of recommendation may have been returned to Misch, as it is not preserved in the National Archives; a presumably identical letter (dated December 1, 1938) is preserved in Misch's collection at the Leo Baeck Institute, New York, https://archives.cjh.org/repositories/5/archival_objects/947063. See also Sam H. Shirakawa, *The Devil's Music Master. The Controversial Life and Career of Wilhelm Furtwängler* (New York: Oxford University Press, 1992), 263.

50. http://lbistories.cjh.org/stories/ludwig-misch; see also Susanne Fontaine, "Umgeben vom Roten Meer. Remigration nach Westberlin," in *Zwischen individueller Biographie und Institution. Zu den Bedingungen beruflicher Rückkehr von Musikern aus dem Exil*, eds. Matthias Pasdzierny and Dörte Schmidt (Schliengen: Edition Argus, 2013), 164–70.

51. Matthias Pasdzierny, *Wiederaufnahme? Rückkehr aus dem Exil und das westdeutsche Musikleben nach 1945* (Munich: edition text + kritik, 2014), 809, on Silbermann, see also 237–55.

52. Alphons Silbermann, *Verwandlungen. Eine Autobiografie* (Bergisch Gladbach: Lübbe, 1989), 148.

53. Albrecht Dümling, *The Vanished Musicians: Jewish Refugees in Australia*, trans. Diana K. Weekes (Oxford: Peter Lang, 2016), 12, 118–20, 521; Matthias Pasdzierny, *Wiederaufnahme?*, 240, 810.

54. Verena Naegele, *Viktor Ullmann. Komponieren in verlorener Zeit* (Köln: Dittrich, 2002), 310–12; Ingo Schultz, *Viktor Ullmann. Leben und Werk* (Kassel: Bärenreiter, 2008), 176–77.

55. Viktor Ullmann to Victor Urbancic, Prague, June 26, 1939 (private collection, Sibyl Urbancic); see also Peter Sarkar, "Ein Brief von Viktor Ullmann nach Reykjavík aus dem Jahr 1939," *mr-Mitteilungen* 108 (2022): 9–11.

56. Saul Friedländer, *The Years of Extermination: Nazi Germany and the Jews 1939–1945* (New York: HarperCollins, 2007), 354.

57. Heinz Edelstein to Icelandic Ministry of Justice, Reykjavík, January 12, 1939, National Archives of Iceland, Cabinet of Iceland I, Ministry of Justice, B/636-7.

58. Icelandic Ministry of Justice to Heinz Edelstein, Reykjavík, January 16, 1939, National Archives of Iceland, Cabinet of Iceland I, Ministry of Justice, B/636-7.

59. https://heritage.statueofliberty.org (search term: Ruth Schepses); see also Renee Schepses Hoffman, interviewed by Andrew Budris. https://bellport.com/vnews/columns/oral-history/vn_oral-history.htm

60. Renee Schepses Hoffman, interviewed by Andrew Budris, https://bellport.com/vnews/columns/oral-history/vn_oral-history.htm; see also Rudolf B. Schmerl, "Place of Birth," *American Jewish Archives Journal* 62 (2010): 49–67.

61. Sarah A. Ogilvie and Scott Miller, *Refuge Denied: The St. Louis Passengers and the Holocaust* (Madison: University of Wisconsin Press, 2006), 15–28.

62. Ida Oberländer, personal identity card, National Archives of the Netherlands.
63. https://jck.nl/en/exhibition/persecution-jews-photographs-netherlands-1940-1945
64. Stefán Edelstein, interview with the author, January 25, 2021.
65. Kathrin Clausing, *Leben auf Abruf*, 312–316. A few letters written by Lilli in Gurs to her friends in Freiburg are preserved in the Caritas Archives, Freiburg, 093.2+284.01 Karton 1, Deportationen 1940–1942.
66. Staatsarchiv Freiburg, Charlotte Edelstein, Wiedergutmachung Report, F 166/3-3569; Stefán Edelstein, interviewed by the author, January 25, 2021.
67. Heinz Edelstein to Helgi P. Briem, Reykjavík, December 23, 1941, National Archives of Iceland, Foreign Ministry 1989, B/7-1.
68. Vigdís Finnbogadóttir, "Charlotte Edelstein," *Morgunblaðið*, September 13, 1997.
69. Victor Urbancic to the Justice Department, Reykjavík, November 13, 1939, National Archives of Iceland, Cabinet of Iceland I, Ministry of Justice, B/635-8; Snorri G. Bergsson, *Erlendur landshornalýður?*, 298.
70. Snorri G. Bergsson, *Erlendur landshornalýður?*, 297.
71. Rigspolitichefen, Copenhagen, report dated February 16, 1940, Rigsarkivet, Copenhagen, Tilsynet for Udlændinge, Udl.sag 76287; see also Snorri G. Bergsson, *Erlendur landshornalýður?*, 298–99; Vilhjálmur Örn Vilhjálmsson, "Eimskipasaga." https://fornleifur.blog.is/blog/fornleifur/entry/1347477
72. Victor and Melitta Urbancic to Valerie Neumann, Reykjavík, April 26, 1940; Victor Urbancic to his family in Vienna, Reykjavík, April 11, 1941 (private collection, Sibyl Urbancic).
73. Helgi P. Briem to Victor Urbancic, Lisbon, April 10, 1942, National Archives of Iceland, Foreign Ministry 1989, B/7.
74. Sibyl Urbancic, interviewed by Sigríður Stephensen, *Heimsmenning á hjara veraldar*, Iceland National Radio, first broadcast 1997.
75. Snorri G. Bergsson, *Erlendur landshornalýður?*, 299.
76. Snorri G. Bergsson, *Erlendur landshornalýður?*, 299; Þór Whitehead, emails to the author, April 14 and 22, 2021. See also Ólafur Þorgrímsson (Reykjavík Music Society) to Ministry of Justice, Reykjavík, September 2, 1938, National Archives of Iceland, Cabinet of Iceland I, Ministry of Justice, B/635-8.
77. Sibyl Urbancic, interviewed by Anna Marsibil Clausen, *Lestin*, Iceland National Radio, first broadcast December 15, 2021.
78. Bohr was related to Danish psychiatrist Edgar Rubin and his uncle Marcus, who was Lis Jacobsen's father; see David Favrholdt, *Niels Bohr's Philosophical Background* (Copenhagen: Det Kongelige Danske Videnskabernes Selskab, 1992), 20.
79. Peter Abraham to Lis Jacobsen, Los Angeles, June 17, 1941; Róbert A. Ottósson to Lis Jacobsen, Reykjavík, August 1, 1960, Lis Jacobsen collection, The Royal Library, Copenhagen.
80. www.imdb.com/name/nm0326588/bio

81. "Mrs. Mathias, Wife of Retired Professor, Dies," *The Capital Times* (Wisconsin), July 4, 1970.

82. Landesamt für Bürger- und Ordnungsangelegenheiten, Berlin, 50.931, Grete Abraham-Nielsen. In order to be allowed permanent residence in Denmark, Grete Abraham entered a marriage of convenience with a Danish painter. She escaped occupied Denmark to Sweden in 1943 and resided there until the end of the war; see Birgit S. Nielsen, "Emigranten und Künstler auf Bornholm," in *Exil in Dänemark. Deutschsprachige Wissenschaftler, Künstler und Schriftsteller im dänischen Exil nach 1933*, eds. Willy Dähnhardt and Birgit S. Nielsen (Heide: Westholsteinische Verlagsanstalt Boyens & Co., 1993), 357–58.

83. Andrew Gosling, "Walter Simon—A Scholar-Librarian and his East Asian Collection," *National Library of Australia News* 11/3 (2000): 3.

84. Grétar Ottó Róbertsson, interview with the author, January 7, 2020.

85. As Marion A. Kaplan has shown, Jews in mixed marriages were not spared from deportations, although these were more sporadic and arbitrary than was otherwise the case; see Kaplan, *Between Dignity and Despair*, 190–91.

Chapter 5

1. The definition is from Eric D. Weitz, *Weimar Germany: Promise and Tragedy* (Princeton, NJ: Princeton University Press, 2007), quoted in Lily E. Hirsch, *A Jewish Orchestra in Nazi Germany*, 7.

2. Ursula Seeber, *Frá hjara veraldar. Melitta Urbancic (1902–1984)—í útlegð frá Austurríki á Íslandi*, trans. Pétur Urbancic (Reykjavík: Landsbókasafn Íslands—Háskólabókasafn, 2014), 16.

3. Jelena Ćirić, "Iceland Officially Recognizes Jewish Community as Religious Organisation," www.icelandreview.com/society/iceland-officially-recognises-jewish-community-as-religious-organisation. On anti-semitism in Iceland, see Vilhjálmur Örn Vilhjálmsson, "Iceland: A Study of Antisemitism in a Country Without Jews," in *Antisemitism in the North: History and State of Research*, eds. Jonathan Adams and Cordelia Heß (Berlin/Boston: De Gruyter, 2020), 69–105.

4. Páll Valsson, *Vigdís*, 96–97.

5. Jón Múli Árnason, *Þjóðsögur Jóns Múla Árnasonar* (Reykjavík: Mál og menning, 1996), 257.

6. Arthúr Björgvin Bollason, "'Svo sú passa þennan strák,'" *Morgunblaðið*, August 16, 2020.

7. Beate Sodian, "SRCD Oral History Interview," Wolfgang Edelstein Max-Planck-Institute for Human Development, Berlin, Germany Part 1: October 17, 2008, and Part 2: March 2, 2009. www.srcd.org/sites/default/files/file-attachments/edelstein_wolfgang_interview.pdf.

8. *Alþingistíðindi 1946–1947, 66. löggjafarþing* (Reykjavík: 1950–1951), B, col. 1873.
9. *Alþingistíðindi 1946–1947, 66. löggjafarþing*, A, 389; B, col. 1872.
10. "N.d. fjallar um ríkisborgararétt," *Vísir*, February 25, 1947.
11. Garðar Sverrisson, interview with the author, June 11, 2024.
12. *Alþingistíðindi 1947–1948, 67. löggjafarþing*, C, col. 160.
13. *Alþingistíðindi 1948–1949, 68. löggjafarþing*, B, cols. 324–27.
14. Páll Valsson, *Myndir úr lífshlaupi Péturs Urbancic*, 20.
15. Sibyl Urbancic, interview with the author, August 18, 2019.
16. Sibyl Urbancic, interview with the author, August 18, 2019.
17. Pétur Urbancic, interview with the author, August 23, 2019.
18. Ingvar Jónasson, interviewed by Óskar Ingólfsson, *Sinfóníuhljómsveit Íslands 40 ára*, Iceland National Radio, first broadcast 1990.
19. Sigrún Löve, interview with the author, March 10, 2020.
20. On lingustic difficulties in exile, see Helene Maimann, "Sprachlosigkeit. Ein zentrales Phänomen der Exilerfahrung," in *Leben im Exil. Probleme der Integration deutscher Flüchtlinge im Ausland 1933–1945*, eds. Wolfgang Frühwald and Wolfgang Schneider (Hamburg: Hoffmann und Campe, 1981), 31–38; Magda Stroińska, "The Role of Language in the Re-Construction of Identity in Exile," in *Exile, Language and Identity*, eds. Magda Stroińska and Vittorina Cecchetto (Frankfurt: Peter Lang, 2003), 95–109.
21. Stefán Edelstein, interview with the author, August 23, 2019.
22. Heinz Edelstein to Björn Jónsson, Detmold, November 13, 1951, National Archives of Iceland, Reykjavík Music Society no. 12/2002, box 2.
23. Arthúr Björgvin Bollason, "'Svo sú passa þennan strák,'" *Morgunblaðið*, August 16, 2020.
24. Páll Björnsson, *Ættarnöfn á Íslandi. Átök um þjóðararf og ímyndir* (Reykjavík: Sögufélag, 2021), 122.
25. "Við mótmælum!," *Alþýðublaðið*, January 12, 1968.
26. Halldór Kiljan Laxness, "Fagur viðburður," *Tímarit Máls og menningar* 3 (1940): 187.
27. "Bæjarpósturinn," *Þjóðviljinn*, January 20, 1948.
28. Páll Björnsson, *Ættarnöfn á Íslandi*, 162.
29. Hermann Hildebrandt to Robert Abraham, Berlin, July 4, 1955; Robert Abraham to Hermann Hildebrandt, Reykjavík, July 9, 1955, National Archives of Iceland, Róbert Abraham Ottósson 2012-002, A/5, 8.
30. Newspaper clippings and programs in National Archives of Iceland, Róbert Abraham Ottósson 2012-002, K/3, 16.
31. Vigdís Finnbogadóttir, "Charlotte Edelstein," *Morgunblaðið*, September 13, 1997.
32. Benjamín Edelstein, interview with the author, July 7, 2022.

33. Charlotte and Heinz Edelstein to Lotte Zier, Reykjavík, November 1949, Hessisches Staatsarchiv Darmstadt, N 25/11025.

34. Charlotte Edelstein to Kurt Zier, Reykjavík, November 23, 1949, Hessisches Staatsarchiv Darmstadt, N 25/11025; see also "Kaffið kemur um næstu mánaðamót," *Vísir*, November 22, 1949.

35. Sibyl Urbancic, quoted in Claudia Geringer, ". . . dass ich wegen unseres Essens gespürt hab, dass wir Emigranten sind. Erinnerungen an das Essen in der Generationenfolge," eds. Veronika Zwerger and Ursula Seeber, *Küche der Erinnerung. Essen & Exil* (Vienna: new academic press, 2018), 319–20.

36. Sibyl Urbancic, email to the author, February 12, 2022.

37. Sibyl Urbancic, emails to the author, February 11 and 12, 2022.

38. Ruth Erb (Urbancic), "Æskuminningar" (typewritten memoir), 9.

39. Stefán Edelstein, interview with the author, August 23, 2019.

40. Tómas Þór Tómasson, *Heimsstyrjaldarárin á Íslandi*, vol. 1 (Reykjavík: Örn og Örlygur, 1983), 63.

41. Stefán Edelstein, interviewed by Sigríður Stephensen, *Heimsmenning á hjara veraldar*, Iceland National Radio, first broadcast 1997.

42. Pétur Urbancic, interview with the author, August 23, 2019.

43. "Roy Hickman syngur í Gamla bíó á föstudaginn," *Alþýðublaðið*, March 31, 1946.

44. Guðrún Egilson, *Spilað og spaugað. Rögnvaldur Sigurjónsson leikur af fingrum fram* (Reykjavík: Almenna bókafélagið, 1978), 93.

45. Leroy Anderson, "Iceland," memoirs from 1947, Leroy Anderson Foundation, Woodbury, CT.

46. Sibyl Urbancic, interview with the author, August 14, 2019.

47. Victor Urbancic to Ernst and Hildegard Urbantschitsch, Reykjavík, April 11, 1941 (private collection, Sibyl Urbancic).

48. See Charmian Brinson and Richard Dove, *A Matter of Intelligence*, 103–14; Andrea Strutz, "Interned as 'Enemy Aliens,'" 46–51.

49. Snorri G. Bergsson, "Fangarnir á Mön," *Ný saga* 8 (1996): 9.

50. Óðinn Melsted, *Með nótur í farteskinu*, 203–4.

51. Carl Billich to Páll Ísólfsson, Isle of Man, October 1, 1943, Páll Ísólfsson Collection, National and University Library, Reykjavík, Lbs 922 NF; Sigurður Pálsson, *Norður í svalann*, 109–11.

52. Óðinn Melsted, *Með nótur í farteskinu*, 58.

53. Stefán Edelstein, interview with the author, August 23, 2019.

54. Stefán Edelstein, interview with the author, August 23, 2019.

55. Stefán Edelstein, interview with the author, August 23, 2019.

56. Stefán Edelstein, interview with the author, August 23, 2019.

57. Páll Ísólfsson, "Heinz Edelstein in memoriam," *Morgunblaðið*, November 8, 1959.

58. Heinz Edelstein, "Isländisches Wandertagebuch," travel diary, June 21–July 4, 1938 (private collection, Stefán Edelstein).

59. Stefán Edelstein, interview with the author, August 23, 2019; "Æfintýralegt ferðalag þriggja Reykvíkinga," *Vísir*, July 30, 1942.

60. A complete listing of Icelandic doctoral theses can be found at https://doktor.landsbokasafn.is/completelist.

61. On the roles of women in exile, see Heike Klapdor, "Überlebensstrategie statt Lebensentwurf. Frauen in der Emigration," in *Frauen und Exil. Zwischen Anpassung und Selbstbehauptung*, eds. Claus-Dieter Krohn, Erwin Rotermund, Lutz Winckler, and Wulf Koepke (Munich: edition text + kritik, 1993), 12–30; Sibille Quack, ed., *Between Sorrow and Strength: Women Refugees of the Nazi Period* (Cambridge: Cambridge University Press, 1995), 4.

62. Pétur Urbancic, "Vielseitig, engagiert, anpassungsfähig . . . ," *Der literarische Zaunkönig* 1 (2008): 54.

63. Björn Franzson, "Framsagnarkvöld frú Urbantschitsch," *Þjóðviljinn*, November 4, 1945.

64. Jana Waldhör, *Zeitspiegel. Eine Stimme des österreichischen Exils in Großbritannien 1939–1946* (Vienna: New Academic Press, 2020), 336–37.

65. Melitta Urbancic, *Frá hjara veraldar / Vom Rand der Welt* (Reykjavík: Stofnun Vigdísar Finnbogadóttur í erlendum tungumálum, 2014).

66. Gauti Kristmannsson, "Bergmál minninganna," 102, 107.

67. Páll Valsson, *Myndir úr lífshlaupi Péturs Urbancic*, 19.

68. "Tvær 10 og 11 ára stúlkur í Reykjavík ætla að koma sér upp býflugnabúum að sumri," *Alþýðublaðið*, September 22, 1953.

69. Gísli Kristjánsson, "Býrækt," *Freyr* 48/3–4 (1953): 58.

70. Cf. Lise Abraham to Melitta Urbancic, Reykjavík, August 14, 1940 (private collection, Sibyl Urbancic).

71. Vigdís Finnbogadóttir, "Charlotte Edelstein," *Morgunblaðið*, September 13, 1997.

72. Vigdís Finnbogadóttir, "Charlotte Edelstein," *Morgunblaðið*, September 13, 1997.

73. Charlotte Edelstein, "An Maria" (private collection, Monika Keller).

74. Deutscher Caritasverband, Freiburg, April 28, 1955; Charlotte Edelstein, Wiedergutmachung report, Staatsarchiv Freiburg, F 196/1-4371.

Chapter 6

1. See, for example, Constanze Stratz, *Ein Wanderer zwischen den Welten. Ernst Toch in der Emigration 1933–1950* (Mainz: Schott Musik, 2013), 218.

2. Kristján Sigurðsson, "Tónlistarskólinn 1930–1940," *Tímarit Tónlistarfélagsins* 2/5 (1940): 18–19.

3. Baldur Andrésson, "Fréttir," *Heimir, söngmálablað* 4 (1938): 18.

4. Emil Thoroddsen, "Hátíðahljómleikar Tónlistarfjelagsins," *Morgunblaðið*, December 10, 1938.

5. Werner Gerlach, memorandum, quoted in Þór Whitehead, *Milli vonar og ótta. Ísland í síðari heimsstyrjöld* (Reykjavík: Vaka-Helgafell, 1995), 44.
6. Sibyl Urbancic, interview with the author, August 14, 2019.
7. "Óratórið Júdas Makkabeus eftir Händel í útvarpinu 14. júní," *Útvarpstíðindi* 10 (1947): 232.
8. "Jóhannesarpassían," *Vísir*, March 3, 1943.
9. Þorsteinn Hannesson, interviewed by Sigríður Stephensen, *Heimsmenning á hjara veraldar*, Iceland National Radio, first broadcast 1997.
10. Jón Nordal, interview with the author, February 9, 2016.
11. Jón Ásgeirsson, interviewed by Rudolf Habringer, September 14, 2003.
12. Eyþór Stefánsson to Victor Urbancic, Sauðárkrókur, April 24, 1943, Victor Urbancic Collection, National and University Library, Reykjavík.
13. Árni Kristjánsson, "Jóhannesarpassían," *Tímarit Máls og menningar* 6 (1943): 19.
14. "Jólaóratoríó eftir Bach flutt af Tónlistarfélaginu," *Vísir*, December 9, 1944.
15. Minutes of the Music Society Choir, January 3, 1946, quoted in Aðalheiður Þorsteinsdóttir, "Dr. Victor Urbancic," BA thesis, Reykjavík College of Music, 1997, 20.
16. "Óratoríið Messías eftir Händel," *Fálkinn*, February 22, 1946, 2; Baldur Andrésson, "'Messías' eftir Händel," *Vísir*, February 21, 1946.
17. Þorsteinn Sveinsson, "Norræna söngmótið í Kaupmannahöfn," *Musica* 1/2 (1948): 4–6.
18. See Árni Heimir Ingólfsson, *Jón Leifs and the Musical Invention of Iceland*, 258–65.
19. Victor Urbancic, "Jón Leifs fimmtugur," *Alþýðublaðið*, May 1, 1949.
20. Tage Ammendrup, "Úr tónlistarlífinu," *Musica* 1/6 (1949): 13.
21. "Mánudagsþankar Jóns Reykvíkings," *Mánudagsblaðið*, November 29, 1948.
22. "Söngför Tónlistarfélagskórsins," *Þjóðviljinn*, August 10, 1951.
23. Páll Ísólfsson, "Þriðju tónleikar Tónlistarfjelagsins," *Morgunblaðið*, February 24, 1938.
24. Sigurður E. Markan, "3. hljómleikar (Kammermusikkvöld) Tónlistarfélagsins," *Alþýðublaðið*, February 25, 1938.
25. "B," "Tónlistarfélagið: 3. hljómleikar," *Þjóðviljinn*, February 27, 1938.
26. "Tríó Tónlistarskólans," *Fálkinn*, April 14, 1939, 2.
27. "Tríó Tónlistarskólans," *Útvarpstíðindi*, January 9, 1939, 188.
28. Hallgrímur Helgason, "Hljómleikalíf Reykjavíkur," *Musica* 4 (1945): 27. In 1938, attempts had been made to create a string quartet under the leadership of violinist Ernst Drucker, who came to Iceland to perform on behalf of the Reykjavík Music Society (see chapter 3), with Edelstein as cellist. The board of the National Radio approved this proposal, but nothing became of the plan, and Drucker emigrated to the United States soon afterward; see Björn Jónsson to Jón

Leifs, Reykjavík, March 20, 1938, and Páll Ísólfsson to Jón Leifs, April 18, 1938, Jón Leifs Collection, National and University Library, Reykjavík, Lbs 751 NF.

29. Haukur Gröndal to Heinz Edelstein, Reykjavík, April 30, 1945 (private collection, Stefán Edelstein).

30. Heinz Edelstein to Haukur Gröndal, Reykjavík, May 1, 1945 (private collection, Stefán Edelstein).

31. Reykjavík Music Society, salary report, Reykjavík Music Society Collection, National and University Library, Reykjavík, Lbs 1146 NF.

32. Þórarinn Óskarsson, interview with the author, January 12, 2020.

33. Stefán Edelstein, interview with the author, August 23, 2019.

34. Stefán Edelstein, interview with the author, August 23, 2019.

35. Stefán Edelstein, interview with the author, January 27, 2020.

36. Stefán Edelstein, interview with the author, August 23, 2019.

37. Haukur Guðlaugsson, interview with the author, March 23, 2020.

38. Stefán Edelstein, interview with the author, August 23, 2019.

39. Gunnar Kvaran, interview with the author, January 6, 2020.

40. Stefán Edelstein, interview with the author, August 23, 2019.

41. Pétur Urbancic, interview with the author, February 17, 2022.

42. Sigrún Löve, interview with the author, March 10, 2020.

43. Pétur Urbancic, interview with the author, February 17, 2022.

44. Páll Kr. Pálsson, "Árstíðirnar," *Þjóðviljinn*, March 17, 1943.

45. Baldur Andrésson, "Tónleikar Tónlistarfélagsins í Trípólíleikhúsinu," *Vísir*, April 24, 1946; see also "6. tónleikar Tónlistarfjel.," *Morgunblaðið*, April 11, 1946.

46. Hallgrímur Helgason, "Samsöngur „Hörpu"," *Alþýðublaðið*, March 11, 1945.

47. Robert Abraham to Paul Hindemith, Reykjavík, May 20, 1945 (private collection, Elín Þ. Ólafsdóttir).

48. "40 manna kór úr Söngfélaginu „Hörpu" fór utan með Drottningunni í gærkvöldi," *Alþýðublaðið*, June 14, 1946.

49. Emil Thoroddsen, "Samsöngur," *Morgunblaðið*, February 2, 1944.

50. "Samsöngur Karlakórs iðnaðarmanna," *Þjóðviljinn*, May 11, 1947.

51. Páll Ísólfsson, "Samsöngur Karlakórs iðnaðarmanna," *Morgunblaðið*, May 17, 1947.

52. Robert Abraham to an unknown recipient, Reykjavík, December 18, 1946 (private collection, Elín Þ. Ólafsdóttir).

53. Gunnar Stefánsson, *Útvarp Reykjavík. Saga Ríkisútvarpsins 1930–1960* (Reykjavík: Sögufélag, 1997), 306.

54. "Yfirlit yfir söngskrár Útvarpskórsins veturinn 1947/1948," typewritten repertoire list, dated May 25, 1948 (private collection, Elín Þ. Ólafsdóttir).

55. "Klassísk tónlist vinsælli en jazz meðal útvarpshlustenda," *Morgunblaðið*, March 14, 1948.

56. Sigurður Þórðarson, "Brjef: Útvarpskórinn," *Morgunblaðið*, March 17, 1948.

57. "Athugasemd frá útvarpsráði," *Morgunblaðið*, May 28, 1948.
58. "Snúlli," "Úr daglega lífinu," *Morgunblaðið*, November 21, 1947.
59. Jakob Benediktsson, "Úr daglega lífinu," *Morgunblaðið*, November 22, 1947.
60. Sigurður Skagfield, "Söngur Útvarpskórsins," *Tíminn*, February 11, 1949; Tage Ammendrup, "Samsöngur Útvarpskórsins," *Musica*, 3/3 (April 1, 1950), 14.
61. Abraham also briefly conducted the Reykjavík Mixed Choir (*Samkór Reykjavíkur*), founded in 1943 by Jóhann Tryggvason, father of Þórunn Ashkenazy. Abraham took over the ensemble in 1952 and directed it for two years, in repertoire ranging from Bach motets to Brahms's *Schicksalslied*, the latter with the Iceland Symphony Orchestra. A high point of his work with the choir was a concert tour of Finland and Norway in summer 1954, but shortly afterward Abraham left his position due to his busy schedule, and the choir was disbanded.
62. "Það er gaman að lifa á þessum þroskaárum íslenzkrar tónlistar," 4.
63. Tage Ammendrup, "Samsöngur Útvarpskórsins," 14; Guðmundur Jónsson, interviewed by Sigríður Stephensen, *Heimsmenning á hjara veraldar*, Iceland National Radio, first broadcast 1997.
64. Ingólfur Margeirsson, *Lífsjátning. Endurminningar Guðmundu Elíasdóttur söngkonu* (Reykjavík: Iðunn, 1981), 115.
65. Jónína Michaelsdóttir, *Líf mitt og gleði. Minningar Þuríðar Pálsdóttur söngkonu* (Reykjavík: Forlagið, 1986), 135–36, 186.
66. Halldór Halldórsson, "Vinarkveðja," *Morgunblaðið*, March 20, 1974; reprinted in *Árbók Vísindafélags Íslendinga* (1974): 142.
67. "Pianissimo—ekki pianó!," *Morgunblaðið*, March 8, 1960.
68. Jón Þórarinsson, "Guðríður Magnúsdóttir—Minning," *Morgunblaðið*, March 16, 1990.
69. "Það er gaman að lifa á þessum þroskaárum íslenzkrar tónlistar," 4.
70. Árni Björnsson, "Dr. Róbert Abraham Ottósson—In memoriam," *Þjóðviljinn*, March 20, 1974.
71. Árni Björnsson, "Dr. Róbert Abraham Ottósson—In memoriam," *Þjóðviljinn*, March 20, 1974.
72. Árni Björnsson, "Dr. Róbert Abraham Ottósson—In memoriam," *Þjóðviljinn*, March 20, 1974.
73. Margrét Heinreksdóttir ["mbj"], "Sveiflur í túlkun tónlistar eins og í öðrum listgreinum," *Morgunblaðið*, November 28, 1973.
74. Lilja Árnadóttir, "Skarpgreindur, víðsýnn og fjölmenntaður mannvinur," *Sunnudagsmogginn*, April 15, 2012.
75. Halldór Halldórsson, "Vinarkveðja," 10.
76. "Góðir Íslendingar," *Vísir*, December 14, 1961; Jón Stefánsson, interview with the author, January 13, 2012.
77. Þorgerður Ingólfsdóttir, interview with the author, February 5, 2012.
78. Þorgerður Ingólfsdóttir, interview with the author, February 5, 2012; Stefán Edelstein, interview with the author, February 6, 2012.

79. Robert Abraham to Halldór Halldórsson, Akureyri, July 12, 1939; Robert Abraham to Halldór Halldórsson, Reykjavík, March 15, 1941 (private collection, Hildigunnur Halldórsdóttir).

80. Grétar Ottó Róbertsson and Elín Þ. Ólafsdóttir, interview with the author, January 8, 2012.

81. Stefán Edelstein, interview with the author, February 6, 2012.

82. Grétar Ottó Róbertsson, interview with the author, January 8, 2012.

83. Þorgerður Ingólfsdóttir, interview with the author, February 5, 2012.

84. "Vikar" [Ólafur Þorgrímsson], "6. hljómleikar Tónlistarfjelagsins," *Morgunblaðið*, May 12, 1939.

85. Þorsteinn Sveinsson, "Fimmtugur í dag: Dr. Victor Urbancic," *Morgunblaðið*, August 9, 1953.

86. Rögnvaldur Sigurjónsson, interviewed by Sigríður Stephensen, *Heimsmenning á hjara veraldar*, Iceland National Radio, first broadcast 1997.

87. Baldur Hermannsson, *Ævars saga Kvaran* (Reykjavík: Örn og Örlygur, 1989), 187–88.

88. Þuríður Pálsdóttir, interviewed by Sigríður Stephensen, *Heimsmenning á hjara veraldar*, Iceland National Radio, first broadcast 1997.

89. Jórunn Viðar, interviewed by Egill Friðleifsson, *Tónlistarmenn*, Iceland National Radio, first broadcast 1981.

90. Gunnar Egilson, interviewed by Sigríður Stephensen, *Heimsmenning á hjara veraldar*, Iceland National Radio, first broadcast 1997.

91. Ragnar Björnsson, "Góð fæðing eftir Þyrnirósar-svefn," *Morgunblaðið*, November 26, 1996.

92. "Dagskrá, 6.-12. febrúar," Iceland National Radio, January 1949.

93. Ragnar Björnsson, "Góð fæðing eftir Þyrnirósar-svefn," *Morgunblaðið*, November 26, 1996.

94. Gunnar Egilson, interviewed by Sigríður Stephensen, *Heimsmenning á hjara veraldar*, Iceland National Radio, first broadcast 1997.

95. "Nýstárlegt kórverk í Landakotskirkju á sunnudaginn kemur," *Morgunblaðið*, May 13, 1941.

96. Emil Thoroddsen, "Tveir tónlistarviðburðir," *Morgunblaðið*, December 23, 1941; see also Baldur Andrésson, "Kvöldsöngur í Landakotskirkjunni," *Vísir*, December 19, 1941.

97. B.G., "Tónleikar í Kristskirkju," *Vísir*, February 2, 1955; Róbert Abraham, "Nýstárlegir hljómleikar," *Morgunblaðið*, May 1, 1945.

98. Johann Sebastian Bach, *Tíu sönglög eftir Joh. Seb. Bach*, ed. Victor Urbancic (Reykjavík: Guðrún Pálsdóttir, 1952).

99. "Mozart-hátíðahöld. Nýr kvöldsöngur í Landakoti o.fl.," *Morgunblaðið*, December 6, 1941.

100. Emil Thoroddsen, "Minningartónleikar Tónlistarfjelagsins," *Morgunblaðið*, December 11, 1941.

101. "Nitouche á leiksviðinu," *Fálkinn*, February 28, 1941, 5.
102. "Saga kaþólsku kirkjunnar á Íslandi," https://catholica.is/biskupsdaemid-saga/.
103. Páll Valsson, *Myndir úr lífshlaupi Péturs Urbancic*, 25.
104. "Dr. Urbancic heldur orgelhljómleika í Kristskirkju á þriðjudag," *Alþýðublaðið*, December 9, 1950.
105. Sibyl Urbancic, interview with the author, August 14, 2019.
106. Sibyl Urbancic, interview with the author, August 18, 2019.
107. Sigurður E. Markan, "5. hljómleikar Tónlistarfélagsins," *Alþýðublaðið*, March 18, 1940.
108. For more on this competition, see Ingólfsson, *Jón Leifs and the Musical Invention of Iceland*, 135–40.
109. Þórarinn Jónsson, "Minningartónleikar um Emil Thoroddsen," *Alþýðublaðið*, May 18, 1954.
110. Jórunn Viðar to Katrín Viðar, New York, July 29, 1945 (private collection, Katrín Fjeldsted).
111. "Bæjarfréttir," *Vísir*, September 28, 1946.
112. Guðrún Guðmundsdóttir, "Þjóðleikhúskórinn á sínum fyrstu árum," https://sarpur.is/Adfang.aspx?AdfangID=539874.
113. "Kynnti íslenzka tónlist í stórborgum Austurríkis," *Vísir*, October 2, 1948; *Neues Österreich*, July 30, 1948.
114. "Dr. Páll Ísólfsson hlaut fyrstu verðlaun fyrir tónverk við Skálholtsljóð," *Morgunblaðið*, April 26, 1956.
115. "Óður Skálholts," *Morgunblaðið*, November 22, 1996.
116. Árni Heimir Ingólfsson, *Jón Leifs and the Musical Invention of Iceland*, 3–4.
117. Pétur Húni Björnsson, "Íslensk þjóðlög? Söfnun, útgáfa og viðtökur þjóðlagasafns séra Bjarna Þorsteinssonar, Íslenzk þjóðlög" (MA thesis in ethnology, University of Iceland, 2019), 96–97.
118. Baldur Andrésson, "Tónskáldið Karl O. Runólfsson," *Vikan*, November 14, 1946, 3 and 7.
119. The libretto is based on a famous play by Icelandic playwright Jóhann Sigurjónsson. Mixa's opera premiered only in 1987, but he gave a partial performance (with piano) for the board of the Reykjavík Music Society before leaving Iceland in 1938 (Georg Zauner, *Franz Mixa. Leben und Werk*, 26).
120. Franz Mixa, "Jón Leifs og afstaða hans til íslenzkra tónskálda," *Lesbók Morgunblaðsins*, November 28, 1937, 369–70.
121. Victor Urbancic, "Jón Leifs fimmtugur," *Alþýðublaðið*, May 1, 1949.
122. Jón Nordal, interview with the author, October 14, 2020.
123. Jón Nordal, interview with the author, February 9, 2016.
124. "Stórkostlegt að lifa þennan atburð," *Morgunblaðið*, November 25, 1982.

125. Black music book without title, dedicated to "Meinen drei Lieben!" (private collection, Sibyl Urbancic).

126. "Komnir heim úr söngför til Norðurlandsins," *Morgunblaðið*, August 2, 1941.

127. Áskell Snorrason, "Kirkjuhljómleikar," *Verkamaðurinn*, July 26, 1941.

128. Music book without title, arrangements of twelve Icelandic folk songs (private collection, Sibyl Urbancic).

129. Ernst Roth (Boosey & Hawkes) to Melitta Urbancic, London, July 18, 1958; Alfred Schlee (Universal Edition) to Melitta Urbancic, Vienna, August 9, 1960; (Victor Urbancic Collection, National and University Library).

130. Melitta Urbancic, "Betrifft: Isländische Volkslieder für gemischten Chor" (private collection, Sibyl Urbancic); Sibyl Urbancic interview with the author, December 27, 2021.

Chapter 7

1. Minutes of the Icelandic Musicians' Union (FÍH), March 3, 1944, FÍH archives, Reykjavík.

2. Minutes of the Icelandic Musicians' Union (FÍH), February 1, 1944, FÍH archives, Reykjavík.

3. Minutes of the Icelandic Musicians' Union (FÍH), February 23, 1944, FÍH archives, Reykjavík.

4. Baldur Andrésson, "Hljómleikar," *Vísir*, May 9, 1944.

5. Minutes of the Reykjavík Symphony Orchestra, 8–9, National Archives of Iceland, Symfóníuhljómsveit Reykjavíkur 2007, A/1-6.

6. Páll Ísólfsson, "Symfóníuhljómsveit Reykjavíkur," *Morgunblaðið*, January 22, 1948.

7. Victor Urbancic, "Bréfabálkur," *Tónlistin* 1/2 (1942): 39.

8. Ólafur Jakobsson, ". . . Ísland er minn starfsvettvangur . . . ," *Musica* 1/3 (1948): 6.

9. Jón Þórarinsson, "Symfóníuhljómsveit Reykjavíkur," *Alþýðublaðið*, March 13, 1948.

10. Óðinn Melsted, *Með nótur í farteskinu*, 219.

11. See also Óðinn Melsted, *Með nótur í farteskinu*, 155–58.

12. Minutes of the Reykjavík Symphony Orchestra, 52–53, National Archives of Iceland, Symfóníuhljómsveit Reykjavíkur 2007, A/1-6.

13. Minutes of the Icelandic Musicians' Union (FÍH), April 13, 1949, FÍH archives, Reykjavík.

14. Minutes of the Icelandic Musicians' Union (FÍH), October 23, 1949, FÍH archives, Reykjavík.

15. Róbert Abraham, "Symfóníuhljómsveit Reykjavíkur. Stjórnandi P. Ísólfsson," *Morgunblaðið*, December 13, 1949.

16. "Nýju Sinfóníuhljómsveitinni fagnað ákaflega," *Morgunblaðið*, March 10, 1950; Sigurður Skagfield, "Sinfóníuhljómleikarnir," *Mánudagsblaðið*, March 13, 1950.

17. Robert Abraham to Kurt Bendix, Reykjavík, October 16, 1950 (private collection, Elín Þ. Ólafsdóttir).

18. Grete Abraham to Robert Abraham, Allinge, April 28, 1952, National Archives of Iceland, Róbert Abraham Ottósson 2012-002, A/5, 8.

19. Bjarki Bjarnason, *Sinfóníuhljómsveit Íslands. Saga og stéttartal* (Reykjavík: Sögusteinn, 2000), 262–64.

20. Þórarinn Jónsson, "Frá Haendel til Stravinsky," *Alþýðublaðið*, December 18, 1951.

21. Þorsteinn Valdimarsson, "Glæsilegir tónleikar Sinfóníuhljómsveitarinnar," *Þjóðviljinn*, November 22, 1950.

22. Ragnar Jónsson, "Þættir úr sögu hljómsveitarmálanna," *Helgafell* 5 (1953): 65. Jónsson's judgment on Abraham is correct; when he directed the Iceland Symphony's inaugural concert in 1950, he had conducted in public only one movement from a Beethoven symphony in Paris (1934), three concerts in Copenhagen (1935), one program (repeated several times) with the FÍH orchestra (1944) and a single concert with the Reykjavík Symphony Orchestra (1948).

23. Trond Olav Svendsen, "Olav Kielland," *Store norske leksikon*. https://snl.no/Olav_Kielland

24. Victor Urbancic, "Opið bréf," *Alþýðublaðið*, May 3, 1952; see also "Yfirlýsing frá stjórn Sinfóníuhljómsveitarinnar," *Morgunblaðið*, May 6, 1952.

25. "Urbancic," *Tíminn*, May 7, 1952.

26. Þórhallur Björnsson, "Hugleiðingar um tónlistarmál," *Tíminn*. June 4, 1952.

27. "Jón Þórarinsson leggur stund á tónlistarfræði," *Morgunblaðið*, January 4, 1944.

28. Jón Þórarinsson, "Merkur tónlistarviðburður," *Helgafell* 2 (1943): 240–42.

29. Jón Nordal, interview with the author, February 9, 2016.

30. Heinz Edelstein to Jón Þórarinsson, ca. 1950 (private collection, Stefán Edelstein).

31. Heinz Edelstein to Jón Þórarinsson, ca. 1950 (private collection, Stefán Edelstein).

32. Stefán Edelstein, interview with the author, January 25, 2021.

33. Iceland Symphony Orchestra program booklets, 1950–55.

34. The Music Society Choir (Tónlistarfélagskórinn) minutes, September 30, 1952, Minutes 1951–1953, The Reykjavík Music Society Collection, National and University Library, Reykjavík, Lbs 1146 NF.

35. Victor Urbancic to the boards of the Reykjavík Music Society and the Music Society Choir, September 15, 1952, Minutes 1951–1953, The Reykjavík Music Society Collection, National and University Library, Reykjavík, Lbs 1146 NF.

36. The Music Society Choir minutes, September 29, 1952, The Reykjavík Music Society Collection, National and University Library, Reykjavík, Lbs 1146 NF.

37. The Music Society Choir minutes, September 30, 1952, The Reykjavík Music Society Collection, National and University Library, Reykjavík, Lbs 1146 NF.

38. The Music Society Choir minutes, October 6, 1952, The Reykjavík Music Society Collection, National and University Library, Reykjavík, Lbs 1146 NF.

39. B.G., "Óratorían 'Davíð konungur,'" *Vísir*, December 11, 1952.

40. See "Hefir stjórnað flutningi flestra stórra kórverka hér," *Tíminn*, February 22, 1953.

41. "Hef aldrei farið með ófrið á hendur tónlistarmönnum," *Morgunblaðið*, March 1, 1953; "Nýr kafli í Þjóðleikhússhljómkviðunni," *Þjóðviljinn*, September 10, 1953.

42. Guðlaugur Rósinkranz, *Allt var þetta indælt stríð. Æviminningar Guðlaugs Rósinkranz þjóðleikhússtjóra* (Reykjavík: Örn og Örlygur, 1977), 142.

43. "Tónlistarmenn vilja frið við Þjóðleikhúsið," *Morgunblaðið*, February 28, 1953.

44. Ragnar Jónsson, "Fyrirspurn til Þjóðleikhússtjóra," *Morgunblaðið*, February 18, 1953.

45. Ragnar Jónsson to Guðlaugur Rósinkranz, no date, February 1953 (Ragnar Jónsson Collection, National and University Library, Reykjavík, Lbs 9 NF); see also "Skæruhernaður í tónlistarmálum breytist í styrjöld," *Vísir*, February 26, 1953.

46. "Nýr kafli í Þjóðleikhússhljómkviðunni," *Þjóðviljinn*, September 10, 1953.

47. "Styrjöld um hljómsveitarstjóra Þjóðleikhússins," *Alþýðublaðið*, February 26, 1953.

48. "Tónlistarfélagið í skotgrafahernaði gegn þjóðleikhúsinu," *Tíminn*, February 27, 1953.

49. "Nýr kafli í Þjóðleikhússhljómkviðunni," *Þjóðviljinn*, September 10, 1953.

50. "Tónlistarmenn vilja frið við Þjóðleikhúsið," *Morgunblaðið*, February 28, 1953.

51. Jón Þórarinsson and Björn Jónsson, "Greinargerð um samningaumleitanir Sinfóníuhljómsveitarinnar við Þjóðleikhúsið," *Morgunblaðið*, January 28, 1953.

52. "Nýr kafli í Þjóðleikhússhljómkviðunni," *Þjóðviljinn*, September 10, 1953.

53. "Fer dr. Urbancic úr landi vegna áreitni og ofríkis í tónlistarmálum?," *Tíminn*, September 10, 1953; "Dr. Urbancic ætlar ekki úr landi nema hann neyðist til að leita sér atvinnu annars staðar," *Alþýðublaðið*, September 12, 1953.

54. See, for example, Arthur Mendel (Princeton University) to Victor Urbancic, Princeton, April 13, 1954; William L. Crosten (Stanford University) to Urbancic, Stanford, April 14, 1954; Theodore Kratt (University of Oregon School of Music) to Urbancic, Eugene (OR), April 15, 1954; Archibald J. Davison (Harvard University) to Urbancic, Cambridge (MA), April 17, 1954; Wilfred C. Bain (Indiana University) to Urbancic, Bloomington, April 20, 1954; Joaquin Nin-Culmell (University of California) to Urbancic, Berkeley, May 24, 1954 (private collection, Sibyl Urbancic).

55. Sæm. Á., "Opið bréf til Ragnars Jónssonar," *Mánudagsblaðið*, March 2, 1953; see also Ragnar Jónsson, "Stutt sögusinfónía í dilentantískum stíl," *Mánudagsblaðið*, March 9, 1953.

56. "Tónskáldafélagið," *Þjóðviljinn*, March 3, 1953.

57. "Hefir stjórnað flutningi flestra stórra kórverka hér," *Tíminn*, February 22, 1953.

58. "Tónlistarmenn vilja frið við Þjóðleikhúsið," *Morgunblaðið*, February 28, 1953.

59. Ragnar Jónsson, "Bréf um tónlistarmál," *Morgunblaðið*, February 22, 1953. See also a response to this open letter, Sæm. Á., "Opið bréf til Ragnars Jónssonar," *Mánudagsblaðið*, March 2, 1953, and Jónsson's reply, "Stutt sögusinfónía í diletantískum stíl," *Morgunblaðið*, March 9, 1953.

60. Ragnar Jónsson to Victor Urbancic, Reykjavík, May 3, 1952 (copy in Páll Ísólfsson Collection, National and University Library, Reykjavík, Lbs 922 NF).

61. Victor Urbancic to Ragnar Jónsson, Reykjavík, May 9, 1952, Ragnar Jónsson Collection, National and University Library, Reykjavík, Lbs 9 NF.

62. Victor Urbancic to Ragnar Jónsson, Reykjavík, May 9, 1952, Ragnar Jónsson Collection, National and University Library, Reykjavík, Lbs 9 NF.

63. Ragnar Jónsson to Victor Urbancic, Reykjavík, May 3, 1952, copy in Páll Ísólfsson Collection, National and University Library, Reykjavík, Lbs 922 NF.

64. Páll Ísólfsson to Sigurður Nordal, Reykjavík, December 2, 1953, Páll Ísólfsson Collection, National and University Library, Reykjavík, Lbs 922 NF.

65. Jón Nordal to Páll Ísólfsson, Mont Pélerin, May 5, 1954, Páll Ísólfsson Collection, National and University Library, Reykjavík, Lbs 922 NF. On Kielland in Iceland, see also Bjarki Bjarnason, *Sinfóníuhljómsveit Íslands* (Reykjavík: Sögusteinn, 2000), 101–4.

66. Stefán Edelstein, interview with the author, January 25, 2021.

67. Heinz Edelstein to Lotte Zier, Reykjavík, November 9, 1952, Hessisches Staatsarchiv Darmstadt, N 25/11027.

68. Stefán Edelstein, interview with the author, January 25, 2021.

69. Iceland Symphony Orchestra program book, November 28, 1952, Victor Urbancic Collection, National and University Library, Reykjavík.

70. Robert Abraham to Hermann Hildebrandt, Reykjavík, April 9, 1955, National Archives of Iceland, Róbert Abraham Ottósson 2012-002, A/5, 8.

71. Robert Abraham to Jón Þórarinsson, Reykjavík, May 7, 1955, Jón Þórarinsson Collection, National and University Library, Reykjavík, Jón Þórarinsson Collection, Lbs 1188 NF.

72. Ragnar Jónsson to Bjarni Benediktsson, Reykjavík, September 13, 1953, Reykjavík Municipal Archives, Private Collection no. 360, Box 2-12.

73. Ragnar Jónsson to Bjarni Benediktsson, Reykjavík, September 13, 1953, Reykjavík Municipal Archives, Private Collection no. 360, Box 2-12.

74. Sibyl Urbancic, interview with the author, September 23, 2022.

75. Guðlaugur Rósinkranz, *Allt var þetta indælt stríð*, 143.
76. Ragnar Jónsson, "Óperettan Káta ekkjan," *Nýtt Helgafell* 1 (1956): 138.
77. Ragnar Jónsson, "Listir: Tvær óperur," *Nýtt Helgafell* 2 (1957): 44.
78. Ragnar Jónsson, "Sinfóníuhljómsveitin og Sovétlistamennirnir," *Morgunblaðið*, September 22, 1954.
79. Sveinn Einarsson, "Þuríður Pálsdóttir—Minningarorð," *Morgunblaðið*, August 29, 2022.
80. Sigurður Grímsson, "Tosca," *Morgunblaðið*, September 25, 1957.
81. "Tríó Tónlistarskólans," *Útvarpstíðindi*, January 9, 1939, 187.
82. Styrmir Gunnarsson, email to the author, April 18, 2020.
83. Heinz Edelstein, "Tónlistaruppeldi," *Tímarit Tónlistarfélagsins* 1 (1938): 19–20.
84. Heinz Edelstein, "Tónlistaruppeldi," *Tímarit Tónlistarfélagsins* 1 (1938): 21.
85. Heinz Edelstein, "Erling Blöndal Bengtson," *Morgunblaðið*, May 9, 1946.
86. Gunnar Björnsson, "Fleiri nótur í farteskinu," *Morgunblaðið*, September 9, 2020.
87. In a letter dated October 1948, Edelstein asked Þórarinsson to write a few songs for a collection of songs for children he hoped to publish; see Heinz Edelstein to Jón Þórarinsson, Velbert, Germany, October 2, 1948, Jón Þórarinsson Collection, National and University Library, Reykjavík, Lbs 1188 NF.
88. Jón Þórarinsson, *Sex gamlir húsgangar með nýjum lögum fyrir börn* (Reykjavík: Helgafell, 1951 [*sic*]).
89. Heinz Edelstein to Lotte and Kurt Zier, Reykjavík, June 30, 1950, Hessisches Staatsarchiv Darmstadt, N 25/11027.
90. *Þjóðviljinn*, March 22, 1951.
91. Heinz Edelstein to Björn Jónsson, Detmold, November 13, 1951, National Archives of Iceland, The Reykjavík Music Society no. 12/2002, box 2.
92. Heinz Edelstein to Björn Jónsson, Detmold, November 13, 1951, National Archives of Iceland, The Reykjavík Music Society no. 12/2002, box 2.
93. Heinz Edelstein, Application for Wiedergutmachung, Staatsarchiv Freiburg, F 196/1-2465.
94. Heinz Edelstein to Ingólfur Guðbrandsson, Hamburg, August 14, 1952 (private collection, Þorgerður Ingólfsdóttir).
95. "Barnamúsíkskólinn hefur starfsemi sína," *Vísir*, October 12, 1956.
96. Bergþóra Jónsdóttir, "Tónmenntaskóli Reykjavíkur 50 ára," *Morgunblaðið*, May 18, 2003.
97. "Ný kennsluaðferð notuð við tónlistarnám barna," *Tíminn*, October 25, 1955.
98. "Barnamúsikskólinn færir út kvíarnar í vetur," *Þjóðviljinn*, October 25, 1955.
99. Stefán Edelstein, interview with the author, August 23, 2019.
100. "Barnamúsíkskólinn flytur söngleik fyrir börn," *Morgunblaðið*, April 8, 1960; "Við ætlum að leika Barnasinfóníuna," *Vísir*, May 13, 1961.

101. Kolbeinn Bjarnason, *Helguleikur. Saga Helgu Ingólfsdóttur og Sumartónleika í Skálholti* (Selfoss: Bókaútgáfan Sæmundur, 2018), 86–87.

102. Gunnar Kvaran, interview with the author, January 6, 2020; Sigrún Löve, interview with the author, March 10, 2020.

103. Heinz Edelstein to Kurt Zier, Reykjavík, March 25, 1953, Hessisches Staatsarchiv Darmstadt, N 25/11027; Heinz Edelstein to Kurt and Lotte Zier, Reykjavík, November 16, 1952, November 29 and December 7, 1953, Hessisches Staatsarchiv Darmstadt, N 25/11027.

104. Heinz Edelstein to Kurt and Lotte Zier, Reykjavík, November 16, 1952, November 29 and December 7, 1953, Hessisches Staatsarchiv Darmstadt, N 25/11027.

105. Ingólfur Guðbrandsson, "Uppeldi og tónlist," *Morgunblaðið*, November 24, 1955.

106. E.P., "Músíkskóli dr. Edelstein," *Tíminn*, May 19, 1955.

107. H.H., "Dr. Edelstein og börnin hans," *Frjáls þjóð*, May 21, 1955.

108. Icelandic National Radio record catalogue, records no. 82043 and 82044.

109. "Almar," "Úr daglega lífinu," *Morgunblaðið*, June 8, 1955.

110. Robert Abraham to Leitung des Städtischen Orchesters Freiburg, Reykjavík, October 17, 1955, National Archives of Iceland, Róbert Abraham Ottósson, 2012-002, A/2.

111. "Róbert A. Ottósson ráðinn hljómsveitarstjóri í Berlín í vetur," *Alþýðublaðið*, August 19, 1956.

112. Yohanan Boem, "Musical Diary," *The Jerusalem Post*, November 21, 1962.

113. Bjarki Bjarnason, *Sinfóníuhljómsveit Íslands*, 262–66.

114. Ásgeir Hjartarson, "Rakarinn í Sevilla," *Þjóðviljinn*, January 4, 1959.

115. Abraham formally suggested that the National Theater perform *The Tales of Hoffmann*, c.f. his letter to the National Theater's Music Committee, Reykjavík, November 17, 1953 (private collection, Elín Þ. Ólafsdóttir).

Chapter 8

1. Stefán Edelstein, "Kurt Zier—Minningarorð," *Morgunblaðið*, October 25, 1969.

2. *Hagskinna. Sögulegar hagtölur um Ísland*, eds. Guðmundur Jónsson and Magnús S. Magnússon (Reykjavík: Hagstofa Íslands, 1997), 199.

3. Rudolf Habringer, "Emigration an der Rand der Welt," 115.

4. Victor Urbancic, "Að lokinni kynnisför til Bandaríkjanna," *Tíminn*, April 27, 1958.

5. Victor Urbancic to Melitta Urbancic, Cambridge (MA), January 27, 1958 (private collection, Sibyl Urbancic).

6. Victor Urbancic, "Að lokinni kynnisför til Bandaríkjanna," *Tíminn*, April 27, 1958.

7. Sibyl Urbancic, interview with the author, August 14, 2019.
8. Sibyl Urbancic, interview with the author, August 14, 2019.
9. Jón Leifs, "Dr. Urbancic minnzt," *Morgunblaðið*, November 27, 1958.
10. Melitta Urbancic, "Til minningar um dr. Victor Urbancic hinn 9. ágúst 1973," *Tíminn*, August 9, 1973.
11. Þorsteinn Sveinsson, "Dr. Victor Urbancic. 75 ára fæðingarafmælis minnst með veglegu stofnframlagi úr minningarsjóði hans til kaupa á heilarannsóknartæki," *Morgunblaðið*, August 9, 1978.
12. Maren Köster, "Musik-Remigration nach 1945. Konturen eines neuen Forschungsfelds," in *"Man kehrt nie zurück, man geht immer nur fort." Remigration und Musikkultur*, 19; see also, however, Matthias Pasdzierny, *Wiederaufnahme? Rückkehr aus dem Exil und das westdeutsche Musikleben nach 1945* (Munich: text + kritik, 2014), 647–54.
13. Johannes Feichtinger, "Remigration Reconsidered. Wiederaufbau und wissenschaftlicher Wandel," *Return from Exile—Rückkehr aus dem Exil. Exiles, Returnees and Their Impact in the Humanities and Social Sciences in Austria and Central Europe*, eds. Waldemar Zacharasiewicz and Manfred Prisching (Vienna: Verlag der Österreichischen Akademie der Wissenschaften, 2017), 27–29.
14. Hans Mommsen, "Rückkehr in eine verwandelte Heimat. Zur Rolle der Emigration in der deutschen Nachkriegsgesellschaft," in *"Man kehrt nie zurück, man geht immer nur fort,"* 32; see also Waldemar Zachariasiewicz, "Introduction," in Zachariasiewicz and Manfred Prisching, eds., *Return from Exile—Rückkehr aus dem Exil. Exiles, Returnees and their Impact in the Humanities and Social Sciences in Austria and Central Europe*, 10–11; Walter Pass, Gerhard Scheit, and Wilhelm Svoboda, *Orpheus im Exil. Die Vertreibung der österreichischen Musik von 1938 bis 1945* (Vienna: Verlag für Gesellschaftskritik, 1995), 185–88.
15. Sibyl Urbancic, interviewed by Sigríður Stephensen, *Heimsmenning á hjara veraldar*, Iceland National Radio, first broadcast 1997.
16. Ólafur Jakobsson, ". . . Ísland er minn starfsvettvangur . . . ," *Musica* 1/3 (1948): 6. In Austria, there seems to have been no interest in calling Urbancic back from exile. In March 1946, Eva Kolmer, on behalf of the Free Austrian Movement in Great Britain, wrote to the Viennese City Councillor for Culture, Viktor Matejka, asking whether there might be a position available for Urbancic there. If Matejka replied, his letter has not survived; see Markus Helmut Lenhart, "Geschichte ohne Brüche? Das Jahr 1938 und 200 Jahre Kunstuniversität Graz," in *Stand und Perspektiven der NS-Forschung in der Musik*, 150.
17. Gauti Kristmannsson, "Bergmál minninganna," 108.
18. "Hátíðahöldin á völlunum 17. júní," *Morgunblaðið*, June 20, 1944.
19. Arnheiður Sigurðardóttir, *Mærin á menntabraut. Skyggnst um öxl—endurminningar* (Reykjavík: Fjölvi, 1997), 227.
20. Arnheiður Sigurðardóttir, *Mærin á menntabraut*, 227.

21. "Presturinn var ekki sá sami—Samt fannst mér ég kominn heim," *Morgunblaðið*, September 18, 1955.

22. "Hljómsveitarstjóri í Berlín," *Þjóðviljinn*, October 13, 1957.

23. Karola Adalsten, *Licht aus dem Norden* (Freiburg: Lambertus Verlag, 1951); *Besonnte Gletscher* (Freiburg: Lambertus Verlag, 1952).

24. Gunnsteinn Ólafsson, "Charlotte Edelstein," *Morgunblaðið*, September 19, 1997.

25. C.f. Matthias Pasdzierny, "»Das Lehrerverzeichnis weist viele Veränderungen auf, aber es ist immerhin noch beinahe die Hälfte, die ich kenne.« Musiker-Remigration an der Musikhochschule Stuttgart," in *Zwischen individueller Biographie und Institution. Zu den Bedingungen beruflicher Rückkehr von Musikern aus dem Exil*, eds. Matthias Pasdzierny and Dörte Schmidt (Schliengen: Edition Argus, 2013), 113–14.

26. Heinz Edelstein to Páll Ísólfsson, Odenwaldschule, July 22, 1958, Páll Ísólfsson Collection, National and University Library, Reykjavík, Lbs 922 NF.

27. Heinz Edelstein to Ingólfur Guðbrandsson, Odenwaldschule, May 12, 1957 (private collection, Þorgerður Ingólfsdóttir).

28. Heinz Edelstein to Ingólfur Guðbrandsson, Odenwaldschule, May 12, 1957 (private collection, Þorgerður Ingólfsdóttir); Heinz Edelstein to German authorities (Entschädigungsbehörde), Odenwaldschule, September 22, 1956 (Landesamt für Bürger- und Ordnungsangelegenheiten, Berlin, papers regarding Ida Edelstein).

29. Heinz Edelstein to Ingólfur Guðbrandsson, Odenwaldschule, April 14, 1959 (private collection, Þorgerður Ingólfsdóttir).

30. Heinz Edelstein to Ingólfur Guðbrandsson, Odenwaldschule, April 14, 1959 (private collection, Þorgerður Ingólfsdóttir).

31. Heinz Edelstein to Ingólfur Guðbrandsson, Odenwaldschule, December 3, 1956 (private collection, Þorgerður Ingólfsdóttir).

32. Heinz Edelstein to Ingólfur Guðbrandsson, Odenwaldschule, December 3, 1956 (private collection, Þorgerður Ingólfsdóttir).

33. Heinz Edelstein to Jónas B. Jónasson, Odenwaldschule, July 20, 1958, Páll Ísólfsson Collection, National and University Library, Reykjavík, Lbs 922 NF.

34. Stefán Edelstein to Ingólfur Guðbrandsson, Freiburg im Breisgau, September 7, 1958 (private collection, Þorgerður Ingólfsdóttir).

35. Stefán Edelstein, interview with the author, August 23, 2019.

36. Heinz Edelstein to Ingólfur Guðbrandsson, Odenwaldschule, May 29, 1959 (private collection, Þorgerður Ingólfsdóttir).

37. Stefán Edelstein, interview with the author, January 12, 2022.

38. Wolfgang Edelstein to Ragnar Jónsson, October 1959, Ragnar Jónsson Collection, National and University Library, Reykjavík, Lbs 9 NF.

39. Wolfgang Edelstein to Ragnar Jónsson, October 1959, Ragnar Jónsson Collection, National and University Library, Reykjavík, Lbs 9 NF.

40. *Dagur*, September 9, 1937; *Vísir*, January 24, 1941.

41. Although the Roman-Catholic church only formally canonized Saint Thorlak in 1984, he had been canonized locally in 1198.

42. "Dvaldist í hálfan mánuð í klaustri að kynna sér gregoríanskan söng," *Alþýðublaðið*, October 4, 1953.

43. Róbert Abraham Ottósson, *Sancti Thorlaci Episcopi Officia Rhytmica et Proprium Missæ in AM 241 a folio*, Bibliotheca Arnamagnæana supplementum vol. III (Copenhagen: Munksgaard, 1959), 48–50.

44. "Þorlákstíðir," *Morgunblaðið*, September 13, 1959.

45. Robert Abraham to Halldór Halldórsson, Reykjavík, November 8, 1959 (private collection, Hildigunnur Halldórsdóttir).

46. Róbert Abraham Ottósson, "Ein fögur Saung Vijsa . . . ," in *Afmælisrit Jóns Helgasonar* (Reykjavík: Heimskringla, 1969), 251–59.

47. Róbert Abraham Ottósson, "Das musiktheoretische Textfragment im Stockholmer Homilienbuch," *Opuscula* 4, Bibliotheca Arnamagnaeana 30 (Copenhagen: Munksgaard, 1970), 169–76; "Ein Prozessionsgesang der Mönche zu Þingeyrar," *Scientia Islandica* 2 (1970): 3–12; "Antifon" (1:162–63), "Diskant" (3:105–7), "Koral, Gregoriansk" (9:116–20), and "Tvesang" (19:83–86), *Kulturhistorisk leksikon for nordisk middelalder fra vikingetid til reformationstid* (Copenhagen: Rosenkilde og Bagger, 1956–1978); "Iceland. II/1,2 [Folk Music]," *The New Grove Dictionary of Music and Musicians* (London: Macmillan, 1980), 9:7–9.

48. Iceland's first PhD in musicology was Hallgrímur Helgason (Zürich University, 1954), but he devoted most of his later career to composition.

49. Jón Þórarinsson, "Afmæliskveðja," *Söngsveitin Fílharmónía 25 ára* (Reykjavík: Söngsveitin Fílharmónía, 1984), 7.

50. "Skemmta sjálfum sér og öðrum," *Þjóðviljinn*, March 31, 1968.

51. "Sálumessa Mozarts flutt," *Vísir*, April 24, 1964.

52. Robert Abraham, 1964 Diary, National Archives of Iceland, Róbert Abraham Ottósson 2012-002, C/1, 2, 40; Páll Kristinn Pálsson, *Góðra vina fundur. Minningar Kristins Hallssonar söngvara* (Reykjavík: Forlagið, 1997), 189.

53. Jónína Michaelsdóttir, *Líf mitt og gleði*, 210–14; Páll Kristinn Pálsson, *Góðra vina fundur*, 189.

54. Árni Heimir Ingólfsson, *Jón Leifs and the Musical Invention of Iceland*, 137.

55. Jón Þórarinsson, "Níunda sinfónían," *Morgunblaðið*, February 15, 1966.

56. Árni Björnsson, interview with the author, January 4, 2020.

57. From the memoirs of Dr. Aðalgeir Kristjánsson (private collection, Kristján Árnason).

58. Árni Björnsson, interview with the author, January 4, 2020.

59. From the memoirs of Dr. Aðalgeir Kristjánsson (private collection, Kristján Árnason).

60. "Verður Missa Solemnis ekki flutt?," *Vísir*, February 16, 1967; "Flutningi Missa Solemnis líklega frestað," *Vísir*, February 23, 1967.

61. "Norðri," "Listgagnrýni á lágu stigi," *Ný vikutíðindi*, March 28, 1970; see also Stefán Edelstein, "Missa Solemnis," *Vísir*, March 7, 1970.

62. Robert Abraham to Hermann Hildebrandt, Reykjavík, August 4, 1970, Hermann-Hildebrandt-Stiftung, Mainz; Þorkell Sigurbjörnsson, "Afrek," *Vísir*, April 3, 1965.

63. The overture to *Dansinn í Hruna* is preserved in National Archives of Iceland, Róbert Abraham Ottósson 2012-002, BA/6, 3; see also BA/1, 10. On the overture to Dickens's play, see Sigurður Grímsson, "Söngbjallan (Cricket on the Hearth)," *Morgunblaðið*, December 29, 1950.

64. National Archives of Iceland, Róbert Abraham Ottósson 2012-002, BA/5, 3; see also BA/3, 13; and BI/2, 2. It seems as if Abraham composed the work for Samkór Reykjavíkur but that nothing came of its performance; in November 1953, he wrote to his Aunt Grete in Denmark that he hoped to perform Psalm 148 with his choir (Robert Abraham to Grete Abraham, Reykjavík, November 1, 1953, private collection, Elín Þ. Ólafsdóttir).

65. "Áheyrandi," "Samkór Róberts Abraham," *Verkamaðurinn*, April 6, 1940; see also "Auditor," "Samkór R. Abrahams," *Dagur*, April 18, 1940; "Söngskemmtun," *Íslendingur*, March 29, 1940.

66. Iceland National Radio Archives, shellac record no. 80396. The recording was made on March 22, 1949, and first broadcast on May 1 that year.

67. The manuscript survives in National Archives of Iceland, Róbert Abraham Ottósson, BA/5, 2.

68. Unnur Arnórsdóttir, "Í hljómleikasal," *Tíminn*, May 29, 1968.

69. See *Árbók Háskóla Íslands háskólaárið 1964–65* (Reykjavík: Háskóli Íslands, 1969), 3, *Árbók Háskóla Íslands háskólaárið 1966–67* (Reykjavík: Háskóli Íslands, 1969), 3; "Skálholtshátíð á sunnudaginn," *Tíminn*, July 18, 1972; "Skálholtshátíð vel heppnuð og hátíðleg," *Morgunblaðið*, July 22, 1975.

70. Áskell Snorrason, "Hljómleikar," *Verkamaðurinn*, October 10, 1936; "Hljómleikar," *Verkamaðurinn*, November 3, 1936.

71. Páll Kristinn Pálsson, *Góðra vina fundur*, 190.

72. "Góðir Íslendingar," *Vísir*, December 14, 1961.

73. See "Prestafélagið," *Prestafélagsritið* 16 (1934): 164; "Messusöngvar," *Kirkjublað* 2 (1934): 144.

74. Þorgerður Ingólfsdóttir, interview with the author, February 5, 2012; see also Andrés Kristjánsson, "Á mítramó," *Tíminn*, February 1, 1967; Sigurbjörn Einarsson, "Í móinn og bláinn," *Tíminn*, February 7, 1967.

75. Kolbeinn Bjarnason, *Helguleikur*, 187.

76. "Búendur æfa söng eftir erfiðan vinnudag," *Morgunblaðið*, July 20, 1963.

77. Sigvaldi S. Kaldalóns, *Söngvasafn Kaldalóns, 9. hefti* (Reykjavík: Kaldalónsútgáfan, 1946).

78. Sigrún Alda Sighvats, "Heyr himna smiður—50 ár frá lagasmíði," www.feykir.is/is/frettir/heyr-himna-smidur-50-ar-fra-lagasmidi; Þorkell Sigurbjörnsson, interview with the author, August 24, 2012.

79. "Skálholtshátíðin á sunnudaginn," *Tíminn*, July 20, 1973.

80. Bragi Þór Valsson, "Heyr, himna smiður: The Sacred A Cappella SATB works of Þorkell Sigurbjörnsson (1938–2013)," PhD dissertation, Stellenbosch University, 2022, 208.

81. Þórir Kr. Þórðarson, "Um starf dr. Róberts A. Ottóssonar í guðfræðideild Háskóla Íslands," *Tíminn*, November 17, 1974.

82. Björn Björnsson, "Kveðja frá guðfræðideild Háskóla Íslands," *Morgunblaðið*, March 20, 1974.

83. "Þakklátur forsjóninni fyrir að fá að lifa með íslenzkri þjóð," *Morgunblaðið*, December 2, 1970.

84. Þ.G.E., "Hvað veldur?," *Stúdentablaðið*, June 17, 1962.

85. Sverrir Garðarsson, "Dr. Róbert Abraham Ottósson," *Tónamál* 5 (1975): 10.

86. Guðrún Egilson, *Með lífið í lúkunum. Rögnvaldur Sigurjónsson í gamni og alvöru* (Reykjavík: Almenna bókafélagið, 1979), 52.

87. Gylfi Þ. Gíslason, "Listin og lotningin fyrir henni," *Alþýðublaðið*, March 20, 1974.

88. See Kolbeinn Þorleifsson, "Íslenzkur kórflutningur," *Dagblaðið*, April 19, 1977.

89. "Píanóleikari lítur um öxl," *Morgunblaðið*, October 15, 1993.

90. www.tonmenntaskoli.is.

91. "Að syngja í kirkjukór," *Morgunblaðið*, March 27, 1975.

92. "Minningartónleikar um Róbert A. Ottósson í Skálholtskirkju á sunnudag," *Þjóðviljinn*, May 8, 1975.

93. Guðmundur Emilsson, "Sumartónleikar í Skálholtskirkju," *Morgunblaðið*, July 25, 1978; Kolbeinn Bjarnason, *Helguleikur*, 190.

94. Björn Franzson, "Minningartónleikar um dr. Victor Urbancic," *Þjóðviljinn*, November 23, 1958.

95. See, for example, Rudolf Habringer, "In dunklen Zeiten"; Markus Helmut Lenhart, "Melitta and Victor Urbancic: Art in Exile in Iceland"; Markus Helmut Lenhart, "Geschichte ohne Brüche? Das Jahr 1938 und 200 Jahre Kunstuniversität Graz"; Alois Kernbauer, *Der Nationalsozialismus im Mikrokosmos*.

96. Melitta Urbancic, *Unter Sternen. Gedichtauswahl* (Vienna: Theodor Kramer, 2022); Agneta Hauber, *Melitta Urbancic: Lyrik am Rand der Welt. Exil und Integration in Island* (Berlin: Peter Lang, 2022).

97. See, for example, Stephan Stompor, *Jüdisches Musik- und Theaterleben unter den NS-Staat* (Hannover: Europäisches Zentrum für Jüdische Musik, 2001); Matthias Pasdzierny, *Wiederaufnahme? Rückkehr aus dem Exil und das westdeutsche Musikleben nach 1945* (Munich: text + kritik, 2014), 699–700.

98. Ylfa Edelstein, email to the author, February 14, 2023.

99. On the Rottberger's story, see Erhard Roy Wiehn, *Jüdische Schicksale von Konstanz* (Konstanz: Hartung-Gorre Verlag, 2021).

100. Einar Heimisson, *Götuvísa gyðingsins* (Reykjavík: Vaka-Helgafell, 1989), 144–45.

101. Einar Heimisson, "Vísað aftur í dauðann af íslenskum stjórnvöldum," *Þjóðlíf* 4 (1988): 33.

102. Hannes Hólmsteinn Gissurarson, "Gyðingastjarnan og hakakrossinn. Örlög tveggja útlendinga á Íslandi," *Þjóðmál* 8 (2012): 57.

103. Böðvar Guðmundsson, email to the author, January 7, 2022.

104. Sjón, *Red Milk*, trans. Victoria Cribb (London: Sceptre, 2021), 57. This scene is built on a passage in Savitri Devi's book, *Gold in the Furnace* (Calcutta, 1952), where she describes her dispute with an unnamed Jew at an afternoon tea in a Reykjavík home, but there the dispute was about hunting animals (Sjón, email to the author, January 6, 2022).

105. Sjón, *Red Milk*, 81–82.

106. Ursula Seeber, trans. Pétur Urbancic, *Frá hjara veraldar*, 22.

Postlude

1. Árni Heimir Ingólfsson, "Victor Urbancic," *Lesbók Morgunblaðsins*, July 7, 2001, 4–5; "Heinz Edelstein," *Lesbók Morgunblaðsins*, July 14, 2001, 8–9; "Róbert A. Ottósson," *Lesbók Morgunblaðsins*, July 21, 2001, 8–9.

2. Styrmir Gunnarsson, "Menning og pólitík," *Morgunblaðið*, August 21, 2021.

3. [Styrmir Gunnarsson], "Reykjavíkurbréf," *Morgunblaðið*, July 15, 2001.

4. [Styrmir Gunnarsson], "Reykjavíkurbréf," *Morgunblaðið*, July 15, 2001.

5. Óðinn Melsted, *Með nótur í farteskinu*. See also a series on foreign musicians by Ingibjörg Eyþórsdóttir, "Erlendir tónlistarmenn á Íslandi á 20. öld," *Lesbók Morgunblaðsins*, April 14, 2007, 4–5; April 21, 2007, 4–5; April 28, 2007, 12–13; May 5, 2007, 12–13.

6. Hannah Jane Cohen, "Artist Eric DeLuca Shows Iceland's Failing in the Holocaust," *The Reykjavík Grapevine*, September 7, 2021. See also Adam Buffington, "Of Nature and Recollection: The Sonic Convergences in Unheard Of." https://artzine.is/of-nature-and-recollection-the-sonic-convergences-in-unheard-of

7. Fríða Björk Ingvarsdóttir, interviewed by Anna Marsibil Clausen, *Lestin*, Iceland National Radio, first broadcast October 6, 2021.

8. Anna Marsibil Clausen, *Lestin*, Iceland National Radio, first broadcast December 13–16, 2021.

9. Sibyl Urbancic, interviewed by Anna Marsibil Clausen, *Lestin*, Iceland National Radio, first broadcast December 15, 2021.

10. Andrew Mellor, "'Anything is Possible': Why Iceland Has Become a Classical Powerhouse," *The Guardian*, April 5, 2023.

Bibliography

Unpublished Documents: Iceland

NATIONAL ARCHIVES OF ICELAND, REYKJAVÍK

Cabinet of Iceland I, Ministry of Justice:

B/498-4. Surveillance of Foreigners, 1935–1936.
B/545-1. Surveillance of Foreigners, 1936–1937.
B/571-3. Foreign Artists, Concert Permissions etc., 1932–1942.
B/598-13. Surveillance of Foreigners, 1938–1939.
B/635-8. Surveillance of Foreigners, 1939–1940.
B/636-1. Surveillance of Foreigners, 1940–1941.

Cabinet of Iceland II, Ministry of Labor:

B/624-4. Ministry of Labor, 1938.
B/648-3. "Þjóðverjar, styrkur til févana manna," 1940–1945.

Foreign Ministry, del. 1967.

B/45-21. Telegrams to the Icelandic Embassy in Copenhagen, 1938.
B/75-2. Applications for Residence and Work Permits, I, 1938–1942.

Foreign Ministry, del. 1989.

B/7-1. Letters to and from attaché Helgi P. Briem, 1932–1942.
B/8, 3–4. Letters to and from attaché Helgi P. Briem. Letters to the Foreign Ministry, 1940–1942.

Ólafur Þorgrímsson Collection, del. 2016-90.

A/3-1. The Reykjavík Music Society.

Reykjavík Music Society Collection, del. 2002-12.

Letters and other materials from the Reykjavík Music Society.

Reykjavík Symphony Orchestra, del. 2007.

A/1-6. Minutes and Programs of the Reykjavík Symphony Orchestra.

Róbert Abraham Ottósson, del. 2012.

Róbert Abraham Ottósson Collection.

NATIONAL AND UNIVERSITY LIBRARY OF ICELAND, REYKJAVÍK

Lbs 9 NF. Ragnar Jónsson Collection.
Lbs 125 NF. Björgvin Guðmundsson Collection.
Lbs 751 NF. Jón Leifs Collection.
Lbs 922 NF. Páll Ísólfsson Collection.
Lbs 1146 NF. Reykjavík Music Society Collection.
Lbs 1188 NF. Jón Þórarinsson Collection.
Victor Urbancic Collection.
Concert programs, 1900–1974.

RÚV: ICELANDIC NATIONAL RADIO ARCHIVES, REYKJAVÍK

Heimsmenning á hjara veraldar, 7 episodes. Producer: Sigríður Stephensen. First broadcast March 23–May 8, 1997.
Lestin. Producer: Anna Marsibil Clausen. First broadcast October 6, 2021.
Lestin. Producer: Anna Marsibil Clausen. First broadcast December 15, 2021.
Lífið og skólinn. Wolfgang Edelstein interviewed by Ágúst Þór Árnason. First broadcast January 1, 2020.
Students of the Children's Music School perform music under the direction of Heinz Edelstein. Shellac discs nos. 82043 and 82044. First broadcast May 30, 1955.
Róbert A. Ottósson. *Svarkurinn.* National Radio Choir. Shellac disc no. 80396. First broadcast May 1, 1949.
Sinfóníuhljómsveit Íslands 40 ára. Producer: Óskar Ingólfsson. First broadcast March 15, 1990.

Tónlistarmenn: Jórunn Viðar. Producer: Egill Rúnar Friðleifsson. First broadcast June 28, 1981.
Vaka. Róbert A. Ottósson interviewed by Þorkell Sigurbjörnsson. First broadcast December 10, 1971.

THE REYKJAVÍK SCHOOL OF MUSIC, REYKJAVÍK

Student records, 1936–1945.

ICELANDIC MUSICIANS' UNION (FÍH), REYKJAVÍK

Minutes, 1932–1955.

REYKJAVÍK MUNICIPAL ARCHIVES, REYKJAVÍK

Private Collection E-258, box 1–2. Philharmonia Choral Society.
Private Collection E-360, box 2–12. Letters from Ragnar Jónsson to Bjarni Benediktsson.

Unpublished Documents: Austria

ARCHIV DER MDW—UNIVERSITÄT FÜR MUSIK UND DARSTELLENDE KUNST, VIENNA

Documents regarding Victor Urbantschitsch.

ARCHIV DER UNIVERSITÄT WIEN

Documents regarding Victor Urbantschitsch.

ÖSTERREICHISCHE NATIONALBIBLIOTHEK, VIENNA

Autogr. 843/12. Letters from Franz Mixa to Joseph Marx.
Autogr. 868/15. Letters from Victor Urbantschitsch to Joseph Marx.

Unpublished Documents: Denmark

THE ROYAL LIBRARY, COPENHAGEN

Det Unge Tonekunstnerselskab. Correspondence 1934. Letters from Lis Jacobsen to Det Unge Tonekunstnerselskab.

Lis Jacobsen Collection. Tilg. 489. Letters from Grete, Lise, Otto, Peter, and Robert Abraham to Lis Jacobsen.
Lis Jacobsen Collection. Tilg. 489. Unpublished memoirs.
NKS 4596 4to. Letters from Otto Abraham to Marcus Rubin.

Niels Bohr Archive, Niels Bohr Institute, Copenhagen

Correspondence between Niels Bohr and Grete, Lise, Peter, and Robert Abraham.

Danish National Archives, Copenhagen

Chief of Police, Surveillance of Foreigners:
Udlændingesag nr. 43752. Peter Abraham.
Udlændingesag nr. 45347. Robert Louis Abraham and Lise Abraham.
Udlændingesag nr. 76287. Valerie Neumann.

Unpublished Documents: England

People's History Museum, Manchester

AM/1/4–5. Letters from Heinz and Charlotte Edelstein to Allan Merson.
AM/2/2/1. "A British Soldier in Iceland, 1941–43." Memoirs of Allan Merson.

Unpublished Documents: Germany

Archiv der Akademie der Künste, Berlin

Hermann Scherchen-Archiv nos. 292 and 293. Deuxième Session d'Études de Hermann Scherchen, Paris, 1934.

Archiv der Universität der Künste, Berlin

Documents regarding Robert Abraham and Emmy Schulz.

Bundesarchiv, Berlin

R 55/21302. "Liste der aus der Reichsmusikkammer ausgeschlossenen Juden, jüdischen Mischlinge und jüdisch Versippten," A–E.
R 55/21303. "Liste der aus der Reichsmusikkammer ausgeschlossenen Juden, jüdischen Mischlinge und jüdisch Versippten," K–L.

NSDAP-Mitgliederkartei. Franz Mixa and Hans Wlach.
Reichsmusikkammer. Papers regarding Victor Urbancic.

LANDESAMT FÜR BÜRGER- UND ORDNUNGSANGELEGENHEITEN, BERLIN

BEG-Akte Reg.-Nr. 50931. Documents regarding Grete Abraham-Nielsen.
BEG-Akte Reg.-Nr. 54069. Documents regarding Ida Edelstein.
BEG-Akte Reg.-Nr. 258018. Documents regarding Robert, Lise, and Peter Abraham.

UNIVERSITÄTSARCHIV DER HUMBOLDT-UNIVERSITÄT ZU BERLIN

Documents regarding Heinz Edelstein.

STAATLICHES GYMNASIUM ZU BONN

Documents regarding Heinz Edelstein.

STADTARCHIV, BONN

Emanuel Edelstein, Meldekarte.

HESSISCHES STAATSARCHIV, DARMSTADT

N 25, 11025. Letters from Charlotte and Wolfgang Edelstein to Kurt and Lotte Zier.
N 25, 11027. Letters from Heinz Edelstein to Kurt and Lotte Zier.

ARCHIV DES DEUTSCHEN CARITASVERBANDES, FREIBURG IM BREISGAU

093.2+284.01. Letters from Lilli Schottländer, 1940–1941.
284.1.016 E. Exchange of letters with Charlotte and Stefán Edelstein, 1956–1959.

LANDESARCHIV BADEN-WÜRTTEMBERG, ABT. STAATSARCHIV, FREIBURG IM BREISGAU

F 196/1. Nr. 2465. Wiedergutmachungsakte Heinz Edelstein.
F 196/1. Nr. 4371. Wiedergutmachungsakte Charlotte Edelstein.
F 166/3. Nr. 3569. Zivilprozessakte Charlotte Edelstein.

STAATSARCHIV DER FREIEN UND HANSESTADT HAMBURG

351-11_7891. Entschädigungsakte Albert und Fanny Klahn.

HERMANN-HILDEBRANDT-STIFTUNG, MAINZ

Letters from Robert Abraham to Hermann Hildebrandt.

STADTARCHIV, MAINZ

90/vor 1962. Personalakte Viktor Urbantschitsch.

LANDESAMT FÜR FINANZEN, AMT FÜR WIEDERGUTMACHUNG, SAARBURG

VA 283357. Wiedergutmachungsakte Victor Urbancic.

Unpublished Documents: The Netherlands

AMSTERDAM CITY ARCHIVES, AMSTERDAM

Identity card (Persoonskaart), Ida Oberländer (Edelstein).

Unpublished Documents: United States

LEO BAECK INSTITUTE, NEW YORK

AR 2073/MF 1084. Ludwig Misch Collection.

LEROY ANDERSON FOUNDATION, WOODBURY, CONNECTICUT

Leroy Anderson. "Iceland." Memoirs, 1947.

NEW YORK PUBLIC LIBRARY, NEW YORK

Emergency Committee in Aid of Displaced Foreign Scholars Records. Exchange of letters between Fritz Redl and Betty Drury, regarding Victor Urbancic.

UNIVERSITY OF PENNSYLVANIA, KISLAK CENTER FOR SPECIAL COLLECTIONS, RARE BOOKS AND MANUSCRIPTS, PENNSYLVANIA

Ms. Coll. 813. Box 19/Folder 969. Letter from Heinz Edelstein to Rudolf Serkin.

Unpublished Documents: Israel

THE CENTRAL ZIONIST ARCHIVES, JERUSALEM

A15/49, A15/61, A15/64. Letters from Max Bodenheimer to Emanuel Edelstein.

Unpublished Documents: Private Collections

Kristján Árnason, Reykjavík:

Dr. Aðalgeir Kristjánsson, unpublished memoirs.

Stefán Edelstein, Reykjavík:

Letters and other documents, Heinz Edelstein.

Katrín and Lovísa Fjeldsted, Reykjavík:

Letters from Jórunn Viðar to Katrín Viðar.

Hildigunnur Halldórsdóttir, Reykjavík:

Letters from Robert and Lise Abraham to Halldór Halldórsson.

Þorgerður Ingólfsdóttir, Reykjavík:

Letters from Heinz Edelstein to Ingólfur Guðbrandsson.

Elín P. Ólafsdóttir, Reykjavík:

Letters and other documents, Robert Abraham.

Monika Keller-Edelstein, Berlin, Germany:

Documents formerly belonging to Charlotte Edelstein.

Heide Sommer, Wacken, Germany:

Letters from Robert and Lise Abraham, Ernest Golm, and Lis Jacobsen to Emmy and Artur Grenz.

Sibyl Urbancic, Vienna, Austria:

Letters and other documents, Victor and Melitta Urbancic.

Interviews

Gerður G. Bjarklind, January 4, 2020.
Árni Björnsson, January 4, 2020.
Stefán Edelstein, June 15, 2001; February 6, 2012; August 23, 2019; January 25, 2021.
Vigdís Finnbogadóttir, January 3, 2020.
Haukur Guðlaugsson, March 23, 2020.
Renee Schepses Hoffman, January 28, 2022.
Þorgerður Ingólfsdóttir, February 5 and March 10, 2012.
Gunnar Kvaran, January 6, 2020.
Sigrún Löve, March 10, 2020.
Ingibjörg Magnúsdóttir, January 11, 2012.
Jón Nordal, February 9, 2016; October 14, 2020.
Elín Þ. Ólafsdóttir, January 8, 2012; January 7, 2020.
Þórarinn Óskarsson, January 12, 2020.
Grétar Ottó Róbertsson, January 8, 2012; January 7, 2020; June 30, 2021.
Þorkell Sigurbjörnsson, August 24, 2012.
Jón Stefánsson, January 13, 2012.
Garðar Sverrisson, June 11, 2024.
Pétur Urbancic, August 23, 2019.
Sibyl Urbancic, August 14 and 18, 2019; September 6, 2022; July 19, 2023.

Email Correspondence

Thomas Becker (Bonn University), March 19, 2021.
Ylfa Edelstein, February 14, 2023.
Heather Forster (Humboldt-University, Berlin), February 22, 2021.
Tim Glander (Stadtarchiv Bonn), November 23, 2022.
Ulrike Grandke (Vienna Symphony Orchestra), May 10, 2021.
Böðvar Guðmundsson, January 7, 2022.
Styrmir Gunnarsson, April 18, 2020.
Sigurjón Birgir Sigurðsson (Sjón), January 6, 2022.
Heide Sommer, April 5, 2020.
Sibyl Urbancic, February 11 and 12, 2022.
Þór Whitehead, April 14 and 22, 2021.

Unpublished Theses

Björnsson, Pétur Húni. "Íslensk þjóðlög? Söfnun, útgáfa og viðtökur þjóðlagasafns séra Bjarna Þorsteinssonar, Íslenzk þjóðlög." MA thesis, University of Iceland, 2019.

Halter, Corinna. "Jüdische Emigration nach Island während des Nationalsozialismus. Fall Wolfgang Edelstein." Cultural studies term paper, Humboldt-Universität, Berlin, 2015.

Heimisson, Einar. "Die Asylsituation in Island in den dreissiger Jahren im Vergleich mit den anderen nordischen Ländern." PhD dissertation, Albert-Ludwigs-Universität, Freiburg im Breisgau, 1992.

Silli, Mona. "Chronik des Johann-Joseph-Fux-Konservatoriums. Die musikgeschichtliche Entwicklung der Instrumentalmusikerziehung von 1815 bis zur Gegenwart." PhD dissertation, Universität für Musik und darstellende Kunst, Graz, 2009.

Sveinbjörnsson, Bjarki. "Tónlistin á Íslandi á 20. öld, með sérstakri áherslu á upphaf og þróun elektrónískrar tónlistar á árunum 1960–90." PhD dissertation, Aalborg University, 1997.

Urbantschitsch, Victor. "Die Sonatenform bei Brahms. Ein Beitrag zur Geschichte der Instrumentalmusik." PhD dissertation, Universität Wien, 1925.

Valsson, Bragi Þór. "Heyr, himna smiður: The Sacred A Cappella SATB works of Þorkell Sigurbjörnsson (1938–2013)." PhD dissertation, Stellenbosch University, 2022.

Windholz, Susanne. "Franz Mixa: Gesamtwerk, Tätigkeiten und Werkaufführungen in Graz." MA thesis, Karl-Franzens-Universität Graz, 2007.

Þorsteinsdóttir, Aðalheiður. "Dr. Victor Urbancic." Final thesis, Reykjavík School of Music, 1997.

Websites

Collections and Data Banks

ANNO—Historische österreichische Zeitungen und Zeitschriften: https://anno.onb.ac.at
DEMOS—Datenbank zur Erforschung der Musik in Österreich: www.demos.ac.at
Exil Archiv: www.exilarchiv.de
exil.arte Zentrum: www.exilarte.at
Lexikon verfolgter Musiker und Musikerinnen der NS-Zeit: www.lexm.uni-hamborg.de
Tímarit.is: www.timarit.is
Tónmenntaskóli Reykjavíkur: www.tonmenntaskoli.is

Articles

Amtliches Fernsprechbuch für den Bezirk der Reichspostdirektion Berlin. https://digital.zlb.de/viewer/image/15849352_1936/45. Accessed February 21, 2022.

"Aus den Städtischen Nachrichten." *Bonner Zeitung*, January 23, 1917. http://bonn 1914-1918.de/chronik-1917/59-januar-1917/980-1917_01_23.html. Accessed April 28, 2022.

"Aus den Städtischen Nachrichten." *Bonner Zeitung*, January 25, 1917. http://bonn 1914-1918.de/59-chronik-1917/januar-1917/982-1917_01_25.html. Accessed April 28, 2022.

"Bericht über die Ereignisse in Graz am 10. November 1938." The Wiener Library nr. 1375/296. www.pogromnovember1938.co.uk/viewer/image/93983/1. Accessed February 27, 2022.

Buffington, Adam. "Of Nature and Recollection: The Sonic Convergences in Unheard Of." https://artzine.is/of-nature-and-recollection-the-sonic-convergences-in-unheard-of. Accessed June 25, 2023.

Edelstein, Wolfgang, interviewed by Christoph Lindenmeyer, Bayerischer Rundfunk, December 12, 2006. www.br.de/fernsehen/ard-alpha/sendungen/alpha-forum/wolfgang-edelstein-gespraech100-attachment.pdf? Accessed December 12, 2021.

Guðmundsdóttir, Guðrún. "Þjóðleikhúskórinn á sínum fyrstu árum." https://sarpur.is/Adfang.aspx?AdfangID=539874. Accessed January 1, 2022.

Hoffman (Schepses), Renee interviewed by Andrew Budris. https://bellport.com/vnews/columns/oral-history/vn_oral-history.htm. Accessed April 3, 2021.

Massar, Kathrin. "Das Symphonieorchester des Jüdischen Kulturbunds Rhein-Main/Frankfurt am Main," on the webpage "Hans Wilhelm Steinberg—In Memoriam." https://oper-frankfurt.de/media/pdf/AusstellungWilliamSteinberg.pdf. Accessed May 2, 2021.

"Moritz Daniel Volkmar." https://de.wikipedia.org/wiki/Moritz_Daniel_Volkmar. Accessed April 8, 2021.

"Saga kaþólsku kirkjunnar á Íslandi." https://catholica.is/biskupsdaemid-saga. Accessed July 30, 2023.

Sighvats, Sigrún Alda. "Heyr himna smiður—50 ár frá lagasmíði." www.feykir.is/is/frettir/heyr-himna-smidur-50-ar-fra-lagasmidi. Accessed December 16, 2022.

Sodian, Beate. "SRCD Oral History Interview, Wolfgang Edelstein, Max-Planck-Institute for Human Development, Berlin, Germany Part I: October 17, 2008 and Part 2: March 2, 2009. www.srcd.org/sites/default/files/file-attachments/edelstein_wolfgang_interview.pdf. Accessed December 10, 2022.

Svendsen, Trond Olav. "Olav Kielland." *Store norske leksikon*. https://snl.no/Olav_Kielland. Accessed August 6, 2022.

"Sögur og tilvitnanir," reminiscences about Robert Abraham. http://filharmonia.is/index.php?option=com_content&view=article&id=115&Itemid=115. Accessed May 17, 2012.

Vilhjálmsson, Vilhjálmur Örn. "Eimskipasaga." https://fornleifur.blog.is/blog/fornleifur/entry/1347477/. Accessed October 23, 2022.

Vilhjálmsson, Vilhjálmur Örn. "Heil Hitler og Hari Krishna." https://fornleifur.blog.is/blog/fornleifur/entry/1385163. Accessed March 23, 2023.

Newspapers and Magazines

Alþýðublaðið, Reykjavík, 1936–1974.
The Capital Times, Wisconsin, 1970.
Dagur, Akureyri, 1936–1940.
DV, Reykjavík, 1994.
Eyjafréttir, Vestmannaeyjar, 2015.
Fálkinn, Reykjavík, 1939–1946.
Fjallkonan, Reykjavík, 1910.
Fréttatíminn, Reykjavík, 2016.
Gjallarhorn, Akureyri, 1910.
The Guardian, London, 2023.
Íslendingur, Akureyri, 1936.
Mánudagsblaðið, Reykjavík, 1948–1953.
Morgunblaðið, Reykjavík, 1914–2022.
Musica, Reykjavík, 1945–1950.
Neue Zürcher Zeitung, Zürich, 1998.
The Reykjavík Grapevine, Reykjavík, 2021.
Stúdentablaðið, Reykjavík, 1962.
Tíminn, Reykjavík, 1949–1974.
Útvarpstíðindi, Reykjavík, 1939–1947.
Verkamaðurinn, Akureyri, 1936.
Vikan, Reykjavík, 1944–1946.
Vísir, Reykjavík, 1914–1970.
Þjóðviljinn, Reykjavík, 1936–1975.

Books and Articles

Abraham, Otto. *Kinderlieder*. Berlin: Madrigal-Verlag, no date.
Abraham, Otto. "Das absolute Tonbewußtsein." *Sammelbände der Internationalen Musikgesellschaft* 3 (1901): 1–86.
Abraham, Otto, and Erich Moritz von Hornbostel. "Studien über das Tonsystem und die Musik der Japaner." *Sammelbände der Internationalen Musikgesellschaft* 4 (1903): 302–60.
Abraham, Otto, and Erich Moritz von Hornbostel. "Phonographierte indische Melodien." *Sammelbände der Internationalen Musikgesellschaft* 5 (1904): 348–401.
Abraham, Otto, and Erich Moritz von Hornbostel. "Über die Harmonisierbarkeit exotischer Melodien." *Sammelbände der Internationalen Musikgesellschaft* 7 (1905): 138–41.
Abraham, Otto, and Erich Moritz von Hornbostel. "Vorschläge für die Transkription exotischer Melodien." *Sammelbände der Internationalen Musikgesellschaft* 11 (1909): 1–25.

Abraham, Otto, and Erich Moritz von Hornbostel. "Suggested Methods for the Transcription of Exotic Music." Translated by George and Eve List. *Ethnomusicology* 38 (1994): 425–56.

Adalsten, Karola [Charlotte Edelstein]. *Licht aus dem Norden. Die heilige Birgitta von Schweden*. Freiburg im Breisgau: Lambertus-Verlag, 1951.

Adalsten, Karola [Charlotte Edelstein], transl. *Besonnte Gletscher. Isländische Erzählungen*. Freiburg im Breisgau: Lambertus-Verlag, 1952.

Agerby, Aksel. "Det unge tonekunstnerselskabs orkester gennem 5 sæsoner." *Dansk Musik Tidsskrift* 10 (1935): 62–65.

Ágústsson, Haukur. *Ferill til frama. Ævisaga Björgvins Guðmundssonar tónskálds*. Akureyri: Ásprent, 2011.

Akademie der Künste, ed. *Geschlossene Vorstellung. Der Jüdische Kulturbund in Deutschland 1933–1941*. Berlin: Edition Hentrich, 1992.

Albertsdóttir, Elín. *Íslenska undrabarnið. Saga Þórunnar Jóhannsdóttur Ashkenazy*. Reykjavík: Bókafélagið, 2009.

Alþingistíðindi 1946–1949. Reykjavík, 1950–1951.

Applegate, Celia, and Pamela Potter. "Germans as 'The People of Music': Genealogy of an Identity." In *Music and German National Identity*, eds. Celia Applegate and Pamela Potter, 1–35. Chicago: University of Chicago Press, 2002.

Árbók Háskóla Íslands háskólaárið 1964–65. Reykjavík: Háskóli Íslands, 1969.

Árbók Háskóla Íslands háskólaárið 1966–67. Reykjavík: Háskóli Íslands, 1969.

Árnason, Jón Múli. *Þjóðsögur Jóns Múla Árnasonar* 1. Reykjavík: Mál og menning, 1996.

Ásgeirsson, Páll Ásgeir. *Fóstbræðralag. Saga Karlakórsins Fóstbræðra í níutíu ár*. Reykjavík: Karlakórinn Fóstbræður, 2001.

Bach, Johann Sebastian. *Tíu sönglög eftir Joh. Seb. Bach*, ed. Victor Urbancic. Reykjavík: Guðrún Pálsdóttir, 1952.

Berg, Sigurd. "Lunn, Sven." *Dansk biografisk leksikon*, 3rd ed., 9:210. Copenhagen: Gyldendal, 1981.

Berger, Peter. "Exiles of Eden: Vienna and the Viennese During and After World War I." In *1914: Austria-Hungary, the Origins, and the First Year of World War I*, eds. Günter Bischof, Ferdinand Karlhofer, and Samuel R. Williamson Jr., 167–86. New Orleans: University of New Orleans Press, 2014.

Bergmeier, Horst J. P., Ejal Jakob Eisler, and Rainer E. Lotz, eds. *Vorbei . . . Beyond Recall. Dokumentation jüdischen Musiklebens in Berlin, 1933–1938*. Hambergen: Bear Family Records, 2001.

Bergsson, Snorri G. "Fangarnir á Mön." *Ný saga* 8 (1996): 4–30.

Bergsson, Snorri G. *Erlendur landshornalýður. Flóttamenn og framandi útlendingar á Íslandi, 1853–1940*. Reykjavík: Almenna bókafélagið, 2017.

Biwald, Brigitte. "Krieg und Gesundheitswesen." In *Im Epizentrum des Zusammenbruchs. Wien im Ersten Weltkrieg*, eds. Alfred Pfoser and Andreas Weigl, 294–301. Vienna: Metroverlag, 2013.

Bjarnason, Bjarki. *Tónlist og tónlistarmenn á Íslandi. Sinfóníuhljómsveit Íslands, Saga og stéttartal.* Reykjavík: Sögusteinn, 2000.

Bjarnason, Kolbeinn. *Helguleikur. Saga Helgu Ingólfsdóttur og Sumartónleika í Skálholti.* Selfoss: Bókaútgáfan Sæmundur, 2018.

Björnsson, Páll. *Ættarnöfn á Íslandi. Átök um þjóðararf og ímyndir.* Reykjavík: Sögufélag, 2021.

Bourdieu, Pierre. *Distinction: A Social Critique of the Judgement of Taste.* Translated by Richard Nice. Cambridge, MA: Harvard University Press, 1987.

Braun, Joachim, Vladimir Karbusický, and Heidi Tamar Hoffmann, eds. *Verfemte Musik. Komponisten in den Diktaturen unseres Jahrhunderts.* Frankfurt am Main: Peter Lang, 1995.

Bräunche, Ernst Otto. "'Die Reichskristallnacht' in Freiburg." *Zeitschrift des Breisgau-Geschichtsvereins ("Schau-ins-Land")* 103 (1984): 149–60.

Brenner, Helmut. *Musik als Waffe?—Theorie und Praxis der politischen Musikverwendung, dargestellt am Beispiel der Steiermark 1938–1945.* Graz: H. Weishaupt, 1992.

Brinkmann, Reinhold, and Christoph Wolff, eds. *Driven into Paradise: The Musical Migration from Nazi Germany to the United States.* Berkeley: University of California Press, 1999.

Brinson, Charmian, and Richard Dove. *A Matter of Intelligence: MI5 and the Surveillance of Anti-Nazi Refugees 1933–50.* Manchester: Manchester University Press, 2014.

Brunnbauer, Heidi. *Im Cottage von Währing/Döbling . . . Interessante Häuser—interessante Menschen.* Gösing/Wagram: Edition Weinviertel, 2003.

Clausing, Kathrin. *Leben auf Abruf. Zur Geschichte der Freiburger Juden im Nationalsozialismus.* Veröffentlichungen aus dem Archiv der Stadt Freiburg im Breisgau 37. Freiburg im Breisgau: Stadtarchiv Freiburg im Breisgau, 2005.

Crawford, Dorothy Lamb. *A Windfall of Musicians: Hitler's Émigrés and Exiles in Southern California.* New Haven: Yale University Press, 2009.

Cullin, Michel, and Primavera Driessen Gruber, eds. *Douce France?: Musik-Exil in Frankreich 1933–1945.* Vienna: Böhlau, 2008.

Dahl, Izabela A. "Dänemark als Zufluchtsland für jüdische Flüchtlinge." In *Skandinavien als Zuflucht für jüdische Intellektuelle 1933–1945*, eds. Izabela A. Dahl and Jorunn Sem Fure, 211–27. Berlin: Metropol, 2014.

Dähnardt, Willi, and Birgit S. Nielsen. *Exil in Dänemark. Deutschsprachige Wissenschaftler, Künstler und Schriftsteller im dänischen Exil nach 1933.* Heide: Westholsteinische Verlagsanstalt Boyens & Co., 1993.

Dümling, Albrecht. "On the Road to the "Peoples' Community" [Volksgemeinschaft]: The Forced Conformity of the Berlin Academy of Music under Fascism." *The Musical Quarterly* 77 (1993): 459–83.

Dümling, Albrecht. *The Vanished Musicians: Jewish Refugees in Australia.* Translated by Diana K. Weekes. Exile Studies 14. Oxford: Peter Lang, 2016.

Düwell, Kurt. "Jewish Cultural Centers in Nazi Germany: Expectations and Accomplishments." In *The Jewish Response to German Culture: From the Enlightenment to the Second World War*, eds. Jehuda Reinharz and Walter Schatzberg, 294–316. Hanover, NH & London: University Press of New England, 1985.

Edelstein, Emanuel. "Die Aufgabe der jüdischen Turner." *Jüdische Turn-Zeitung* 7 (1900): 73–75.

Edelstein, Heinz. *Die Musikanschauung Augustins nach seiner Schrift „De musica."* Ohlau: Eschenhagen, 1929.

Edelstein, Heinz. "Tónlistaruppeldi." *Tímarit Tónlistarfélagsins* 1 (1938): 18–22.

Edelstein-Schottländer, Charlotte. *Der Solidarismus als wirtschaftstheoretisches System*. Freiburg im Breisgau: Günther, 1929.

Egilson, Guðrún. *Spilað og spaugað. Rögnvaldur Sigurjónsson leikur af fingrum fram*. Reykjavík: Almenna bókafélagið, 1978.

Egilson, Guðrún. *Með lífið í lúkunum: Rögnvaldur Sigurjónsson í gamni og alvöru*. Reykjavík: Almenna bókafélagið, 1979.

Egilson, Guðrún. *Tvístirni. Saga Svanhvítar Egilsdóttur*. Reykjavík: Almenna bókafélagið, 2002.

Elíasdóttir, Guðmunda. *Lífsjátning*. Ingólfur Margeirsson, ed. Reykjavík: Iðunn, 1982.

Fabrizius, Peter. "Brief aus San Francisco." *Aufbau*, June 18, 1948.

Favrholdt, David. *Niels Bohr's Philosophical Background*. Copenhagen: Det Kongelige Danske Videnskabernes Selskab, 1992.

Faye, Jan. *Niels Bohr: His Heritage and Legacy*. Science and Philosophy 6. Dordrecht: Kluwer Academic Publishers, 1991.

Fetthauer, Sophie. *Musiker und Musikerinnen im Shanghaier Exil, 1938–1949*. Musik im „Dritten Reich" und im Exil 21. Neumünster: von Bockel Verlag, 2021.

"ff." "Jüdischer Kulturbund Hannover." *Nachrichtenblatt, Amtliches Organ der Synagogen-Gemeinde Hannover*, May 21, 1937.

Fischer, Jens Malte. *Richard Wagners Das Judentum in der Musik. Eine kritische Dokumentation als Beitrag zur Geschichte des Antisemitismus*. Wagner in der Diskussion 15. Würzburg: Königshausen & Neumann, 2015.

Friedländer, Saul. *The Years of Extermination: Nazi Germany and the Jews 1939–1945*. New York: HarperCollins, 2007.

Fritsch-Vivié, Gabriele. *Gegen alle Widerstände: Der Jüdische Kulturbund 1933–1941. Fakten, Daten, Analysen, biographische Notizen und Erinnerungen*. Berlin: Hentrich & Hentrich, 2013.

Garðarsson, Sverrir. "Dr. Róbert Abraham Ottósson," *Tónamál* 5 (1975): 10.

Geisel, Eike, and Henryk M. Broder. *Premiere und Pogrom. Der Jüdische Kulturbund 1933–1941. Texte und Bilder*. Berlin: Siedler, 1992.

Genée, Rudolph. *Síðustu dagar Mozarts. Frásögn eftir heimildum*. Translated by Robert Abraham. Reykjavík: Tónlistarfélagið, 1941.

Geringer, Claudia. ". . . dass ich wegen unseres Essens gespürt hab, dass wir Emigranten sind. Erinnerungen an das Essen in der Generationenfolge." In

Küche der Erinnerung. Essen & Exil, eds. Veronika Zwerger and Ursula Seeber, 308–25. Vienna: New Academic Press, 2018.

Gissurarson, Hannes Hólmsteinn. "Gyðingastjarnan og hakakrossinn. Örlög tveggja útlendinga á Íslandi." *Þjóðmál* 8 (2012): 57–71.

Goldsmith, Martin. *The Inextinguishable Symphony. A True Story of Music and Love in Nazi Germany*. New York: John Wiley & Sons, Inc., 2000.

Gosling, Andrew. "Walter Simon—A Scholar-Librarian and his East Asian Collection." *National Library of Australia News* 11/3 (2000): 3–6.

Gratzer, Wolfgang, and Nils Grosch. *Musik und Migration*. Münster: Waxmann, 2018.

Griffioen, Pim, and Ron Zeller. "Comparing the Persecution of Jews in the Netherlands, France and Belgium, 1940–1945: Similarities, Differences, and Causes." In *The Persecution of the Jews in the Netherlands, 1940–1945: New Perspectives*, 55–92. Amsterdam: Vossiuspers UvA, 2012.

Grünbaum [Urbancic], Melitta. *Der fünffüssige Jambus bei Grabbe*. Vienna: Melitta Grünbaum, 1927.

Grünbaum [Urbancic], Melitta. *Begegnungen mit Gundolf*, ed. Gunilla Eschenbach. Aus dem Archiv 5. Marbach am Neckar: Deutsche Schillergesellschaft, 2012.

Guðmundsson, Böðvar. *Enn er morgunn*. Akranes: Uppheimar, 2009.

Habringer, Rudolf. "Emigration an den Rand der Welt. Die Geschichte des Musikers Victor Urbancic." *Zwischenwelt* 20 (2003): 33–41.

Habringer, Rudolf. *Island-Passion*. Vienna: Picus, 2008.

Habringer, Rudolf. "In dunklen Zeiten—Über das Wirken des Musikers Victor Urbancic am Grazer Konservatorium." In *Gradus ad musicam. 200 Jahre Johann-Joseph-Fux-Konservatorium*, ed. Eduard Lanner, 48–55. Graz: Johann-Joseph-Fux-Konservatorium, 2016.

Habringer, Rudolf. *Das Unergründliche und das Banale. Essays*. Wels: Mitter Verlag, 2017.

Halbrainer, Heimo, Susanne Korbel, and Gerald Lamprecht, eds. *Der „schwierige" Umgang mit dem Nationalsozialismus an österreichischen Universitäten. Die Karl-Franzens-Universität Graz im Vergleich*. Graz: CLIO, 2021.

Hanau, Eva. *Musikinstitutionen in Frankfurt am Main 1933 bis 1939*. Cologne: Studio, 1994.

Harich-Schneider, Eta. *Charaktere und Katastrophen. Augenzeugenberichte einer reisenden Musikerin*. Berlin: Ullstein, 1978.

Hauber, Agneta. *Melitta Urbancic: Lyrik am Rand der Welt. Exil und Integration in Island*. Nordeuropäische Arbeiten zur Literatur, Sprache und Kultur 16. Berlin: Peter Lang, 2022.

Haumann, Heiko. "Das Schicksal der Juden." In *Geschichte der Stadt Freiburg im Breisgau*, eds. Heiko Haumann and Hans Schadek, 3:325–339. Stuttgart: Konrad Theiss Verlag, 2001.

Heer, Hannes, Sven Fritz, Heike Drummer, and Jutta Zwilling. *Verstummte Stimmen. Die Vertreibung der „Juden" und „politisch Untragbaren" aus den hessischen*

Theatern 1933 bis 1945. Schriften der Kommission für die Geschichte der Juden in Hessen 27. Berlin: Metropol, 2011.

Heimisson, Einar. *Götuvísa gyðingsins*. Reykjavík: Vaka-Helgafell, 1989.

Heimisson, Einar. "Vísað aftur í dauðann af íslenskum stjórnvöldum." *Þjóðlíf* 4 (1988): 31–34.

Heister, Hanns-Werner, Claudia Maurer Zenck, and Peter Petersen, eds. *Musik im Exil. Folgen des Nazismus für die internationale Musikkultur*. Frankfurt am Main: Fischer, 1993.

Hermannsson, Baldur. *Ævars saga Kvaran*. Reykjavík: Örn og Örlygur, 1989.

Himmelmann, Werner. *Das Schicksal der jüdischen Rechtsanwälte und Notare während der Zeit des Nationalsozialismus: am Beispiel Dortmund*. Dortmund: Anwalt- und Notarverein, 1993.

Hirsch, Lily E. *A Jewish Orchestra in Nazi Germany. Musical Politics and the Berlin Jewish Culture League*. Ann Arbor: The University of Michigan Press, 2010.

Hirsch, Lily E. "Germany's Commemoration of the Jüdischer Kulturbund." In *Dislocated Memories: Jews, Music, and Postwar German Culture*, eds. Tina Frühauf and Lily E. Hirsch, 243–64. Oxford: Oxford University Press, 2014.

Hornbostel, Erich Moritz von. "Otto Abraham †." *Psychologische Forschung* 7 (1926): 291–93.

Hornbostel, Erich Moritz von. *Tonart und Ethos. Aufsätze zur Musikethnologie und Musikpsychologie*. Wilhelmshaven: Florian Noetzel, 1999.

Höroldt, Dietrich. *Bonn. Von einer französischen Bezirksstadt zur Bundeshauptstadt, 1794–1989*. Geschichte der Stadt Bonn 4. Bonn: Dümmler, 1989.

Hvidt, Kristian. *Forsker, furie, frontkæmper. En bog om Lis Jacobsen*. Copenhagen: Gyldendal, 2011.

Ingólfsson, Árni Heimir. "Konur, karlar og kórsöngurinn. Viðbrögð við grein Ingu Dóru Björnsdóttur." *Saga* 40/2 (2002): 207–15.

Ingólfsson, Árni Heimir. "Róbert Abraham Ottósson." *Andvari* 137 (2012): 11–63.

Ingólfsson, Árni Heimir. *Jón Leifs and the Musical Invention of Iceland*. Bloomington: Indiana University Press, 2019.

Ingólfsson, Árni Heimir. "Starting from Scratch: Nation Building and the Creation of an Icelandic Choral Tradition." In *The Nature of Nordic Music*, ed. Tim Howell, 71–86. Abingdon: Routledge, 2019.

Jackman, Jarrell C., and Carla M. Borden, eds. *The Muses Flee Hitler: Cultural Transfer and Adaptation, 1930–1945*. Washington, DC: Smithsonian Institution Press, 1983.

Jakobsson, Ólafur. ". . . Ísland er minn starfsvettvangur . . ." *Musica* 1/3 (1948): 4–6.

Jeserich, Philipp. *Musica Naturalis. Speculative Music Theory and Poetics, from Saint Augustine to the Late Middle Ages in France*. Translated by Michael J. Curley and Steven Rendall. Baltimore: Johns Hopkins University Press, 2013.

Johannessen, Matthías. *Hundapúfan og hafið*. Reykjavík: Bókfellsútgáfan, 1961.

Jonsson, Dehnow [Fritz Dehnow]. *Aires escandinavos, 33 canciones islandesas, noruegas, suecas y dinamarquesas*. Buenos Aires: Ricordi americana, 1957.

Jónsson, Guðmundur, and Magnús S. Magnússon, eds. *Hagskinna. Sögulegar hagtölur um Ísland*. Reykjavík: Hagstofa Íslands, 1997.

Kaldalóns, Sigvaldi S. *Söngvasafn Kaldalóns, 9. hefti*. Reykjavík: Kaldalónsútgáfan, 1946.

Kaplan, Marion A. *Between Dignity and Despair. Jewish Life in Nazi Germany*. New York: Oxford University Press, 1998.

Karner, Stefan. *Die Steiermark im Dritten Reich 1938–1945. Aspekte ihrer politischen, wirtschaftlich-sozialen und kulturellen Entwicklung*. Graz: Leykam, 1986.

Kater, Michael H., and Albrecht Riethmüller, eds. *Music and Nazism: Art Under Tyranny*. Laaber: Laaber, 2003.

Kaufmann, Hans, and Inge Kaufmann. *Verfolgung, Widerstand, Neubeginn in Freiburg 1933–1945*. Freiburg im Breisgau: Offensiv-Verlag, 1989.

Kelbetz, Ludwig. "Lied und Chormusik in der Hitler-Jugend." *Zeitschrift für Musik* 105 (1938): 1088–90.

Kernbauer, Alois. *Der Nationalsozialismus im Mikrokosmos. Die Universität Graz 1938. Analyse—Dokumentation—Gedenkbuch*. Publikationen aus dem Archiv der Universität Graz 48. Graz: Akademische Druck- u. Verlagsanstalt, 2019.

Killy, Walter, et al., ed. *Dictionary of German Biography*. Munich: K.G. Saur, 2006.

Klapdor, Heike. "Überlebensstrategie statt Lebensentwurf. Frauen in der Emigration." In *Frauen und Exil. Zwischen Anpassung und Selbstbehauptung*, eds. Claus-Dieter Krohn, Erwin Rotermund, Lutz Winckler, and Wulf Koepke, 12–30. Exilforschung 11. Munich: edition text + kritik, 1993.

Krohn, Claus-Dieter, Patrik von zur Mühlen, Gerhard Paul, and Lutz Winckler, eds. *Handbuch der deutschsprachigen Emigration 1933–1945*. Darmstadt: Primus Verlag, 1998.

Köster, Maren, and Dorte Schmidt, eds. *„Man kehrt nie zurück, man geht immer nur fort." Remigration und Musikkultur*. Munich: edition text + kritik, 2005.

Lenhart, Markus Helmut. "Geschichte ohne Brüche? Das Jahr 1938 und 200 Jahre Kunstuniversität Graz." In *Stand und Perspektiven der NS-Forschung in der Musik*, eds. Klaus Aringer, Susanne Kogler, and Markus Helmut Lenhart, 141–52. Musikwissenschaftliche Beiträge der Kunstuniversität Graz 2. Graz: Leykam, 2021.

Lenhart, Markus Helmut. "Melitta and Victor Urbancic: Art in Exile in Iceland." In *Cultural Translations and Knowledge Transfer on Alternative Routes of Escape from Nazi Terror: Mediations through Migrations*, eds. Susanne Korbel and Philipp Strobl, 234–46. Milton: Routledge, 2021.

Levi, Erik, ed. *The Impact of Nazism on Twentieth-Century Music*. exil-arte Schriften 3. Vienna: Böhlau, 2014.

Magnússon, Björn, and Gunnar Þorsteinsson. "Dr. Róbert Abraham Ottósson heimsóttur." *Stúdentablaðið* 48 (1971): 10–11.

Maimann, Helene. "Sprachlosigkeit. Ein zentrales Phänomen der Exilerfahrung." In *Leben im Exil. Probleme der Integration deutscher Flüchtlinge im Ausland 1933–1945*, eds. Wolfgang Frühwald and Wolfgang Schneider, 31–38. Historische Perspektiven 18. Hamburg: Hoffmann und Campe, 1981.

Margeirsson, Ingólfur. *Ragnar í Smára*. Reykjavík: Lögberg, 1982.
Martini, Joachim Carlos. *Musik als Form geistigen Widerstandes. Jüdische Musikerinnen und Musiker 1933–1945, Das Beispiel Frankfurt am Main*. Frankfurt am Main: Brandes & Apsel, 2010.
Maurer Zenck, Claudia. "Kein schleichender Übergang. Das Musikleben in Österreich 1938." *Die Tonkunst* 3/4 (2009): 411–27.
Medawar, Jean, and David Pyke. *Hitler's Gift: The True Story of the Scientists Expelled by the Nazi Regime*. New York: Arcade Publishing, 2000.
Melsted, Óðinn. *Með tónlist í farteskinu. Erlendir tónlistarmenn á Íslandi, 1930–1960*. Reykjavík: Sögufélag, 2016.
Michaelsdóttir, Jónína. *Líf mitt og gleði. Minningar Þuríðar Pálsdóttur söngkonu*. Reykjavík: Forlagið, 1986.
Misch, Ludwig. *Beethoven Studies*. Norman: University of Oklahoma Press, 1953.
Misch, Ludwig. "Berufsverbot als Musikkritiker." In *Sie durften nicht mehr Deutsche sein. Jüdischer Alltag in Selbstzeugnissen 1933–1938*, eds. Margarete Limberg and Hubert Rübsaat, 241–44. Frankfurt am Main: Campus Verlag, 1990.
Morreau, Annette. *Emanuel Feuermann*. New Haven: Yale University Press, 2002.
Naegele, Verena. *Viktor Ullmann. Komponieren in verlorener Zeit*. Köln: Dittrich, 2002.
Notley, Margaret. *Lateness and Brahms: Music and Culture in the Twilight of Viennese Liberalism*. Oxford: Oxford University Press, 2007.
Ogilvie, Sarah A., and Scott Miller. *Refuge Denied: The St. Louis Passengers and the Holocaust*. Madison: University of Wisconsin Press, 2006.
Ottósson, Róbert A. *Sancti Thorlaci episcopi officia rhytmica et proprium missæ in AM 241 a folio*. Bibliotheca Arnamagnæana Supplementum 3. Copenhagen: Ejnar Munksgaard, 1959.
Ottósson, Róbert A. "Ein føgur Saung Vijsa . . ." In *Afmælisrit Jóns Helgasonar, 30. júní 1969*, ed. Jakob Benediktsson, 251–59. Reykjavík: Heimskringla, 1969.
Ottósson, Róbert A. "Ein Prozessionsgesang der Mönche zu Þingeyrar." *Scientia Islandica* 2 (1970): 3–12.
Ottósson, Róbert A. "Das musiktheoretische Textfragment im Stockholmer Homilienbuch." *Opuscula* 4 (1970): 169–76. Bibliotheca Arnamagnaeana 30. Copenhagen: Munksgaard.
Ottósson, Róbert A. "Antifon," "Diskant," "Koral, Gregoriansk," and "Tvesang." In *Kulturhistorisk leksikon for nordisk middelalder fra vikingetid til reformationstid*, ed. Magnús Már Lárusson et al., 1:162–63; 3:105–07; 9:116–20; 19:83–86. Copenhagen: Rosenkilde og Bagger, 1956–78.
Ottósson, Róbert A. "Iceland. II/1,2 [Folk Music]." In *The New Grove Dictionary of Music and Musicians*, ed. Stanley Sadie, 9:7–9. London: Macmillan, 1980.
Paisey, David. "Adolphus Asher (1800–1853): Berlin Bookseller, Anglophile, and Friend to Panizzi." *The British Library Journal* 23 (1997): 131–53.
Pálsson, Heimir. "Syngjandi sendiherrar." In *Menntaskólinn við Hamrahlíð 30 ára*, ed. Heimir Pálsson, 67–85. Reykjavík: Menntaskólinn við Hamrahlíð, 1997.

Pálsson, Hrafn. *Félag íslenzkra hljómlistarmanna 50 ára*. Reykjavík: Félag íslenzkra hljómlistarmanna, 1982.
Pálsson, Páll Kristinn. *Góðra vina fundur. Minningar Kristins Hallssonar söngvara*. Reykjavík: Forlagið, 1997.
Pálsson, Sigurður. *Norður í svalann. Viðtöl við aðflutta Íslendinga*. Reykjavík: Bókaútgáfan Salt, 1982.
Pasdzierny, Matthias. *Wiederaufnahme? Rückkehr aus dem Exil und das westdeutsche Musikleben nach 1945*. Munich: edition text + kritik, 2014.
Pasdzierny, Matthias, and Dörte Schmidt, eds. *Zwischen individueller Biographie und Institution. Zu den Bedingungen beruflicher Rückkehr von Musikern aus dem Exil*. Forum Musikwissenschaft 9. Schliengen: Edition Argus, 2013.
Pass, Walter, Gerhard Scheit, and Wilhelm Svoboda. *Orpheus im Exil. Die Vertreibung der österreichischen Musik von 1938 bis 1945*. Antifaschistische Literatur und Exilliteratur—Studien und Texte 13. Vienna: Verlag für Gesellschaftskritik, 1995.
Potter, Pamela M. *Most German of the Arts: Musicology and Society from the Weimar Republic to the End of Hitler's Reich*. New Haven, CT: Yale University Press, 1998.
Prieberg, Fred K. *Musik im NS-Staat*. 2nd edition. Cologne: Dittrich, 2000.
Prieberg, Fred K. *Handbuch Deutsche Musiker*. Kiel, 2005.
Quack, Sibylle, ed. *Between Sorrow and Strength: Women Refugees of the Nazi Period*. New York: Cambridge University Press, 1995.
Rilke, Rainer Maria, and Erika Mitterer. *Besitzlose Liebe. Der poetische Briefwechsel*, ed. Katrin Kohl. Berlin: Insel, 2018.
"rb." "Opernfragmente im Musikverein." *Grazer Tagespost*, December 9, 1935.
Rósinkranz, Guðlaugur. *Allt var þetta indælt stríð. Æviminningar Guðlaugs Rósinkranz þjóðleikhússtjóra*. Reykjavík: Örn og Örlygur, 1977.
Ryding, Erik, and Rebecca Pechefsky. *Bruno Walter—A World Elsewhere*. New Haven, CT & London: Yale University Press, 2001.
"S." "Það er gaman að lifa á þessum þroskaárum íslenzkrar tónlistar." *Heimilispósturinn* 2/3 (1951): 1–5.
Sarkar, Peter. "Ein Brief von Viktor Ullmann nach Reykjavík aus dem Jahr 1939." *mr-Mitteilungen* 108 (2022): 9–11.
Schmerl, Rudolf B. "Place of Birth." *American Jewish Archives Journal* 62 (2010): 49–67.
Schultz, Ingo. *Viktor Ullmann. Leben und Werk*. Kassel: Bärenreiter, 2008.
Schwalbach, Leopoldine. *Zum Bericht über eine Generation*, ed. Thomas Lindemann. Karlsruhe: Info Verlagsgesellschaft, 1997.
Seeber, Ursula. *Frá hjara veraldar. Melitta Urbancic (1902–1984)—í útlegð frá Austurríki á Íslandi*. Translated by Pétur Urbancic. Reykjavík: Landsbókasafn Íslands–Háskólabókasafn, 2014.
Shirakawa, Sam H. *The Devil's Music Master. The Controversial Life and Career of Wilhelm Furtwängler*. New York: Oxford University Press, 1992.

Sigurðardóttir, Arnheiður. *Mærin á menntabraut. Skyggnst um öxl—endurminningar*. Reykjavík: Fjölvi, 1997.
Sigurðsson, Kristján. "Tónlistarskólinn 1930–1940." *Tímarit Tónlistarfélagsins* 2 (1940): 1–25.
Silbermann, Alphons. *Verwandlungen. Eine Autobiographie*. Bergisch Gladbach: Lübbe, 1989.
Sjón. *Red Milk*. Translated by Victoria Cribb. London: Sceptre, 2021.
Sommer, Heide. *Lassen Sie mich mal machen. Fünf Jahrzehnte als Sekretärin berühmter Männer*. Berlin: Ullstein, 2019.
Sponheuer, Bernd. "Musik auf einer «kulturellen und physischen Insel.» Musik als Überlebensmittel im Jüdischen Kulturbund 1933–1941." In *Musik in der Emigration 1933–1945*, ed. Horst Weber, 108–35. Berlin: Springer-Verlag, 1994.
Stalla, Robert. *Theater in der Josefstadt, 1788–2030*. Munich: Hirmer, 2021.
Steege, Benjamin. "Between Race and Culture: Hearing Japanese Music in Berlin." *History of the Humanities* 2 (2017): 361–74.
Stefánsson, Gunnar. *Útvarp Reykjavík. Saga Ríkisútvarpsins 1930–1960*. Reykjavík: Sögufélag, 1997.
Stengel, Theo, and Herbert Gerigk. *Lexikon der Juden in der Musik*. Veröffentlichungen des Instituts der NSDAP zur Erforschung der Judenfrage 2. Berlin: Bernhard Hahnefeld Verlag, 1940.
Stephan, Alexander. *Exile and Otherness. New Approaches to the Experience of Nazi Refugees*. Exile Studies 11. Oxford: Peter Lang, 2005.
Stompor, Stephan. *Jüdisches Musik- und Theaterleben unter den NS-Staat*. Schriftenreihe des Europäischen Zentrums für Jüdische Musik 6. Hannover: Europäisches Zentrum für Jüdische Musik, 2001.
Stratz, Constanze. *Ein Wanderer zwischen den Welten: Ernst Toch in der Emigration 1933–1950*. Mainz: Schott Musik, 2013.
Stroińska, Magda. "The Role of Language in the Re-Construction of Identity in Exile." In *Exile, Language and Identity*, eds. Magda Stroińska and Vittorina Cecchetto, 95–109. Frankfurt: Peter Lang, 2003.
Strutz, Andrea. "Interned as 'Enemy Aliens': Jewish Refugees from Austria, Germany and Italy in Canada." In *Refugees from Nazi-Occupied Europe in British Overseas Territories*, eds. Swen Steinberg and Anthony Grenville, 46–67. Yearbook of the Research Centre for German and Austrian Exile Studies 20. Leiden: Brill, 2020.
Stumpf, Carl. *The Origins of Music*. Edited and translated by David Trippett. Oxford: Oxford University Press, 2012.
Svenstrup, Thyge. *Arup: En biografi om den radikale historiker Erik Arup, hans tid og miljø*. Copenhagen: Museum Tusculanum, 2006.
Tkaczyk, Viktoria. "The Testing of a Hundred Listeners: Otto Abraham's Studies on 'Absolute Tone Consciousness.'" In *Testing Hearing: The Making of Modern Aurality*, eds. Viktoria Tkaczyk, Mara Mills, and Alexandra Hui, 49–76. Oxford: Oxford University Press, 2020.

Tómasson, Tómas Þór. *Heimsstyrjaldarárin á Íslandi*, vol. 1. Reykjavík: Örn og Örlygur, 1983.
Touhamin, Mira Delavec, and Franc Križnar, eds. *Josipina Urbančič Turnograjska*. Preddvor: KD Josipine Turnograjske, 2018.
Traber, Habakuk, and Elmar Weingarten. *Verdrängte Musik. Berliner Komponisten im Exil*. Berlin: Argon Verlag, 1987.
Urbancic, Melitta. *Frá hjara veraldar*. Gauti Kristmannsson, ed., Sölvi Björn Sigurðsson transl. Reykjavík: Stofnun Vigdísar Finnbogadóttur í erlendum tungumálum, 2014.
Urbancic, Melitta. *Unter Sternen*. Vienna: Theodor Kramer, 2022.
Urbancic, Pétur. "Vielseitig, engagiert, anpassungsfähig . . ." *Der literarische Zaunkönig* 1 (2008): 54–58.
Urbantschitsch, Victor. "Die Entwicklung der Sonatenform bei Brahms." *Studien zur Musikwissenschaft* 14 (1927): 265–85.
Urbantschitsch, Victor. "Zur Situation der musikalischen Privatschule: Aus einem Gespräch mit Direktor Josef Reitler vom Neuen Wiener Konservatorium." *Musikblätter des Anbruch* 16 (1934): 147–50.
Urbantschitsch, Victor. "Beethoven in immer neuer Deutung. Das Problem der Musikbiographie." *Musikblätter des Anbruch* 16 (1934): 171–74.
Urbantschitsch, Victor. "Neuer Wind im Grazer Musikverein." *Musikblätter des Anbruch* 16 (1934): 192–94.
Valsson, Páll. *Vigdís. Kona verður forseti*. Reykjavík: JPV, 2009.
Valsson, Páll. *Myndir úr lífshlaupi Péturs Urbancic*. Reykjavík: Nostrum, 2021.
Víkingur, Sveinn. *Skálholtshátíðin 1956. Minning níu alda biskupsdóms í Skálholti*. Hafnarfjörður: Bókaútgáfan Hamar, 1958.
Vilhjálmsson, Vilhjálmur Örn. *Medaljens bagside. Jødiske flygtningeskæbner i Danmark, 1933–1945*. Copenhagen: Forlaget Vandkunsten, 2005.
Vilhjálmsson, Vilhjálmur Örn. "Iceland: A Study of Antisemitism in a Country without Jews." In *Antisemitism in the North: History and State of Research*, eds. Jonathan Adams and Cordelia Heß, 69–105. Berlin/Boston: De Gruyter, 2020.
Waldhör, Jana. *Zeitspiegel. Eine Stimme des österreichischen Exils in Großbritannien 1939–1946*. Vienna: new academic press, 2020.
Weber, Horst, and Stefan Drees, eds. *Quellen zur Geschichte emigrierter Musiker, 1933–1950. 2:New York*. Munich: K.G. Saur, 2005.
Whitehead, Þór. *Ófriður í aðsigi. Ísland í síðari heimsstyrjöld*. Reykjavík: Almenna bókafélagið, 1980.
Whitehead, Þór. *Milli vonar og ótta. Ísland í síðari heimsstyrjöld*. Reykjavík: Vaka-Helgafell, 1995.
Wiehn, Erhard Roy. *Jüdische Schicksale von Konstanz*. Konstanz: Hartung-Gorre Verlag, 2021.
Wlach, Hans. "Franz Mixa. 30 Lieder aus 'Des Knaben Wunderhorn.'" *Zeitschrift für Musik* 104 (1937): 495–97.
Wlach, Hans. "Konzert und Oper." *Zeitschrift für Musik* 106 (1939): 661.

Würthle, Stefan. *Der Birklehof—Ein deutsches Landerziehungsheim in nationalsozialistischer Zeit.* 2nd ed. Freiburg im Breisgau: Albert-Ludwigs-Universität, Historisches Seminar, 1998.

Wyn Jones, David. *Music in Vienna, 1700, 1800, 1900.* Woodbridge: Boydell Press, 2016.

Zacharasiewicz, Waldemar, and Manfred Prisching, eds. *Return from Exile—Rückkehr aus dem Exil. Exiles, Returnees and Their Impact in the Humanities and Social Sciences in Austria and Central Europe.* Vienna: Verlag der Österreichischen Akademie der Wissenschaften, 2017.

Zauner, Georg. *Der Komponist Franz Mixa. Leben und Werk.* Tutzing: Hans Schneider, 2002.

Ziegler, Susanne. *Die Wachszylinder des Berliner Phonogramm-Archivs.* Veröffentlichungen des Ethnologisches Museums Berlin 73. Berlin: Staatliche Museen zu Berlin—Preußischer Kulturbesitz, 2006.

Zweig, Stefan. *Die Welt von Gestern. Erinnerungen eines Europäers.* Ditzingen: Reclam, 2023.

Þórarinsson, Jón. "Afmæliskveðja." In *Söngsveitin Fílharmónía 25 ára.* Reykjavík: Söngsveitin Fílharmónía, 1984.

Index

Abraham, Grete, 87, 108
Abraham, Lise (Louise), 20–21, 23, 84–85, 86, 87, 107
Abraham, Otto, 18–23, 39, 42, 44, 87
Abraham, Peter, 18, 42, 43, 87, 106–7
Abraham, Robert, 1–2, 3, 87, 101, 103, 106, 108, 111, 120, 129, 138, 167, 185–86
  acculturation of, 115, 204
  adaptation of name, 116–17
  arrangements by, 109, 143, 145, 164, 209, 218, 219, 224–25
  arrival in Iceland, 57, 62–65
  as choral conductor, 66–68, 85–86, 120, 139–46, 201, 211–15, 223–24
  as composer, 216–17
  as music critic, 153, 171
  as orchestral conductor, 168–70, 170–72, 173, 196–98, 215
  as teacher, 66, 119, 183, 193, 194, 206
  career in Akureyri, 65–70
  childhood and studies of, 21–25, 38–41
  Church Music Director, 218–22
  citizenship of, 112–113
  death and legacy of, 199, 222–23, 229, 232
  early career in Reykjavík, 84–86
  exile in Copenhagen, 42–45
  exile in Paris, 41
  in fiction, 227–28
  marriage of, 86–87, 148, 176
  personality of, 146–51
  research on Icelandic music, 109, 161, 196, 197, 208–11, 217
  return to Berlin, 196–97, 204
  works:
    Dansinn í Hruna (*The Dance at Hruni*), 216
    Intrada on Themes from Þorlákstíðir, 218
    Miskunnarbæn (*Icelandic Kyrie*), 217, 225
    Nóttin var sú ágæt ein (*That Wondrous Night*), 217
    Overture on Old English Folk Songs, 216
    Svarkurinn (*The Shrew*), 216
    Þingvallareið (*Ride to Þingvellir*), 86, 216
Abrahamsen, Erik, 44
Adler, Guido, 9, 52
Adler, Rigmor, 107
Anderson, Leroy, 120
Angerer, Edmund, 193
anti-Semitism
  in Germany, 27–32, 38–39, 50, 56, 76, 93, 97–101

anti-Semitism *(continued)*
  in Iceland, 69–71, 73, 88, 89–91, 97–101, 109–10, 186. *See also* xenophobia
Arason, Jón, 156
Arason, Páll, 123
Arcadelt, Jacques, 129, 141
Arup, Erik, 64–65
Ashkenazy, Vladimir, 85, 116, 152, 198
Augustine, Saint, 16
Árnason, Jón Múli, 95, 110–11
Árnason, Þórhallur, 92, 93
Ásgeirsson, Jón, 133, 152, 163

Bach, Johann Sebastian, 2, 6, 24, 29, 59, 66, 129, 138, 143, 153, 157, 213
  The Art of Fugue, 153
  Cantata no. 6, 143
  Cantata no. 79, 140
  Cantata no. 80, 144, 147
  Cantata no. 161, 143
  Christmas Oratorio, 49, 131, 134
  Magnificat, 212
  Mass in B minor, 153
  The Musical Offering, 41
  O Jesulein süß, 155
  St John Passion, 120, 131–34, 173–74, 184
  St Matthew Passion, 134
  Ten Songs by (ed. Urbancic), 153–55
Bartók, Béla, 18, 171
Beethoven, Ludwig van, 3, 6, 12, 14, 29, 35, 58, 68, 99, 136, 137, 170, 218
  Coriolan, overture, 66, 170
  Egmont, overture, 66, 171
  Fidelio, 141, 198
  Missa solemnis, 212, 214–15
  Piano Concerto no. 4, 151, 170
  Piano Sonata op. 57 (*Appassionata*), 58

Piano Sonata op. 109, 66
Piano Sonata op. 110, 66
Symphony no. 1, 171
Symphony no. 2, 43, 185
Symphony no. 4, 41
Symphony no. 5, 21, 172
Symphony no. 6 ("Pastoral"), 198
Symphony no. 7, 186
Symphony no. 9, 24, 86, 148, 212, 213–14
Benary, Ferdinand, 20
Bendix, Kurt, 172
Benediktsson, Bjarni, 85, 186
Benediktsson, Einar, 65
Benediktsson, Jakob, 45, 143, 144
Berg, Alban, 132
Bergsson, Snorri G., 106
Bernstein, Leonard, 200
Bethge, Hans, 159
Biber, Heinrich Ignaz Franz, 129, 153
Biggs, E. Power, 200
Billich, Carl, 63, 113, 121, 230
Birkis, Sigurður, 218
Björk, 224, 232
Björnsson, Árni, 152, 157
Björnsson, Ragnar, 152, 153
Björnsson, Sveinn, 45
Björnsson, Tómas, 68–69
Björnsson, Þórarinn, 65
Bodenheimer, Max, 14
Bohr, Hans, 107
Bohr, Margrethe, 43, 107
Bohr, Niels, 43, 106, 107
Brahms, Johannes, 2, 3, 9, 29, 44, 59, 62, 66, 68, 137, 143
  Alto Rhapsody, 141
  Begräbnisgesang, 144
  A German Requiem, 66, 201, 212, 224
  Liebeslieder Waltzes, 146
  Lullaby, 196
  Schicksalslied, 140
  Symphony no. 2, 198

Index

Brandes, Georg, 42
Briem, Helgi, 105
Britten, Benjamin, 126, 130
Bruckner, Anton, 215
Burgstaller, Valesca, 23
Busch, Adolf, 119
Busoni, Ferruccio, 18
Böðvarsson, Bjarni, 91

Caldwell, Katherine, 231
Camphausen, Rudolf, 121
Cherkassky, Shura, 198
Chopin, Frédéric, 6, 137, 184
Christoffersen, Henry, 44
Clausen, Anna Marsibil, 231
Colda, Marina, 226
Cook, Walter, 32
Corelli, Arcangelo, 43

Danziger, Ludwig, 17
Dehnow, Fritz, 97
Dehnow, Ilse, 97
DeLuca, Eric, 230–31
Despić, Minna, 159
Devi, Savitri, 228
Djúpalæk, Kristján (Einarsson) frá, 145
Donizetti, Gaetano, 198
Drucker, Ernst, 37, 53, 73, 136
Drucker, Eugene, 37
Dvořák, Antonín, 35, 37
   Cello Concerto, 187, 198
   Slavonic Dances, 36
   Te Deum, 149, 213

Edelstein, Alexander Smári
   Kristjánsson, 208
Edelstein, Charlotte, 17, 81, 83,
   103–4, 108, 111, 123, 207, 208
   culinary efforts in Iceland, 117–18
   in the Third Reich, 34, 74–76, 78
   journey to Iceland, 78–80
   life in Iceland, 124, 125–27
   life story of, 226–27
   remigration to Germany, 127, 138,
   194, 205
Edelstein, Emanuel, 13–14, 33
Edelstein, Heinz, 1–2, 3, 25, 34, 60,
   72, 81, 87, 96, 101, 102, 103–4,
   108, 111, 120, 121, 124, 129,
   145, 167, 228
   arrival in Iceland, 57, 62, 73–75,
   76–77
   as pedagogue, 15, 119, 137–39,
   188–96, 198
   boycott by Nazis, 30, 32–33
   career in Freiburg, 18
   childhood and studies of, 13–16
   citizenship of, 113
   death and legacy of, 199, 223–24,
   229–30, 232
   hiking in Iceland, 122–23
   knowledge of Icelandic language,
   114–15
   marriage of, 17, 74–75, 78
   performer in Iceland, 131, 132–33,
   136–37, 168, 169, 185
   Radio Quartet snub, 174–75
   remigration to Germany, 205–8
   with *Jüdischer Kulturbund* orchestra,
   35–37, 226
Edelstein, Ida, 14, 16, 102–3
Edelstein, Kristján, 208
Edelstein, Ruth, 14–15, 16, 102
Edelstein, Stefán, 17, 34, 62, 74, 76,
   78, 79, 103, 119, 122, 138, 175,
   199, 207, 208, 215
Edelstein, Wolfgang, 17, 33, 34, 75,
   76, 78, 79, 81, 110, 111–12,
   113, 115–16, 205, 207, 208
Edelstein, Ylfa, 226–27
Edison, Thomas Alva, 19
Egilson, Gunnar, 152, 153
Einarsson, Sigfús, 58, 161, 219
Einarsson, Sigurður, 160

Elíasdóttir, Guðmunda, 147
Erasmus of Rotterdam, 18
Erb, James, 164, 204
Erdensohn, Caesar, 98
Erdensohn, Paul, 97–98, 101
Ernst, Robert, 52

Fakouri, Elham, 231
Falla, Manuel de, 46
Felzmann, Josef, 62
Ferrier, Kathleen, 216
Feuermann, Emanuel, 16, 18, 38
Finnbogadóttir, Vigdís, 81, 104, 110, 117, 125
Fleischmann, Friedrich, 73, 136
Freud, Sigmund, 4, 5
Friedman, Ignaz, 68
Froelicher, Helen, 75
Furtwängler, Wilhelm, 23, 24, 99

Gál, Hans, 47, 121
Genée, Rudolph, 85
Gerigk, Herbert, 30
Gerlach, Werner, 131
Giannini, Vittorio, 157
Gíslason, Gylfi Þ., 222
Gluck, Christoph Willibald, 66
Gmeindl, Walter, 23, 38
Goebbels, Joseph, 29
Goethe, Johann Wolfgang von, 125
Golm, Ernest, 107
Golm, Eugen, 20
Golm, Gerhard, 107
Golm, Lisa, 107
Golm, Lise (Louise), *see* Abraham, Lise
Golm, Rudolf, 107
Gorodnitzki, Sascha, 170
Grabbe, Christian Dietrich, 11
Grenz, Artur, 40
Grieg, Edvard, 6, 161
Grünbaum, Alfred, 10, 53, 54
Grünbaum, Alberta, 10

Grünbaum, Ilma, 10, 54, 104, 105, 106
Grünbaum, Jenny, 10
Grünbaum, Melitta, *see* Urbancic, Melitta
Guðbrandsson, Ingólfur, 192, 206
Guðlaugsson, Haukur, 139
Guðmundsdóttir, Björk, *see* Björk
Guðmundsdóttir, Fanney, 70
Guðmundsson, Björgvin, 69, 70–71, 156, 169, 224
Guðmundsson, Böðvar, 227–28
Guðmundsson, Lúðvíg, 74
Guðmundsson, Sigurður, 71, 84
Guðmundsson, Þórarinn, 57, 62, 158, 204
Guðnadóttir, Hildur, 232
Gulda, Friedrich, 198
Gundolf, Friedrich, 11
Gunnarsson, Styrmir, 189, 230, 232
Gurlitt, Wilibald, 16

Habringer, Rudolf, 228
Hafstein, Jóhann, 113
Halldórsson, Halldór, 65, 66, 71, 147, 149
Halldórsson, Páll, 141
Hallsson, Kristinn, 188
Handel, George Frideric, 59, 68, 129, 151, 153
  Judas Maccabeus, 131
  Laudate pueri, 153
  Messiah, 120, 131, 135, 149, 169, 212, 213, 224
  Water Music, 172
Hannesson, Þorsteinn, 132, 211
Harich-Schneider, Eta, 23
Haydn, Joseph, 3, 36, 58, 66, 137, 143, 172, 198
  The Creation, 131, 213
  Divertimento in B-flat, 171
  Missa brevis in B-flat, 144

The Seasons, 120, 140, 146–47
Symphony no. 100, 170
Symphony no. 103 ("Drumroll"), 121
Heidegger, Martin, 15, 16
Heimisson, Einar, 227
Helgason, Hallgrímur, 165
Helgason, Þröstur, 229
Heller, Karl, 136
Henrietta (nun), 81
Hermannsson, Benedikt H., 231
Hervé (Louis-Auguste Florimond Ronger), 155
Hesse, Hermann, 159
Hickman, Roy, 120
Hildebrandt, Hermann, 117, 119, 172, 182, 196
Hildegard of Bingen, 14
Himmler, Heinrich, 227
Hindemith, Paul, 18, 40, 46, 130, 141, 143, 173, 193
Hirsch, Martha, 37
Hitler, Adolf, 24, 27, 78, 83, 100, 102, 181, 192, 199
Honegger, Arthur, 130, 177
Hornbostel, Erich Moritz von, 19, 23, 39
Horowitz, Vladimir, 24
Hughes, Dom Anselm, 209
Humperdinck, Engelbert, 12
Hunger, Martin, 223

Iceland, immigration policy of, 89–92
    naming conventions, 115–16
    occupation of (World War II), 119–20, 161
Iceland National Radio, 62, 68, 77, 85, 86, 91, 136, 137, 156, 158, 173, 193
Iceland National Radio Choir, 142–46, 147, 216, 223
Iceland Symphony Orchestra, 95, 138, 145–46, 167, 171–73, 223–24
    and Robert Abraham, 25, 149, 198, 212, 214, 215
    and Heinz Edelstein, 167, 175, 185, 191
    and Hermann Hildebrandt, 119, 172
    and Aram Khachaturian, 190
    and Olav Kielland, 209
    and Victor Urbancic, 157, 158, 160, 178–87, 201
Icelandic Musicians' Union, 65, 89, 91–92, 94–96, 168–69, 171
Icelandic Musicians' Union Orchestra, 140, 168–80
Ingólfsdóttir, Helga, 225
Ingólfsdóttir, Þorgerður, 150, 223
Ingvarsdóttir, Fríða Björk, 231
Íslandi, Stefán, 187
Ísólfsson, Páll, 62, 65, 123, 180, 185, 205
    as composer, 158, 160, 188, 224
    as conductor, 59, 93, 131, 168, 171, 213
    as critic, 136, 141, 170
    as dean, 60, 168, 174
    as organist, 57, 132, 145, 227

Jacobsen, Lis, 42, 43, 45, 64
Jalas, Jussi, 172
Jaspers, Karl, 11
Jewish Culture League, see *Jüdischer Kulturbund*
Joachim, Joseph, 97
Jóhannsdóttir (Ashkenazy), Þórunn, 85, 152
Jóhannsson, Magnús Blöndal, 151
Jónasson, Hermann, 64, 65, 84, 89–90, 104, 106, 231
Jónsdóttir, Margrét, 153, 155
Jónsson, Björn, 62, 177, 191

Jónsson, Guðmundur, 149, 188
Jónsson, Jakob, 188
Jónsson, Magnús, 188
Jónsson, Pétur, 187
Jónsson, Ragnar, 61–62, 73–74, 80–81, 82, 172, 177, 178–87, 189, 191, 192, 208, 211
Jónsson, Sigurður, 132
Jung, Wilhelm, 47
Jüdischer Kulturbund, 35–37, 73, 74, 99, 136, 226

Karp, Richard, 36
Kartz (Klahn), Fanny, 93, 95
Kazantseva, Nadezhda, 190
Kelbetz, Ludwig, 50, 51, 53, 160
Khachaturian, Aram, 190
Kielland, Olav, 160, 172–73, 182–86, 209
Klabund (Alfred Henschke), 188
Klahn, Albert, 92–95, 169
Kleiber, Erich, 23, 132
Klemperer, Otto, 23, 24
Klimt, Gustav, 4
Korngold, Erich Wolfgang, 46
Krauss, Clemens, 9
Kress, Bruno, 227
Kristallnacht, 30–31, 56, 78–79, 89, 99
Kristinsson, Sigursveinn, 165
Kristjánsson, Árni, 58, 60, 77, 96, 134, 136, 137, 214
Kristmannsson, Gauti, 125
Kroner, Irmgard, 83, 113
Kroner, Karl, 83, 228
Kvaran, Gunnar, 139
Kvaran, Ævar, 151

Laufey, 232
Laxness, Halldór, 62, 116
Lárusson, Magnús Már, 210

Lehár, Franz, 4, 155, 187
Leifs, Jón, 73, 77, 135, 143, 162, 181, 198, 201, 214, 224
Lunn, Sven, 44
Luther, Martin, 141
Löve, Sigrún, 139

Magnúsdóttir, Guðríður, 86–87, 113, 138, 143, 148, 150, 176, 194, 197, 221, 222, 223
Mahler, Gustav, 2, 3, 29, 35, 159
  Das Lied von der Erde, 215–16
  Symphony no. 1, 215
Markan, María, 187
Marteau, Henri, 59–60, 97
Marx, Joseph, 8, 159
Mathias, Emmy, 107
Melsted, Óðinn, 230
Mendelssohn, Felix, 29–30, 35, 36, 37, 143, 161
  A Midsummer Night's Dream, 29–30, 188
Menotti, Gian Carlo, 147, 198
Merson, Allan, 121
Meyerbeer, Giacomo, 21
Michaelis, Kurt, 37
Misch, Ludwig, 98–99, 101
Mitterer, Erika, 11
Mixa, Franz, 51–53, 60, 62, 81–82, 130, 136, 162, 173, 230
Mixa, Katrín, *see* Ólafsdóttir, Katrín
Morávek, Jan, 53, 171, 230
Moses, Grandma (Anna Mary Robertson), 87
Mozart, Leopold, 193
Mozart, Wolfgang Amadeus, 2, 3, 6, 7, 24, 35, 49, 51, 58, 66, 68, 136, 170, 172, 197, 198, 218
  Ave verum corpus, 86
  Kegelstatt Trio, 139
  The Magic Flute, 151, 187, 188, 198

Piano Concerto no. 24, 185
Requiem, 131, 212, 213
Symphony no. 39, 155
Musorgsky, Modest, 141, 198

Neumann, Valerie, 104–5, 106
Nielsen, Carl, 42, 198
Nordal, Jón, 86, 133, 152, 163, 174, 185
Nordal, Sigurður, 86, 185
Norðmann, Jórunn, 67

Oberländer, Ida, *see* Edelstein, Ida
Offenbach, Jacques, 46, 198
Orff, Carl, 29, 191, 212
 Carmina Burana, 212, 213
Ormandy, Eugene, 200
Ottósson, Róbert Abraham, *see* Abraham, Robert
Ólafsdóttir, Katrín, 51, 82, 162
Ólafsson, Björn, 58, 60, 136, 137, 145, 168, 174, 180, 226
Ólafsson, Gunnsteinn, 205
Ólafsson, Sigurjón, 224
Ólafsson, Víkingur, 224, 232
Óskarsson, Þórarinn, 138

Palestrina, Giovanni Pierluigi da, 129
Partridge, Ian, 120
Pálsdóttir, Þuríður, 143, 147, 151, 188, 213
Pears, Peter, 216
Pergolesi, Giovanni Battista, 153
Petzold, Christian, 155
Pétursson, Hallgrímur, 132, 179
Philharmonia Choral Society, 148, 149, 211–15, 216, 217, 223–24
Pjeturss, Anna, 142
Polignac, Princess Edmond de, *see* Singer, Winnaretta
Porter, Cole, 200

Praetorius, Michael, 196
Prokofiev, Sergei, 172
Prunières, Henry, 41
Prüwer, Julius, 36

Quiquerez, Hans, 73

Rachmaninoff, Sergei, 24
Ravel, Maurice, 136
Redl, Fritz, 51
Reichsmusikkammer, 27–28, 32–33, 53, 93, 247n116
Reinhardt, Max, 11, 12
Reykjavík Music Society, 37, 61, 83, 151, 167, 168, 173, 186, 223
 and Heinz Edelstein, 73, 74, 76–77, 136–38
 and Hans Stepanek, 95
 and Victor Urbancic, 52, 55, 82, 130, 134, 138, 155, 177, 177–84, 186
Reykjavík Music Society Choir, 114, 119, 130–35, 153, 164, 176–77, 224
Reykjavík Orchestra, The, 58–59, 61, 62, 95, 130, 168–70
 and Robert Abraham, 140
 and Heinz Edelstein, 137
 and Franz Mixa, 51
 and Victor Urbancic, 82, 110, 114, 131, 134, 153, 155, 157
Reykjavík School of Music, 51, 60, 61, 62, 73, 77, 90, 95, 97, 137–38, 155, 157, 168, 174, 177, 188–91
Reykjavík Symphony Orchestra, 170
Rilke, Rainer Maria, 11, 125
Rosenberg, Alfred (Nazi ideologue), 30, 38
Rosenberg, Alfred (restaurateur), 91
Rossini, Gioachino, 147, 198
Rostropovich, Mstislav, 163, 187

Rottberger, Hans, 227
Rottberger, Olga, 227
Róbertsson, Grétar Ottó, 87, 150, 197, 223
Rósinkranz, Guðlaugur, 178–81, 187
Rubin, Marcus, 42
Runólfsson, Karl Ottó, 91, 94, 157, 162, 163, 164, 198

Sachs, Curt, 23, 39, 85, 244n72
Schepses, Erwin, 79, 102
Scherchen, Hermann, 41
Schiller, Friedrich, 125
Schnabel, Artur, 18, 24, 38
Schoenberg, Arnold, 4, 18, 31, 35, 100, 107
 Pierrot lunaire, 41
Schottländer, Arnold, 17
Schottländer, Charlotte, *see* Edelstein, Charlotte
Schottländer, Jenny, 17, 103
Schottländer, Lilli, 79, 103
Schreker, Franz, 23, 38
Schubert, Franz, 3, 10, 35, 36, 58, 66, 68, 70, 136, 198
 Das Dreimäderlhaus (music by), 155
 Mass in G major, 130
 Piano Sonata in B-flat, D. 960, 153
 Symphony no. 5, 168
 Unfinished symphony, 66, 171
Schulz, Emmy, 39–40, 44, 64
Schumann, Robert, 12, 15, 44, 66, 70, 198, 218
 Brautgesang, 86
 Piano Quintet, 224
 Symphony no. 1, 198
Schwalbach, Leopoldine, 16
Serkin, Rudolf, 119
Shakespeare, William, 29
Shattuck, Arthur, 58
Shostakovich, Dmitri, 137

Sibelius, Jean, 141, 172
Sigfúsdóttir, Kristín, 86
Sigurbjörnsson, Þorkell, 139, 220
Sigurðardóttir, Elín, 95
Sigurðsson, Einar, 217
Sigurðsson, Haraldur, 58
Sigurjónsson, Rögnvaldur, 151, 170, 222, 224
Silbermann, Alphons, 99–100, 101
Simon, Clara Henriette, 108
Simon, Walter, 108
Singer, Winnaretta, 41
Símonar, Guðrún Á., 188
Sjón, 228
Smári, Jakob, 132
Smetana, Bedřich, 49, 187
Smyth, Ethel, 24
Snorrason, Áskell, 68, 70, 218
Sommer, Heide, 40–41
Stefánsson, Davíð, 188
Stefánsson, Eggert, 163
Stefánsson, Eyþór, 134
Stefánsson, Stefán Jóhann, 106
Steffensen, Valdimar, 68, 70
Steinberg, Wilhelm, 36
Stepanek, Hans, 60, 62, 77, 95–96, 136, 224
Stephensen, Sigríður, 230
Stradella, Alessandro, 153
Straube, Karl, 57
Strauss, Johann jr., 30
 Die Fledermaus, 188
Strauss, Richard, 7
 Der Rosenkavalier, 44
Stravinsky, Igor, 24, 130
 Les noces, 41
 Oedipus Rex, 23, 141–42, 215
 The Rite of Spring, 200
 Symphony of Psalms, 212, 215
Stumpf, Carl, 19
Stäblein, Bruno, 210, 211

Sveinbjörnsson, Sveinbjörn, 149, 161
Sveinsson, Atli Heimir, 189
Sveinsson, Jón (Nonni), 78
Sveinsson, Þorsteinn, 151
Szell, George, 200
Söngsveitin Fílharmónía, *see*
 Philharmonia Choral Society

Takács, Georg, 91
Tchaikovsky, Pyotr Ilyich, 35, 136
 Serenade for Strings, 36
 Symphony no. 5, 185
Telemann, Georg Philipp, 196
Thalau, Gustav, 16
Thomsen, Grímur, 216–17
Thorlak, Saint, 209–10, 218, 219, 220
Thoroddsen, Emil, 62, 153, 157, 164, 204
Thors, Ólafur, 106
Tinhof, Julia, 226
Toch, Ernst, 35, 37
Tónlistarfélagið í Reykjavík, *see*
 Reykjavík Music Society
Tónlistarfélagskórinn, *see* Reykjavík
 Music Society Choir
Tónlistarskólinn í Reykjavík, *see*
 Reykjavík Music School
Tryggvason, Jóhann, 152
Tumason, Kolbeinn, 220
Töpper, Hertha, 53

Ullmann, Viktor, 100–101
Urbancic, Eiríka, 118, 164, 199, 204, 225
Urbancic, Melitta, 10–12, 45–46, 49, 50, 51, 83, 108, 114, 131, 164, 186
 bust of Victor Urbancic, 224, 225
 conversion of, 53–54, 156
 culinary efforts in Iceland, 118–19
 flight from Mainz, 47–48
 flight to Iceland, 55–56, 78
 Grünbaum/Neumann affair, 104–6
 husband's illness and death, 200–202
 life in Iceland, 124–25, 127, 203
 poetry of, 125, 159, 226, 231
 publication of folk song volume, 165
Urbancic, Pétur (Peter), 46, 49, 50, 54, 55, 113–14, 118, 121, 131, 139, 152, 163, 164, 203, 204
Urbancic, Ruth, 46, 49, 54, 55, 114, 118, 121, 131, 152, 163, 164, 203–4
Urbancic, Sibyl, 11, 48, 49, 55, 82, 106, 113–14, 118, 119, 120, 156, 164, 186, 199, 203, 204, 231–32
Urbancic, Victor, 1–2, 25, 60, 72, 87, 100, 101, 103, 111, 120, 124, 129, 167, 175, 185, 203
 arrangements of Icelandic folk songs, 109, 160, 161–65
 arrival in Iceland, 62, 81–84
 as choral conductor, 120, 130–35, 174, 176–77, 211, 213
 as composer, 8, 159–161
 as lecturer, 158, 200
 as opera conductor, 155
 as orchestral conductor, 151, 153, 155, 157, 168, 170, 171, 172, 173
 as organist, 156, 183
 as pianist, 153, 158, 183
 as teacher, 86, 151–53, 157–58, 162, 173–74, 177, 181, 183
 at the National Theater, 135, 178–88, 198, 200
 career in Mainz, 45–48
 career in Graz, 48–55
 change in spelling of name, 116
 childhood and studies of, 3–12

Urbancic, Victor *(continued)*
   culinary efforts in Iceland, 118–19
   death and legacy of, 199–202,
     223–26, 228, 229, 232
   Grünbaum/Neumann affair, 104–6
   in fiction, 227–28
   knowledge of Icelandic language,
     114–15
   National Theater controversy,
     178–88
   works:
   Caprices mignons über ein Kinderlied,
     12, 13, 226
   Call of Spring, 160
   Concertino for three saxophones,
     160, 161, 226
   Concerto for Orchestra, 160
   Death and the Fool, overture, 159
   Elisabeth (song cycle), 49, 159
   Fantasy-Sonata, 12, 159, 226
   Hymnus, 160
   Lieder, 159, 226
   Missa in honorem Jesu Christi regis,
     160
   Ode to Skálholt, 160–61, 226
   Overture to a Comedy, 160, 161,
     225, 226
   Partita for cello and piano, 49
   Sonatina for Piano, 12, 226
   Sonata for Violin and Piano, 12,
     159, 226
   Sonata no. 2 for Violin and Piano,
     159–60
Urbančič (Turnogradska), Josipina, 4
Urbantschitsch, Erich, 4, 5, 7, 203
Urbantschitsch, Ernst, 4, 5–6, 10
Urbantschitsch, Hildegard, 4, 5–6, 7,
   201, 203, 247n116
Urbantschitsch, Rudolf, 4–5
Urbantschitsch, Viktor, 4

Valdemarsson, Hallgrímur, 70

Valdimarsson, Þorsteinn, 132, 172,
   189, 213
Verdi, Giuseppe, 2
   La forza del destino, 200
   Requiem, 24, 66, 144, 213
   Rigoletto, 36, 178, 188
   La traviata, 179
Victoria, Tomás Luis de, 129, 153
Viðar, Jórunn, 152, 157–158, 163,
   198, 226
Vigfússon, Einar, 174–75
Vivaldi, Antonio, 43
Volkmar, Moritz Daniel, 21

Wagner, Otto, 4
Wagner, Richard, 7, 10, 12, 29, 35
   Die Meistersinger von Nürnberg, 150
   Tannhäuser, 24
   Tristan und Isolde, 24, 36
Walter, Bruno, 23–25, 29, 215–16
Waltz, Christoph, 5
Weber, Carl Maria von, 49, 198
Weill, Kurt, 31
Weingarten, Paul, 8
Weingartner, Felix, 6
Weisshappel, Fritz, 63, 91, 169
Wellesz, Egon, 9
Wiesler, Manuela, 49
Wlach, Hans, 51–52
Wodiczko, Bohdan, 214
Wolf, Hugo, 159
Wolf-Rottkay, Wolf Helmuth, 79–80

xenophobia in Iceland, 88,
   89–101, 110–11, 165. *See also*
   anti-Semitism

Zeisel, Arnold, 122
Zier, Kurt, 133, 138, 190, 191, 193,
   194, 199, 204, 205, 228
Zier, Lotte, 117, 204
Zweig, Stephan, 4

Þorgrímsson, Ólafur, 62, 177, 184
Þorleifsson, Hallur, 111
Þorsteinsdóttir, Guðrún, 68, 69
Þorsteinsson, Bjarni, 161, 162, 163
Þorvaldsdóttir, Anna, 211, 232
Þórarinsson, Jón, 144, 148, 152, 173–74, 185, 189, 211–12
  as music critic, 170, 214
  dispute with Edelstein, 174–75
  National Theater controversy, 178, 179, 180, 181, 183
  Of Love and Death, 198
Þórðarson, Sigurður, 71, 144, 155, 156
Þórhallsson, Þorlákur, *see* Thorlak, Saint

www.ingramcontent.com/pod-product-compliance
Lightning Source LLC
Chambersburg PA
CBHW030117240426
43673CB00041B/1308